Universal's
Concise Commentary
on

# The Juvenile Justice (Care and Protection of Children) Act, 2000

**(56 of 2000)**

with

Exhaustive Case Law

First Edition 2015
**Reprint August 2015**

Universal's
Concise Commentary
on

# The Juvenile Justice (Care and Protection of Children) Act, 2000

**(56 of 2000)**

with
Exhaustive Case Law

Universal
Law Publishing
an imprint of LexisNexis

LexisNexis®

This book is a publication of **LexisNexis®**
(A Division of Reed Elsevier India (Pvt) Ltd)
14th floor, Building No 10, Tower–B, DLF Cyber City, Phase-II,
Gurgaon–122002, Haryana, India.
Tel : + 91 124 4774444 Fax: + 91 124 4774100
Website : www.lexisnexis.co.in / E-mail : help.in@lexisnexis.com

---



Universal's Concise Commentary - *The Juvenile Justice (Care and Protection of Children) Act, 2000*
First Edition 2015, Reprint August 2015

ISBN: 978-93-5035-546-6

Printed by: Deepak Printers, Delhi



Printed and bound in India.

# THE JUVENILE JUSTICE (CARE AND PROTECTION OF CHILDREN) ACT, 2000



## CONTENTS

*CHAPTER I*

**PRELIMINARY**



*CHAPTER II*

**JUVENILE IN CONFLICT WITH LAW**

*CHAPTER IV*

**REHABILITATION AND SOCIAL REINTEGRATION**



*CHAPTER V*

**MISCELLANEOUS**

# THE JUVENILE JUSTICE (CARE AND PROTECTION OF CHILDREN) RULES, 2007

**Rules**

*CHAPTER I*
**PRELIMINARY**

## CHAPTER II
## FUNDAMENTAL PRINCIPLES OF JUVENILE JUSTICE AND PROTECTION OF CHILDREN



## CHAPTER III
## JUVENILE IN CONFLICT WITH LAW



## CHAPTER IV
## CHILD IN NEED OF CARE AND PROTECTION



## CHAPTER V
## REHABILITATION AND SOCIAL REINTEGRATION



## CHAPTER VI
## STANDARDS OF CARE FOR INSTITUTIONS

## NATIONAL CHARTER FOR CHILDREN, 2003

# TABLE OF CASES

# THE JUVENILE JUSTICE (CARE AND PROTECTION OF CHILDREN) ACT, 2000

## INTRODUCTION

To provide for the care, protection, treatment, development and rehabilitation of neglected or delinquent juveniles and for the adjudication of certain matters relating to, and disposition of, delinquent juveniles the Juvenile Justice Act, 1986 (53 of 1986) was enacted by Parliament. Several provisions of the Constitution including clause (3) of article 15, clauses (e) and (f) of article 39, articles 45 and 47 also impose on the State a primary responsibility of ensuring that all the needs of children are met and that their basic human rights are fully protected. On 20th November, 1989 General Assembly of the United Nations adopted the Convention on the Rights of the Child wherein a set of standards to be adhered to by all State parties in securing the best interests of the child has been prescribed. The Convention emphasises social re-integration of child victims, to the extent possible, without resorting to judicial proceedings. The Government of India, having ratified the Convention, has found it expedient to re-enact the existing law relating to juveniles bearing in mind the standards prescribed in the Convention on the Rights of the Child, the United Nations Standard Minimum Rules for the Administration of Juvenile Justice, 1985 (The Beijing Rules), the United Nations Rules for the Protection of Juveniles Deprived of their Liberty (1990), and all other relevant international instruments. To achieve this objective the Juvenile Justice (Care and Protection of Children) Bill was introduced in the Parliament.

### SYNOPSIS

1. Speeches by Members of Legislature – Importance of
2. Beneficial Legislation – Concept of
3. Classification –Law on
4. External and Internal Aids – Comments on
5. General Later Law and Earlier Special Law – Comments on
6. Grammar – Effect of
7. Convention on Rights of Child – Comments on
8. Interpretation – Role of
9. Juvenile Offenders – Law on
10. Parliament and State Legislatures – Comments on
11. Penal Provision – Construction of
12. Special Law and General Law – Comments on
13. Validity of Legislation – Challenge for
14. Welfare Legislation – Construction of

### COMMENTS

**1. Speeches by Members of Legislature – Importance of –** Now it is true that the speeches made by the Members of the Legislature on the floor of the House when a Bill for enacting a statutory provision is being debated are inadmissible for the purpose of interpreting the statutory provision but the speech made by the Mover of the Bill explaining the reason for the introduction of the Bill can certainly be referred to for the purpose of ascertaining the mischief sought to be remedied by the legislation and the object and purpose for which the legislation is enacted. This is in accord with the recent trend in juristic thought not only in Western countries but also in India that interpretation of a statute being an exercise in the ascertainment of meaning, everything which is logically relevant should be admissible; *K.P. Varghese* v. *Income-Tax Officer, Ernakulam*, AIR 1981 SC 1922: 1981 (3) SCALE 1315: 1981 (4) SCC 173.

**2. Beneficial Legislation – Concept of –** The concept of beneficial legislation becomes relevant only when two views are possible; *Manipal Academy of Higher Education* v. *Provident Fund Commissioner*, AIR 2008 SC 1951: 2008 (4) SCALE 53: 2008 (5) SCC 428.

**3. Classification –Law on –** The power of Courts to declare a statute unconstitutional is subject to two guiding principles of decision which ought not to be absent from judicial consciousness. One is that Courts are concerned only with the power to enact statutes, not with their wisdom. The other is that while unconstitutional exercise of power by the Executive and Legislative branches of the government is subject to judicial restraint, the only check upon our exercise of power is our own sense of self-restraint. For the removal of unwise laws from the statute books appeal lies not to the Courts but to the ballot and to the processes of democratic Government. Certain principles which bear upon classification may be mentioned here. It is true that a State may classify persons and objects for the purpose of legislation and pass laws for the purpose of obtaining revenue or other objects. Every differentiation is not discrimination. But classification can be sustained only if it is founded on pertinent and real differences as distinguished from irrelevant and artificial ones. The constitutional standard, by which the sufficiency of the differentia which forms a valid basis for classification may be measured, has been repeatedly stated by the Courts. If it rests on a difference which bears a fair and just relation to the object for which it is proposed, it is constitutional. To put it differently, the means must have nexus with the ends. Even so, large latitude is allowed to the State for classification upon a reasonable basis and what is reasonable is a question of practical details and a variety of factors which the Court will be reluctant and perhaps ill-equipped to investigate. In this imperfect world perfection even in grouping is an ambition hardly ever accomplished. In this context, we have to remember the relationship between the Legislative and Judicial departments of Government in the determination of the validity of classification. Of course, in the last analysis Courts possess the power to pronounce on the constitutionality of the acts of the other branches whether a classification is based upon substantial differences or is arbitrary, fanciful and consequently illegal. At the same time, the question of classification is primarily for Legislative judgment and ordinarily does not become a Judicial question. A power to classify being extremely broad and based on diverse considerations of executive pragmatism, the Judicature cannot rush in where even the Legislature warily treads. All these operational restraints on Judicial power must weigh more emphatically where the subject is taxation"; *Subramanian Swamy* v. *Raju*, 2014 (4) SCALE 305: AIR 2014 SC 1649: 2014 (2) Crimes 307 (SC) *Nirbhaya* case [Hon'ble Judges: P. Sathasivam, Ranjan Gogoi, Shiva Kirti Singh].

**4. External and Internal Aids – Comments on –** A statute is best understood if we know the reason for it. The reason for a statute is the safest guide to its interpretation. The words of a statute take their colour from the reason for it. How do Courts discover the reason for a statute? There are external and internal aids. The external aids are Statement of Objects and Reasons when the Bill is presented to Parliament, the reports of Committees which preceded the Bill and the reports of Parliamentary Committees. Occasional excursions into the debates of Parliament are permitted. Internal aids are the preamble, the scheme and the provisions of the Act. Having discovered the reason for the statute and so having set the sail to the wind, the interpreter may proceed ahead. No provision in the statute and no word of the statute may be construed in isolation. Every provision and every word must be looked at generally before any provision or word is attempted to be construed. The setting and the pattern are important. It is again important to remember that Parliament does not waste its breath unnecessarily. Just as Parliament, is not expected to use unnecessary expressions, Parliament is also not expected to express itself unnecessarily. Even as Parliament does not use any word without meaning something, Parliament does not legislate where no legislation is called for. Parliament cannot be assumed to legislate for the sake of legislation; nor can it be assumed to make pointless legislation. Parliament does not indulge in legislation merely to state what it is unnecessary to state or to do what is already validly done. Parliament may not be assumed to legislate unnecessarily. Again, while the words of an enactment are important, the context is no less important. For instance, "the fact that general words are used in a statute is not in itself a conclusive reason why every case falling literally within them should be governed by that statute, and the context of any Act may well indicate that wide or general words should be given a restrictive meaning"; *Utkal Contractors and Joinery Pvt. Ltd.* v. *State of Orissa*, AIR 1987 SC 1454: 1987 (1) SCALE 1162: 1987 (3) SCC 279 (*See* Halsbury, 4th Edn., Vol. 44, para 874).

**5. General Later Law and Earlier Special Law – Comments on –** A general later law does not abrogate an earlier special one by mere implication. *Generalia specialibus non derogant*, or, in other words, "where there are general words in a later Act capable of reasonable and sensible application without extending them to subjects specially dealt with by earlier legislation, you are not to hold that earlier and special legislation indirectly repealed, altered, or derogated from merely by force of such general words, without any indication of a particular intention to do so". In such cases it is presumed to have only general cases in view, and not particular cases which have been already otherwise provided for by the Special Act; *Maharaja Pratap Singh Bahadur* v. *Man Mohan Dev*, AIR 1966 SC 1931 (1934).

**6. Grammar – Effect of –** The law of the Constitution is not only for those who govern or for the theorist, but also for the bulk of the people for the common man for whose benefit and pride and safeguard the Constitution has also been written. Unless and until these fundamental provisions are altered by the constituent processes of Parliament they must be interpreted in a sense which the common man, not versed in the niceties of grammar and dialectical logic, can understand and appreciate so that he may have faith and confidence and unshaken trust in that which has been enacted for his benefit and protection; *State of West Bengal* v. *Anwar Ali Sarkar*, AIR 1952 SC 75: 1952 Cr LJ 510: 1952 SCJ 55: 1952 SCR 284

**7. Convention on Rights of Child – Comments on –** The Convention on the Rights of the Child, 1990 ("CRC"), in article 1, adopts a chronological definition of a "child", *viz.*, less than 18 years old, unless majority under national legislation is attained earlier:

> "For the purposes of the present Convention, a child means every human being below the age of eighteen years unless under the law applicable to the child, majority is attained earlier."

Article 37(a) of the CRC prohibits the imposition of capital punishment and life imprisonment without possibility of release on offenders below 18 years of age. The CRC further obliges State Parties to establish a minimum age below which children shall be presumed not to have the capacity to infringe the penal law [Article 40(3)(a)].

Rule 1-2 of the Havana Rules provides that a juvenile shouid be deprived of his/her liberty only as a measure of the last resort limited to exceptional cases and for the minimum necessary period. Even then, detention should be in such a manner and in conditions that respect the human rights of juveniles (Rule 12).

Rule 11(a) of the Havana Rules, 1990 define a juvenile as every person under the age of 18, and allow national laws to determine a minimum age below which such person will not be detained.

Under article 43 of the CRC, constitution of a Committee for the purpose of examining the progress made by the State parties on the rights of the child is contemplated. The first meeting of the Committee under article 44 was to be within 2 years of the coming into force of the convention so far as a particular State party, in respect of whom review of the progress is made, is concerned. Thereafter, the Committee is required to meet every 5 years. In January, 2000, the Committee considered the initial report of India submitted on 19-3-1997 and adopted certain "concluding observations" the relevant part of which are extracted hereinbelow:

"79. The Committee is concerned over the administration of juvenile justice in India and its incompatibility with articles 37, 40 and 39 of the Convention and other relevant international standards. The Committee is also concerned at the very young age of criminal responsibility 7 years and the possibility of trying boys between 16 and 18 years of age as adults. Noting that the death penalty is *de facto* not applied to persons under 18, the Committee is very concerned that *de jure*, this possibility exists. The Committee is further concerned at the overcrowding and unsanitary conditions of detenained children, including detention with adults; lack of application and enforcement of existing juvenile justice legislation; lack of training for professionals, including the Judiciary, lawyers and law enforcement officers, in relation to the Convention, other existing international standards and the 1986 Juvenile Justice Act; and the lack of measures and enforcement thereof to prosecute officials who violate these provisions.

80. The Committee recommends that the State party review its laws in the administration of juvenile justice to ensure that they are in accordance with the Convention, especially articles 37, 40 and 39, and other relevant international standards such as the United Nations Standard Minimum Rules for the Administration of Juvenile Justice (the Beijing Rules), the United Nations Guidelines for the Prevention of Juvenile Delinquency (the Riyadh Guidelines), the United Nations Rules for the Protection of Juveniles Deprived of their Liberty and the Vienna Guidelines for Action on Children in the Criminal Justice System.

81. The Committee recommends that the State party abolish by law the imposition of the death penalty on persons under 18. The Committee also recommends that the State party consider raising the age of criminal responsibility and ensure that persons under 18 years are not tried as adults. In accordance with the principle of non-discrimination contained in article 2 of the Convention, the Committee recommends article 29(h) of the 1986 Juvenile Justice Act be amended to ensure that boys under 18 years are covered by the definition of juvenile, as girls already are. The Committee recommends that the 1986 Juvenile Justice Act be fully enforced and that the Judiciary and lawyers be trained and made aware of it. The Committee further recommends that measures be taken to reduce overcrowding, to release those who cannot be given a speedy trial and to improve prison facilities as quickly as possible. The Committee recommends that the State party ensure regular, frequent and independent monitoring of institutions for juvenile offenders." It is pursuant to the aforesaid concluding observations of the Committee made in the year 2000 that the JJ Act was amended in the later part of that year by having a uniform age of 18 for both male and female juveniles. It needs to be clarified that the concluding observations of the Committee under article 45 of the UN Convention (CRC) are *qua* a particular State party whereas general comments of the Committee under the same article are authoritative interpretations addressed to all State parties. The above distinction between "concluding observations" and "general comments" is highlighted to draw attention to the fact that in the meeting of the Committee held in Geneva in the year 2007 certain general observations with regard to MCAR of 18 years were made which would be applicable to State parties other than India as the law had already been amended in our country pursuant to the concluding observations made by the Committee in the year 2000 specifically *qua* India. The views of the Committee in respect of other member States may be usefully taken note at this stage by extracting the recommendations in the nature of general comments in paras 36, 37 and 38 of the Report:

"36. The Committee also wishes to draw the attention of States parties to the upper age-limit for the application of the rules of juvenile justice. These special rules - in terms both of special procedural rules and of rules for diversion and special measures - should apply, starting at the MACR set in the country, for all children who, at the time of their alleged commission of an offence (or act punishable under the criminal law), have not yet reached the age of 18 years.

"37. The Committee wishes to remind States parties that they have recognized the right of every child alleged as, accused of, or recognized as having infringed the penal law to be treated in accordance with the provisions of article 40 of CRC. This means that every person under the age of 18 years at the time of the alleged commission of an offence must be treated in accordance with the rules of juvenile justice.

"38. The Committee, therefore, recommends that those States parties which limit the applicability of their juvenile justice rules to children under the age of 16 (or lower) years, or which allow by way of exception that 16 or 17-year-old children are treated as adult criminals, change their laws with a view to achieving a non- discriminatory full application of their juvenile justice rules to all persons under the age of 18 years. The Committee notes with appreciation that some States parties allow for the application of the rules and regulations of juvenile justice to persons aged 18 and older, usually till the age of 21, either as a general rule or by way of exception"; *Subramanian Swamy* v. *Raju*, JT 2014 (4) SC 328: 2014 (4) SCALE 305: AIR 2014 SC 1649, *Nirbhaya* case [Hon'ble Judges: P. Sathasivam, Ranjan Gogoi, Shiva Kirti Singh].

**8. Interpretation – Role of –** That interpretation is best which makes the textual interpretation match the contextual. A statute is best interpreted when we know why it was enacted. Most fair and rational method for interpreting a statute is by exploring the intention of the Legislature through the most natural and probable signs which are either the words, the context, the subject-matter, the effects and consequences, or the spirit and reason of the law. In the Court of law what the Legislature intended to be done or not to be done can only be legitimately ascertained from that what it has chosen to enact, either in express words or by reasonable and necessary implication. But the whole of what is enacted 'by necessary implication' can hardly be determined without keeping in mind the purpose or object of the statute. A bare mechanical interpretation of the words and application of legislative intent devoid of concept or purpose will reduce most of the remedial and beneficent legislation of futility. The Courts however, are always warned that they are not entitled to usurp legislative function under the disguise of interpretation and that they must avoid the danger of determination of the meaning of a provision based on their own pre-conceived notions of ideological structure or scheme into which the provision to be interpreted is somehow fitted; *District Mining Officer* v. *Tata Iron and Steel Co. Ltd.*, AIR 2001 SC 3134: 2001 (4) SCALE 680: 2001 (7) SCC 358.

**9. Juvenile Offenders – Law on –** It cannot be questioned that children are amongst the most vulnerable sections in any society. They represent almost one-third of the world's population, and unless they are provided with proper opportunities, the opportunity of making them grow into responsible citizens of tomorrow will slip out of the hands of the present generation. International community has been alive to the problem for a long time. After the aftermath of the First World War, the League of Nations issued the Geneva Declaration of the Rights of the Child in 1924. Following the gross abuse and violence of human rights during the Second World War, which caused the death of millions of people, including children, the United Nations had been formed in 1945 and on 10th December, 1948 adopted and proclaimed the Universal Declaration of Human Rights. While articles 1 and 7 of the Declaration proclaimed that all human beings are born free and equal in dignity and rights and are equal before the law, article 25 of the Declaration specifically provides that motherhood and childhood would be entitled to special care and assistance. The growing consciousness of the world community was further evidenced by the Declaration of the Rights of the Child, which came to be proclaimed by the United Nations on 20th November, 1959, in the best interests of the child. This was followed by the Beijing Rules of 1985, the Riyadh Guidelines of 1990, which specially provided guidelines for the prevention of juvenile delinquency, and the Havana Rules of 14th December, 1990. The said three sets of Rules intended that social policies should be evolved and applied to prevent juvenile delinquency, to establish a Juvenile Justice System for juveniles in conflict with law, to safeguard fundamental rights and to establish methods for social re-integration of young people who had suffered incarceration in prison or other corrective institutions. One of the other principles which was sought to be reiterated and adopted was that a juvenile should be dealt with for an offence in a manner which is different from an adult. The Beijing Rules indicated that efforts should be made by member countries to establish within their own national jurisdiction, a set of laws and rules especially applicable to juvenile offenders. It was stated that the age of criminal responsibility in legal systems that recognize the concept of the age of criminal responsibility for juveniles should not be fixed at too low an age-level, keeping in mind the emotional, mental and intellectual maturity of children; *Salil Bali* v. *Union of India*, 2013 (9) SCALE 140: 2013 Cr LJ 4597: AIR 2013 SC 3743.

**10. Parliament and State Legislatures – Comments on –** Constitution vested only legislative power in Parliament and in the State Legislatures. A House of Parliament or State Legislature could not try anyone or any case directly, as a court of justice could. It could proceed *quasi*-judicially in cases of contempt of its authority and take up motions concerning its privileges and immunities because, in doing so, it sought removal of obstructions to the due performance of its legislative functions. If any question of jurisdiction arose, it had to be decided by the courts in appropriate proceedings; *P.V. Narasimha Rao* v. *State (CBI/SPE)*, AIR 1998 SC 2120: 1998 Cr LJ 2930: 1998 (3) SCALE 53 [Five Judges-Bench].

**11. Penal Provision – Construction of –** A penal provision has to be strictly construed; *Rib Tapes (India) Pvt. Ltd.* v. *Union of India*, AIR 1986 SC 2014: 1986 (2) SCALE 367: 1986 (4) SCC 185.

**12. Special Law and General Law – Comments on –** It is stated therein that for the general principle that the special law prevails over general law there is one exception and that is a later general law prevails over earlier special law if it clearly indicates the intention to supersede the special law; *R.S. Raghunath* v. *State of Karnataka*, AIR 1992 SC 81: 1991 (2) SCALE 808: 1992 (1) SCC 335.

**13. Validity of Legislation – Challenge for –** When validity of legislation is challenged on the ground of want of legislative competence and it becomes necessary to ascertain to which entry in the three lists the legislation is referable to, the Court has evolved the theory of pith and substance. If in pith and substance a legislation falls within one entry or the other but some portion of the subject-matter of the legislation incidentally trenches upon and might enter a field under another List, the Act as a whole would be valid notwithstanding such incidental trenching. This is well established by a catena of decisions; *Ishwari Khetan Sugar Mills (P.) Ltd.* v. *State of Uttar Pradesh*, AIR 1980 SC 1955: 1980 (4) SCC 136: 1980 (3) SCR 331 [*see* also: *Union of India* v. *H.S. Dhillon*, (1972) 2 SCR 33: AIR 1972 SC 1061 and *Kerala State Electricity Board* v. *Indian Aluminium Co. Ltd.*, (1976) 1 SCR 552: AIR 1976 SC 1031; *State of Karnataka* v. *Ranganatha Reddy*, (1978) 1 SCR 641: AIR 1978 SC 215].

**14. Welfare Legislation – Construction of –** It is well settled that in construing the provision of welfare legislation, Courts should adopt, what is described as a beneficent rule of construction; *Workmen of Firestone Tyre and Rubber Co. of India P. Ltd.* v. *Management*, AIR 1973 SC 1227: 1973 (1) SCC 813: 1973 (3) SCR 587.

## STATEMENT OF OBJECTS AND REASONS

A review of the working of the Juvenile Act, 1986 (53 of 1986) would indicate that much greater attention is required to be given to children in conflict with law or those in need of care and protection. The justice system as available for adults is not considered suitable for being applied to a juvenile or the child or any one on their behalf including the police, voluntary organisations, social workers, or parents and guardians, throughout the country. There is also an urgent need for creating adequate infrastructure necessary for the implementation of the proposed legislation with a larger involvement of informal systems specially the family, the voluntary organisations and the community.

2. In this context, the following further proposals have been made—

(i) to lay down the basic principles for administering justice to a juvenile or the child in the Bill;

(ii) to make the juvenile system meant for a juvenile or the child more appreciative of the developmental needs in comparison to criminal justice system as applicable to adults;

(iii) to bring the juvenile law in conformity with the United Nations' Convention on the Rights of the Child;

(iv) to prescribe a uniform age of eighteen years for both boys and girls;

(v) to ensure speedy disposal of cases by the authorities envisaged under this Bill regarding juvenile or the child within a time limit of four months;

(vi) to spell out the role of the State as a facilitator rather than doer by involving voluntary organisations and local bodies in the implementation of the proposed legislation;

(vii) to create special juvenile police units with a humane approach through sensitisation and training of police personnel;

(viii) to enable increased accessibility to a juvenile or the child by establishing Juvenile Justice Boards and Child Welfare Committees and Homes in each district or group of districts;

(ix) to minimise the stigma and in keeping with the developmental needs of the juvenile or the child, to separate the Bill into two parts—one for juveniles in conflict with law and the other for the juvenile or the child in need of care and protection;

(x) to provide for effective provisions and various alternatives for rehabilitation and social reintegration such as adoption, foster care, sponsorship and aftercare of abandoned, destitute, neglected and delinquent juvenile and child.

3. The Bill seeks to repeal and re-enact the Juvenile Justice Act, 1986 with a view to achieving the above objects.

## ACT 56 OF 2000

The Juvenile Justice (Care and Protection of Children) Bill having been passed by both the Houses of Parliament received the assent of the President on 30th December, 2000. It came on the Statute Book as THE JUVENILE JUSTICE (CARE AND PROTECTION OF CHILDREN) ACT, 2000 (56 of 2000) (*Came into force on 1-4-2001*).

## LIST OF AMENDING ACTS

1. The Juvenile Justice (Care and Protection of Children) Amendment Act, 2006 (33 of 2006) (w.e.f. 22-8-2006).
2. The Juvenile Justice (Care and Protection of Children) Amendment Act, 2011 (12 of 2011) (w.e.f. 1-1-2012).

### SYNOPSIS

**1.** Articles 14 of Constitution – Comments on
**2.** Constitutional Laws – Comments on
**3.** Directive Principles of State Policy – Comments on
**4.** Directory Provision – Considerations for
**5.** International Conventions on Juvenile Justice – Comments on
**6.** International Law – Importance of
**7.** Juvenile Justice Act, 2000 – Purpose of
**8.** Juveniles in Conflict with Law – Law for
**9.** Legislation – Rule for
**10.** Legislative Classification – Principle of
**11.** Pith and Substance – Doctrine of
**12.** Principle of Equality – Comments on
**13.** Reasonable Classification – Legality of
**14.** Sovereign Powers – Comments on
**15.** Statement of Objects and Reasons – Comments on
**16.** Statement of Objects and Reasons – Necessity of
**17.** Statement of Objects and Reasons – Need of
**18.** Statement of Objects and Reasons – No Use of
**19.** Statement of Objects and Reasons – Admissibility of
**20.** Statement of Objects and Reasons and Preamble – Law for
**21.** Statement of Objects and Reasons – Law on
**22.** Statute – Presumption for
**23.** Legislative Function – Guidelines for

### COMMENTS

**1. Articles 14 of Constitution – Comments on –** The principles underlying article 14 of the Constitution are well-settled. The only difficulty which arises is in regard to the application of those principles to the facts of a particular case and the Court has to consider the terms of the impugned legislation having regard to the background and the surrounding circumstances so far as it may be necessary to do so in order to arrive at a conclusion when it infringes the fundamental right in question; *A. Thangla Kunju Musaliar* v. *M. Venkatachalam Potti, Authorised Official and Income-Tax Officer*, AIR 1956 SC 246: 1956 SCJ 323: 1955 (2) SCR 1196 (FB).

**2. Constitutional Laws – Comments on –** The preamble to the Constitution mentions one of the objects to be to secure to all its citizens equality of status and opportunity. Article 14 provides: "the State shall not deny to any person equality before the law or the equal protection of the laws within the territory of India. Then follow articles 15 and 16, the former prohibiting discrimination on grounds of religion, race, caste, sex, place of birth, or any of them, and the latter providing of equality of opportunity in matters of public employment. Leaving aside article 17 to 19 as irrelevant for present purposes, article 20, 21, and 22, which deal with prosecutions and convictions for offences and cases of preventive detention and prescribe, in rough and general outline, certain matters of procedure. Article 21, is so to say, the key of this group of bunch and it is in these terms: No person shall be deprived of his life or personal liberty except according to procedure established by law"; *State of West Bengal; Habib Mohammad, State of Hyderabad State of Mysore* v. *Anwar Ali Sarkar*, AIR 1952 SC 75: 1952 Cr LJ 510: 1952 SCR 284.

**3. Directive Principles of State Policy – Comments on –** Function of the State has long since ceased to be confined to the preservation of the public peace, the exaction of taxes and the defence of its frontiers. It is now the function of the State to secure to its citizens 'social, economic and political justice', to preserve 'liberty of thought, expression, belief, faith and worship' and to ensure 'equality of status and of opportunity and 'the dignity of the individual' and the unity of the nation'. That is what the Preamble to our Constitution says and that is what is elaborated in the two vital Chapters of the Constitution on Fundamental Rights and Directive Principles of State Policy. The desire to attain these objectives has necessarily resulted in intense legislative activity touching every aspect of the life of the citizen and the nation. Executive activity in the field of delegated or subordinate legislation has increased in direct, geometric progression. It has to be and it is as it should be. The Parliament and the State Legislature are not bodies of experts or specialists. They are skilled in the art of discovering the aspirations, the expectations and the needs, the limits to the patience and the acquiescence and the articulation of the views of the people whom they represent. They function best when they concern themselves with general principles, broad objectives and fundamental issues instead of technical and situational intricacies which are better left to better equipped full time expert executive bodies and specialist public servants. Parliament and the State Legislatures have neither the time nor the expertise to be involved in detail and circumstances. Nor can Parliament and the State Legislature visualise and provide for new, strange, unforeseen and unpredictable situations arising from the complexity of modern life and the ingenuity of modern man. That is the raison *d'etre* for delegated legislation. That is what makes delegated legislation inevitable and indispensable. The Indian Parliament and the State Legislatures are endowed with plenary power to legislate upon any of the subjects entrusted to them by the Constitution, subject to the limitations imposed by the Constitution itself. The power to legislate carries with it the power to delegate. But excessive delegation may amount to abdication. Delegation unlimited may invite despotism uninhibited. So, the theory has been evolved that the Legislature cannot delegate its essential legislative function. Legislate it must by laying down policy and principle and delegate it may to fill in detail and carry out policy. The Legislature may guide the delegate by speaking through the express provision empowering delegation or the other provision of the statute, the preamble, the scheme or even the very subject-matter of the statute. If guidance there is, wherever it may be found, the delegation is valid. A good deal of latitude has been held to be permissible in the case of taxing statutes and on the same principle a generous degree of latitude must be permissible in the case of welfare legislation, particularly those statutes which are designed to further the Directive Principles of State Policy; *Registrar of Co-Operative Societies* v. *K. Kunjabmu*, AIR 1980 SC 350: 1980 (1) SCC 340: 1980 (2) SCR 260.

**4. Directory Provision – Considerations for –** Thus two considerations for regarding a provision as directory are: (1) absence of any provision for the contingency of a particular provision not being complied with or followed and (2) serious general inconvenience and prejudice that would result to the general public if the act of the Government or an instrumentality is declared invalid for non-compliance with the particular provision; *Atlas Cycle Industries Limited* v. *State of Haryana,* AIR 1979 SC 1149: 1979 Cr LJ 927: 1979 (2) SCC 196.

**5. International Conventions on Juvenile Justice – Comments on –** The Geneva declaration of 1924 on the rights of the child adopted by the League of Nations on 26th September, 1924 provided that mankind owe to the child the best that it has to give, declare and accept it as their duty. Thus, the child must be given the means requisite for its normal development, both materially and spirituality. A hungry child must be fed and further recognised various child rights included that the delinquent child must be reclaimed. The declaration of the right of the child adopted by the United Nations on 20th November, 1959, provides that the child by reason of his physical and mental immaturity needs special safeguards and care including his appropriate legal protection before as well as after birth. The United Nations adopted Standard Minimum Rules for the Administration of Juvenile Justice (The Beijing Rules) dated November 29, 1985. India is a signatory to the Declaration and effectively participated in bringing the Declaration into force. The Rules guide the States to protect children's rights and respect their needs during the development of separate and particular system of juvenile justice. It is also in favour of meeting the best interests of the child while conducting any proceedings before any authority. If children are processed through the criminal justice system, it results in the stigma of criminality and this in fact amplifies criminality of the child. The Rules say that depriving a child/juvenile of his liberty should be used as the last resort and that too, for the shortest period. These Rules direct the Juvenile Justice System to be fair and humane, emphasising the well- being of the child. Besides that, the importance of rehabilitation is also stressed demanding necessary assistance in the form of education, employment or shelter to be given to the child. The Juvenile Justice Act, 1986 was enacted in pursuance of the Constitutional obligations cast under article 39, clause (f) of the Constitution of India as well as of commitment to the aforesaid International Conventions. The Convention postulates that State Parties recognise that every child has the inherent right to life. States Parties shall ensure that no child shall be subjected to torture or other cruel, inhuman or degrading treatment or punishment. Neither capital punishment nor life imprisonment without possibility of release shall be imposed for offences committed by persons below 18 years of age. Aims of juvenile justice provide that the juvenile Justice system shall emphasize the well-being of the juvenile and shall ensure that any reaction to juvenile offenders shall always be in proportion to the circumstances of both the offenders and the offence. The said Rules further lays down that restrictions on the personal liberty of the juvenile shall be imposed only after careful consideration and shall be limited to the possible minimum; and deprivation of personal liberty shall not be imposed unless the juvenile is adjudicated of a serious act involving violence against another person or of persistence in committing other serious offences and unless there is no other appropriate response. The Statement of Objects and Reasons of JJ Act reveal that the Act is in consonance with the provisions under article 21 of the Constitution read with clause (f) of article 39 of the Constitution which provides that the State shall direct its policy towards securing the children or give opportunities and facilities to develop in a healthy manner and in conditions of freedom and dignity and the childhood and youth are protected against exploitation and against moral and material abandonment; *Essa @ Anjum Abdul Razak Memon* v. *State of Maharashtra*, 2013 (3) Supreme 195: JT 2013 (6) SC 1: 2013 (3) SCALE 1 (SC).

**6. International Law – Importance of –** The Juvenile Justice Act specially refers to international law. The relevant provisions of the Rules are incorporated therein. The international treatises, covenants and conventions although may not be a part of our municipal law, the same can be referred to and followed by the courts having regard to the fact that India is a party to the said treatises. A right to a speedy trial is not a new right. It is embedded in our Constitution in terms of articles 14 and 21 thereof. The international treaties recognize the same. It is now trite that any violation of human rights would be looked down upon. Some provisions of the international law although may not be a part of our municipal law but the courts are not hesitant in referring thereto so as to find new rights in the context of the Constitution. Constitution of India and other ongoing statutes have been read consistently with the rules of international law. Constitution is a source of, and not an exercise of, legislative power. The principles of International law whenever applicable operate as a statutory implication but the Legislature in the instant case held itself bound thereby and, thus, did not legislate in disregard of the constitutional provisions or the international law as also in the context of articles 20 and 21 of the constitution of India. The law has to be understood, therefore, in accordance with the international law. Part III of our Constitution protects substantive as well as procedural rights. Implications which arise therefrom must effectively be protected by the Judiciary. A contextual meaning of the statute is required to be assigned having regard to the Constitutional as well as International Law operating in the field; *Pratap Singh* v. *State of Jharkhand*, AIR 2005 SC 2731: 2005 (1) SCALE 763: 2005 (3) SCC 551.

**7. Juvenile Justice Act, 2000 – Purpose of –** The Juvenile Justice (Care and Protection of Children) Act, 2000 is an Act to consolidate and amend the law relating to juveniles in conflict with law and children in need of care and protection by providing for proper care, protection and treatment by catering to their development needs and by adopting the child-friendly approach in the adjudication and disposition of matters in the "best interest of children and for their ultimate rehabilitation". Reference is made in this regard to article 15(3), 39(e), (f), 45 and 47 of the Constitution; *Vidya* v. *Government of India*, 2010 Cr LJ 1387: 2010 (3) AICLR 308: 2009 (4) Ker LT 937 (Ker).

**8. Juveniles in Conflict with Law – Law for –** The 2000 Act came into force w.e.f. 1st April, 2001. It is an act to consolidate and amend the law relating to juveniles in conflict with law and children in need of care and protection, by providing for proper care, protection and treatment by catering to their development needs, and by adopting a child-friendly approach in the adjudication and disposition of matters in the best interest of children and for their ultimate rehabilitation and for matters connected therewith or incidental thereto; *Lakhan Lal* v. *State of Bihar*, 2011 (1) SCALE 504: 2011 (2) SCC 251: 2011 (1) SCR 770.

**9. Legislation – Rule for –** Legislation enacted for the achievement of a particular object or purpose need not be all embracing. It is for the Legislature to determine what categories it would embrace within the scope of legislation and merely because certain categories which would stand on the same footing as those which, are covered by the legislation are left out would not render legislation which has been enacted in any manner discriminatory and violative of the fundamental right guaranteed by article 14 of the Constitution." Social legislation would be impossible, social reform would be impossible, if the Legislature was to be expected to pass legislation embracing the whole people, and therefore if social reform is enacted by stages that would be permissible under article 14, Bhagwati J. himself points out that if you go by stages you must apply the law to a particular category and postpone the application of the law to another category for a future time; *S.C. Prashar* v. *Vasantsen Dwarkadas*, AIR 1956 Bom 530: 1956 (58) BLR 184: 1956 (29) ITR 857 (DB).

**10. Legislative Classification – Principle of –** The principle of legislative classification is an accepted principle whereunder persons may be classified into groups and such groups may differently be treated if there is a reasonable basis for such difference or distinction. The rule of differentiation is that in enacting laws differentiating between different persons or things in different circumstances which govern one set of persons or objects such laws may not necessarily be the same as those governing another set of persons or objects so that the question of unequal treatment does not really arise between persons governed by different conditions and different set of circumstances. The limit of valid classification must not be arbitrary but scientific and rational. It must always rest upon some real and substantial distinction bearing reasonable and just relation to the needs in respect of which the classification is made; *Kartar Singh; Kripa Shankar Rai* v. *State of Punjab*, 1994 Cr LJ 3139: JT 1994 (2) SC 423: 1994 (2) SCR 375.

**11. Pith and Substance – Doctrine of –** This doctrine of 'pith and substance is applied when the legislative competence of a Legislature with regard to a particular enactment is challenged with reference to the entries in the various lists *i.e.*, a law dealing with the subject in one list is also touching on a subject in another list. In such a case, what has to be ascertained is the pith and substance of the enactment. On a scrutiny of the Act in question, if found, that the legislation is in substance one on a matter assigned to the Legislature enacting that statute, then that Act as a whole must be held to be valid notwithstanding any incidental trenching upon matters beyond its competence *i.e.*, on a matter included in the List, belonging to the other Legislature. To say differently, incidental encroachment is not altogether forbidden; *Kartar Singh; Kripa Shankar Rai* v. *State of Punjab,* 1994 Cr LJ 3139: JT 1994 (2) SC 423: 1994 (2) SCR 375.

**12. Principle of Equality – Comments on –** The framers of the Constitution have referred to equality in the Preamble, and have devoted as many as five articles, namely, articles 14, 15, 16, 17 and 18 in the Chapter on Fundamental Rights to ensure equality in all its aspects. Some of these articles are confined to citizens only and some can be availed of by non-citizens also; but on reading these provisions as a whole, one can see the great importance attached to the principle of equality in the Constitution; *State of West Bengal* v. *Anwar Ali Sarkar,* AIR 1952 SC 75: 1952 Cr LJ 510: 1952 SCR 284.

**13. Reasonable Classification – Legality of –** It is well settled that equality before the law or the equal protection of laws does not mean identity abstract symmetry of treatments. Distinctions have to be made for different classes and groups of persons and a rational or reasonable classification is permitted, as otherwise it would be almost impossible to carry on the work of Government of any State or country; *State of West Bengal* v. *Anwar Ali Sarkar,* AIR 1952 SC 75: 1952 Cr LJ 510: 1952 SCR 284.

**14. Sovereign Powers – Comments on –** Every student of Constitutional Law is well aware that constitutional lawyers classify the State's sovereign power into three categories, namely the power of taxation, the power of eminent domain and the police power. These are distinct categories of sovereign powers with different connotations subserving different needs of the society and the State; *State of West Bengal* v. *Subodh Gopal Bose,* AIR 1954 SC 92: 1954 SCJ 127: 1954 SCR 587.

**15. Statement of Objects and Reasons – Comments on –** It is now well settled that though the Statement of Objects and Reasons accompanying a legislative Bill cannot be used to determine the true meaning and effect of the substantive provisions of a statute, it is permissible to refer to the Statement of Objects and Reasons accompanying a Bill for the purpose of understanding the background, the antecedent state of affairs, the surrounding circumstances in relation to the statute, and the evil which the statute sought to remedy; *Narain Khamman* v. *Parduman Kumar Jain,* AIR 1985 SC 4: 1984 (2) SCALE 650: 1985 (1) SCC 1.

**16. Statement of Objects and Reasons – Necessity of –** The Statement of objects and reasons cannot be taken into account for the purpose of interpreting the plain words of the section. But it gives an indication as to what the Legislature wanted to achieve; *Workmen of Firestone Tyre and Rubber Co. of India P. Ltd.* v. *Management,* AIR 1973 SC 1227: 1973 (1) SCC 813: 1973 (3) SCR 587.

**17. Statement of Objects and Reasons – Need of –** The Statement of Objects and Reasons of the Act may suggest something if there are any type of confusion; *State of West Bengal* v. *Swapan Kumar Guha,* AIR 1982 SC 949: 1982 (1) SCALE 38: 1982 (1) SCC 561.

**18. Statement of Objects and Reasons - No Use of –** If the meaning of the provision of a statute is clear and explicit, it is not necessary to advert to the Statement of objects and reasons thereof; *Raymond Ltd.* v. *State of Chhattisgarh,* AIR 2007 SC 2854: 2007 (3) SCALE 341: 2007 (3) SCC 79.

**19. Statement of Objects and Reasons – Admissibility of –** The Statement of Objects and Reasons is not admissible, however, for construing the section; far less can it control the actual words used; *Central Bank of India* v. *Their Workmen,* (1960) 1 SCR 200: AIR 1960 SC 12 (21).

**20. Statement of Objects and Reasons and Preamble – Law for –** Statement of objects and reasons for introducing a Bill in the Legislature is not admissible as an aid to the construction of the statute as enacted; far less can it control the meaning of the actual words used in the Act. It can only be referred to for the limited purpose of ascertaining the circumstances which actuated the sponsor of the Bill to introduce it and the purpose for doing so. The preamble of a statute which is often described as a key to the understanding of it may legitimately be consulted to solve an ambiguity or to ascertain and fix the meaning of words in their context which otherwise bear more meanings than one. It may afford useful assistance as to what the statute intends to reach, but if the enactment is clear and unambiguous in itself then no preamble can vary its meaning. While construing a statute one has also to bear in mind the presumption that the Legislature does not intend to make any substantial alteration in the existing law beyond what it expressly declares or beyond the immediate scope and object of the statute; *A.C. Sharma* v. *Delhi Administration*, AIR 1973 SC 913: 1973 Cr LR 292: 1973 (1) SCC 726.

**21. Statement of Objects and Reasons – Law on –** It is however well settled that the Statement of Objects and Reasons accompanying a bill, when introduced in Parliament cannot be used to determine the true meaning and effect of substantive provisions of the statute. They cannot be used except for the limited purpose of understanding the background and the antecedent state of affairs leading up to the legislation. But we cannot use this statement as an aid to the construction of the enactment or to show that the Legislature did not intend to acquire the proprietary rights vested in the State or in any way to affect the State Governments' rights as owner of minerals. A statute, as passed by Parliament, is the expression of the collective intention of the Legislature as a whole, and any statement made by an individual, albeit a Minister, of the intention and objects of the Act cannot be used to cut down the generality of the words used in the statute"; *State of West Bengal* v. *Union of India*, (1964) 1 SCR 371 (382): AIR 1963 SC 1241 (1247).

**22. Statute – Presumption for –** The presumption is always in favour of the constitutionality of an enactment, since it must be assumed that the Legislature understands and correctly appreciates the needs of his own people that its law is directed to problems made manifest by experience and its discriminations are based on adequate grounds. The presumption may be rebutted in certain cases by showing that on the face of the statute, there is no classification at all and no difference peculiar to any individual or class and not applicable to any other individual or class, and yet the law hits only a particular individual or class. The principle of equality does not mean that every law must have universal application for all persons who are not by nature, attainment or circumstances in the same position, and the varying needs of different classes of persons often require separate treatment. The principle does not take away from the State the power of classifying persons for legitimate purposes. Every classification is in some degree likely to produce some inequality, and mere production of inequality is not enough. If a law deals equally with members of a well defined class, it is not obnoxious and it is not open to the charge of denial of equal protection on the ground that it has no application to other persons. While reasonable classification is permissible, such classification must be based upon some real and substantial distinction bearing a reasonable and just relation to the object sought to be attained, and the classification cannot be made arbitrarily and without any substantial basis; *State of West Bengal* v. *Anwar Ali Sarkar*, AIR 1952 SC 75: 1952 Cr LJ 510: 1952 SCR 284.

**23. Legislative Function – Guidelines for –** The Legislature cannot delegate its function of laying down legislative policy in respect of a measure and its formulation as a rule of conduct. The Legislature must declare the policy of the law and the legal principles which are to control any given cases and must provide a standard to guide the officials or the body in power to execute the law. The essential legislative function consists in the determination or choice of the legislative policy and of formally enacting that policy into a binding rule of conduct; *Harishankar Bagla* v. *State of Madhya Pradesh*, (1955) 1 SCR 380.

# THE JUVENILE JUSTICE (CARE AND PROTECTION OF CHILDREN) ACT, 2000

(56 of 2000)

[*30th December, 2000*]

*An Act to consolidate and amend the law relating to juveniles in conflict with law and children in need of care and protection, by providing for proper care, protection and treatment by catering to their development needs, and by adopting a child-friendly approach in the adjudication and disposition of matters in the best interest of children and for their ultimate rehabilitation* [1][*and for matters connected therewith or incidental thereto*].

WHEREAS the Constitution has, in several provisions, including clause (3) of article 15, clauses (e) and (f) of article 39, articles 45 and 47, impose on the State a primary responsibility of ensuring that all the needs of children are met and that their basic human rights are fully protected;

AND WHEREAS, the General Assembly of the United Nations has adopted the Convention on the Rights of the Child on the 20th November, 1989;

AND WHEREAS, the Convention on the Rights of the Child has prescribed a set of standards to be adhered to by all State parties in securing the best interests of the child;

AND WHEREAS, the Convention on the Rights of the Child emphasises social reintegration of child victims, to the extent possible, without resorting to judicial proceedings;

AND WHEREAS, the Government of India has ratified the Convention on the 11th December, 1992.

AND WHEREAS, it is expedient to re-enact the existing law relating to juveniles bearing in mind the standards prescribed in the Convention on the Rights of the Child, the United Nations Standard Minimum Rules for the Administration of Juvenile Justice, 1985 (the Beijing Rules), the United Nations Rules for the Protection of Juveniles Deprived of their Liberty (1990), and all other relevant international instruments.

BE it enacted by Parliament in the Fifty-first Year of the Republic of India as follows:—

**SYNOPSIS**

1. Government of India – Policy of
2. Preamble and Directive Principles – Role of
3. Preamble – Aid of
4. Preamble – Effect of
5. Preamble – Law on
6. Preamble – Need of
7. Preamble – No Need of
8. Preamble – Role of

**COMMENTS**

**1. Government of India – Policy of –** The great concern for the welfare of the children at the international level culminated in the Declaration of the Rights of the Child adopted by the General Assembly of the United Nations on 20th November, 1959. The declaration in its Preamble points out that "the child, by reason of his physical

1. Subs. by Act 33 of 2006, sec. 2, for "through various institutions established under this enactment" (w.e.f. 22-8-2006).

and mental immaturity, needs special safeguards and care, including appropriate legal protection, before as well as after birth", and that "mankind owes to the child the best it has to give". It is the experience of the society that a child can be moulded so that he can become a good citizen. Today's children are tomorrows citizens. If we are successful in treating the children with love and affection and take proper care for their welfare, then those children in future will become good citizens and they would know their duties towards their nation, fellow human beings and family members. Responsible attitude, lovely and kind treatment of the parents, teachers and other family members and elders mould the children as healthy children and in future responsible and duty minded citizens. The children who are loved and treated with care and affection would certainly become good citizens and they love the human beings and treat other living beings kindly. If the children are ill-treated and tortured, then the seeds of hatred would develop in their minds and in future they may become criminals. A study of the children kept in observation homes reveals that 70% of the children are from disturbed families. The children, when abandoned by both the parents or either of them and neglected by the near and dear, and who have no support would be forced to work in hazardous conditions. When they run away from such situations and found wandering, sometimes they are made as bonded labourers or implicated in false criminal cases and in some other cases antisocial elements, bootleggers, smugglers may take control of such children and use them for their anti-social and anti-national activities. Thus the ill-treatment and the torture of the children make the children hatred and sometimes make them hardened criminals. Thus it is the socio-economic conditions particularly the poverty which force the children to leave their houses and therefore, a great responsibility lies on the society, on the government and social organizations to pick up such children and provide them basic needs and treat them with love and affection and see that they become good citizens. These constitutional provisions show great anxiety of the constitution makers to protect and safeguard the interests and welfare of the children in the country. The Government of India has also in pursuance of these constitutional provisions evolved a national policy for the welfare of the children; *Chagalamarri Subbaiah* v. *State Rep. by its Public Prosecutor,* 2010 Cr LJ 655: 2009 (2) ALD (Cri) 121: 2009 (3) ALT (Cri) 36 (AP).

**2. Preamble and Directive Principles – Role of –** When Courts consider the question whether a statute offends article 14 of the Constitution Courts must also consider whether a classification that the Legislature may have made is consistent with the socialist goals set out in the Preamble and the Directive Principles enumerated in Part IV of the Constitution. A classification which is not in tune with the Constitution is *per se* unreasonable and cannot be permitted; *Atam Prakash* v. *State of Haryana,* AIR 1986 SC 859: 1986 (1) SCALE 260: 1986 (2) SCC 249.

**3. Preamble – Aid of –** The preamble provides the key to the general purpose of the Act; *Superintendent and Remembrancer of Legal Affairs, West Bengal* v. *Girish Kumar Navalkha,* AIR 1975 SC 1030: 1975 (4) SCC 754: 1975 (3) SCR 802.

**4. Preamble – Effect of –** Preamble cannot control the Provision of any enactment where the language is plain and unambiguous; *State of West Bengal* v. *Anwar Ali Sarkar,* AIR 1952 SC 75: 1952 Cr LJ 510: 1952 SCR 284.

**5. Preamble – Law on –** The policy and the wisdom of the Legislature cannot be tested by taking aid of the preamble of the Act particularly when the language of section inclusive, unambiguous, specific and explicit. Preamble of the Act is the key to open the mind of the Legislature when the language of the statute is ambiguous; *Sita Devi* v. *State of Bihar,* JT 1995 (1) SC 410: 1994 (5) SCALE 86: 1995 (Supp) 1 SCC 670.

**6. Preamble – Need of –** The preamble and the provisions of statute no doubt assist the Court in finding out its object and policy but its object and policy need not always be strictly confined to its preamble and the provisions contained therein; *Punjab*

*Tin Supply Co., Chandigarh* v. *Central Government,* AIR 1984 SC 87: 1983 (2) SCALE 503: 1984 (1) SCC 206.

**7. Preamble – No Need of –** The preamble of each Act need not be resorted to for construing its provisions and in particular for understanding the meaning of the word; *Burrakur Coal Co. Ltd.* v. *Union of India,* AIR 1961 SC 954: 1962 (2) SCJ 216: 1962 (1) SCR 44.

**8. Preamble – Role of –** A preamble is a key to the interpretation of a Statute but is not ordinarily an independent enactment conferring rights or taking them away and cannot restrict or widen the enacting part which is clear and unambiguous. The motive for legislation is often recited in the preamble but the remedy may extend beyond the cure of the evil intended to be removed; *R. Venkataswami Naidu* v. *Narasram Naraindas,* AIR 1966 SC 361: 1966 (1) Mad LJ 1: 1966 (1) SCR 110 (FB). See *Maxwell on Interpretation of Statutes,* 11th Edn., p. 45.

## *CHAPTER I*

## PRELIMINARY

**1. Short title, extent [1][, commencement and application].—**(1) This Act may be called the Juvenile Justice (Care and Protection of Children) Act, 2000.

(2) It extends to the whole of India except the State of Jammu and Kashmir.

(3) It shall come into force on such date[2] as the Central Government may, by notification in the Official Gazette, appoint.

[3][(4) Notwithstanding anything contained in any other law for the time being in force, the provisions of this Act shall apply to all cases involving detention, prosecution, penalty or sentence of imprisonment of juveniles in conflict with law under any such law.]

### SYNOPSIS

1. International Treaty – Comments on
2. Notable Distinction – Comments on
3. Object of Act – Comments on
4. Penal Statute – Construction of
5. Act – Salient Features – Comments on
6. Act – Salient Features of
7. Construction – Cardinal Principle of
8. Construction – Comments on
9. Construction – Rule of
10. Construction – Rule on
11. Legislature – Intention of
12. Provisions of Statute – Interpretation of
13. Statutory Notification – Comments on

### COMMENTS

**1. International Treaty – Comments on –** It can therefore be seen that there is no automatic acceptance of an international treaty, even post ratification, as domestic law in India. It only becomes binding as law once Parliament has indicated its acceptance of the ratified treaty through enabling legislation. Since no such legislation exists, this treaty is not binding, and therefore, non-compliance with its provisions does not result in a violation of the procedure established by law. The only rider is that if the standard postulated in the covenant or international treaty is consistent with Indian law, the same can be considered as an aid to interpretation of the relevant provision of municipal law; *Jamal Mirza* v. *State,* 2012 (2) AD (Del) 366: 2013 (6) RCR (Cri) 2775 (Del) (DB).

---

1. Subs. by Act 33 of 2006, sec. 3, for "and commencement" (w.e.f. 22-8-2006).
2. Came into force on 1-4-2001, *vide* S.O. 177(E), dated 28th February, 2001, published in the Gazette of India, Extra., Pt. II, Sec. 3(ii), dated 28th February, 2001.
3. Ins. by Act 33 of 2006, sec. 3 (w.e.f. 22-8-2006).

**2. Notable Distinction – Comments on –** Sub-section (1) of section 2 of 2000 Act defines "juvenile in conflict with law" means a juvenile who is alleged to have committed an offence. The notable distinction between the definitions of 1986 Act and 2000 Act is that in 1986 Act "juvenile in conflict with law" is absent. The definition of delinquent juvenile in 1986 Act is referable to an offence said to have been committed by him. It is the date of offence that he was in conflict with law. When a juvenile is produced before the competent authority and or court he has not committed an offence on that date, but he was brought before the authority for the alleged offence which he has been found to have committed. What was implicit in 1986 Act has been made explicit in 2000 Act; *Pratap Singh* v. *State of Jharkhand*, AIR 2005 SC 2731: 2005 (1) SCALE 763: 2005 (3) SCC 551.

**3. Object of Act – Comments on –** Whole object of the Act is to provide for the care, protection, treatment, development and rehabilitation of neglected delinquent juveniles. It is a beneficial legislation aimed at to make available the benefit of the Act to the neglected or delinquent juveniles. It is settled law that the interpretation of the Statute of beneficial legislation must be to advance the cause of legislation to the benefit for whom it is made and not to frustrate the intendment of the legislation; *Pratap Singh* v. *State of Jharkhand*, AIR 2005 SC 2731: 2005 (1) SCALE 763: 2005 (3) SCC 551.

**4. Penal Statute – Construction of –** In construing a penal statute, the object of the law must be clearly borne in mind. The importance of time-bound investigation and a trial in relation to an offence allegedly committed by a juvenile is explicit as has been dealt with in some details hereinbefore. While making investigation it is expected that the accused would be arrested forthwith. He, upon his arrest; if he appears to be a juvenile, cannot be kept in police custody and may be released on bail. If he is not released on bail by the arresting authority, he has to be produced before the competent Court or Board. Once he appears to be juvenile, the competent court and/or board may pass an appropriate order upon releasing him on bail or send him to a protective custody. An inquiry for the purpose of determination of age of the juvenile need not be resorted to if the person produced is admitted to be a juvenile. An inquiry would be necessary only if a dispute is raised in that behalf. A decision thence is required to be taken by the competent court and/or board having regard to the status of the accused as to whether he is to be released on bail or sent to a protective custody or remanded to police or judicial custody. For the said purpose what is necessary would be to find out as to whether on the date of commission of the offence he was a juvenile or not as otherwise the purpose for which the Act was enacted would be defeated. The provisions of the said Act, as indicated hereinbefore, clearly postulate that the necessary steps in the proceedings are required to be taken not only for the purpose of adopting a special procedure at the initial stage but also for the intermediary and final stage of the proceedings. If the person concerned is a juvenile, he cannot be tried along with other adult accused. His trial must be held by the Board separately. Having regard to rule 20.1 of the Rules his case is required to be determined, without any unnecessary delay. In the trial, the right of the juvenile as regard his privacy must be protected. He is entitled to be represented by a legal adviser and for free legal aid, if he applies therefor. His parents and/or guardian are also entitled to participate in the proceedings. The court would be entitled to take into consideration the social Inquiry Reports wherein the background and the circumstances in which the juvenile was living and the condition in which the offence had been created may be properly investigated so as to facilitate juvenile adjudication of the case by the competent authority. At all stages, the Court Board is required to pass an appropriate order expeditiously. Right of a juvenile to get his case disposed of expeditiously is a statutory as also a constitutional right; *Pratap Singh* v. *State of Jharkhand*, AIR 2005 SC 2731: 2005 (1) SCALE 763: 2005 (3) SCC 551.

**5. Act – Salient Features – Comments on –** The salient features of the 2000 Act may be noticed at the outset. Section 1(3) of the said Act states that it would come into force on such date as the Central Government may, by notification in the Official Gazette, appoint. The Central Government had issued an appropriate notification in terms whereof; 1-4-2001 has been specified as the 'appointed date' from which the provisions of the said Act will come into force. The Act, thus, is prospective in its operation. However, the 2000 Act has repealed the Act of 1986. It has obliterated the distinction between juvenile of different sex by reason whereof, a male juvenile would also be juvenile if he has not crossed the age of 18; *Bijender Singh* v. *State of Haryana,* AIR 2005 SC 2262: 2005 (3) SCALE 467: 2005 (3) SCC 685.

**6. Act – Salient Features of –** The salient features of the Act of 2000 may be noticed at the outset. Section 1(3) of the Act of 2000 states that it would come into force on such date as the Central Government may, by notification in the official Gazette, appoint. The Central Government had issued an appropriate notification in terms whereof; 1-4-2001 has been specified as the 'appointed date' from which the provisions of the said Act will come into force. The Act, thus, is prospective in its operation. However, the Act of 2000 has repealed the Act of 1986. It has obliterated the distinction between juvenile of different sex by reason whereof, a male juvenile would also be juvenile if he has not crossed the age of 18; *Pratap Singh* v. *State of Jharkhand,* AIR 2005 SC 2731: 2005 (1) SCALE 763: 2005 (3) SCC 551.

**7. Construction – Cardinal Principle of –** It is a cardinal principle of construction of a statute that when the language of the statute is plain and unambiguous, then the court must give effect to the words used in the statute and it would not be open to the courts to adopt a hypothetical construction on the grounds that such construction is more consistent with the alleged object and policy of the Act; *Union of India* v. *Hansoli Devi,* 2002 (7) SCC.

**8. Construction – Comments on –** It is true that the consequences of a suggested construction cannot alter the meaning of a statutory provision but it can certainly help to fix its meaning. It is a well recognised rule of construction that a statutory provision must be so construed, if possible, that absurdity and mischief may be avoided; *K.P. Varghese* v. *Income-Tax Officer, Ernakulam,* AIR 1981 SC 1922: 1981 (3) SCALE 1315: 1981 (4) SCC 173.

**9. Construction – Rule of –** It is a settled rule of construction that to ascertain the legislative intent, all the constituent parts of a statute are to be taken together and each word, phrase or sentence is to be considered in the light of the general purpose and object of the Act itself; *Poppatlal Shah* v. *State of Madras,* AIR 1953 SC 274: 1953 Cr LJ 1105: 1953 SCR 677.

**10. Construction – Rule on –** It is well-settled that the statement of objects and reasons is not admissible as an aid to the construction of the statute; *State of West Bengal* v. *Subodh Gopal Bose,* AIR 1954 SC 92: 1954 (1) Mad LJ 314: 1954 SCR 587.

**11. Legislature – Intention of –** Where the language is clear, the intention of the Legislature has to be gathered from the language used; *Grasim Industries Limited* v. *Collector of Customs,* 2002 (4) SCC 297 [*Vide* also: *Union of India* v. *Hamsoli Devi,* 2002 (7) SCC 273].

**12. Provisions of Statute – Interpretation of –** It is a well settled rule that in interpreting the provisions of a statute the court will presume that the legislation was intended to be *intra vires* and also reasonable; *All Saints High School* v. *Government of Andhra Pradesh,* AIR 1980 SC 1042: 1980 (2) SCC 478: 1980 (2) SCR 924.

**13. Statutory Notification – Comments on –** The validity of the statutory notification cannot be judged merely on the basis of Statement of Objects and Reasons accompanying the Bill. Nor it could be tested by the Government policy taken from time to time. The executive policy of the Government, or the Statement of Objects and Reasons of the Act or Ordinance cannot control the actual words used in the legislation; *Utkal Contractors* *and Joinery Pvt. Ltd.* v. *State of Orissa,* AIR 1987 SC 2310: 1987 (2) SCALE 639: 1988 (1) SCR 314.

**2. Definitions.**—In this Act, unless the context otherwise requires,—

(a) "advisory board" means a Central or a State advisory board or a district and city level advisory board, as the case may be, constituted under section 62;

[1][(aa) "adoption" means the process through which the adopted child is permanently separated from his biological parents and become the legitimate child of his adoptive parents with all the rights, privileges and responsibilities that are attached to the relationship;]

(b) "begging" means—

(i) soliciting or receiving alms in a public place or entering into any private premises for the purpose of soliciting or receiving alms, whether under any pretence;

(ii) exposing or exhibiting with the object of obtaining or extorting alms, any sore, wound, injury, deformity or disease, whether of himself or of any other person or of an animal;

(c) "Board" means a Juvenile Justice Board constituted under section 4;

(d) "child in need of care and protection" means a child—

(i) who is found without any home or settled place or abode and without any ostensible means of subsistence,

[1][(ia) who is found begging, or who is either a street child or a working child,]

(ii) who resides with a person (whether a guardian of the child or not) and such person—

(a) has threatened to kill or injure the child and there is a reasonable likelihood of the threat being carried out, or

(b) has killed, abused or neglected some other child or children and there is a reasonable likelihood of the child in question being killed, abused or neglected by that person,

(iii) who is mentally or physically challenged or ill children or children suffering from terminal diseases or incurable diseases having no one to support or look after,

(iv) who has a parent or guardian and such parent or guardian is unfit or incapacitated to exercise control over the child,

(v) who does not have parent and no one is willing to take care of or whose parents have abandoned [1][or surrendered] him or who is missing and run away child and whose parents cannot be found after reasonable injury,

(vi) who is being or is likely to be grossly abused, tortured or exploited for the purpose of sexual abuse or illegal acts,

1. Ins. by Act 33 of 2006, sec. 4 (w.e.f. 22-8-2006).

(vii) who is found vulnerable and is likely to be inducted into drug abuse or trafficking,

(viii) who is being or is likely to be abused for unconscionable gains,

(ix) who is victim of any armed conflict, civil commotion or natural calamity;

(e) "children's home" means an institution established by a State Government or by voluntary organisation and certified by that Government under section 34;

(f) "Committee" means a Child Welfare Committee constituted under section 29;

(g) "competent authority" means in relation to children in need of care and protection a Committee and in relation to juveniles in conflict with law a Board;

(h) "fit institution" means a governmental or a registered non-governmental organisation or a voluntary organisation prepared to own the responsibility of a child and such organisation is found fit by the [1][State Government on the recommendation of the competent authority;]

(i) "fit person" means a person, being a social worker or any other person, who is prepared to own the responsibility of a child and is found fit by the competent authority to receive and take care of the child;

(j) "guardian", in relation to a child, means his natural guardian or any other person having the actual charge or control over the child and recognised by the competent authority as a guardian in course of proceedings before that authority;

(k) "juvenile" or "child" means a person who has not completed eighteenth year of age;

[2][(l) "juvenile in conflict with law" means a juvenile who is alleged to have committed an offence and has not completed eighteenth year of age as on the date of commission of such offence;]

[3][***]

(n) "narcotic drug" and "psychotropic substance" shall have the meanings respectively assigned to them in the Narcotic Drugs and Psychotropic Substances Act, 1985 (61 of 1985);

---

1. Subs. by Act 33 of 2006, sec. 4, for "competent authority" (w.e.f. 22-8-2006).
2. Subs. by Act 33 of 2006, sec. 4, for clause (l). Clause (l), before substitution, stood as under:

   '(l) "juvenile in conflict with law" means a juvenile who is alleged to have committed an offence;' (w.e.f. 22-8-2006).'.
3. Clause (m) omitted by Act 33 of 2006, sec. 4 (w.e.f. 22-8-2006). Clause (m), before omission stood as under:

   '(m) "local authority" means Panchayats at the village and Zila Parishad at the district level and shall also include a Municipal Committee or Corporation or a Cantonment Board or such other body legally entitled to function as local authority by the Government;'.

(o) "observation home" means a home established by a State Government or by a voluntary organisation and certified by that State Government under section 8 as an observation home for the juvenile in conflict with law;

(p) "offence" means an offence punishable under any law for the time being in force;

(q) "place of safety" means any place or institution (not being a police lock-up or jail), the person incharge of which is willing temporarily to receive and take care of the juvenile and which, in the opinion of the competent authority, may be a place of safety for the juvenile;

(r) "prescribed" means prescribed by rules made under this Act;

(s) "probation officer" means an officer appointed by the State Government as a probation officer under the Probation of Offenders Act, 1958 (20 of 1958);

(t) "public place" shall have the meaning assigned to it in the Immoral Traffic (Prevention) Act, 1956 (104 of 1956);

(u) "shelter home" means a home or a drop-in-centre set up under section 37;

(v) "special home" means an institution established by a State Government or by a voluntary organisation and certified by that Government under section 9;

(w) "special juvenile police unit" means a unit of the police force of a State designated for handling of juveniles or children under section 63;

(x) "State Government", in relation to a Union territory, means the Administrator of that Union territory appointed by the President under article 239 of the Constitution;

(y) all words and expressions used but not defined in this Act and defined in the Code of Criminal Procedure, 1973 (2 of 1974), shall have the meanings respectively assigned to them in that Code.

**SYNOPSIS**

## COMMENTS

**1. Heading of a Section – Importance of –** Heading of a section is inserted by a Draftsman, and strictly speaking is not a law. It is only a guide to the contents of the part or sections which follow. It may be construed as preamble to the section. It cannot control the plain words of a section. It cannot also be referred to, for the purpose of construing the provision, when the words used in the provisions are clear and unambiguous. It cannot be used for cutting down the plain meaning of the words used in the section. It is not meant to control the operation of the enacting words. When the Court is reading a section to construe it, if the language employed is ambiguous and not clear, a doubt arises in the mind of the Court, to dispel such doubt and understand the real meaning of the section, the heading of a section aids in resolving that doubt. It will always be a useful pointer as to the intention of the Legislature in enacting the section. Beyond this, it serves no other purpose; *Y.L. Services Private Limited* v. *Silverline Business and Tech Park Private Limited,* AIR 2008 Kar 127: 2008 (4) Kar LJ 259: 2008 AIHC 1983.

**2. Statutory Definitions – Effect of –** It is well settled that all statutory definitions or abbreviations must be read subject to the qualification variously expressed in the definition clauses which created them and it may be that even where the definition is exhaustive inasmuch as the word defined is said to mean a certain thing, it is possible for the word to have a somewhat different meaning in different sections of the Act depending upon the subject or the context. That is why all definitions in statutes generally begin with the qualifying words similar to the words used in the present case, namely, unless there is anything repugnant in the subject or context; *Vanguard Fire and General Insurance Co. Ltd., Madras* v. *Fraser and Ross,* AIR 1960 SC 971: 1960 (30) Comp Cas 13: 1960 (3) SCR 857.

**3. Definition – Comments on –** Now it is well settled that where the definition of a word has not been given, it must be construed in its popular sense if it is a word of every day use, Popular sense means 'that sense which people conversant with the subject-matter with which the statute is dealing would attribute to it'; *C.I.T., Andhra Pradesh* v. *M/s. Taj Mahal Hotel, Secunderabad,* (1972) 1 SCR 168: AIR 1972 SC 168.

**4. Expression – Meaning of –** It is not correct to give as wide a meaning as possible to terms used in a statute simply because the statute does not define an expression. The correct rule is that Courts have to endeavour to find out the exact sense in which the words have been used in a particular context. Courts are entitled to look at the statute as a whole and give an interpretation in consonance with the purposes of the statute and what logically follows from the terms used; *Commissioner of Wealth-Tax, A.P.* v. *Officer-in-Charge (Court of Wards), Paigah,* AIR 1977 SC 113: 1976 (3) SCC 864: 1977 (1) SCR 146.

**5. Term – *Explanation* of –** Different statutes may use the same term for different purposes. A term or a word may be interpreted in the statute itself for fulfilling the purport and object mentioned therein whereas in another statute it may be defined differently; *Naresh Kumar Madan* v. *State of Madhya Pradesh,* AIR 2008 SC 385: 2007 (5) SCALE 510: 2007 (4) SCC 766.

**6. Juvenile – Determination of –** As per section 2(h) of the old Juvenile Justice Act, 1986, the detenu herein, who had not completed 18 years of age as on the date of commission of offence, is not a juvenile. But, as per section 2(k) of the new Juvenile Justice Act, 2000, he is a juvenile. On the date of offence, he was below 18 years of age, but, subsequently he had crossed 18 years of age and before 1-4-2001, he was above 18 years of age. As per section 2(1) of the new Act, he is a juvenile in conflict with law; *Kalai Selvi* v. *State Represented by Inspector of Police,* 2013 (4) Mad LJ (Cri) 101 (Mad) (DB).

**7. Child – Meaning of** – The word child connotes 'one who is between birth and full growth'. This would reflect upon the biological aspect. The word 'childlike' has been defined by Oxford as 'cedulous', 'foolish', 'immature', 'infantile', 'juvenile', and 'naive'. Whether a person is a juvenile, it would depend upon both, his physical growth which exemplifies adolescence coupled with his behaviour, with emphasis on the latter, because it is his conduct or rather grave misconduct that has brought him in conflict with law and society; *Shimil Kumar* v. *State of Haryana,* 2013 (4) RCR (Cri) 16: 2014 (1) Crimes 74 (P&H): 2014 (1) Crimes 528 (P&H).

**8. Borderline Juvenile – Comments on** – Where a borderline juvenile delinquent is allegedly compelled into crime due to circumstances of poverty and lack of social empowerment at the behest of overpowering malevolent forces beyond his control, denial of the healing balm of juvenile law to him would be a travesty of justice. The accused should be declared to be a juvenile in conflict with law.

**9. Child in Need of Care and Protection and Child – Law on** – A reading of the various clauses of definition makes it clear that there is difference between the child and the child in need of care and protection. A child is a person, who has not completed eighteenth year of age and the child in need of care and protection means a child, coming within the categories, as stated in section 2(d) of the Act; *Seva Chakkara Samajam* v. *Chairman, Child Welfare Committee,* 2012 (5) LW 293 (Mad).

**10. Juvenile Offender – Comments on** – One misunderstanding of the law relating to the sentencing of juveniles needs to be corrected. The general understanding of a sentence that can be awarded to a juvenile under section 15(1)(g) of the Juvenile Justice (Care and Protection of Children) Act, 2000, prior to its amendment in 2006, is that after attaining the age of eighteen years, a juvenile who is found guilty of a heinous offence is allowed to go free. The essence of the Juvenile Justice (Care and Protection of Children) Act, 2000, and the Rules framed thereunder in 2007, is restorative and not retributive, providing for rehabilitation and re-integration of children in conflict with law into mainstream society. The age of eighteen has been fixed on account of the understanding of experts in child psychology and behavioural patterns that till such an age the children in conflict with law could still be redeemed and restored to mainstream society, instead of becoming hardened criminals in future. There are, of course, exceptions where a child in the age group of sixteen to eighteen may have developed criminal propensities, which would make it virtually impossible for him/her to be re-integrated into mainstream society, but such examples are not of such proportions as to warrant any change in thinking, since it is probably better to try and re-integrate children with criminal propensities into mainstream society, rather than to allow them to develop into hardened criminals, which does not augur well for the future; *Salil Bali* v. *Union of India*, 2013 (9) SCALE 140: 2013 Cr LJ 4597: AIR 2013 SC 3743: 2013 (7) SCC 705.

**11. Juvenility – Law on** – A conjoint reading of sections 2(k), 2(1), 7A, 20 and 49 of the Juvenile Justice Act, 2000 read with rules 12 and 98 makes the position of law very clear and establishes beyond all doubts that all persons who were below the age of 18 years on the date of commission of the offence even prior to commencement of the Juvenile Justice Act, 2000 on 1-4-2001, would be treated as juveniles even if the claim of juvenility would be raised after they had attained the age of 18 years on or before the date of commencement of the Act and were undergoing sentence upon being convicted; *Subash Sahu* v. *State of Orissa*, 2012 Cr LJ 4607: 2013 (7) RCR (Cri) 2646 (Ori) (DB).

**12. Juvenile – Ambit of** – The issue is no longer *res integra* that if an offence has been committed by a person who was less than 18 years of age before the Act of 2000 came into force and even if the person has attained the age of more than 18 years during the pendency of the proceedings (including the proceedings before the Appellate Court) he will be treated as a juvenile; *Surjeet Singh* v. *State*, 2013 (204) DLT 325 (Del).

**13. Distinction between Male and Female Juveniles – Law on –** One of the basic distinctions between 1986 Act and 2000 Act relates to age of males and females. Under the 1986 Act, a juvenile means a male juvenile who has not attained the age of 16 years, and a female juvenile who has not attained the age of 18 years. In the 2000 Act, the distinction between male and female juveniles on the basis of age has not been maintained. The age limit is 18 years for both male and female; *Bijender Singh* v. *State of Haryana,* AIR 2005 SC 2262: 2005 (3) SCALE 467: 2005 (3) SCC 685.

**14. Offence – Comments on –** Clause (n) of section 2 of the JJ Act defines 'offence', as an offence punishable under any law for the time being in force. Thus, the said provision does not make any distinction between offences punishable under the IPC or one that is punishable under any local or special law. The provisions of the JJ Act have been interpreted by this Court time and again, and it has been clearly explained that raising the age of "juvenile" to 18 years from 16 years would apply retrospectively; *Union of India* v. *Ex-Gnr. Ajeet Singh,* 2013 Cr LJ 2215: 2013 (5) SCALE 107: 2013 (4) SCC 186.

**15. Principle of *Utres Magis Valeat Quam Pereat* – Law on –** The statute, it is well known, must be construed in such a manner so as to make it effective and operative on the principle of *utres magis valeat quam pereat*. The courts lean strongly against any constructions which tend to reduce a statute to a futility. When two meanings, one making the statute absolutely vague, wholly intractable and absolutely meaningless and the other leading to certainty and meaningful are given, in such an event the latter should be followed; *Pratap Singh* v. *State of Jharkhand,* AIR 2005 SC 2731: 2005 (1) SCALE 763: 2005 (3) SCC 551; *See* Also, *Tinsukhia Electric Supply Co. Ltd.* v. *State of Assam,* (1989) 3 SCC 709 [see *Andhra Bank* v. *B. Satyanarayana,* (2004) 2 SCC 657] and *Indian Handicrafts Emporium* v. *Union of India,* (2003) 7 SCC 5891.

**16. Courts – Definition of –** The Juvenile Justice (Care and Protection of Children) Act, 2000 does not define a court. However, section 2(y) of the Act declares that all words and expression used; but not defined in this Act and defined in the Code of Criminal procedure shall have the meanings respectively assigned to them in that code. Under the Code of Criminal procedure, there is no definition of the expression court though the Code Speaks of constitution of criminal courts in Chapter 2 of the Code. Section 2(y) of the Cr.P.C. further states that words and expressions used in the Code and not defined; but defined in the Indian Penal Code shall have the meanings respectively assigned to them in that Code; but unfortunately the I.P.C. does not also define the expression "court". Assistance was sought from the General Clauses Act. The same does not also define the expression "court". The Code of Civil Procedure also does not define the expression "court" though the said code also refers to constitution of courts; *Andrew Mendez* v. *State of Kerala,* 2008 Cr LJ 2368: 2008 (1) Ker LJ 647: 2008 (1) Ker LT 1000 (Ker).

**17. Adoption – Comments on –** The JJ Act, 2000 is an enabling legislation that gives a prospective parent the option of adopting an eligible child by following the procedure prescribed by the Act, Rules and the Central Adoption Resource Agency Guidelines, as notified under the Act. The Act does not mandate any compulsive action by any prospective parent leaving such person with the liberty of accessing the provisions of the Act, if he so desires. Such a person is always free to adopt or choose not to do so and, instead, follow what he comprehends to be the dictates of the personal law applicable to him. To us, the Act is a small step in reaching the goal enshrined by article 44 of the Constitution. Personal beliefs and faiths, though must be honoured, cannot dictate the operation of the provisions of an enabling statute. At the cost of repetition we would like to say that an optional legislation that does not contain an unavoidable imperative cannot be stultified by principles of personal law which, however, would always continue to govern any person who chooses to so submit himself until such time that the vision of a uniform Civil Code is achieved. The same can only happen by the collective decision of the generation(s) to come to sink conflicting faiths and beliefs that are still active as on date; *Shabnam Hashmi* v. *Union of India,* 2014 (2) SCALE 529: 2014 (4) SCC 1: AIR 2014 SC 1281.

**18. Competent Authority – Comments on –** Section 2(g) of the Act of 2000 prescribes the 'competent authority'. It means in relation to children in need of care and protection a Committee and in relation to juveniles in conflict with law a Board; *Vikram Saini* v. *State of Rajasthan,* 2011 (2) Raj LW 1455: 2013 (7) RCR (Cri) 3527 (Raj).

**19. Rules of Construction – Comments on –** In construing a statutory provision the first and foremost rule of construction is the literary construction. All that the Court has to see at the very outset is what does the provision say. If the provision is unambiguous and if from the provision the legislative intent is clear, the Court need not call into aid the other rules of construction of statutes. The other rules of construction are called into aid only when the legislative intent is not clear; *M/s. Hiralal Ratanlal* v. *STO,* AIR 1973 SC 1034.

**20. Interpretation – Cardinal Principle of –** It is a cardinal principle of interpretation of statute that the words of a statute must be understood in their natural, ordinary or popular sense and construed according to their grammatical meaning, unless such construction leads to some absurdity or unless there is something in the context or in the object of the statute to suggest to the contrary. The golden rule is that the words of a statute must *prima facie* be given their ordinary meaning. It is yet another rule of construction that when the words of the statute are clear, plain and unambiguous, then the Courts are bound to give effect to that meaning, irrespective of the consequences. It is said that the words themselves best declare the intention of the law-giver. The Courts are adhered to the principle that efforts should be made to give meaning to each and every word used by the Legislature and it is not a sound principle of construction to brush aside words in a statute as being inapposite surpluses, if they can have a proper application in circumstances conceivable within the contemplation of the statute"; *Gurudevdatta V.K.S.S.S. Maryadit* v. *State of Maharashtra,* AIR 2001 SC 1980.

**21. Interpretation – Constructive Approach for –** The primary duty of the Court while construing the provisions of such an Act is to adopt a constructive approach subject to that it should not do violence to the language of the provisions and is not contrary to attempted objective of the enactment. 'Include' is very generally used (in) interpretation clauses in order to enlarge the meaning of the words or phrases occurring in the body of the statute, and when it is so used these words or phrases must be construed as comprehending, not only such things as they signify according to their natural, import, but also those things which the definition clause declares that they shall include; *Lucknow Development Authority* v. *M.K. Gupta,* AIR 1994 SC 787: 1993 (4) SCALE 370: 1994 (1) SCC 243 [*Vide* also, *Regional Director, Employees' State Insurance Corporation* v. *Highland Coffee Works of P.F.X. Saldanha and Sons,* (1991) 3 SCC 617: AIR 1991 SCW 2821 and *C.I.T., Andhra Pradesh* v. *M/s. Taj Mahal Hotel, Secunderabad,* (1971) 3 SCC 550: AIR 1972 SC 168].

**22. Interpretation – Function of Court –** The function of the Court is only to expound the law and not to legislate; *District Mining Officer* v. *Tata Iron and Steel Company,* 2002 (7) SCC 358.

**23. Interpretation – Law on –** Interpretation must depend on the text and the context. They are the bases of interpretation. One may well say if the text is the texture, context is what gives the colour. Neither can be ignored. Both are important. That interpretation is best which makes the textual interpretation match the contextual. A statute is best interpreted when we know why it was enacted. With this knowledge, the statute must be read, first as a whole and then section by section, clause by clause, phrase by phrase and word by word. If a statute is looked at, in the context of its enactment, with the glasses of the statute-maker, provided by such context, its scheme, the sections, clauses, phrases and words may take colour and appear different than when the statute is looked at without the glasses provided by the context. With those glasses we must look at the Act as a whole and discover what each section, each clause, each phrase and each word is meant and designed to say as to fit into the scheme of the entire Act. No part of a statute and no word of a statute can be construed in isolation. Statutes have to be construed so that every word has a place and everything is in its place; *Reserve Bank of India* v. *Peerless General Finance and Investment Company Limited*, AIR 1987 SC 1023: 1987 (1) SCALE 100: 1987 (1) SCC 424.

**24. Interpretation – Requirement of –** Where the language is clear, the intention of the legislature has to be gathered from the language used; *Grasim Industries Limited* v. *Collector of Customs*, 2002 (4) SCC 297 [*Vide* also *Union of India* v. *Hamsoli Devi*, 2002 (7) SCC 273].

**25. Interpretation – Restriction for –** In a case where the statutory provision is plain and unambiguous, the court shall not interpret the same in a different manner, only because of harsh consequences arising therefrom; *Nasiruddin* v. *Sita Ram Agarwal*, 2003 (2) SCC 577 (*vide* para 35).

**26. Interpretation – Restriction for Courts –** When the language is plain and explicit and does not admit of any doubt, the Court cannot by reference to an assumed legislative intent expand or alter the plain meaning of an expression employed by the legislature; *Ombalika Das* v. *Hulisa Shaw*, 2002 (4) SCC 539.

**27. Interpretation – Rule of –** First and foremost principle of interpretation of a statute in every system of interpretation is the literal rule of interpretation. The other rules of interpretation *e.g.*, the mischief rule, purposive interpretation etc., can only be resorted to when the plain words of a statute are ambiguous or lead to no intelligible results or if read literally would nullify the very object of the statute. Where the words of a statute are absolutely clear and unambiguous, recourse cannot be had to the principles of interpretation; *Raghunath Rai Bareja* v. *Punjab National Bank*, JT 2007 (1) SC 542: 2006 (13) SCALE 511: 2007 (2) SCC 230. There is no doubt that when the Act itself provides dictionary for the words used, Courts must look into that dictionary first for an interpretation of the word used in the statute; AIR 1957 SC 121: 1957 (1) SCR 121: 1957 SCR 121.

**28. Functional Interpretation – Comments on –** Once Parliamentary intention is ascertained and the object and purpose of the legislation is known, it then becomes the duty of the Court to give the statute a purposeful or a functional interpretation. This is what is meant when, for example, it is said that measures aimed at social amelioration should receive liberal or beneficent construction. Again, the words of a statute may not be designed to meet the several uncontemplated forensic situations that may arise. The draftsman may have designed his words to meet what Lord Simon of Glaisdale calls the 'primary situation'. It will then become necessary for the Court to impute an intention to Parliament in regard to 'secondary situations'. Such 'secondary intention' may be imputed in relation to a secondary situation so as to best serve the same purpose as the primary statutory intention does in relation to a primary situation; *Girdhari Lal and Sons* v. *Balbir Nath Mathur*, AIR 1986 SC 1499: 1986 (1) SCALE 272: 1986 (2) SCC 237.

**29. Terms – Interpretation of –** The same word may be used in different senses in the same statute, and even in the same section; *Maxwell's Interpretation of Statutes*, p. 322.

**30. Literal Interpretation – Rule of –** Once Courts depart from the literal rule, then any number of interpretations can be put to a statutory provision, each Judge having a free play to put his own interpretation as he likes. This would be destructive of judicial discipline, and also the basic principle in a democracy that it is not for the Judge to legislate as that is the task of the elected representatives of the people. Even if the literal interpretation results in hardship or inconvenience, it has to be followed. Hence departure from the literal rule should only be done in very rare cases, and ordinarily there should be judicial restraint in this connection; *Raghunath Rai Bareja* v. *Punjab National Bank,* AIR 2006 SCW 6446: 2006 (13) SCALE 511: 2007 (2) SCC 230.

**31. Literal Rule of Interpretation – Comments on –** Literal rule of interpretation is not only followed by Judges and lawyers, but it is also followed by the lay man in his ordinary life. To give an illustration, if a person says "this is a pencil", then he means that it is a pencil; and it is not that when he says that the object is a pencil, he means that it is a horse, donkey or an elephant. In other words, the literal rule of interpretation simply means that we mean what we say and we say what we mean. If we do not follow the literal rule of interpretation, social life will become impossible, and we will not understand each other. If we say that a certain object is a book, then we mean it is a book. If we say it is a book, but we mean it is a horse, table or an elephant, then we will not be able to communicate with each other. Life will become impossible. Hence, the meaning of the literal rule of interpretation is simply that we mean what we say and we say what we mean; *Raghunath Rai Bareja* v. *Punjab National Bank,* AIR 2006 SCW 6446: 2006 (13) SCALE 511: 2007 (2) SCC 230.

**32. Same Words – Different Interpretation of –** It is said to be a presumption in construction that the same words are used in the same meaning in the same statute and particularly in the same section or sub-section. The presumption is, however, of the slightest, and there are many instances where the application of this rule or presumption is impossible. The same words may often receive a different interpretation in different parts of the same Act, for words used with reference to one set of circumstances "may convey an intention quite different from what the self-same set of words used with reference to another set of circumstances would or might have produced; *Commissioner of Income-Tax, Madhya Pradesh and Bhopal* v. *Sodra Devi,* AIR 1957 SC 832: 1958 SCJ 1: 1958 SCR 1 (FB).

**33. Term – Interpretation on –** Interpretation of a term in one statute, however, cannot be done with reference to its definition contained in another Act; *Raymond Ltd.* v. *State of Chhattisgarh,* 2007 (3) SCALE 341.

**34. Terms or Expressions – Interpretation of –** It is well settled that whenever the Legislature uses certain terms or expressions of well-known legal significance or connotation the courts must interpret them as used or understood in the popular sense; *Sonia Bhatia* v. *State of Uttar Pradesh,* AIR 1981 SC 1274: 1981 (1) SCALE 58: 1981 (2) SCC 585.

**3. Continuation of inquiry in respect of juvenile who has ceased to be a juvenile.**—Where an inquiry has been initiated against a juvenile in conflict with law or a child in need of care and protection and during the course of such inquiry the juvenile or the child ceases to be such, then, notwithstanding anything contained in this Act or in any other law for the time being in force, the inquiry may be continued and orders may be made in respect of such person as if such person had continued to be a juvenile or a child.

**COMMENTS**

**Provisions – Comments on –** Section 3 provides that where an inquiry has been initiated against a juvenile even, during the course of such inquiry a juvenile ceased to be such, then, notwithstanding anything contained therein or any other law for the time being in force, the inquiry may be continued and orders may be made in respect of such persons as if such person had continued to be a juvenile. Chapter II of the Act speaks of competent authorities and institutions for juveniles such as Juvenile Welfare Boards, Juvenile courts, Juvenile Homes, special homes, observation homes and aftercare organisations. Chapter III makes provision for neglected juveniles. Section 17 makes provision for uncontrollable juveniles. Chapter IV deals with delinquent juveniles. Sections

18 to 26 provide for bail and custody of juveniles, accused of a bailable or non-bailable offence, the manner of dealing with them and the orders that may be passed regarding or against delinquent juveniles. Proceedings as laid down in Chapter VIII of the Code of Criminal Procedure are not competent against a juvenile. A juvenile and a person who is not a juvenile cannot be jointly tried. No disqualification attaches to conviction of a juvenile for any offence under any law. Special provisions are contained in section 26 as regard the proceedings in respect of juveniles pending in any court on the date of the coming into force of the Act. Chapter V (Sections 27 to 40) lay down the procedure of competent authorities generally under the Act and appeals and revisions from orders of such authorities. Chapter VI (Sections 41 to 45) provides for Special offences in respect of juveniles. Chapter VII (Sections 46 to 63) contains miscellaneous provisions; *Pratap Singh* v. *State of Jharkhand*, AIR 2005 SC 2731: 2005 (1) SCALE 763: 2005 (3) SCC 551.

## *CHAPTER II*

## JUVENILE IN CONFLICT WITH LAW

**4. Juvenile Justice Board.**—(1) Notwithstanding anything contained in the Code of Criminal Procedure, 1973 (2 of 1974), the State Government may, [1][within a period of one year from the date of commencement of the Juvenile Justice (Care and Protection of Children) Amendment Act, 2006, by notification in the Official Gazette, constitute for every district], one or more Juvenile Justice Boards for exercising the powers and discharging the duties conferred or imposed on such Boards in relation to juveniles in conflict with law under this Act.

(2) A Board shall consist of a Metropolitan Magistrate or a Judicial Magistrate of the first class, as the case may be, and two social workers of whom at least one shall be a woman, forming a Bench and every such Bench shall have the powers conferred by the Code of Criminal Procedure, 1973 (2 of 1974), on a Metropolitan Magistrate or, as the case may be, a Judicial Magistrate of the first class and the Magistrate on the Board shall be designated as the principal Magistrate.

(3) No Magistrate shall be appointed as a member of the Board unless he has special knowledge or training in child psychology or child welfare and no social worker shall be appointed as a member of the Board unless he has been actively involved in health, education, or welfare activities pertaining to children for at least seven years.

(4) The term of office of the members of the Board and the manner in which such member may resign shall be such as may be prescribed.

(5) The appointment of any member of the Board may be terminated after holding inquiry, by the Sate Government, if—

(i) he has been found guilty of misuse of power vested under this Act,

(ii) he has been convicted of an offence involving moral turpitude, and such conviction has not been reversed or he has not been granted full pardon in respect of such offence,

---

1. Subs. by Act 33 of 2006, sec. 6, for "by notification in the Official Gazette, constitute for a district or a group of districts specified in the notification" (w.e.f. 22-8-2006).

(iii) he fails to attend the proceedings of the Board for consecutive three months without any valid reason or he fails to attend less than three-fourth of the sittings in a year.

**SYNOPSIS**



**COMMENTS**

**1. Provision – Comments on –** Chapter II of 2000 Act deals with juvenile in conflict with law. This Chapter comprises of sections 4 to 28. Section 4 provides for constitution of Juvenile Justice Board and its composition. Section 5 provides for procedure, etc., in relation to Juvenile Justice Board; *Abuzar Hossain @ Gulam Hossain* v. *State of West Bengal*, AIR 2013 SC 1020: 2012 (10) SCALE 101: 2012 (10) SCC 489 [Hon'ble Judges: R.M. Lodha, Anil R. Dave, T.S. Thakur].

**2. Juvenile Justice Board – Comments on –** A close reading of section 4(1) of the Act would make it abundantly clear that a Juvenile Justice Board is a forum to be constituted by the Government by issuance of a Notification in the Official Gazette which shall function at the particular notified place. After constitution of the Board, it is the further duty of the Government to appoint the members of the said Board. As per section 4(2) of the Act, the Board shall consist of a Metropolitan Magistrate or a Judicial Magistrate of the first class, as the case may be, and two social workers, of whom, one shall be a woman and it is a Bench. The Magistrate shall be designated as the Principal Magistrate. Section 4(3) of the Act stipulates that no Magistrate shall be appointed as a member of the Board, unless, he has special knowledge or training in child psychology or child welfare. This clearly indicates that it is only an individual, who happens to be a Magistrate, who shall be appointed as Principal Magistrate of the Juvenile Justice Board. The Principal Magistrate of the Board is not an *ex-officio* Member on account of his being the Presiding Officer of a Court of Metropolitan Magistrate. So, while making appointment as Principal Magistrate of the Juvenile Justice Board, it is for the Government to examine as to, whether a particular individual Magistrate possesses the required qualifications such as special knowledge or training in child psychology or child welfare. For any reason, if a Magistrate, who has been appointed as a Principal Magistrate ceases to hold the office, then, a fresh appointment has to be made, thereby, appointing an individual Magistrate possessing qualifications as the Principal Magistrate. Thus, it is crystal clear that under sub-section (3) of section 4 of the said Act, the term "Magistrate" does not refer to an *ex officio* but to an individual Officer; *Idukkan* v. *Inspector of Police*, 2012 (4) CTC 718 (Mad).

**3. High Court and Court of Session – Powers of –** A Juvenile Justice Board is contemplated under section 4 which prescribes as well the composition thereof. This statutory body has been empowered to exercise the powers and to discharge the duties in relation to juveniles in conflict with law under the Act. Under section 6(2), the powers conferred on the Board by or under the Act are exercisable by the High Court and the Court of Session, when the proceeding comes before them in appeal, revision or otherwise; *State of Assam (in re:)*, 2012 Cr LJ 471: 2011 (4) Gau LR 235: 2013 (6) RCR (Cri) 2190 (Gau) (DB).

**4. Juvenile Courts – Comments on –** Juvenile Courts contain well intentional feature and they originated as an institution which reforms, envisioned a body that would handle juvenile cases with an eye on their rehabilitation and in their best interest and for their welfare. Section 7A of the Act is an important safeguard against unjust, unconstitutional and erroneous conviction and sentence; *Gurdarshan Singh* v. *State of Punjab*, 2012 (4) RCR (Cri) 909 (P&H).

**5. Juvenile Welfare Board – Comments on –** The Juvenile Welfare Board will have no competence to deal with cases of children who are in prostitution or have been trafficked. Such children are to be considered as children in need of care and protection. However, in States where the Child Welfare Committees have not been constituted, these matters should be referred to the Juvenile Welfare Board; *Bachpan Bachao Andolan* v. *Union of India*, AIR 2011 SC 3361: 2011 (4) SCALE 769: 2011 (5) SCC 1.

**6. Principal Magistrate – Comments on –** A conjoint reading of section 4, and rules 4 & 5, would go a long way to show that the Board is a structure and the members are its components and irrespective of the fact that there are no members, the Board will survive. But, if there is no Board, the office of members will not survive as the term of office of the members is co-terminus with the Board [*vide* rule 21]. The Chairperson of the Board shall be the Magistrate. First of all, there is no post of Chair Person at all provided in the Act. There is only a Principal Magistrate to be designated by the Government. If the Magistrate presiding over the Magistrate Court does not possess required qualification as provided in sub-section (3) of section 4 the Act, then certainly, he cannot act as the Principal Magistrate; *Idukkan* v. *Inspector of Police*, 2012 (4) CTC 718 (Mad).

**5. Procedure, etc., in relation to Board.**—(1) The Board shall meet at such times and shall observe such rules of procedure in regard to the transaction of business at its meetings, as may be prescribed.

(2) A child in conflict with law may be produced before an individual member of the Board, when the Board is not sitting.

(3) A Board may act notwithstanding the absence of any member of the Board, and no order made by the Board shall be invalid by reason only of the absence of any member during any stage of proceedings:

Provided that there shall be at least two members including the principal Magistrate present at the time of final disposal of the case.

(4) In the event of any difference of opinion among the members of the Board in the interim or final disposition, the opinion of the majority shall prevail, but where there is no such majority, the opinion of the Principal Magistrate shall prevail.

**SYNOPSIS**



**COMMENTS**

**1. Special Public Prosecutor – Comments on –** Section 25 of Code deals with the Assistant Public Prosecutors. According to the said provision, the State Government shall appoint in every district one or more Assistant Public Prosecutors for conducting the prosecutions in the Courts of Magistrates. Therefore, no Assistant Public Prosecutor can be appointed under section 25 of Cr.P.C. for the purpose of conducting the prosecution before the Juvenile Justice Board since the Board cannot be equated to a Court of Magistrate. Prosecuting Officer before the Juvenile Justice Board should be a Special Public Prosecutor to be appointed under section 24(8) of Cr.P.C. Section 24(8) of Cr.P.C. empowers the State Government to appoint, for the purposes of any case or class of cases, a person who has been in practice as an Advocate for not less than ten years as a Special Public Prosecutor. In addition to the said qualification, the person to be appointed as Special Public Prosecutor for the Juvenile Justice Board may be a person having special knowledge or skill in child psychology or child welfare. Such persons need to be appointed by Government to conduct the prosecution before the Juvenile Justice Boards; *Idukkan* v. *Inspector of Police*, 2012 (4) CTC 718 (Mad).

**2. Competent Authority – Requirement for –** From a bare reading of the provision, it is clear that it merely provides that when it appears to the competent authority *viz.*, the Board that the person brought before it is a juvenile. The Board is obliged to make an enquiry as to the age of that person; for that purpose it shall take evidence as may be necessary and then record a finding whether the person in question is a juvenile or not; *Babloo Pasi* v. *State of Jharkhand*, AIR 2009 SC 314: 2008 (13) SCC 133: 2008 (13) SCALE 137.

**6. Powers of Juvenile Justice Board.**—(1) Where a Board has been constituted for any district [1][***], such Board shall, notwithstanding anything contained in any other law for the time being in force but save as otherwise expressly provided in this Act, have power to deal exclusively with all proceedings under this Act relating to juvenile in conflict with law.

(2) The powers conferred on the Board by or under this Act may also be exercised by the High Court and the Court of Session, when the proceeding comes before them in appeal, revision or otherwise.

**SYNOPSIS**

1. Chapter II – Comments on
2. Provision – Comprehension of
3. Juvenile Justice Board – Powers of
4. Order of Juvenile Justice Board – Comments on
5. Board – Obligations of
6. Board – Powers of
7. Child-Friendly Approach – Comments on
8. Disposed off Cases – Law on
9. Further Determination of Age – Law on
10. High Court – Powers of
11. Overriding Effect – Comments on
12. Separate Forum or Special Court for Holding Trial of Juvenile – Law on
13. Sessions Judge – Powers of
14. Set-off of Period Already Spent by Juvenile – Law on
15. High Court – Powers of

**COMMENTS**

**1. Chapter II – Comments on –** Sections 4 to 28 occur in Chapter II which deal with juvenile in conflict with law and section 64 occurs in Chapter V dealing with miscellaneous provisions. It is interesting to note that all the provisions occurring in Chapter II or section 20 do not use the expression juvenile in conflict with law whereas section 64 specifically uses that expression. Chapter II provides for constitution of a Juvenile Justice Board. Its power had been outlined in section 6. Section 7 mandates that a Magistrate before whom a juvenile is produced must without any delay record his opinion, and if it is found that a person brought before him is a juvenile, he shall record the same and forward him with the record of the proceeding to the competent authority having jurisdiction over the proceeding. Sections 8 and 9 provide for observation homes and special homes. Section 10 provides that on apprehension of a juvenile in conflict with law; he shall be placed under the charge of a special juvenile police unit or the designated police officer who shall immediately report the matter to a member of the Board. Section 12 provides for bail. In no circumstances, a person who appears to be juvenile is to be placed in a police lock-up. He is to be kept in an observation home in the prescribed manner until he can be brought before the court. Sub-section (3) of section 12 mandates the Board to make an order sending a juvenile to the observation home instead of committing him to prison. Section 14 provides for holding of an inquiry by the Board regarding a juvenile within a period of four months. Section 15 provides for an order that may be passed regarding juvenile; *Pratap Singh* v. *State of Jharkhand*, AIR 2005 SC 2731: 2005 (1) SCALE 763: 2005 (3) SCC 551.

**2. Provision – Comprehension of –** Section 6(2) of the said Act stipulates that the powers conferred on the Board by or under the said Act, may also be exercised by the High Court and the Court of Session, when the proceedings comes before them in appeal,

1. The words "or a group of districts" omitted by Act 33 of 2006, sec. 7 (w.e.f. 22-8-2006).

revision or otherwise. Thus, instead of forwarding the accused to the Board for passing an appropriate order, by virtue of section 6(2) read with section 7A(2), High Court can pass the appropriate order; *Surender Khare* v. *State*, 2011 (10) AD (Del) 24: 2012 Cr LJ 1: 2012 (3) RCR (Cri) 456.

**3. Juvenile Justice Board – Powers of –** Section 6 thereof refers to the powers of the Juvenile Justice Board (the Board for short). It states that notwithstanding anything contained in any other law for the time being in force but save as otherwise expressly provided in the said Act, the Juvenile Justice Board shall have power to deal exclusively with all proceedings under the said Act relating to juvenile in conflict with law. Sub-section (2) of section 6 states that the powers conferred on the Board by or under the said Act may also be exercised by the High Court and the Court of Sessions, when the proceeding comes before them in appeal, revision or otherwise; *Gangaram Dushanna Dandil* v. *State of Maharashtra*, 2009 (4) Crimes 697 (Bom): 2009 (2) BCR (Cri) 277: 2009 (5) AIR BomR 45.

**4. Order of Juvenile Justice Board – Comments on –** The courts are not left with no discretion but they can hold an enquiry and give a finding regarding age in the manner prescribed. For the guidance of the subordinate courts, it may be noted that rule 12 of the Central Rules, 2007 and rule 22 of the U.P. Rules, 2004 prescribe a detailed procedure for holding such kind of enquiries, if the documents namely birth certificate or birth certificate from the school last attended or matriculation or equivalent certificate are not available then only matter shall be referred to the Medical Board for ascertaining the age of such offender. It is also crystal clear that once a person is declared to be juvenile, then in terms of section 49 of the Act that order would be final and in terms of sub-section (2) thereof, subsequently no proof can be taken as against it. If the order of the Juvenile Justice Board is against the person claiming to be juvenile or in favour of the juvenile then section 52 of the Act provides for an appeal to the Court of Session and section 53 provides for a revision to the High Court; *Sudhakar Dwivedi* v. *State of Uttar Pradesh*, 2012 (6) ADJ 649: 2012 (2) ACrR 2250 (All).

**5. Board – Obligations of –** If Board has not given any ground for believing that the release of juvenile is likely to bring him into association with any known criminal or expose him to moral, physical or psychological danger or his release would defeat the ends of justice then such Order is revisable.

**6. Board – Powers of –** Board under the Act had got the power to deal with Juvenile offenders notwithstanding anything contained in any other law for the time being in force but save as "otherwise expressly provided under this Act." Thus even though Board under the Act has got superintendence over any other law for the time being in force but its powers are subject to other express provision under the Act. Power of the Board thus is not absolute but it is subject to other express provision under the Act. Sub-section (2) of section 6 of the Act thus assumes much importance as it provides that High Court or Court of Session may also exercise power conferred on the Board in Appeal, Revision or otherwise. Thus the power which has been conferred on Juvenile Justice Board though section 6(1) of the Act has also been conferred on the High Court and Court of session through section 6(2) of the Act. Sub-section (2) of section 6 of the Act has got a salutary purpose. The Act was incorporated for the benefit of juvenile offenders providing for proper care, protection, treatment and rehabilitation for them. The purpose of enactment is "An Act to consolidate and amend the law relating to juveniles in conflict with law and children in need of care and protection, by providing for proper care, protection and treatment by catering to their development needs, and by adopting a child - friendly approach in the adjudication and disposition of matters in the best interest of children and for their ultimate rehabilitation through various institutions established under this enactment; *Manish Tyagi* v. *State of Uttar Pradesh*, 2007 (5) ADJ 102: 2007 (4) All LJ 103: 2007 Cr LJ 3165.

**7. Child-Friendly Approach – Comments on –** It is clear, therefore, that the Juvenile Act is intended to protect the juvenile from the rigours of a trial by a criminal court. It prohibits sentencing of a juvenile and committing him to prison. As its preamble suggests it seeks to adopt a child-friendly approach in the adjudication and disposition of matters in the best interest of children and for their ultimate rehabilitation; *Kalu @ Amit* v. *State of Haryana,* AIR 2012 SC 3212: 2012 Cr LJ 4244: 2012 (7) SCALE 404.

**8. Disposed off Cases – Law on –** Rule 97 of the Juvenile Justice (Care and Protection of Children) Rules, 2007 says that no juvenile shall be denied the benefits of the Act and the Rules made there under and that all pending cases, which have not received finality, shall be dealt with and disposed of in terms of the provisions of the Act and the Rules made there under. A conjoint reading of section 7A of the Juvenile Justice (Care and Protection of Children) Act, 2000 as amended by Act 33 of 2006, rules 12 and 98 of the Juvenile Justice (Care and Protection of Children) Rules, 2007, shall make it clear that in disposed off cases, the Government or the Board may either *suo motu* or on an application, review the case of a person or a juvenile in conflict with law and determine his juvenility as on the date of commission of the offence and grant the relief in accordance with the provisions of the Act; *A. Chinnaponnu W/o Annamalai* v. *State of Tamil Nadu,* 2011 (3) Mad LJ (Cri) 433: 2011 (8) RCR (Cri) 663 (Mad) (DB).

**9. Further Determination of Age – Law on –** The provisions of section 6(2) of the said Act also make it clear that the powers conferred on the Board by or under the said Act may also be exercised by the High Court and the Court of Session, when the proceeding comes before them in appeal, revision or 'otherwise'. Therefore, no further determination of age was necessary by the Juvenile Justice Board; *Sakir Mewati* v. *State of Madhya Pradesh,* 2011 Cr LJ 4469: 2011 (2) Jab LJ 245 (MP) (Gwalior Bench).

**10. High Court – Powers of –** As per the provision of section 20, the Court is not required to pass any sentence in respect of juvenile but he is required to be forwarded to the Board, which shall pass orders in accordance with the provisions of the said Act as if it had been satisfied, on inquiry, that he had committed the offence. As per section 6(2) of the Act, the powers conferred on the Board under the Act, may also be exercised by the High Court and the Court of Session, when the proceeding comes before them in appeal, revision or otherwise. Thus, reading the provisions of section 20 along with section 6(2), it is apparent that after a finding is recorded against juvenile he can be dealt with by High Court in the same manner as he would be dealt with by the Board for the purposes of the order that is to be passed deeming the same to be a satisfaction on inquiry under the Act that juvenile had committed the offence; *Chatpal @ Satpal* v. *State,* 2011 (123) DRJ 131 (Del) (DB).

**11. Overriding Effect – Comments on –** The children if come in contact with hardened criminals in jail; it would have the effect of dwarfing the development of the child, exposing him to baneful influences, coarsening his conscience and alienating him from the society. Therefore, there can be no doubt that the J & J Act is beneficial in nature *i.e.,* socially oriented legislation. In case the provisions are not complied with, the object of its enactment would be frustrated. Section 6 of JJ Act contains a *non-obstante* clause giving overriding effect to any other law for the time being in force and provides that Juvenile Justice Board, where it has been constituted, shall "have power to deal exclusively" with all proceedings under this Act relating to juvenile in conflict with law. Section 18(i) further provides that notwithstanding contained in section 223 of the Code or any other law for the time being in force, no juvenile shall be charged with or tried for any offence together with a person who is not a juvenile. More so, *non-obstante* clause contained in various provisions thereof, particularly, sections 15, 16, 18, 19 and 20 make the legislative intent unambiguous that the JJ Act being a special law would have override effect on any other statute for the time being in force. Such a view stand further fortified in view of the provisions of sections 29 and 37 which provide for constitution of a Child

Welfare Committee which provides for welfare of the children including rehabilitation; *Essa @ Anjum Abdul Razak Memon;* v. *State of Maharashtra,* 2013 (3) Supreme 195: JT 2013 (6) SC 1: 2013 (3) SCALE 1 (SC).

**12. Separate Forum or Special Court for Holding Trial of Juvenile – Law on –** Juvenile Justice Act was enacted with a laudable object of providing a separate forum or a special court for holding trial of children/juvenile by the juvenile court as it was felt that children become delinquent by force of circumstance and not by choice and hence they need to be treated with care and sensitivity while dealing and trying cases involving criminal offence; *Om Prakash* v. *State of Rajasthan,* AIR 2012 SC 1608: 2012 (4) SCALE 348: 2012 (5) SCC 201.

**13. Sessions Judge – Powers of –** It is well within the powers of the Sessions Court to embark upon an inquiry as to the age of a person instead of referring the matter to the Juvenile Court/Juvenile Justice Board. It is also clear that if the Sessions Court comes to the opinion that the person before it is not a juvenile then the matter ends there and need not be referred to the Juvenile Court/Juvenile Justice Board. However, this opinion of the Sessions Court would still be subject to correction by a superior Court. Hence, the Sessions Judge can exercise powers of the Board in view of the provisions of section 6(2) of the said Act. No doubt true that under section 6(2) of the Juvenile Justice Act, 2000, the Court of Session could exercise the powers conferred on the Board only when the proceedings of a case came before it in appeal or revision or in connection with any other proceedings under the Act. The words 'or otherwise' clearly show that the Additional Sessions judge could pass such an order in a proceeding even other than appeal or revision before, him; *Sakir Mewati* v. *State of Madhya Pradesh,* 2011 Cr LJ 4469: 2011 (2) Jab LJ 245 (MP) (Gwalior Bench).

**14. Set-off of Period Already Spent by Juvenile – Law on –** The Juvenile Justice (Care and Protection of Children) Act, 2000 does not provide any provision for set-off of the period already spent by the juvenile, but it also does not provide contrary provisions for drawing inference of non-application of the provisions of section 428 of the Code. *Inter alia,* in absence of contrary provisions, the provisions of section 428 of the Code in accordance with sub-section (2) of section 4 and section 5 of the Code would be applicable, in case of juvenile; *Pradeep Kashyap* v. *State of Chhattisgarh,* 2013 (1) Cg LRW 101: 2013 (1) MPHT (Chh) 60: 2013 (2) Cg LJ 206.

**15. High Court – Powers of –** In view of section 6(2) of the said Act High Court can exercise powers conferred on the Board under the said Act in this appeal; *Gangaram Dushanna Dandil* v. *State of Maharashtra,* 2009 (4) Crimes 697 (Bom): 2009 (2) BCR (Cri) 277: 2009 (5) AIR BomR 45.

**7. Procedure to be followed by a Magistrate not empowered under the Act.**—(1) When any Magistrate not empowered to exercise the powers of a Board under this Act is of the opinion that a person brought before him under any of the provisions of this Act (other than for the purpose of giving evidence), is a juvenile or the child, he shall without any delay record such opinion and forward the juvenile or the child and the record of the proceeding to the competent authority having jurisdiction over the proceeding.

(2) The competent authority to which the proceeding is forwarded under sub-section (1) shall hold the inquiry as if the juvenile or the child had originally been brought before it.

**SYNOPSIS**

1. Magistrate – Duties of
2. Judicial Magistrate – Comments on
3. Competent Authority – Role of
4. Determination of Juvenility – Law on
5. Juvenility – Claim for
6. Proviso to sub-section (1)

**COMMENTS**

**1. Magistrate – Duties of –** It becomes obligatory for every Magistrate before whom an accused is produced to ascertain, in the first instance or as soon thereafter as may be possible, whether the accused person is an adult or a juvenile in conflict with law. The reason for this, obviously, is to avoid a two-fold difficulty: *first,* to avoid a juvenile being subjected to procedures under the normal criminal law and de hors the Act and the Rules, and *second,* a resultant situation, where the "trial" of the juvenile is required to be set aside and quashed as having been conducted by a court not having jurisdiction to do so or a juvenile, on being found guilty, going 'unpunished'. This is necessary not only in the best interests of the juvenile but also for the better administration of criminal justice so that the Magistrate or the Sessions Judge (as the case may be) does not waste his time and energy on a "trial". It must be appreciated by every Magistrate that when an accused is produced before him, it is possible that the prosecution or the investigating officer may be under a mistaken impression that the accused is an adult. If the Magistrate has any iota of doubt about the juvenility of an accused produced before him, rule 12 provides that a Magistrate may arrive at a *prima facie* conclusion on the juvenility, on the basis of his physical appearance. In our opinion, in such a case, this *prima facie* opinion should be recorded by the Magistrate. Thereafter, if custodial remand is necessary, the accused may be sent to jail or a juvenile may be sent to an observation home, as the case may be, and the Magistrate should simultaneously order an inquiry, if necessary, for determining the age of the accused. Apart from anything else, it must be appreciated that such an inquiry at the earliest possible time would be in the best interests of the juvenile, since he would be kept away from adult under-trial prisoners and would not be subjected to a regimen in jail, which may not be conducive to his well being. As mentioned above, it would also be in the interests of better administration of criminal justice. It is, therefore, enjoined upon every Magistrate to take appropriate steps to ascertain the juvenility or otherwise of an accused person brought before him or her at the earliest possible point of time, preferably on first production; *Jitendra Singh @ Babboo Singh* v. *State of Uttar Pradesh,* 2013 (11) SCC 193: 2013 (9) SCALE 18: 2013 (83) All Cri C 651.

**2. Judicial Magistrate – Comments on –** It is needless to say that as on today, there is only one Magistrate in each District who is empowered, as a member of the Board, to exercise the powers of the Board. Section 7 stipulates that when any Magistrate who is not empowered to exercise the power of a Board is of the opinion that a person brought before him is a Juvenile or the child, he shall record such opinion and without delay forward the juvenile or child to the competent authority having jurisdiction over the proceeding. The competent authority prescribed in section 7 in relation to a juvenile is the Juvenile Justice Board, which shall hold the enquiry. In view of the above, no Judicial Magistrate other than the member of the Board shall send the Juvenile or child directly to observation homes or special homes contemplated under section 8 and section 9 of the Act. As stated earlier, it is the duty of such Magistrates, who are not empowered to exercise the powers of the Board under the Act, to send the Juvenile immediately to the Juvenile Justice Board; *Jyothi W/o S. Babu* v. *Director General of Police, Police Head Quarters, Chennai,* 2013 (6) RCR (Cri) 2219 (Mad) (DB).

**3. Competent Authority – Role of –** When any Magistrate not empowered to exercise the powers of the board under this Act is of opinion that a person brought before him under any provisions of this Act (other than for purpose of giving evidence) is juvenile or the child, he shall without delay record such opinion and forward the juvenile or the child and record of the proceeding to the competent authority having jurisdiction over the proceeding. Then the competent authority shall hold the inquiry as if the juvenile or the child has been brought before it. It clearly indicates as soon as the trial court not having jurisdiction under the Act found *prima facie* that the accused present before the court is juvenile, it shall forward the juvenile or the child along with the record of the proceeding to the Board having jurisdiction under the Act for making an inquiry under section 49 of the Act; *Narayan Sharma* v. *State of Madhya Pradesh*, 2012 Cr LJ 736: 2013 (6) RCR (Cri) 1672 (MP) (Gwalior Bench).

**4. Determination of Juvenility – Law on –** A joint reading of sections 7 and 7A leaves no manner of doubt and makes it manifest or indubitable that whenever a plea of juvenility is raised by "a person' before "any Court' or "a Court', an inquiry into that question of juvenility, in accordance with the procedure prescribed under the Act, is indispensable which cannot be overlooked. The preposition of law that "if a thing is required to be done in a particular manner then either it should be done in that manner or not at all' is too well settled to be ignored. The fallout of this trite law is that no person can be determined to be a juvenile or otherwise unless an inquiry into that aspect has been conducted by "a Court' or by "any Court' in consonance with the procedure established under the Act or the Rules made their under. The natural corollary therefore is that if a person has been declared to be a juvenile or otherwise without conducting an inquiry into that aspect in accordance with the provisions of the Act or the Rules made thereunder, then that determination will be wholly illegal. Sections 14 and 49 of the Act and other sections re-emphasize conducting of an inquiry for such a determination; *Surendra* v. *State of Uttar Pradesh*, 2013 (3) All Cri R 3385: 2013 (83) All Cri C 568: 2014 (3) All LJ 188 (All) (DB).

**5. Juvenility – Claim for –** As per proviso to section 7(A)(1) of the Act, a claim of juvenility may be raised before any Court, at any stage, even, after disposal of the case and such claim shall be determined in terms of provisions contained in Act; *Jai Parkash* v. *State of Haryana*, 2013 (4) RCR (Cri) 509 (P&H).

**6. Proviso to sub-section (1) –** does lay down that a claim of juvenility may be raised at any stage, even after final disposal of the case; *Pawan* v. *State of Uttaranchal*, 2009 Cr LJ 2257: 2009 (15) SCC 259: 2009 (3) SCALE 195 [Hon'ble Judges: S.B. Sinha, Asok Kumar Ganguly, R.M. Lodha].

[1][**7A. Procedure to be followed when claim of juvenility is raised before any court.**—(1) Whenever a claim of juvenility is raised before any court or a court is of the opinion that an accused person was a juvenile on the date of commission of the offence, the court shall make an inquiry, take such evidence as may be necessary (but not an affidavit) so as to determine the age of such person, and shall record a finding whether the person is a juvenile or a child or not, stating his age as nearly as may be:

Provided that a claim of juvenility may be raised before any court and it shall be recognised at any stage, even after final disposal of the case, and such claim shall be determined in terms of the provisions contained in this Act and the rules made thereunder, even if the juvenile has ceased to be so on or before the date of commencement of this Act.

(2) If the court finds a person to be a juvenile on the date of commission of the offence under sub-section (1), it shall forward the juvenile to the Board for passing appropriate orders and the sentence, if any, passed by a court shall be deemed to have no effect.]

**SYNOPSIS**

1. Court – Role of
2. Provision – Comments on
3. Procedure – Comments on
4. Term "May Be Raised before Any Court" – Comments on
5. Definition of Court – Comments on

1. Ins. by Act 33 of 2006, sec. 8 (w.e.f. 22-8-2006).

**6.** Claim of Juvenility – Law on
**7.** Claim of Juvenility – Comments on
**8.** Question of Juvenility – Law on
**9.** Courts – Duties of
**10.** Courts – Role of
**11.** Effect of Sentence – Law on
**12.** Evidence – Law on
**13.** Further Evidence – Law on
**14.** Ex-Juvenile in Conflict with Law – Relief for
**15.** Final Disposal of Case – Law on
**16.** High Court – Obligations of
**17.** Writ Jurisdiction – Comments on
**18.** Writ of *Mandamus* – Maintainability of
**19.** Magistrate – Obligations of
**20.** Review Case of Juvenile in Conflict with Law – Law on
**21.** Review – Law on
**22.** Special Home – Law on
**23.** Trial of Juvenile – Law on
**24.** Rules – Comments on
**25.** Trials of Summons Cases by Magistrates – Comments on
**26.** Sentence – Law on
**27.** Technicalities and Irregularities – Law on
**28.** Two Views Possible – Law on

**COMMENTS**

**1. Court – Role of –** According to section 7A, whenever a question of juvenility is raised on behalf of the accused, the court shall hold an enquiry into question of juvenility of the accused and shall take all such evidence as may be necessary to determine the age of the accused as merely as may be. To hold an enquiry into a question of juvenility of an accused, does not amount to criminal trial but the court must take an active part in the enquiry and must not act simply as a referee between two litigating factions; *Darshan Singh* v. *State of Uttar Pradesh,* 2013 (5) ALJ 406: 2014 (1) Crimes 426 (All): 2013 (82) ACC 796 (All).

**2. Provision – Comments on –** Entire object and purpose of the Juvenile Justice Act which is in the nature of beneficial legislation would be defeated and frustrated, if the application for determination of the juvenility of the accused is postponed indefinitely. The determination of accrual of benefits under this Act must be ascertained at earliest; otherwise it would amount to depriving a person, in case his juvenility at the time of offence is confirmed, from enjoying his legal and constitutional rights and protection flowing from this Act. Therefore, section 7A of the Act is very wide in its ambit to encompass the ascertainment of the question of juvenility of an accused/person, at any stage even after the disposal of the case; *Ishtikhar* v. *State of Uttar Pradesh,* 2012 (5) SCALE 47: 2012 (12) SCC 307 (SC).

**3. Procedure – Comments on –** Section 7A deals with the procedure to be followed if the claim of juvenility is raised before any court. It states that whenever a claim of juvenility is raised before any court or a court is of the opinion that an accused person was a juvenile on the date of commission of the offence, the court shall make an enquiry, take such evidence as may be necessary so as to determine the age of such person. Proviso to section 7A of the Act clearly states that a claim of juvenility may be raised before any court and it shall be recognised at any stage, even after disposal of the case; *A. Kabeer* v. *State of Kerala,* 2013 (2) Ker LJ 107 (Ker).

**4. Term "May Be Raised before Any Court" – Comments on –** The term "may be raised before any court" does not empower a Court, which is subordinate on judicial side, to set aside the order of conviction and sentence passed by the superior Court. In such a situation, the juvenile accused may either approach the same Court by way of any application or otherwise or before the superior Court for setting aside the order of conviction and sentence. If the order was passed by the Division Bench and Single Bench, even in exercise of its power under article 226 of the Constitution, set aside the order of the Division Bench under the provisions of section 7A of the Act, 2000 that may create judicial chaos and will be opposed to the judicial propriety and discipline. No writ/ direction can be issued by a Single Bench to make an order passed by the Division Bench even in exercise of power under section 7A of the Act, 2000 as redundant; *Susen Kumar Ray* v. *State of Chhattisgarh,* 2013 Cr LJ 4742: 2013 (4) CgLJ 361 (Chhat).

**5. Definition of Court – Comments on** – Clause 1 of section 7A obligates the Court to make an inquiry and determine the age of the accused person whenever a claim of juvenility is raised before it. The Court contemplated under section 7A has not been defined under the said Act. Section 2, however, lays down that where words and expressions defined used in the Act but not defined therein and defined in the Code of Criminal Procedure, shall have the meaning as assigned in the code. Thus, for purposes of definition of the Court one has to fall back on the Code of Criminal Procedure to find out the definition of the expression Court envisaged under section 7A. Section 6 of the Code of Criminal Procedure under Chapter 2 deals with the constitution of criminal Courts and offices. Thus, the Court for purposes of section 7A could be any class/category of Court exercising criminal jurisdiction which includes the High Court as well. Thus, the question of juvenility can be decided by the Court of Sessions, Judicial Magistrates of the 1st Class, Judicial Magistrate IInd Class and Executive Magistrates including the High Court exercising the criminal jurisdiction. It appears that the High Court can also decide the question of juvenility but while exercising criminal jurisdiction. Chapter 2 of the Code of Criminal Procedure deals with the constitution of the criminal Courts only. Delinquent should have approached any class or category of criminal Court as defined under section 6 for purposes of section 7A and not the writ Court; *Sunil Kumar* v. *State of Haryana*, 2010 (4) RCR (Cri) 414 (P&H).

**6. Claim of Juvenility – Law on** – Whenever a claim of juvenility is raised before any court, the court is bound to make an enquiry and to take all such evidence as may be necessary so as to deter-mine the age of the accused. Opportunity to lead evidence is necessary; *Monu @ Chhota @ Ashish* v. *State of Uttar Pradesh*, 2010 (2) Crimes 788 (All): 2010 (2) ADJ 205: 2010 (1) ACR 756.

**7. Claim of Juvenility – Comments on** – It is clear from the sub-section (1) of section 7A of the Act that whenever a claim of juvenility is raised, before any Court, that Court is bound to hold an inquiry and take all such evidence, as may be necessary (but not on affidavit) so as to determine the age of such person and shall record a finding whether the person is juvenile or a child or not, stating his age as clearly as may be. As per rule 12(3) of the Juvenile Justice (Care and Protection of Children) Rules, 2007, the question of juvenility has to be decided on the basis of matriculation certificate or equivalent certificate or in the absence whereof the date of birth recorded in the school first attended and in the absence whereof the date of birth recorded in the Municipal records, Panchayat, Corporation etc., and in the absence of above three certificates, age has to be determined on the basis of a certificate of the Medical Board duly constituted for the purpose of ascertaining the age of the accused; *Neelu Chaurasia @ Arvind Kumar Chaurasia* v. *State of Uttar Pradesh*, 2013 (5) ADJ 69: 2013 (6) All LJ 54: 2013 (8) RCR (Cri) 1389.

**8. Question of Juvenility – Law on** – Section 7A of the amended Act shows that a claim of juvenility can be raised at any time. Lest, there be any confusion, the proviso to section 7A of the Act declares that the question of juvenility can be raised and can be recognised at any stage even after the final disposal of the case and the claim must be determined in terms of the provisions contained in the Act even if the juvenile had ceased to be so on or before the date of commencement of the Act; *Selvi* v. *State of Kerala*, 2009 (3) Crimes 662 (Ker): 2008 (4) Ker LT 329 (Ker).

**9. Courts – Duties of** – Section 7A of the Juvenile Justice (Care and Protection of Children) Act, 2000 as amended by Act 33 of 2006 allows the claim of juvenility to be raised before any court at any stage of the proceedings on the ground that an accused was a juvenile on the date of commission of the offence. It also enjoins a duty on the court to make an enquiry regarding the age of the accused in all cases wherein the claim of juvenility is raised or the court is of the opinion that an accused person was a juvenile on the date of commission of the offence. In such a case, the court is to take such evidence as may be necessary so as to determine the age of such person and record a finding as to whether he was a juvenile or not as on the date of commission of offence. The proviso also makes it clear that a claim of juvenility may be raised before any court and it shall be recognised at any stage, even after final disposal of the case and that such claim shall be determined in terms of the provisions of the Act and the rules made there under, even if the juvenile had ceased to be so on or before the date of commencement of the Act; *A. Chinnaponnu W/o Annamalai* v. *State of Tamil Nadu,* 2011 (3) Mad LJ (Cri) 433: 2011 (8) RCR (Cri) 663 (Mad) (DB).

**10. Courts – Role of** – For conducting an enquiry under section 7A of the Act, a Judge or the Board is not a moot spectator or a referee between two parties, but should adopt an active role and must take all such evidence, which may be necessary for just decision on the point of determination of the age of the accused on the date of offence. If Sessions Judge was not satisfied with the certificate or the Mark-sheet, he could have summoned the relevant school authorities or the authorities of the Board of High School and Intermediate Examination to summon the documents relating to date of birth of the accused. A copy of the High School Mark-sheet cannot be ignored simply on the ground that it has not been proved. Judge is competent to summon every witness or document to get the same proved in accordance with law. In accordance with rule 12(3) of the Rules, 2007, the age of the accused on the date of offence is to be determined on the basis of matriculation or equivalent certificate and in absence thereof on the basis of date of birth recorded in the school first attended and in the absence thereof on the basis of birth certificate issued by a Corporation or Municipal Authority or a Panchayat and only in the absence of these certificates, medical opinion can be preferred. When the evidence regarding matriculation or equivalent certificate is available, the medical evidence has no relevance; *Ram Sajiwan* v. *State of Uttar Pradesh,* 2011 (1) ACR 1009: 2011 (1) ALJ 617: 2011 Cr LJ 1121.

**11. Effect of Sentence – Law on** – Section 7A(2) provides that if the court finds a person to be a juvenile on the date of commission of the offence, it shall forward the juvenile to the Board for passing appropriate order, and the sentence if any, shall be deemed to have no effect; *Shyam Pado Mandal* v. *State of Jharkhand,* 2013 (4) JLJR 565: 2014 (1) AIR Jhar HCR 714 (Jhar) (DB).

**12. Evidence – Law on** – Sub-section (1) of section 7A of the Act provides that whenever a claim of juvenility is raised before any Court, the Court shall make an enquiry, take such evidence as may be necessary so as to determine the age of such person and shall record a finding whether the person is a juvenile stating his age as nearly as may be. The Proviso to this section provides that if a claim of juvenility is raised then such claim shall be determined in terms of the provisions contained in the Act and the rules made thereunder. This provision clearly shows that although an enquiry is required to be made if a claim of juvenility is raised before any Court, but evidence is required to be taken only when, the Court feels that it is necessary to take evidence. The provision also indicates that the claim of juvenility shall be determined in terms of the provisions contained in the Act and rules made thereunder. The Central Government has framed Rules of 2007 under the Act. The procedure of enquiry for the determination of juvenility is provided in rule 12 of the Rules of 2007, which has already been quoted in entirety as above; *Dalip Kumar* v. *State of Rajasthan,* 2013 (2) Raj LW 972: 2013 (2) Crimes 287 (Raj): 2013 Cr LJ 1097 (Raj).

**13. Further Evidence – Law on** – A close look at rule 12 reveals that this rule provides a complete code in which "inquiry" referred to in section 7A of the Act about determination as to the age of a juvenile is to be conducted and if any of the documents referred to in this rule is available on record then no further evidence is required to be taken and the Court on the basis of the document referred to in the rule itself shall determine the age of the person. According to rule 12(3)(a)(i), first of all the age determination enquiry shall be conducted by seeking evidence by obtaining the matriculation or equivalent certificate. Once the matriculation certificate or any other equivalent certificate is available on record, no further evidence is required to be taken by the reason that by obtaining the matriculation certificate or equivalent certificate the enquiry is complete. If in a case the matriculation certificate or equivalent certificate is available that shall be conclusive proof of the age of the person by whom the claim of juvenility was made but if in a case such certificate is not available then the Court proceed to make further enquiry; *Dalip Kumar* v. *State of Rajasthan*, 2013 (2) Raj LW 972: 2013 (2) Crimes 287 (Raj): 2013 Cr LJ 1097 (Raj).

**14. Ex-Juvenile in Conflict with Law – Relief for –** The new Act 2000 covers cases under the old Act 1986 even subsequent to the date of the offence, when the juvenile in conflict with law had crossed 18 years of his age. If a juvenile, who has committed an offence when he was below 18 years of age, even after disposal of his case and even after crossing his 18 years of age, as per section 7A and *Explanation* to section 20, can claim juvenility at any stage of the case means trial, revision, appeal or in any other criminal proceedings. Hence, even if the case is over in the trial Court or in the next Appellate Court or Revisional Court or even in the Supreme Court, subsequently, in an independent proceeding, for the first time, the ex-juvenile in conflict with law can claim benefit under the new Act, 2000, based on his juvenility on the date of his commission of the offence; *Kalai Selvi* v. *State Represented by Inspector of Police*, 2013 (4) Mad LJ (Cri) 101 (Mad) (DB).

**15. Final Disposal of Case – Law on –** Section 7A makes it obligatory for the court before which a claim of juvenility is raised to make an inquiry, take such evidence as may be necessary so as to determine the age of such person and record a finding as to whether he/she is a juvenile or a child or not and state his/her age as nearly as may be. That a claim of juvenility may be raised before any court even after the final disposal of the case and that in such an eventuality, the claim has to be determined in terms of the provisions of the Act and the Rules made there under, even if, the juvenile has ceased to be so on or before the date of the commencement thereof, is clearly stipulated in the proviso to section 7A. Section 7A(2) mandates that if a court finds a person to be juvenile on the date of the commission of the offence under sub-section (1), it would forward the juvenile to the Board for passing appropriate orders and the sentence, if any, passed by a court shall be deemed to have no effect; *State of Assam (in re:)*, 2012 Cr LJ 471: 2011 (4) Gau LR 235: 2013 (6) RCR 2190 (Cri) (Gau) (DB).

**16. High Court – Obligations of –** Under sub-section 1 of section 7A of the said Act of 2000, High Court is under an obligation to make an enquiry so as to determine the age of the accused on the date of commission of the offence. Sub-section 2 of section 7(A) of the Act of 2000 requires High Court to forward a person found to be juvenile to the Board constituted under the said Act of 2000 for passing appropriate order and the sentence, if any passed by this Court shall be deemed to have no effect; *Balu Bapusaheb Gade* v. *State of Maharashtra*, 2010 All MR (Cri) 167: 2010 (2) Crimes (Bom) 724: 2011 (8) RCR (Cri) 1425.

**17. Writ Jurisdiction – Comments on –** Having carefully examined the historical background and the very nature of writ jurisdiction, which is a supervisory jurisdiction over inferior courts/tribunals, in our view, on principle a writ of *certiorari* cannot be issued to coordinate courts. Thus, it follows that a High Court cannot issue a writ to another High Court, nor can one Bench of a High Court issue a writ to a different Bench of the same High Court; much less can writ jurisdiction of a High Court be invoked to seek issuance of a writ of *certiorari* to the Supreme Court. Though, the judgment/orders of the High Courts are liable to be corrected by the Supreme Court in its appellate jurisdiction under article 132, 133 and 134 as well as under article 136 of the Constitution, the High Courts are not constituted as inferior courts in our constitutional scheme. Therefore, the

Supreme Court would not issue a writ under article 32 to the High Court. Further, neither a smaller Bench nor a larger Bench of the Supreme Court can issue a writ under article 32 of the Constitution to any other Bench of the Supreme Court. It is pointed out above that article 32 can be invoked only for the purpose of enforcing the fundamental rights conferred in Part III and it is a settled position in law that no judicial order passed by any superior court in judicial proceedings can be said to violate any of the fundamental rights enshrined in Part III. It may further be noted that the superior courts of justice do not also fall within the ambit of State or other authorities under article 12 of the Constitution; *Rupa Ashok Hurra* v. *Ashok Hurra*, 2002 4 SCC 388.

**18. Writ of *Mandamus* – Maintainability of –** Section 7A clearly provides for holding an inquiry, so is the position under rule 12(3) which enjoins upon the Court or the Board a duty to conduct an inquiry by seeking evidence by obtaining the matriculation or equivalent certificates, date of birth certificates, date of birth certificate from the school and such other evidence. Section 7A also clearly empowers the Court dealing with the matter to hold an inquiry by taking evidence. Similarly, rule 12 sub-rule 1 also empowers the Court or the Board or Committee referred to in rule 19 to determine the age of the juvenile in conflict with law by taking evidence. There is no provision whereunder the State can determine the age of the accused claiming to be juvenile at the time of commission of offence. Thus, Writ of *Mandamus* sought by delinquent is misconceived in this regard. The State or any of its agencies has no authority or jurisdiction to determine the age of juvenile. It is only the criminal Court dealing with the matter at any stage or the Board constituted under section 4 or a Committee constituted under rule 19 of the Rules framed under the Act which is competent to determine the age of the accused claiming to be juvenile; *Sunil Kumar* v. *State of Haryana*, 2010 (4) RCR (Cri) 414 (P&H).

**19. Magistrate – Obligations of –** Whenever an accused, who physically appears to be a juvenile, is produced before a Magistrate, he or she should form a *prima facie* opinion on the juvenility of the accused and record it. If any doubt persists, the Magistrate should conduct an age inquiry as required by section 7A of the Juvenile Justice (Care and Protection of Children) Act, 2000 to determine the juvenility or otherwise of the accused person. In this regard, it is better to err on the side of caution in the first instance rather than have the entire proceedings reopened or vitiated at a subsequent stage or a guilty person go unpunished only because he or she is found to be a juvenile on the date of occurrence of the incident; *Jitendra Singh @ Babboo Singh* v. *State of Uttar Pradesh*, 2013 (11) SCC 193: 2013 (3) Crimes 319 (SC): 2013 (9) SCALE 18.

**20. Review Case of Juvenile in Conflict with Law – Law on –** Section 7A of the Juvenile Justice (Care and Protection of Children) Act, 2000, has been inserted by the Juvenile Justice (Care and Protection of Children) Amendment Act, 2006, which deals with the procedure to be followed when juvenility is claimed before any court even after final disposal of the case but this provision does not provide as to where the petition for determining the juvenility would be filed by such person, who is serving out the sentence after final disposal of the case in appeal even by the Hon'ble Apex Court. The provision of section 64 of the Juvenile Justice (Care and Protection of Children) Act, 2000, provides that the State Government, or as the case may be the Board, may, pass appropriate order and review the case of a juvenile in conflict with law undergoing a sentence by giving the adequate and special reason. Rule 98 of the Juvenile Justice (Care and Protection of Children) Rules, 2007, supplements the provision of section 64 of the Juvenile Justice (Care and Protection of Children) Act, 2000. The aforesaid Rule provides that the State Government or as the case may be the Board may, either *suo motu* or on an application made for the purpose, review the case of a person or a juvenile in conflict with law, determine his juvenility in terms of the Act and pass appropriate order in the interest of juvenile in conflict with law under section 64 of the Act; *Majbul Hoda; Izharul Haque* v. *State of Bihar*, 2013 Cr LJ 3167: 2013 (8) RCR (Cri) 851 (Pat).

**21. Review – Law on –** Claim of juvenility may be raised before any court and it shall be recognized at any stage, even after final disposal of the case, and such claim shall be determined in terms of the provisions contained in this Act and the rules made thereunder, even if the juvenile has ceased to be so on or before the date of commencement of this Act. Reading of the section 7A makes it clear that the claim of juvenility can be raised before any court at any stage, even after final disposal of the case and sets out the procedure which the court is required to adopt, when such claim of juvenility is raised. Apart from the aforesaid provisions of the Act as amended, and the rule 98 of the Rules, in particular, has to be read along with section 20 of the Act as amended by the Amending Act, 2006 which provides that even after disposal of cases of juveniles in conflict with law, the State Government or the Board can, either *suo motu* or on an application made for the purpose, review the case of juvenile, determine the juvenility and pass an appropriate order under section 64 of the Act for immediate release of the juvenile whose period of detention has exceeded the maximum period provided in section 15 of the Act *i.e.,* 3 years; *Gurdarshan Singh* v. *State of Punjab,* 2012 (4) RCR (Cri) 909 (P&H).

**22. Special Home – Law on –** Accused was juvenile at the relevant time of occurrence; he is entitled to the benefit of the provisions of Juvenile Justice (Care and Protection of Children) Act, 2000 and Rules made thereunder and as envisaged in section 7A. Consequently, he cannot possibly be directed to be sent to special home for a period not more than three years as contemplated under section 15(1)(g) & 16 of the Act. This matter is no more *res integra* and is now well settled; *Surinder* v. *State of Haryana,* 2013 (4) RCR (Cri) 73: 2014 (1) Crimes 60 (P&H).

**23. Trial of Juvenile – Law on –** For the purpose of the determination of the question as to whether an accused was or was not a juvenile on the date of the alleged commission of offence, it is not at all necessary to determine as to what offence(s) the accused has committed or whether the accused is or is not guilty of the offence(s), which, he is alleged to have committed. It shall be borne in mind that as a matter of principle as well as procedure, whenever a question of juvenility of an accused is raised, the Court must hold an enquiry and determine the answer to the question, so raised, so that the accused, if found to be a juvenile, can be dealt with, at the earliest, in accordance with law contained in that behalf. Such a determination, at the earliest is imperative, because, a juvenile cannot be tried by any Court, in any case, except in accordance with the scheme as embodied in the said Act. To put it a little differently, a Court of ordinary criminal jurisdiction cannot try a juvenile and, hence, when a juvenile, in conflict with law, cannot be tried by a Court of ordinary criminal jurisdiction, the question of juvenility of an accused, facing a trial, in a Court of ordinary criminal jurisdiction, would have to be determined, the moment such a question arises for determination in a given case; *Apurba Das* v. *State of Assam,* 2010 Cr LJ 803: 2010 (1) Gau LR 574: 2009 (3) Gau LT 406 (Gau).

**24. Rules – Comments on –** Section 7A lays down measures to be taken when claim of juvenility is made. It does not enjoin framing of any Rules, much less the mode or nature of evidence to be taken in regard to age of an accused; *Jai Prakash Tiwari* v. *State of Uttar Pradesh,* 2012 (10) ADJ 478: 2013 (2) ACrR 1383 (All).

**25. Trials of Summons Cases by Magistrates – Comments on –** Section 54A reference to the provisions of Chapter XX of the Code which deals with trials of summons cases by Magistrates will have to be made. It will be necessary to make a reference to sections 251 and 252 of the said Code which read thus:—

> *251. Substance of accusation to be stated.*—When in a summons-case the accused appears or is brought before the Magistrate the particulars of the offence of which he is accused shall be stated to him, and he shall be asked whether he pleads guilty or has any defence to make, but it shall not be necessary to frame a formal charge.

252. *Conviction on plea of guilty.*—If the accused pleads guilty, the Magistrate shall record the plea as nearly as possible in the words used by the accused and may, in his discretion, convict him thereon.

**26. Sentence – Law on –** Determination of the juvenility of the accused is a jurisdictional question for the Courts to proceed on the merits of the case. Therefore, it is always desirable for the Courts to determine the question of juvenility at the first instance. In this regard section 7A(2) provides that if the accused is found juvenile at the time of offence, even after the sentence has been passed by a Court, then such sentence would be deemed to have no effect and accused would be forwarded to the Juvenile Board for appropriate orders; *Ishtikhar* v. *State of Uttar Pradesh*, 2012 (5) SCALE 47: 2012 (12) SCC 307 (SC).

**27. Technicalities and Irregularities – Law on –** The expression "failure of justice" would appear, sometimes, as an etymological chameleon. The Court has to examine whether there is really a failure of justice or whether it is only a camouflage. Justice is a virtue which transcends all barriers. Neither the rules of procedure, nor technicalities of law can stand in its way. Even the law bends before justice. The order of the court should not be prejudicial to anyone. Justice means justice between both the parties. The interests of justice equally demand that the "guilty should be punished" and that technicalities and irregularities, which do not occasion the "failure of justice"; are not allowed to defeat the ends of justice. They cannot be perverted to achieve the very opposite end as this would be counter-productive. "Courts exist to dispense justice, not to dispense with justice. And, the justice to be dispensed is not palm-tree justice or idiosyncratic justice". Law is not an escape route for law breakers. If this is allowed, this may lead to greater injustice than upholding the rule of law. The guilty man, therefore, should be punished, and in case substantial justice has been done, it should not be defeated when pitted against technicalities; *Union of India* v. *Ex-Gnr Ajeet Singh*, JT 2013 (4) SC 415: 2013 (5) SCALE 107: 2013 (4) SCC 186; Vide *Ramesh Kumar* v. *Ram Kumar*, AIR 1984 SC 1029; *S. Nagaraj* v. *State of Karnataka*, 1993 Supp (4) SCC 595; *State Bank of Patiala* v. *S.K. Sharma*, AIR 1996 SC 1660 and *Shaman Saheb M. Multani* v. *State of Karnataka*, AIR 2001 SC 921.

**28. Two Views Possible – Law on –** Except for urging that if a discretion is to be exercised when two views are possible about the age of the accused and one of them permits accepting the accused as a juvenile, then that must be followed . However, this again has to be done on the basis of an enquiry conducted by the Court after providing an opportunity of examination to the other side; *Puneet Vasudeva* v. *State*, 2009 (110) DRJ 350: 2009 (5) AD (Del) 129: 2009 (3) Crimes 291 (Del).

**8. Observation homes.**—(1) Any State Government may establish and maintain either by itself or under an agreement with voluntary organisations, observation homes in every district or a group of districts, as may be required for the temporary reception of any juvenile in conflict with law during the pendency of any inquiry regarding them under this Act.

(2) Where the State Government is of opinion that any institution other than a home established or maintained under sub-section (1), is fit for the temporary reception of juvenile in conflict with law during the pendency of any inquiry regarding them under this Act, it may certify such institution as an observation home for the purposes of this Act.

(3) The State Government may, by rules made under this Act, provide for the management of observation homes, including the standards and various types of services to be provided by them for rehabilitation and social integration of a juvenile, and the circumstances under which, and the manner in which, the certification of an observation home may be granted or withdrawn.

(4) Every juvenile who is not placed under the charge of parent or guardian and is sent to an observation home shall be initially kept in a reception unit of the observation home for preliminary inquiries, care and classification for juveniles according to his age group, such as seven to twelve years, twelve to sixteen years and sixteen to eighteen years, giving due considerations to physical and mental status and degree of the offence committed, for further induction into observation home.

**COMMENTS**

The expression 'natural guardian' is defined in section 4(c) of Hindu Minority and Guardianship Act, 1956 as any of the guardians mentioned in section 6. The term 'guardian' is defined in section 4(b) of Hindu Minority and Guardianship Act, 1956 as a person having the care of the person of a minor or of his property or of both, his person and property, and includes a natural guardian among others. Thus, it is seen that the definitions of 'guardian' and 'natural guardian' do not make any discrimination against mother and she being one of the guardians mentioned in section 6 would undoubtedly be a natural guardian as defined in section 4(c). The only provision to which exception is taken is found in section 6(a) which reads "the father, and after him, the mother". (underlining ours). That phrase, on a cursory reading, does give an impression that the mother can be considered to be natural guardian of the minor only after the life time of the father. In fact that appears to be the basis of the stand taken by the Reserve Bank of India also. It is not in dispute and is otherwise well settled also that welfare of the minor in the widest sense is the paramount consideration and even during the life time of the father, if necessary, he can be replaced by the mother or any other suitable person by an order of Court, where to do so would be in the interest of the welfare of the minor. Whenever a dispute concerning the guardianship of a minor, between the father and mother of the minor is raised in a Court of law, the word 'after' in the section would have no significance, as the Court is primarily concerned with the best interests of the minor and his welfare in the widest sense while determining the question as regards custody and guardianship of the minor. The question, however, assumes importance only when the mother acts as guardian of the minor during the lifetime of the father, without the matter going to Court, and the validity of such an action is challenged on the ground that she is not the legal guardian of the minor in view of section 6(a); *Githa Hariharan* v. *Reserve Bank of India,* AIR 1999 SC 1149: 1999 (2) SCC 228: 1999 (1) SCR 669.

**9. Special homes.**—(1) Any State Government may establish and maintain either by itself or under an agreement with voluntary organisations, special homes in every district or a group of districts, as may be required for reception and rehabilitation of juvenile in conflict with law under this Act.

(2) Where the State Government is of opinion that any institution other than a home established or maintained under sub-section (1), is fit for the reception of juvenile in conflict with law to be sent there under this Act, it may certify such institution as a special home for the purposes of this Act.

(3) The State Government may, by rules made under this Act, provide for the management of special homes, including the standards and various types of services to be provided by them which are necessary for re-socialisation of a juvenile, and the circumstances under which, and the manner in which, the certification of a special home may be granted or withdrawn.

(4) The rules made under sub-section (3) may also provide for the classification and separation of juvenile in conflict with law on the basis of age and the nature of offences committed by them and his mental and physical status.

**SYNOPSIS**



**COMMENTS**

**1. Interest of Other Juveniles in Special Home – Law on –** Section 15 of the Act of 2000 provides for various orders which "the Board" may pass against a juvenile when it is satisfied that the juvenile has committed an offence, which includes an order directing the juvenile to be sent to a special home for a period of three years. Section 16 of the Act of 2000 stipulates that where a juvenile who has attained the age of sixteen years has committed an offence and "the Board" is satisfied that the offence committed is so serious in nature that it would not be in his interest or in the interest of other juveniles in a special home to send him to such special home and that none of the other measures provided under the Act is suitable or sufficient, the Board may order the juvenile in conflict with law to be kept in such place of safety and in such manner as it thinks fit and shall report the case for the order of the State Government. Proviso to sub-section (2) of section 16 of the Act of 2000 provides that the period of detention so ordered shall not exceed in any case than thirty five years; *Gurdarshan Singh* v. *State of Punjab,* 2012 (4) RCR (Cri) 909 (P&H).

**2. Custody of Child – Law on –** The purpose of enacting the Act of 2000 is for the welfare of the juvenile. Therefore, it is the responsibility of the Board and Appellate Court and also of the District Probationary Officer to discharge their respective duties with seriousness and in a responsible manner. It was the duty of all the three to discharge such responsibility with care and caution. It is true that a juvenile should not be kept unnecessarily in a protective home but at the same time it is equally important that he should not be exploited, after his release, by criminals and unscrupulous persons of the society, who may use the juvenile for their own benefit. It is also to be looked into whether the mother and father of such juvenile are competent enough to have proper control over such child and if it is found that they can not discharge their duty towards the juvenile in a proper way they can not be given the custody of the child. In such circumstances it is better to keep the juvenile in the protection of the State; *Nihal* v. *State of Uttar Pradesh,* 2013 (4) ADJ 476: 2013 (3) ACrR 3156: 2013 (81) ACC 722 (All).

**3. Detention – Law on –** Juvenile, who is under going a sentence when this Act came into force, would be required to be sent to a special home or a fit institution for the remainder of the period of the sentence, but such sentence was not to exceed, in any case, the maximum period provided in section 15 of the Act. In other words, even where a juvenile in conflict with law had been sentenced and was undergoing the sentence when the Act came into force, he cannot be detained in prison and he is required to be sent to a special home or a fit institution for the remainder period of the sentence with the condition that the sentence shall not, in any case, exceed the maximum period provided in section 15 of the said Act; *Chatpal @ Satpal* v. *State,* 2011 (123) DRJ 131 (Del) (DB).

**4. Word "May" – Comprehension of –** There is no doubt that the word "may" generally does not mean "must" or "shall". But it is well-settled that the word "may" is capable of meaning, "must" or "shall" in the light of the context. It is also clear that where a discretion is conferred upon a public authority coupled with an obligation, the word "may" which denotes discretion should be construed to mean a command. Sometimes, the Legislature uses the word "may" out of deference to the high status of the authority on whom the power and the obligation are intended to be conferred and imposed; *State of Uttar Pradesh* v. *Jogendra Singh,* AIR 1963 SC 1618: 1963 (2) LLJ 444.

**10. Apprehension of juvenile in conflict with law.**—[1][(1) As soon as a juvenile in conflict with law is apprehended by police, he shall be placed under the charge of the special juvenile police unit or the designated police officer, who shall produce the juvenile before the Board without any loss of time but within a period of twenty-four hours of his apprehension excluding the time necessary for the journey, from the place where the juvenile was apprehended, to the Board:

Provided that in no case, a juvenile in conflict with law shall be placed in a police lockup or lodged in a jail.]

(2) The State Government may make rules consistent with this Act,—

(i) to provide for persons through whom (including registered voluntary organisations) any juvenile in conflict with law may be produced before the Board;

(ii) to provide the manner in which such juvenile may be sent to an observation home.

**SYNOPSIS**

1. *Actus Curiae Nerninern Gravabit* – Comments on
2. Apprehension of Juvenile – Law on
3. Benefits of Act – Law on
4. Juvenile – Law on
5. Police Officer – Duties of

**COMMENTS**

**1. *Actus Curiae Nerninern Gravabit* – Comments on** – No man is above the law but at the same time Courts reiterate and declare that no man can be denied his rights under the Constitution and the laws. He has a right to be dealt with in accordance with the law and not in derogation of it. It has been said long time ago that "*Actus Curiae Nerninern Gravabit*" an act of the Court shall prejudice no man. This maxim is founded upon justice and good sense and affords a safe and certain guide for the administration of the law; *Gurdarshan Singh* v. *State of Punjab,* 2012 (4) RCR (Cri) 909 (P&H).

**2. Apprehension of Juvenile – Law on** – The procedures laid down in the Code, in as much as they are for the benefit of a juvenile or a child; apply with full rigour to an apprehension made of a juvenile in conflict with law under section 10 of the Act. If these procedures are followed, the probability of a juvenile, on apprehension, being shown as an adult and sent to judicial custody in a jail, will be considerably minimized. If these procedures are followed, as they should be, along with the requirement of a Magistrate to examine the juvenility or otherwise of an accused person brought before him, subjecting a juvenile in conflict with law to a trial by a regular Court may become a thing of the past; *Jitendra Singh @ Babboo Singh* v. *State of Uttar Pradesh,* 2013 (11) SCC 193: JT 2013 (11) SC 152: 2013 (9) SCALE 18.

**3. Benefits of Act – Law on** – Therefore, the only criteria that is necessary for determining the juvenility of a person is whether on the date of the offence he was below the age of 18 years or not. If he was then he is to be treated as a juvenile and then the benefits of the Act would accrue to him; *Anil* v. *State (Govt. of NCT of Delhi),* 2009 (111) DRJ 102: 2009 (3) Crimes 443 (Del) (DB).

---

1. Subs. by Act 33 of 2006, sec. 9, for sub-section (1) (w.e.f. 22-8-2006). Sub-section (1), before substitution, stood as under:

"(1) As soon as a juvenile in conflict with law is apprehended by police, he shall be placed under the charge of the special juvenile police unit or the designated police officer who shall immediately report the matter to a member of the Board.".

**4. Juvenile – Law on –** As per section 10 of the Act and rule 95 of the Tamil Nadu Juvenile Justice [Care and Protection of Children] Rules, 2001, as soon as the juvenile is apprehended by any Police, he shall be placed under the charge of the Special Juvenile Police Unit or designated Police officer. Thereafter, it is for the Juvenile Police to take care of the juvenile and also to investigate the matter; *Idukkan* v. *Inspector of Police,* 2012 (4) CTC 718 (Mad).

**5. Police Officer – Duties of –** The rule 11 of the Juvenile Justice (Care and Protection of Children) Rules, 2007 provides as soon as a juvenile alleged to be in conflict with law is apprehended by the police, the concerned Police officer shall inform the concerned designated Juvenile or the Child Welfare Officer, parents or guardian of the juvenile, the concerned probation officer. The rule 11 further provides how the case of the juvenile or child is to be dealt with. The rule 12 provides procedure for determination of age of child or a juvenile in conflict with law; *Naushad Ali @ Nishu Son of Kamal Deen* v. *State of Himachal Pradesh,* 2013 (3) Crimes 57 (HP): 2012 (3) Shim LC 1719 (HP).

**11. Control of custodian over juvenile.**—Any person in whose charge a juvenile is placed in pursuance of this Act shall, while the order is in force have the control over the juvenile as he would have if he were his parents, and shall be responsible for his maintenance, and the juvenile shall continue in his charge for the period stated by competent authority, notwithstanding that he is claimed by his parents or any other person.

**COMMENTS**

**Parents – Ambit of –** As the definition of the word parent means both father and mother; *Rajinder Kaur* v. *Union of India,* 1975 ACJ 272 (Del).

**12. Bail of juvenile.**—(1) When any person accused of a bailable or non-bailable offence, and apparently a juvenile, is arrested or detained or appears or is brought before a Board, such person shall, notwithstanding anything contained in the Code of Criminal Procedure, 1973 (2 of 1974) or in any other law for the time being in force, be released on bail with or without surety [1][or placed under the supervision of a Probation Officer or under the care of any fit institution or fit person] but he shall not be so released if there appear reasonable grounds for believing that the release is likely to bring him into association with any known criminal or expose him to moral, physical or psychological danger or that his release would defeat the ends of justice.

(2) When such person having been arrested is not released on bail under sub-section (1) by the officer incharge of the police station, such officer shall cause him to be kept only in an observation home in the prescribed manner until he can be brought before a Board.

(3) When such person is not released on bail under sub-section (1) by the Board it shall, instead of committing him to prison, make an order sending him to an observation home or a place of safety for such period during the pendency of the inquiry regarding him as may be specified in the order.

**SYNOPSIS**

1. Observation Home – Comments on
2. Provision – Comments on
3. Provision – Nature of
4. Mandate of Provision – Attraction
5. Intention of Legislature – Law on
6. Second Part of Provision – Comments on
7. Benefit of Provisions – Law on
8. Accusation for having Nude Photos of Woman – Bail for
9. Bail of Co-Accused – Law on

1. Ins. by Act 33 of 2006, sec. 10 (w.e.f. 22-8-2006).

## COMMENTS

**1. Observation Home – Comments on –** If it is found that the person is a juvenile and, hence a juvenile in conflict with law, then the first thing is that by virtue of section 12 of the Act his bail plea has to be disposed of. In other words, as provided under the said Act, he may or may not be released on bail, but in either of the case he cannot be remanded to the judicial custody. His case has to be placed before the Juvenile Justice Board which can instead of releasing him make an order sending him to observation home or a place of safety by virtue of section 12(3) of the Act. Then orders in terms of section 17 may be passed keeping in mind orders by virtue of section 16 of the Act which may not be passed. However, by virtue of section 18 of the Act it is prohibited to try a juvenile together with a person who is not juvenile but that trial would also be by and before Juvenile Justice Board and not in any Court of the juvenile in conflict with law; *Sudhakar Dwivedi* v. *State of Uttar Pradesh,* 2012 (6) ADJ 649: 2012 (2) ACrR 2250 (All).

**2. Provision – Comments on –** From the bare reading of the provision contained under section 12 of Juvenile Justice (Care & Protection of Children) Act, 2000 it is clear that word 'shall' occurred under clause (1) of section 12 of the aforesaid Act connotes an idea that the release of a juvenile in a criminal case is mandatory unless there appears reasonable grounds for believing that release is likely to bring him into association with any known criminal or expose him to moral, physical or psychological danger or that his release would defeat the ends of justice. It is hereby made clear that mere saying in the impugned order that the release of a juvenile is likely to bring him into association with any known criminal or expose him to moral, physical, psychological danger or that his release would defeat the ends of justice is not enough rather the courts are under legal obligation and duty bound to record reasons based on material and evidence available on record for the aforesaid findings because the aforesaid provision enacted by the Parliament is not a mere idle formality rather it attaches with it a legal sanctity and the courts of law are supposed to ensure its strict compliance in its letter and spirit in the matter of dispensation of justice otherwise the very object and reasons behind the legislation of the aforesaid provision shall loose its legal import; *Kabutar @ Indrasen Singh* v. *State of Uttar Pradesh,* 2014 (2) ADJ 219 (All).

**3. Provision – Nature of –** Harmonious construction of section 12 of the Act is that the gravity of the offence is not a ground for rejection of application for bail under section 12 of the Act. Once the legislature has not provided the gravity of the offence as one of the grounds for rejection of the bail, the bail to a juvenile cannot be denied on the ground of gravity of the offence. The legislative intent is clear in this regard and the provision is mandatory in nature; *Rajvir* v. *State of Haryana,* 2013 Cr LJ 2880 (P&H).

**4. Mandate of Provision – Attraction –** The mandate of section 12 of the Act to release any person accused of a bailable or non-bailable offence and apparently a juvenile when arrested or detained or having appeared or is brought before a Board is subject to only three exceptions. A reasonable ground must exist for believing that the release is:

(i) likely to bring the juvenile into association with any known criminal; or

(ii) expose him to moral physical or psychological danger; or

(iii) that his release would defeat the ends of justice.

Unless there appear reasonable grounds to justify the existence of one or more of the three conditions mentioned above, the mandate of section 12 to release the juvenile on bail would be attracted; *Vikki Singh* v. *State of Chhattisgarh,* 2006 (1) Cg LJ 447: 2006 Cr LJ 1892 (Chhat).

**5. Intention of Legislature – Law on –** Language of section 12 of the Act using the word "shall, is mandatory and it provides *non-obstante* clause by using the expression "notwithstanding anything contained in the Code of Criminal Procedure, 1973 or any other law for the time being in force, which conveys the intention of the Legislature to grant bail to the juvenile irrespective of nature or gravity of the offence alleged to have been committed by him and the bail can be denied only in the case where there appear reasonable grounds for believing that the release is likely to bring him into association with any known criminal or expose him to moral, physical or psychological danger or that his release would defeat the ends of justice; *Amandeep Singh @ Amna* v. *State of Rajasthan*, 2012 (7) RCR (Cri) 3023 (Raj).

**6. Second Part of Provision – Comments on** – According to sub-section (1) of section 12 of the Act, a juvenile shall be released on ball with or without surety notwithstanding anything contained in the Code of Criminal Procedure, 1973 or In any other law for the time being in force, the first part of the provision appears to be mandatory in nature for releasing on bail but the second part is equally appears to be mandatory for refusing the bail as a Juvenile shall not be so released if there appears reasonable grounds for believing that;

(1) the release is lively to bring him into association with any known criminal; or

(2) expose him to moral, physical or psychological danger; or

(3) that his release would defeat the ends of justice.

In case of the refusal of the bail, some reasonable grounds for believing abovementioned exceptions must be brought before the court concerned by the prosecution; *Sanjay Chaurasia* v. *State of Uttar Pradesh*, 2006 (55) All Cri C 480: 2006 (4) All LJ 353: 2006 Cr LJ 2957.

**7. Benefit of Provisions – Law on** – If Courts apply sections 2(k), 2(l), 7A, 20 and 49 of the 2000 Act read with rules 12 and 98 of the Juvenile Justice (Care and Protection of Children) Rules, 2007 (for short 'the Rules') all persons who were below the age of 18 years on the date of commission of the offence even prior to 1-4-2001, would be treated as juveniles even if the claim of juvenility is raised after they have attained the age of 18 years on or before the date of the commencement of the 2000 Act and were undergoing sentences upon being convicted. The age of the accused as on the date of the commission of the offence was 17 years, 11 months and 5 days and hence less than 18 years, and hence when we apply provisions of the 2000 Act, the appellant has to be treated as a juvenile, being less than 18 years of age on the date of the crime and hence entitled to get the benefit of the provisions of the 2000 Act read with Rules; *Ketankumar Gopalbhai Tandel* v. *State of Gujarat*, 2013 (5) Supreme 582: 2013 (9) SCALE 487: 2013 (4) BCR (Cri) 56.

**8. Accusation for having Nude Photos of Woman – Bail for** – Only allegation against the accused was that the principal accused had transferred the nude photograph of the girl on the cell phone of the accused but no cell phone bearing nude photograph could be recovered from the possession of the accused and Courts further find that the case of the accused does not come within the proviso of section 12 of the Juvenile Justice (Care and Protection of Children) Act, 2000 so as to deny the statutory right of the accused of his bail wherein his bail has been made rule and refusal exception; *Manish Kumar* v. *State of Jharkhand*, AIR 2011 Jhar 794: 2011 (4) Crimes 204 (Jhar): 2011 (8) RCR (Cri) 2121.

**9. Bail of Co-Accused – Law on** – From perusal of the F.I.R. that the only allegation against the accused was that the principal accused had transferred the nude photograph of the girl on the cell phone of the accused but no cell phone bearing nude photograph could be recovered from the possession of the accused. So the case of the accused does not come within the proviso of section 12 of the Juvenile Justice (Care and Protection of Children) Act, 2000 so as to deny the statutory right of the accused of his bail wherein his bail has been made rule and refusal exception; *Manish Kumar* v. *State of Jharkhand*, AIR 2011 Jhar 794: 2011 (4) Crimes 204 (Jhar): 2011 (8) RCR (Cri) 2121.

**10. Bail to Juvenile – Three *Exceptions* for** – A juvenile who is accused of a bailable or non-bailable offence "shall" be released on bail or placed under the care of a suitable person/institution. This is subject to three *Exceptions*: (i) where his release would bring him into association with a known criminal, (ii) where his release would expose him to moral, physical or psychological danger, or (iii) where his release would defeat the ends of justice. Even where bail is refused, the juvenile is to be kept in an observation home or a place of safety (and not jail); *Subramanian Swamy* v. *Raju*, JT 2014 (4) SC 328: 2014 (4) SCALE 305: AIR 2014 SC 1649. *Nirbhaya* case [Hon'ble Judges: P. Sathasivam, Ranjan Gogoi, Shiva Kirti Singh].

**11. Enquiry Stage – Effect of** – The case is at the enquiry stage and the accused is in custody for about one year and nine months, in that manner he has already served out more than half of the sentence though he has not yet been convicted by a competent Court of law. If the case of the accused does not come in any manner within the proviso of section 12 of the Act so denial of the statutory right of the accused for his bail is bad; *Naresh Saw @ Naresh Sah* v. *State of Jharkhand*, 2012 (1) Crimes 151 (Jhar): 2011 Cr LJ 3642: 2011 (7) RCR (Cri) 389 (Jhar).

**12. Psychological Danger for Juvenile – Law on** – Bail to a juvenile can be denied in case there appear reasonable grounds for believing that his release would not be in his own interest or it may expose him to moral, physical or psychological danger or that his release would frustrate the very purpose or defeat the ends of justice; *Pradhan Singh* v. *State of Rajasthan*, 2013 (3) Raj LW 2710: 2013 (3) Crimes 313 (Raj): 2013 (1) WLN 159 (Raj) (Jaipur Bench).

**13. Bail – *Exception* for** – The position of law with regard to grant of bail to a juvenile under section 12 of the Act, is clear that a juvenile has to be released on bail mandatorily unless and until the exceptions carved out in the section itself are made out. The *first Exception* is a reasonable ground for believing that the release is likely to bring the juvenile into association with any known criminal. The *second Exception* is that the release of the juvenile is likely to expose him to any moral, physical or psychological danger. Both these Exceptions are not made out because there is no material available in the record of the case to suggest any such association or exposure. The *third Exception* is that the release of the juvenile would defeat the ends of the justice; *Hakam* v. *State of Madhya Pradesh*, 2011 ILR 2237 (MP).

**14. Refusal of Bail – Law on** – As per section 15 of the Act 2000 where a Board after having satisfied on inquiry that a juvenile has committed an offence, then notwithstanding anything to the contrary of any other law for the time being in force, may, if it so thinks fit, make an order at the most directing the juvenile to be sent to a Special Home for a period of three years only. There must be some material and evidence on record to refuse bail prayer of a juvenile for believing that his release was likely to bring him into association with any known criminal or would expose him to moral, physical and psychological danger and that his release would defeat the ends of justice. The bail to a juvenile cannot be refused on hypothetical considerations. A juvenile shall not be released on bail, if there appear reasonable grounds for believing that (i) the release is likely to bring him into association with any known criminal or; (ii) expose him to moral, physical and psychological danger or; (iii) his release would defeat the ends of justice; *Parvez (Minor)* v. *State of Uttar Pradesh*, 2014 (3) ADJ 191 (All).

**15. Specific Overt Act – Law on** – No specific overt act has been attributed against the accused except that he was friend of co-accused and as such his prayer for bail requires reasonably consideration; *Krishna Munda and; Etwa Munda @ Salik Munda* v. *State of Jharkhand*, AIR 2011 Jhar 773: 2011 (8) RCR (Cri) 2106: 2011 (2) JCR 540 (Jhar).

**16. Surrounding Facts and Circumstances – Law on** – Section no where ordains that bail to a juvenile is a must in all cases as it can be denied for the reasons if there appears reasonable grounds for believing that the release is likely to bring him into association with any known criminal or expose him to moral, physical or psychological danger or that his release would defeat the ends of justice. In the light of statutory provision bail prayer of the juvenile revisionist has to be considered on the surrounding facts and circumstances. Merely by declaration of being a juvenile does not entitle a juvenile in conflict with law to be released on bail as a matter of right. The Act has a solemn purpose to achieve betterment of juvenile offenders but it is not a shelter home for those juvenile offenders who have got criminal proclivities and a criminal psychology. It has a reformative approach but does not completely shun retributive theory. Legislature has preserved larger interest of society even in cases of bail to a juvenile. The Act seeks to achieve moral physical and psychological betterment of juvenile offender and therefore if, it is found that the ends of justice will be defeated or that goal desired by the Legislature can be achieved by detaining a juvenile offender in a juvenile home, bail can be denied to him. This is perceptible from phraseology of section 12 itself. Legislature in its wisdom has therefore carved out exceptions to the rule of bail to a juvenile; *Monu* v. *State of Uttar Pradesh,* 2011 (88) ALR 11: 2011 (4) Crimes 118 (All): 2011 Cr LJ 4496.

**17. Age of Accused – Determination of –** Evidence relevant for purpose of determining the age is first to take matriculation certificate or birth certificate etc. as mentioned in section 12(3)(a)(i)(ii)(iii) and in the absence of these document only the Court proceed to consider the Medical Board. The Court is expected to make enquiry under the Act about the juvenility or age of the accused. The enquiry for determination of the age of accused a juvenility is required to be done by the Court not in an enquiry during investigation. There is specific provision for manner of enquiry about the age of juvenile enshrined rule framed by Central Government rule 12 of the Juvenile Justice (Care and Protection of Children) Rules, 2007 and rule 22(3) of Bihar Juvenile Rules, 2003; *Usha Devi* v. *State of Bihar,* 2013 (3) PLJR 871 (Pat).

**18. Age of Person – Law on –** It is well settled that it is neither feasible nor desirable to lay down an abstract formula to determine the age of a person. The date of birth is to be determined on the basis of material on record and on appreciation of evidence adduced by the parties. The Medical evidence as to the age of a person, though a very useful guiding factor, is not conclusive and has to be considered along with other, cogent evidence; *Narayan Sharma* v. *State of Madhya Pradesh,* 2012 Cr LJ 736: 2013 (6) RCR (Cri) 1672 (MP) (Gwalior Bench).

**19. Aggravated Offences – Comments on –** Court has the discretion to ordinarily release a juvenile on bail but can also decline it if it has reasonable ground to believe that his release is likely to bring him into association with any known criminal or expose him to moral, physical and psychological danger or that his release would defeat the ends of justice. In the cases of aggravated offences, what is of importance to establish whether a person is a child or not, is his ability to comprehend what is right and what is wrong, what is lawful and what is unlawful and whether he understands the consequences of his actions. It is the advancement of his mental faculty that would suggest whether he is an adult or a juvenile and for this purpose, there has to be a specialized examination of the child at the hands of experts who can evaluate the ability of such a child to segregate good and bad, the lawful and unlawful and the consequences ensuing therefrom and this would show his maturity or immaturity to answer for his deeds; *Ajit* v. *State of Haryana,* 2013 (4) RCR (Cri) 476 (P&H).

**20. Anticipatory Bail to Lady – Law on –** Accused is a young lady. However, taking into account the seriousness of the offence and the role attributed to her by the prosecutrix in her statement under sections 161 and 164 of the Cr.P.C. coupled with the call details between her and other co-accused, it would not be proper to grant the concession of anticipatory bail to the Accused/Lady when the investigation is still incomplete; *Sanchita Gupta @ Shilpi* v. *State of Rajasthan,* 2014 (1) Crimes 26 (Raj): 2014 (1) Raj LW 340 (Raj).

**21. Arrested Juvenile – Relief for –** Act being a beneficiary and social-oriented legislation should be given full effect by all concerned whenever the matter relating to juvenile comes to consideration before them. It appears that for protection of juveniles. Special Act has been enacted. Section 12 of the Act indicates that if a juvenile is arrested or detained or appears or is brought before a Board, such person shall be released on bail with or without surety or placed under the supervision of a Probation Officer or under the care of any fit institution; *Amandep Singh* alias *Amna* v. *State of Rajasthan,* 2011 Cr LJ 1599 (Raj).

**22. Association with any Known Criminal – Law on –** A bare reading of section 12(1) makes it clear that any person accused of a bailable or non-bailable offence, and apparently a juvenile, is arrested or detained or appears or is brought before a Board, such person shall, notwithstanding anything contained in the Code of Criminal Procedure, 1973 (2 of 1974) or in any other law for the time being in force be released on bail with or without surety. It further says that such person shall not be so released if there appear reasonable grounds for believing that the release is likely to bring him into association with any known criminal or expose him to moral, physical or psychological danger or that his release would defeat the ends of justice; *Vishwajeet* alias *Krishna Bharadwaj* v. *State of Chhattisgarh,* 2012 (2) MPHT 55 (Chh): 2012 (1) Cg BCLJ 465: 2012 Cr LJ 2810 (Chhat); *Vide* Also, *Jayprakash Son of Nandlal* v. *State of Chhattisgarh,* 2012 (3) Crimes 495 (Chhat).

**23. Association with any Known Criminal – Comments on –** Juvenile should be granted bail unless his case falls within one of the *Exceptions* engrafted therein and those are that "there appear reasonable grounds for believing that the release is likely to bring him into association with any known criminal or expose him to moral, physical, or psychological danger or that his release would defeat the ends of justice." Unless the aforesaid rider is satisfied bail to a juvenile should not be refused. It is significant to note that gravity of offence or its seriousness alone, divorced from above *Exceptional* reasons, and has not been taken as a rider by the Legislature to deny bail to a juvenile in conflict with law. It is only danger to his moral, physical and psychological qualities and likely hood of his attaching himself with criminals or his release defeating ends of justice that Board or the courts may not exercise discretion in his favour and enlarge him on bail. For such a determination no hard and fast rule of inflexible nature can be laid down as it depends on facts and circumstances peculiar to each case; *Kushagra Mokhriwale* v. *State of Uttar Pradesh,* 2012 (1) Crimes 69 (All): 2012 Cr LJ 164: 2011 (74) ACC 703.

**24. Association with any Known Criminal – View on –** Section 12 of the Act of 2000 indicates that if a juvenile is arrested or detained or appears or is brought before a Board, such juvenile shall be released on bail, with or without surety, or placed under the supervision of a Probation Officer or under the care of any fit institution. The language of section 12 of the Act conveys the intention of the Legislature to grant bail to the juvenile, irrespective of nature or gravity of the offence, alleged to have been committed by him and bail can be denied only in the case where there appears reasonable grounds for believing that the release is likely to bring him into association with any known criminal, or expose him to moral, physical or psychological danger, or that his release would defeat ends of justice; *Sonu @ Somveer* v. *State of Rajasthan,* 2012 (5) RCR (Cri) 453: 2012 (4) Crimes 279 (Raj).

**25. Association with Criminal Father – Law on –** Legislative intent has to be kept into consideration while considering bail prayer of a juvenile. If on a petty dispute, father instigated his son to murder the deceased, this occurred after many hours of previous altercation. Ostensibly, there was no immediate cause for the Accused to carry the murder weapon with him in day time and to stab the deceased at the bacons call. The act of the accused indicates his criminal intent and psychology. If the accused would have been released on bail, naturally he would have association of his father who had also criminal proclivity and does not care about welfare of his child. Mother of the accused who wants his release, has not shown any reason which can even remotely indicate that she can take care of the accused in his moral, physical and psychological developments; *Mohd. Navi* v. *State of Uttar Pradesh*, 2011 (3) ALJ 717: 2012 (1) Crimes 75 (All): 2011 Cr LJ 2828.

**26. Bail to Juvenile – View on –** A perusal of section 12 of the Juvenile Act reveals that a juvenile is entitled to bail notwithstanding gravity of the crime. His bail can be refused only when there are reasonable grounds for believing that his release is likely to bring him into association with any known criminal or expose him to moral, physical or psychological danger or that his release would defeat the ends of justice. It is also manifest that the said section 12 of the Juvenile Act over-rides the Code of Criminal Procedure, 1973 (for short 'the Code') and other laws for the time being in force and, therefore, in the event of any inconsistency, section 12 of the Juvenile Act will prevail. Bail to the juvenile can only be refused if anyone of the grounds envisaged in section 12 of the Juvenile Act exist. So far as the ground of gravity is concerned, it is not covered under the provisions of the Act. If the bail application of the juvenile was to be considered under the provisions of the Code of Criminal Procedure, there would have been absolutely no necessity for the implementation of the act. The language that notwithstanding anything contained in the Code of Criminal Procedure, 1973 (2 of 1974) or in any other law for the time being in force, the juvenile accused shall be released. Not only this, the Parliament re-considered the entire matter and repealed the old Act of 1986 by introducing new Act No. 56 of 2000, raising the age from 16 to 18 years. This has been done keeping in view the welfare of the child so that even after committing an offence, a child may not become a hardened criminal but he may reform himself; *Shakti Singh* v. *State of Rajasthan*, 2014 (1) Raj LW 276: 2014 (2) Crimes 749 (Raj).

**27. Bail with or without Surety – Law on –** Normal rule as spelt out by sub-section (1) of section 12 of the Act is that the juvenile in conflict with law is to be released on bail with or without surety or placed under the supervision of Probation Officer or under the care of institution or fit person except in cases where the Board has reason to believe that his release would bring him into association with any known criminal or expose him to moral, physical or psychological danger or that his release would defeat the ends of justice; *Afsal Ibrahim* v. *State of Kerala*, 2013 (44) ILR 260 (Ker): 2013 Cr LJ 4945: 2013 (4) Ker LT 181.

**28. Best Interest of Children – Law on –** Section 12 of the Act of 2000, is overriding in nature, inasmuch as, it provides that whenever a juvenile is arrested, detained or appears or is brought before a Board, such person shall, notwithstanding anything contained in the Code of Criminal Procedure, 1973 or in any other law for the time being in force, be released on bail with or without surety but he shall not be so released if there appear reasonable grounds for believing that the release is likely to bring him into association with any know criminal or expose him to moral, physical or psychological danger or that his release would defeat the ends of justice. Thus, the Act of 2000 which is an Act, as per the aims and objects to consolidate and amend the law relating to "juvenile in conflict with law" and "children in need of care and protection", by providing for proper care, protection and treatment by catering to their development needs, and by adopting a child-friendly approach in the adjudication and disposition of matters in the best interest of children and for their ultimate rehabilitation through various institutions established under this Act. The Legislature has enacted the aforesaid Act of 2000 providing special procedure for dealing with juvenile; *Tara Chand* v. *State of Rajasthan*, 2008 (2) Raj LW 1013: 2007 Cr LJ 3047: 2007 (2) Cr LR 1179.

**29. Case under Investigation and Mystery not Solved – Law on –** Nothing incriminating material was recovered either from possession or from Juvenile's house, as such; there was no legal evidence against him. The case was still under investigation and the mystery of murder could not be solved. Accused is a juvenile against whom there is no material except confessional statement of the co-accused and no incriminating material was recovered so as to connect him *prima facie* with the alleged offence, Courts find his prayer for bail reasonably requires consideration in view of the provisions of section 12 of the Juvenile Justice (Care and Protection of Children) Act, 2000; *Anuj Kumar Dubey* v. *State of Jharkhand*, 2011 (2) JCR 377 (Jhar).

**30. Company with "Known Criminals" – Law on –** Accused is keeping company with a criminal Named *X* against whom five cases are pending. Thus, he is keeping company with "known criminals". The intention of the Legislature is to prevent a juvenile delinquent from going back to a criminal gang and to a criminal way of life. Undisputedly, criminal *X* heads a criminal gang to which the accused belongs. Therefore, in case the juvenile were released on bail, undoubtedly, he would go back to the same criminal gang to resume his criminal activities; *Amarlal* v. *State of Rajasthan*, 2009 Cr LJ 1692: 2010 (1) Crimes 875 (Raj) (Jaipur Bench).

**31. Conclusive Proof of Age – Law on –** Court or the Board or as the case may be the Committee, for the reasons to be recorded by them, may, if considered necessary, give benefit to the child or the juvenile by considering his/her age on lower side within the margin of one year and while passing orders in such case shall after taking into consideration such evidence as may be available or the medical opinion as the case may be, record a finding in respect of his age and either of the evidence specified in any of the clause (A) (i), (ii), (iii) or in the absence whereof, clause (B) shall be the conclusive proof of the age as regards such child or the juvenile in conflict with law; *Hariom Soni* v. *State of Madhya Pradesh*, 2012 (6) RCR (Cri) 1269: 2012 (1) Crimes 111 (MP).

**32. Criminal Statute – Duty of Prosecution for –** "While invoking a criminal statute, such as the Act, the prosecution is duty bound to show from the record of the case and the documents collected in the course of investigation that facts emerging therefrom *prima facie* constitute an offence within the letter of the law. When a statute provides special or enhanced punishments as compared to the punishments prescribed for similar offences under the ordinary penal laws of the country, a higher responsibility and duty is cast on the Judges to make sure there exists *prima facie* evidence for supporting the charge leveled by the prosecution. Therefore, when a law visits a person with serious penal consequences extra care must be taken to ensure that those whom the legislature did not intend to be covered by the expression language of the statute are not roped in by stretching the language of the law. But that does not mean that the judicial officer called upon to decide whether or not a case for framing a charge under the Act is made out should adopt a negative attitude. He should frame a charge if the prosecution shows that the material placed on record and the documents relied on give rise to a strong suspicion of the accused having committed the crime alleged against him"; *Niranjan Singh K.S. Punjabi* v. *Jitendra Bhimraj Bijjaya*, (1990) 4 SCC 76.

**33. Date of Birth – Law on –** From the perusal of rule 12(3) of the Rules of 2007, it is evident that the certificates as mentioned in this Rule have to be relied on in order of precedence. Thus, if a Matriculation Certificate is available, the date of birth mentioned in any other certificate cannot be gone into. If a Matriculation Certificate is not available, then date of birth as mentioned in the birth certificate from the school first attended is to be taken into consideration. If the said certificate is also not available, then the date of birth certificate given by the Corporation or a Municipal Authority or Panchayat has to be considered. Clause (b) of rule 12(3) of the Rules of 2007 regarding medical evidence comes into operation only when the three certificates as mentioned in rule 12(3)(a) are not available. According to the applicant, he has not studied beyond 5th standard; *Mahender Singh* v. *State*, 2014 (3) AD 125 (Del) (DB).

**34. Date of Birth of Juvenile – Determination of –** Even though rule 12 is strictly applicable only to determine the age of a child in conflict with law, Statutory provision should be the basis for determining age, even for a child who is a victim of crime. There is hardly any difference in so far as the issue of minority is concerned, between a child in conflict with law, and a child who is a victim of crime. Therefore it would be just and appropriate to apply rule 12 of the 2007 rules, to determine the age of the prosecutrix. The manner of determining age conclusively has been expressed in sub-rule (3) of rule 12. Under the provision, the age of a child is ascertained, by adopting the first available basis, out of a number of options postulated in rule 12(3). If, in the scheme of options under rule 12(3), an option is expressed in a preceding clause, it has overriding effect over an option expressed in a subsequent clause. The highest rated option available, would conclusively determine the age of a minor. In the scheme of rule 12(3), matriculation (or equivalent) certificate of the concerned child is the highest rated option. In case, the said certificate is available, no other evidence can be relied upon. Only in the absence of the said certificate, rule 12(3), envisages consideration of the date of birth entered, in the school first attended by the child. In case such an entry of date of birth is available, the date of birth depicted therein is liable to be treated as final and conclusive, and no other material is to be relied upon. Only in the absence of such entry, rule 12(3) postulates reliance on a birth certificate issued by a corporation or a municipal authority or a panchayat. Yet again, if such a certificate is available, then no other material whatsoever is to be taken into consideration, for determining the age of the child concerned, as the said certificate would conclusively determine the age of the child. It is only in the absence of any of the aforesaid, that rule 12(3) postulates the determination of age of the concerned child, on the basis of medical opinion; *Jarnail Singh* v. *State of Haryana,* AIR 2013 SC 3467: 2013 (7) SCALE 764: 2013 (7) SCC 263.

**35. Default of Furnishing Security – Law on –** Section 16 of the 2000 Act provides that no juvenile shall be sentenced to death or imprisonment for life or committed to prison in default of payment of fine or in default of furnishing security. Section 20 provides for special provisions in respect of pending cases. The 2000 Act came into force on 1-4-2001; *Satish @ Dhanna* v. *State of Madhya Pradesh,* 2009 (14) SCC 187: AIR 2009 SC 2643: 2009 (5) SCALE 702.

**36. Delinquency – Law on –** It is incorrect to say that the preamble speaks of the things of post-delinquency only. The Act not only refers to the obligations of the country to re-enact the existing law relating to juveniles bearing in the mind, the standards prescribed in various conventions but also all other international instruments. It states that the said Act was enacted *inter alia* to consolidate and amend the law relating to juveniles. Once the law relates to delinquent juveniles or juveniles in conflict with law, the same would mean both pre and post-delinquency. The field covered by the Act includes a situation leading to juvenile delinquency visa-vis commission of an offence. In such an event he is to be provided the post delinquency care and for the said purpose the date when delinquency took place would be the relevant date. It must, therefore, be held that the relevant date for determining the age of the juvenile would be one on which the offence has been committed and not when he is produced in court; *Pratap Singh* v. *State of Jharkhand,* AIR 2005 SC 2731: 2005 (1) SCALE 763: 2005 (3) SCC 551.

**37. Denial of Bail to Juvenile – Grounds for –** Bail can be denied to the juvenile only when there is a material on record suggesting that juvenile may join the company of any known-criminal; on release likely to exposes him to moral, physical or psychological danger. There must be some material before the Court to form such opinion and bail should not be denied to juvenile merely on the basis of some assumption or presumption; *Ankit (Minor)* v. *State of Uttarakhand,* 2013 Cr LJ 4989 (Uttra) (Nainital Bench).

**38. Direct Allegation – Law on –** Bail of the juvenile has been made rule and the rejection is exception and if the case of the juvenile did not come within the ambit of *Exception* clause and if there was no *prima facie* direct allegation against the juvenile for making out an offence under section 302 of the Indian Penal Code against him then bail should be granted; *Amarendra Kumar* v. *State of Jharkhand,* 2011 (2) East CriC 410 (Jhar).

**39. Doubtful School Admission Record – Law on –** The benefit of the principle of benevolent legislation attached to Juvenile Justice Act would thus apply to only such cases wherein the accused is held to be a juvenile on the basis of at least *prima facie* evidence regarding his minority as the benefit of the possibilities of two views in regard to the age of the alleged accused who is involved in grave and serious offence which he committed and gave effect to it in a well planned manner reflecting his maturity of mind rather than innocence indicating that his plea of juvenility is more in the nature of a shield to dodge or dupe the arms of law, cannot be allowed to come to his rescue. Hence if the plea of juvenility or the fact that he had not attained the age of discretion so as to understand the consequence of his heinous act is not free from ambiguity or doubt, the said plea cannot be allowed to be raised merely on doubtful school admission record and in the event it is doubtful, the medical evidence will have to be given due weightage while determining the age of the accused; *Om Prakash* v. *State of Rajasthan*, AIR 2012 SC 1608: 2012 Cr LJ 2266: 2012 (4) SCALE 348.

**40. Words "Ends of Justice" – Law on –** Once a person is held to be a juvenile in conflict with law, then section 12 of the Act would govern the question of grant of bail and the custody of juvenile and it will not be governed by the provisions of the Code of Criminal Procedure. It is important to note that gravity or seriousness of the offence, divorced from above exceptional reasons, has not been taken as an obstacle or hindrance by the Legislature to refuse bail to a delinquent juvenile. No straight jacket formula of inflexible nature can be laid down as it would depend on facts and circumstances of each case. Words "ends of Justice" should be confined to those facts which show that the grant of bail itself is likely to result in injustice. For example, there is likelihood of the juvenile delinquent, to whom the bail is granted, interfering with the course of justice or he may pressurize the prosecution witnesses; he is likely to abscond from the jurisdiction of the Court. There may be other examples also. Burden to show that if delinquent juvenile is released on bail there appears a reasonable ground for believing that the release is likely to bring him into association with any known criminal or expose him to moral, physical or psychological danger or that his release would defeat the ends of justice is on the prosecution; *Mohit* v. *State of Uttar Pradesh*, 2013 (3) ACR 2408: 2013 (8) ADJ 216: 2013 (83) ACC 242 (All).

**41. Ends of Justice – Law on –** Accused is a student and he has taken his Class XIIth Examination recently. Accused used to sexually harass deceased Smt. *X* whose husband was in jail in some criminal case and because of sexual harassment caused by the accused, the lady was compelled to commit suicide by hanging herself from a ceiling fan. The report was lodged by the brother of the lady. The matter is at the stage of investigation. If such juvenile delinquent is enlarged on bail, then certainly it will defeat the ends of justice. To check the rising trend of serious crimes which are being committed by juvenile delinquents these days, it is necessary for Courts to see that ends of justice should not be allowed to be defeated by untimely release of such juvenile delinquents; *Aditya Kumar @ Bebby* v. *State of Rajasthan*, 2013 (4) Raj LW 3172: 2013 (3) WLN 261 (Raj): 2014 (1) WLN 449 (Raj).

**42. Ends of Justice – Comments on –** A close scrutiny of provision of section 12 of the Juvenile Justice (Care and Protection of Children) Act, 2000 goes to show that a person may not be released if there appear reasonable grounds for believing that the release is likely to bring him into association with any known criminal or expose him to moral, physical or psychological danger or that his release would defeat the ends of justice; *Ashok* v. *State*, 2010 (3) Crimes 132 (Raj): 2011 (8) RCR (Cri) 1325 (Raj).

**43. Equitable Considerations – Law for –** Equitable considerations have no place where the statute contained express provisions; *E. Palanisamy* v. *Palanisamy (Dead) by LRs.*, 2003 (1) SCC 123 (*vide* para 5).

**44. Exception – Law on –** The provision contained in section 12 of the Act lays down that if a juvenile accused is arrested or detained or appears or is brought before a Board, such person shall not be released if there appears reasonable grounds for believing that the release is likely to bring him into association with any known criminal or expose him to moral, physical or psychological danger or that this release would defeat the ends of justice. Thus, every juvenile for whatsoever offence he is charged with, shall be released on bail except under the above circumstances. Of course, the bail application of juvenile can be refused, if the above grounds or any one of the grounds exists. Thus, the *Exception* would be that he shall not be so released if there appears reasonable grounds for believing that the release is likely to bring him into association with any known criminal or expose him to moral, physical or psychological danger or that would defeat the ends of justice; *Dushyant* v. *State of Madhya Pradesh*, 2012 (1) MPHT 233 (MP) (Gwalior Bench).

**45. Guesswork – Ignorance of –** On bare perusal of provision of section 12(1) of the Juvenile Justice (Care and Protection of Children) Act, 2000, it appears that Juvenile in conflict with law shall be released on bail unless there appear reasonable grounds for believing that the release is likely to bring him into association with any known criminal or expose him to moral, physical or psychological danger or that his release would defeat the ends of Justice. The existence of the aforesaid ground should not mean guesswork but it should be supported by some evidence on record; *Ashish Kumar Bharti @ Suman Kumar Yadav* v. *State of Bihar*, 2013 (2) PLJR 966: 2013 (8) RCR (Cri) 1987 (Pat).

**46. Human Rights – Comments on –** The Fundamental Rights embodied in Part III of the Constitution constitute the basic human rights which inhere in every person and such other rights which are fundamental to the dignity and well being of citizens; *Shabnam Hashmi* v. *Union of India*, 2014 (2) SCALE 529: 2014 (4) SCC 1: AIR 2014 SC 1281.

**47. Increasing Crimes by Juveniles – Law on –** The injured was 17 years only. He has narrated in his statement under section 161, Cr.P.C. that in a small scuffle in a game of football, both the juvenile delinquents with the help of *X* fatally attacked on him and he was badly stabbed in his stomach by *X*, with the help of two juvenile delinquents who had instigated *X* to stab him. The injury report of another injured aged 13 years is on record and his one of the injury is found to be liver deep and dangerous to life. He had to be referred to higher centre for treatment. If the benefit of bail at this early stage is given to the juvenile delinquents, then it will defeat the ends of justice. Looking to rising trend of increasing crimes by juveniles, untimely release of juveniles is not advisable some times; *Shahbaj Ali* v. *State of Rajasthan*, 2013 (3) Crimes 606 (Raj): 2014 (1) Raj LW 24 (Raj).

**48. Juvenile – Comprehension of –** It must also be appreciated that due to his juvenility, a juvenile in conflict with law may be presumed not to know or understand the legal procedures making it difficult for him to put forth his claim for juvenility when he is produced before a Magistrate. Added to this are the factors of poor education and poor economic set up that are jointly the main attributes of a juvenile in conflict with law, making it difficult for him to negotiate the legal procedures; *Jitendra Singh @ Babboo Singh* v. *State of Uttar Pradesh*, 2013 (11) SCC 193: JT 2013 (11) SC 152: 2013 (9) SCALE 18.

**49. Juveniles – Ambit of –** It is, thus, manifest from a conjoint reading of sections 2(k), 2(1), 7A, 20 and 49 of the Act of 2000, read with rules 12 and 98 of the Juvenile Justice (Care and Protection of Children) Rule, 2007 that all persons who were below the age of eighteen years on the date of commission of the offence even prior to 1st April: 2001 would be treated as juveniles even if the claim of juvenility is raised after they have attained the age of eighteen years on or before the date of the commencement of the Act of 2000 and were undergoing sentences upon being convicted; *Lakhan Lal* v. *State of Bihar*, 2011 Cr LJ 1116: AIR 2011 SC 842: 2011 (1) SCALE 504.

**50. Magistrate – Duties of –** There are many instances, where in the remand report, police mentions inflated version as to the age of the Juvenile to show him as an adult accused. Some times, the person in police captivity will be tutored to declare falsely that he is a major before the Magistrate. It is because of the reason that there are many practical difficulties for the police to produce the arrested person before the Juvenile Justice Board and the procedure there is also not conducive for the regular police. Some times, the Juvenile themselves pretend to be adult person making false statement as to their age as they wish to be along with the company of the adult co-accused in an adult prison than the Government observation Home, where there is more restriction for the Juvenile in Conflict with law. It is pertinent here to mention that at that stage, if the Magistrate has got reason to entertain a doubt as to the age of the person produced, it is his duty to hold a preliminary enquiry as to his age, on the date of commission of the offence and take further action as prescribed under the Juvenile Justice (Care and Protection of Children) Act, 2000; *Master Jithu* v. *State of Tamil Nadu,* 2013 (4) Mad LJ (Cri) 311 (Mad).

**51. Matriculation or Equivalent Certificate – Law on** – It is thus clear that the matriculation or equivalent certificate, if available, is the best evidence on the basis of which it can be decided as to whether the accused was a juvenile or not and in the absence of matriculation or equivalent certificate, the date of birth certificate from the school first attended or the birth certificate given by the Corporation or Municipal Authority or Panchayat could have been relied upon. In the absence of above three certificates, the medical evidence has to be relied upon. It is thus obvious that if matriculation or equivalent certificate is available, then other evidence is not required; *Ranjana Yadav* v. *State of Uttar Pradesh,* 2013 (3) ADJ 673: 2013 (4) ALJ 40: 2013 (82) ACC 188 (All).

**52. Member of Unlawful Assembly – Law on** – Accused was a juvenile but his prayer for bail was rejected by the Juvenile Justice Board as well as by the Sessions Judge only on the ground of the gravity of the alleged offence, though no specific overt act was attributed against the juvenile except that he was the member of unlawful assembly. His case does not come within the *Exception* clause of section 12 of the Act wherein in certain situations have been illustrated wherein bail of a juvenile can be refused; *Umesh Mistry* v. *State of Jharkhand,* 2011 (2) East Cri C 428: 2011 (2) JCR 394 (Jhar).

**53. Nature of Offence – Law on** – It is well settled legal position that once a person is held to be a juvenile delinquent, then section 12 of the Act, 2000 would govern the question of grant of bail and custody of juvenile and it will not be governed by the provisions of the Code of Criminal Procedure, 1973.The position of law with regard to grant of bail to a juvenile under section 12 of the Act, is clear that a juvenile has to be released on bail mandatorily unless and until the *Exceptions* carved out in the section itself are made out. The *first Exception* is a reasonable ground for believing that the release is likely to bring the juvenile into association with any known criminal. The *second Exception* is that the release of the juvenile is likely to expose him to any moral, physical or psychological danger. Both these *Exceptions* are not made out because there is no material available in the record of the case to suggest any such association or exposure. The *third Exception* is that the release of the juvenile would defeat the ends of the justice. The nature of the offence is not one of the conditions on which bail can be granted or refused to the juvenile. Bail, in respect of a juvenile, has to be considered purely under the parameters of section 12 of the Act which requires bail to be granted mandatorily unless the court feels that the release of the juvenile is likely to bring him in the association of any known criminal or expose him to moral, physical or psychological danger or that his release would defeat the ends of justice; *Hakam* v. *State of Madhya Pradesh,* 2011 ILR 2237 (MP).

**54. Nature or Gravity of Offence – Comments on** – The Act of 2000 being a beneficiary and social reforms oriented legislation, should be given full effect by all concerned, whenever matters relating to juvenile come for consideration before them. The language of section 12 of the Act of 2000 conveys the intention of the Legislature to grant bail to the juvenile, irrespective of nature or gravity of the offence, alleged to have been committed by him and bail can be denied only in the case where there appears reasonable grounds for believing that the release is likely to bring him into association with any known criminal, or expose him to moral, physical or psychological danger, or that his release would defeat ends of justice; *Raja Singh @ Nirbho Singh* v. *State of Rajasthan*, 2013 (3) WLN 164 (Raj) (Jaipur Bench).

**55. No More Concession – Law on –** In view of statutory relief already available to the accused on account of his status as a juvenile, no more concession can be granted to him by exercise of powers under section 438, Cr.P.C., especially when the juvenile is accused of three other criminal cases. It is not a case where extra-ordinary exceptional circumstances can be said to be existing for granting the relief; *Amit Kumar* v. *State of Haryana*, 2013 (3) Crimes 191 (P&H).

**56. No Specific Overt Act – Effect of –** In the facts and circumstances, Courts find *prima facie* that no specific overt act has been attributed against the accused except that he was friend of co-accused and as such his prayer for bail requires reasonably consideration, accordingly, Accused is directed to be released under section 12 of the Act; *Krishna Munda* v. *State of Jharkhand*, AIR 2011 Jhar 773: 2011 (8) RCR (Cri) 2106: 2011 (2) JCR 540 (Jhar).

**57. Observation Home – Comments on –** If it is found that the person is a juvenile and, hence a juvenile in conflict with law, then the first thing is that by virtue of section 12 of the Act his bail plea has to be disposed of. In other words, as provided under the said Act, he may or may not be released on bail, but in either of the case he cannot be remanded to the judicial custody. His case has to be placed before the Juvenile Justice Board which can instead of releasing him make an order sending him to observation home or a place of safety by virtue of section 12(3) of the Act. Then orders in terms of section 17 may be passed keeping in mind orders by virtue of section 16 of the Act which may not be passed. However, by virtue of section 18 of the Act it is prohibited to try a juvenile together with a person who is not juvenile but that trial would also be by and before Juvenile Justice Board and not in any Court of the juvenile in conflict with law; *Sudhakar Dwivedi* v. *State of Uttar Pradesh*, 2012 (6) ADJ 649: 2012 (2) ACrR 2250 (All).

**58. Offence under Narcotic Drugs and Psychotropic Substances Act – Bail for –** No criminal antecedent has been reported against the accused and accused is a juvenile, who is in custody since long time and the entire liability of the alleged offence under the Act cannot be fastened on the juvenile who was found sitting in the scorpio vehicle with the co-accused. Courts do not find that the case of the juvenile comes with the *Exception* clause of section 12 of the Juvenile Justice (Care and Protection of Children) Act, 2000 so as to deny his statutory right of bail under benevolent Act for offence under sections 17, 18, 27(A) of the Narcotic Drugs and Psychotropic Substances Act; *Ashish Kumar Keshri @ Ashish Keshri His Mother Sunita Devi* v. *State of Jharkhand*, 2011 (2) East Cri C 565.

**58. Denial of Bail – Grounds for –** According to the 1st part of section 12 of Juvenile Justice (Care and Protection of Children) Act, 2000 reveals that bail shall be allowed by the Board. Second part of section 12 of the Act reveals that the bail may be refused on the following grounds:

(1) If there appear reasonable grounds available believing that the release is likely to bring him into associations with any known criminal,

(2) Or expose may to moral, physical, psychological danger,

(3) Or that his release would defeat the ends of justice.

Therefore, the bail application of the juvenile may be refused if the sufficient ground is available regarding anyone of the exception; *Anil Kumar S/o Karey Singh (In Jail)* v. *State of Uttar Pradesh through Principle Secretary Government of Uttar Pradesh*, 2006 (7) ADJ 709: 2006 (6) ALJ 205: 2007 Cr LJ 200 (All).

**59. One Year Margin – Comments on –** In terms of rule 12 of the Juvenile Justice (Care and Protection of Children) Act, 2000, giving the one year margin on the lower side of the age as opined on the medical examination; *Noor Jahan @ Haseena* v. *State NCT of Delhi,* 2013 (2) JCC 896 (Del) (DB).

**60. Opinion to be Formed by Board – Law on –** The Juvenile Justice Board may be justified in denying bail to a juvenile involved in a heinous crime only if there is material before it to form a *prima facie* opinion on the aspects carved out as *Exception* to rule of bail in section 12 of the Act itself. There must be some mechanism with the Juvenile Justice Board to gather material and form an opinion as to whether the juvenile need to be denied bail by bringing his case under the *Exceptions* to bail engrafted in section 12. The opinion to be formed by the Board, by no means, can be subjective and has to be objective. Either the prosecution should place some *prima facie* material before the Board or the Court to show that release of a juvenile on bail may expose him to moral, physical or psychological danger or the Board may obtain a report from the Probation Officer attached to the Board regarding antecedents and circumstances attended to the juvenile, both pre and post crime and it is only thereafter the Board or the Court should crystallised its opinion regarding release or non-release of the juvenile on bail, though involved in a heinous crime. A reference to the statutory provisions governing bail to a juvenile contained in section 12 would show that there is a mandate of law that the juvenile has to be released on bail, except only in those cases where the case falls in one or the other *Exception* engrafted by the Legislature in section 12 itself. A presumption or assumption has no place in law; *Narayan Sharma* v. *State of Madhya Pradesh,* 2012 (2) MPHT 274: 2012 (1) MPWN 125: 2012 ILR 796 (MP) (Gwalior Bench).

**61. Overriding Effect – Comments on –** Provisions of section 12 have an overriding effect over the provisions contained not only in the Code but over all other laws in force. It also takes care of the situation in which the case of a juvenile comes up before the Board (High Court/Court of Session) (i) after arrest; or (ii) in detention; or (iii) appears himself or is brought before the Board, then it is mandatory for the Board except in the circumstances enumerated in section 12 on the Board being satisfied, to be released on bail; *Tara Chand* v. *State of Rajasthan,* 2008 (2) Raj LW 1013: 2007 Cr LJ 3047: 2007 (2) Cr LR 1179.

**62. Physical Danger – Law on –** The provision provides that a juvenile accused has to be released on bail unless there are reasonable grounds for believing that the release is likely to bring him into association with any known criminal or expose him to moral, physical or psychological danger or that his release would defeat the ends of justice. There is no evidence on record to bring the case of the revisionist within the *Exceptions* provided in section 12 of the Act; *Umesh* v. *State of Uttar Pradesh,* 2011 (8) ADJ 7: 2011 (3) ACrR 3255 (All).

**64. Presiding Judge – Duties of –** The Courts administering criminal justice cannot turn blind eye to the ground realities, if, Criminal Court is to be an effective instrument in dispensing justice then Presiding Judge must cease to be a spectator and a mere recording machine. He must become a participant in trial; *Gurdarshan Singh* v. *State of Punjab,* 2012 (4) RCR (Cri) 909 (P&H).

**65. Protection of Society – Law on –** Section 12 deals with the bails of a juvenile. It is the established position of law that while considering the bail application of the juveniles, the gravity of the offence is not to be seen but that does not mean that a juvenile should be released in all the cases only because he was a juvenile on the date of the alleged commission of offence. The Legislature has mentioned in the latter part of sub-section 1 of section 12 of the Act which says that the juvenile shall not be so released if there appear reasonable grounds for believing that the release is likely to bring him into association with any known criminal or expose him to moral, physical or psychological danger or that his release would defeat the ends of justice. These are the riders which are against the bail to the juveniles but at the same time they are for protection of the juveniles and also for the society at large. The Act has been enacted for the benefit of a juvenile. Latter part of section 12 of the Act, is also for his benefit because he should not be allowed to be exposed to moral, physical and psychological dangers if he is allowed to remain outside the protective home. At the same time, the interest of justice is also to be taken into consideration; *Dushyant* v. *State of Uttar Pradesh,* 2011 (3) Crimes 41 (All): 2011 (4) ADJ 25: 2011 (73) ACC 482.

**66. Psychological Danger to Juvenile – Law on –** The Act of 2000 being a beneficiary and social reforms oriented legislation, should be given full effect by all concerned, whenever matters relating to juvenile come for consideration before them. The language of section 12 of the Act of 2000 conveys the intention of the Legislature to grant bail to the juvenile, irrespective of nature or gravity of the offence, alleged to have been committed by him and bail can be denied only in the case where there appears reasonable grounds for believing that the release is likely to bring him into association with any known criminal, or expose him to moral, physical or psychological danger, or that his release would defeat ends of justice; *Rishikesh @ Hansikesh* v. *State of Rajasthan,* 2013 (3) WLN 172 (Raj) (Jaipur Bench).

**67. Reasoning – Importance of –** Moreover, a judicial order is always required to be passed on reasoning and if the order is unreasoned, the same cannot be sustained in the eyes of law. Reasons are live links between the minds of the decision taker to the controversy in question and the decision or conclusion arrived at. Failure to give reasons amounts to denial of justice; *Sandeep* v. *State of Chhattisgarh,* 2007 Cr LJ 1942 (Chhat).

**68. Reconsideration of Bail Prayer – Law on –** Earlier rejections of the bail prayer of the accused were without following the required mandatory procedure established by law and hence that cannot divest Court from reconsidering bail prayer of the accused afresh; *Surendra* v. *State of Uttar Pradesh,* 2013 (3) All CriR 3385: 2013 (83) All CriC 568: 2014 (3) All LJ 188 (All) (DB).

**69. Refusal of Bail – Satisfaction Based on Relevant Material for –** A bare reading of the provisions of section 12 of the Act would show that the juvenile in conflict with law shall be released on bail, notwithstanding anything contained in the Code of Criminal Procedure or in any other law for the time being in force, except in three contingencies specified under section 12(1) itself. Thus, it becomes clear that so far as the gravity of offence is concerned, the same can not be pressed into service for denying the concession of bail to juvenile under section 12 of the Act. Juvenile can be denied the concession of bail, if any of the three situations specified under section 12(1) is available in any given fact situation. These three situations are: (i) if there appear reasonable grounds for believing that the release of the juvenile is likely to bring him into association with any known criminal; (ii) the release will expose the juvenile to moral, physical or psychological danger and; (iii) his release would defeat the ends of justice. The court while denying the benefit of bail to a juvenile in conflict with law on either of the above said three grounds noted above, will record its satisfaction based on relevant material available on the record that release of the juvenile will either bring him into association with any known criminal or will expose him to moral, physical or psychological danger or his release would defeat the ends of justice; *Rajvir* v. *State of Haryana,* 2013 Cr LJ 2880 (P&H).

**70. Rejection of Bail – Law on –** In absence of any ground for denial of bail available under section 12 of the Act, denial/rejection of bail is not in accordance with the provisions of section 12 of the Act; *Mangal Singh* v. *State of Chhattisgarh,* 2009 (1) Crimes 38 (Chhat).

**71. Rejection of Bail – Comments on –** The accused is 15 years of age and, therefore, he is a juvenile and consequently, deemed to be a 'juvenile offender' within the meaning of the Act. The prosecutrix is also a child (girl) and she is less than 16 years of age. Application for bail of the accused can be rejected on the ground that there appears reasonable grounds for believing that the release of the accused on bail would defeat the ends of justice; *Kishore Kunwar Raj S/o Gangaram* v. *State of Madhya Pradesh,* 2013 (4) Crimes 355 (MP): 2013 ILR 2260 (MP) (Gwalior Bench).

**72. Report of District Probationary Officer – Comments on –** After receiving the report of the District Probationary Officer the Board shall dispose of the bail application of the juvenile moved before it under section 12 of the Act within a period of 15 days after hearing all concerned; *Nihal* v. *State of Uttar Pradesh,* 2013 (4) ADJ 476: 2013 (3) ACrR 3156: 2013 (81) ACC 722 (All).

**73. Report of Probation Officer – Significance of –** In view of certain paragraphs of the case diary that the release of the accused on bail would defeat the ends of justice and the social investigation report submitted by the Probation Officer indicated that the father of the accused had already fled away from his house and was traceless and there was no guardian to take care of him but bail of the juvenile has been guaranteed whereas its denial is *Exception; Mukesh Sao @ Mukesh Kumar Sao* v. *State of Jharkhand,* 2011 (105) All Ind Cas 552: 2011 (2) JCR 379: 2011 (7) RCR (Cri) 329 (Jhar).

**74. Rider by Legislature – Law on –** A bare reading of section 12 of the Act, 2000 makes it clear that any person accused of a bailable or non-bailable offence, and apparently a juvenile, is arrested or detained or appears or is brought before a Board, such person shall, notwithstanding anything contained in the Code of Criminal Procedure, 1973 or in any other taw for the time being in force, be released on bail with or without surety. A juvenile should be granted bail unless his case falls within one of the *Exceptions* engrafted therein and those are that there appear reasonable grounds for believing that the release is likely to bring him into association with any known criminal or expose him to moral, physical or psychological danger or that his release would defeat the ends of justice. Unless the aforesaid rider is satisfied, bail to a juvenile should not be refused. It is significant to note that gravity of offence or its seriousness alone, divorced from above exceptional reasons, and has not been taken as a rider by the Legislature to deny bail to a juvenile in conflict with law. It is only danger to his moral, physical and psychological qualities and likelihood of his attaching himself with criminals or his release defeating ends off justice that Board or the courts may not exercise discretion in his favour and enlarge him on bail. For such a determination, no hard and fast rule of inflexible nature can be laid down as it depends on facts and circumstances peculiar to each case; *Ankit Upadhyaya @ Chotu* v. *State of Chhattisgarh,* 2013 (2) Cg LRW 70: 2013 (3) Crimes 252: 2013 (4) MPHT 40 (Chhat).

**75. Right of Bail – Law on –** Section 12 of the Act mandates that whenever a juvenile is arrested or detained or appears or brought before the Board, such juvenile shall be released on bail with or without surety or shall be placed under the supervision of probation officer under the care of any fit institution or fit person, but shall not be so released if there appears reasonable ground that the release is likely to bring him into association with any known criminal or expose him to moral, physical or psychological danger or that his release would defeat the ends of justice. Finding of the Court that he is involved in the serious offence of murdering another young boy and he may tamper with the evidence shall not be construed to mean that his release would defeat the ends of justice. Bail to the juvenile under section 12 of the Act is a right and rejection thereof is an exception; *Satbir* v. *State of Haryana,* 2011 (2) RCR(Cri) 621 (P&H).

**76. Satisfaction on Rider – Law on –** What is discernible from the statutory provision governing bail to a juvenile is that a juvenile in conflict with law should normally be granted bail unless his case falls within one of the *Exceptions* engrafted thereunder and those *Exceptions* are that there appears reasonable grounds for believing that his release is likely to bring him into association with any known criminal or expose him to moral, physical or psychological danger or that his release would otherwise defeat the ends of justice. Unless the rider is satisfied, bail to a juvenile should not be refused. It is significant to note that the gravity of the offence or its seriousness alone, divorced from the exceptional reasons, has not been taken as a rider by the Legislature to deny bail to a juvenile in conflict with law. It is only when there is danger to his moral, physical or psychological qualities or likelihood of his attaching himself with criminals or that his release may otherwise defeat the ends of justice, the Board or the Court may not exercise discretion in his favour and enlarge him on bail. For such a determination, no hard and fast rule of inflexible nature can be laid down as it depends on the facts and circumstances peculiar to each case; *Narayan Sharma* v. *State of Madhya Pradesh,* 2012 (2) MPHT 274: 2012 (1) MPWN 125: 2012 ILR 796 (MP).

**77. School Leaving Certificate – Validity of –** If the school leaving certificate was proved by examining the head mistress of the school and she has recognized the signatures of the principal who issued the school leaving certificate. The evidence adduced by the head mistress was not challenged. Consequently, there is no reason to discard that document; *Ranjeet Goswami* v. *State of Jharkhand,* 2013 Cr LJ 4895: 2014 (1) SCC 588: 2013 (11) SCALE 577.

**78. Second and Third Bail Application – Law on –** The application under section 12 of Act of 2000 is not decided after considering the facts of the offence but looking to the statutory provisions itself. The bail to the juvenile is considered after taking note of the *Exceptions* provided under section 12 of the Act of 2000 *i.e.,* release of juvenile may not defeat the ends of justice or there is likelihood that on release is likely to bring him in company of any known criminal or expose him to moral, physical or physiological danger. These are the only considerations for denial of bail to the juvenile. Once such considerations are made and application is decided up to the High Court, thereafter, an application cannot be maintained again for seeking benefit of bail. It cannot be used like second or third bail application. The second and third bail application can be made with the change in the facts and circumstances because there is a consideration of the case after taking note of the facts relevant to the occurrence or the offence. The situation while considering the application under section 12 of the Act of 2000 is quite different, thus same yard stick cannot be applied; *Ashok Kumar* v. *State of Rajasthan,* 2010 (2) WLN 571 (Raj) (Jaipur Bench).

**79. Subsequent Central Legislation – Law on –** A look at the above provision goes to show that the applicability of the provision of section 438, Cr. P.C. has been excluded. However, unlike sections 6 and 12 of the Act of 2000 relating to Juvenile, the words "or any other law for the time being in force" are conspicuous by their absence. Thus, the subsequent central legislation of the year 2000 enacted specially in relation to Juvenile after a review of the Juvenile Act, 1986, and more particularly section 12 thereof would have an overriding effect on section 18 of the Scheduled Castes and Scheduled Tribes (Prevention of Atrocities) Act, 1989; *Tara Chand* v. *State of Rajasthan,* 2008 (2) Raj LW 1013: 2007 Cr LJ 3047: 2007 (2) Cr LR 1179.

**80. Superfluity – Law on –** According to section 12(3) of the Act, wherever the Court is concerned with the determination of age of a child or a juvenile, who is in conflict with law, it can conduct an inquiry by seeking evidence by obtaining the matriculation or equivalent certificates, if available; and in the absence thereof, the date of birth certificate from the school first attended, and in the absence thereof, the birth certificate given by a corporation or a municipal authority or a panchayat. It is well settled principle of interpretation that the Legislature does not waste its words and say anything in vain. The presumption is always against superfluity in a Statute. Thus, every part of the Statute should be given as far as possible its full meaning and effect and no issue or clause should ordinarily be rejected or superfluitied. In section 12(3)(a)(i) of the Act, the Legislature has intentionally used the word "the matriculation or equivalent certificates, if available;" and "in the absence whereof". Similarly in section 12(3)(a)(ii) of the Act, words "the date of birth certificate from the school (other than a play school) first attended;" and "in the absence whereof" have been used and in the section 12(3)(a)(iii), the words "the birth certificate given by a corporation or a municipal authority or a panchayat" have been used. In my view, the Legislature had dealt with various segments of the society wherein some people have passed matriculation or equivalent class, some people had not reached upto matric or equivalent course and are drop out from the school and some people are totally illiterate. Keeping all the three segments in view, the aforesaid provisions of section 12(3)(a)(i), (ii) and (iii) were enacted and the word "shall" has been used in section 12(3) of the Act for the purpose of conducing an inquiry by seeking evidence by obtaining matriculation or equivalent certificates if it is found that the person concerned is educated upto that standard and if that is not available, as the word "if available" and "in the absence whereof" sound the same sense, then the Court may switch over to the date of birth certificate from the school first attended (other than a play school) and if that is also not available, where the said person has not even gone to the school at all, then the reliance is to be placed upon the birth certificate issued by the corporation, municipal authority of a panchayat. Thus, in the presence of matriculation or equivalent certificates, the Court cannot give preference to the birth certificate issued by the municipal authority; *Hardeep Singh* v. *State of Haryana,* 2012 (3) RCR (Cri) 363 (P&H).

**81. Tamil Nadu Borstal Schools Act, 1925 – Comments on –** There is distinction between Juvenile Justice Act and Borstal Schools Act. J.J. Act is intended to deal with 'Juveniles in conflict with law'. A Juvenile is one either male or female, below 18 years of age. The parallel enactment is Tamil Nadu Borstal Schools Act, 1925. Though their object is same, they differ in their schemes. Under J.J. Act, the crucial date is 'date of commission of the offence'. But, under the Borstal Schools Act, 'it is date of conviction'. Under J.J. Act, on the date when the offence was committed the 'juvenile in conflict with law' must be 'below 18 years', whereas under the Borstal Schools Act, on the date of conviction the 'adolescent offender' must be 'above 18 years but below 21 years'. Under the J.J. Act, at the most, a Juvenile in conflict with law can be detained in a Special Observation Home up to 3 years whereas under the Borstal Schools Act, an 'adolescent offender' shall be kept in a Borstal School for not less than 2 years, but not more than 5 years but in no case beyond 23 years of his age; *Jayavel* v. *State,* 2013 (1) LW (Cri) 643: 2013 (2) Mad LJ (Cri) 889: 2013 (8) RCR (Cri) 1812 (Mad) (DB).

**82. Three Contingencies – Law on –** Three contingencies provided under section 12 (1) in which the bail can be refused to the juvenile in conflict with law are concerned, the denial has to be based on reasonable grounds for believing that anyone out of three contingencies, as a matter of fact, was available, in a given fact situation. The court will record its satisfaction for denying the concession of bail to a juvenile in conflict with law under any of the above noted three contingencies, if the Court comes to the conclusion that there were reasonable grounds to believe that any of the contingency was existing and supported with the relevant material available on the record of the case; *Pankaj* v. *State of Haryana,* 2013 (7) RCR (Cri) 1105 (P&H).

**83. Accused Served Out More Than Half of Sentence – Effect of –** The case is at the enquiry stage and the accused is in custody for about one year and nine months, in that manner he has already served out more than half of the sentence though he has not yet been convicted by a competent Court of law. The case of the accused does not come in any manner within the proviso of section 12 of the Act so as to deny the statutory right of the Petitioner for his bail; *Naresh Saw @ Naresh Sah* v. *State of Jharkhand,* 2012 (1) Crimes 151 (Jhar): 2011 Cr LJ 3642: 2011 (3) East CriC 294.

**84. Allegations Proved by Medical Report – Effect of –** Accused wife had committed suicide after consuming poison within two years of her marriage and there was allegation by the informant-father of the deceased that the accused persons had been extending torture for payment of dowry and the accused persons had forcibly administered poison as a result of which she died. In the post-mortem examination, suspected case of poisoning was found by the Doctor, who held autopsy but Court should not reject the prayer of the accused only on merit without considering the benevolent legislation as contained in section 12 of the Act wherein the bail of a juvenile has been made rule and rejection as *Exception*. There is certain proviso of section 12 of the Act which speaks that in certain circumstances the prayer for bail of a juvenile may be refused. Bail should be granted; *Kartik Vishwakarma* v. *State of Jharkhand*, 2012 (3) Crimes (Jhar) 314: 2011 (3) East CriC 260 (Jhar).

**85. Bail Order – Law on –** The Court is conscious of the fact that while deciding bail, a detailed order on merits may not be appropriate lest it prejudices the case of either of parties; *Saint Shri Asharam Bapu* v. *State of Rajasthan*, 2013 (4) Raj LW 3361 (Raj).

**86. Date of Birth – Document for –** Rules of 2007 made by Central Government are much exhaustive as compared to Rules framed by State of Uttar Pradesh sub-rule 5 of rule 22 of U.P. Rules, 2004 has not given any preference but has used the word "either" which means that either of the documents mentioned in sub clause I to IV may be obtained while the Central Rules, 2007 makes it very clear that the first preference shall be given to matriculation or equivalent certificate and in absence whereof the date of birth certificate from the school first attended may be obtained and in absence whereof birth certificate given by the Corporation or a Municipality and in absence of all the above three, the medical opinion shall be taken into consideration; *Vinod* v. *State of Uttar Pradesh*, 2014 (2) ADJ 167: 2014 (1) All Cri R 647: 2014 (85) All CriC 466 (All).

**87. Date of Birth – Relevant Document for –** The U.P. Juvenile Justice (Care and Protection of Children) Rules, 2004 also recognize the date of birth certificate from the school first attended and *i.e.*, in preference to matriculation or equivalent certificate if available. No one at the entry level of Nursery Class will mention a higher age group because that may be detrimental to his whole career; *Vinod* v. *State of Uttar Pradesh*, 2014 (2) ADJ 167: 2014 (1) All Cri R 647: 2014 (85) All CriC 466 (All).

**88. Date of Birth as per Medical Conclusion – Law on –** The age of accused as per medical conclusion comes to 19 years on the alleged date of occurrence. Having privilege of one year in his favour in terms of rule 4 itself, the age of the accused is further reduced to less than 18 years; *Vijay Prakash* v. *State of Bihar*, 2013 (3) PLJR 625: 2013 (8) RCR (Cri) 2911 (Pat).

**89. Interpretation – *Ejusdem Generis* Rule of –** *Ejusdem generis* rule rule reflects an attempt to reconcile incompatibility between the specific and general words, in view of the other rules of interpretation, that all words in a statute are given effect if possible, that a statute is to be construed as a whole and that no words in a statute are presumed to be superfluous. *Ejusdem Generis* rule being one of the rules of interpretation, only serves, like all such rules, as an aid to discover the legislative intent; it is neither final nor conclusive and is attracted only when the specific words enumerated, constitute a class, which is not exhausted and are followed by general terms and when there is no manifestation of intent to give broader meaning to the general words; *Tribhuban Parkash Nayyar* v. *Union of India*, AIR 1970 SC 540: 1969 (3) SCC 99: 1970 (2) SCR 732.

**90. Judges – Guidelines for –** It does not mean that judges are to determine what is for the good of the people and substitute their individual and personal opinions for that of the government of the day, or that they may usurp the functions of the Legislature. That is not their province and though there must always be a narrow margin within which judges, who are human, will always be influenced by subjective factors, their training and their tradition makes the main body of their decisions speak with the same voice and reach impersonal results whatever their personal predilections or their individual backgrounds It is the function of the legislature alone, headed by the government of the day, to determine what is, and what is not, good and proper for the people of the land; and they must be given the widest latitude to exercise their functions within the ambit of their powers, else all progress is barred. But, because of the Constitution, there are limits beyond which they cannot go and even though it falls to the lot of judges to determine where those limits lie, the basis of their decision cannot be whether the Court thinks the law is for the benefit of the people or not. Cases of this type must be decided solely on the basis whether the Constitution forbids it; *State of West Bengal* v. *Anwar Ali Sarkar*, AIR 1952 SC 75: 1952 Cr LJ 510: 1952 SCJ 55.

**91. Law and Equity – Rule of –** It is now well settled that when there is a conflict between law and equity the former shall prevail; *R. Bhattad* v. *State of Maharashtra*, 2003 (5) SCC 413 (*vide* para 73).

**92. Legislative Intendment – Use of Preamble for –** A preamble though a key to open the mind of the Legislature, cannot be used to control or qualify the precise and unambiguous language of the enactment. It is only in case of doubt or ambiguity that recourse may be had to the preamble to ascertain the reason for the enactment in order to discover the true legislative intendment; *Y.A. Mamarde* v. *Authority Under Minimum Wages Act (Small Causes Court), Nagpur*, AIR 1972 SC 1721: 1972 (2) LLJ 136: 1972 (2) SCC 108.

**93. Material Evidence – Comments on –** If Prosecution has not collected any material to show that there is any likelihood to bring accused into association with the known criminals or to expose any moral, physical or psychological danger or their release would defeat the ends of justice then bail should be granted. The provisions of section 12 is mandatory in nature and in the absence of any ground shown in section 12 of the Act, denial of bail to juvenile would not be in accordance with the provisions of section 12 of the Act; *Virendra Kumar* v. *State of Chhattisgarh*, 2009 (2) Cg LJ 247: 2009 (2) Crimes (Chh) 7: 2009 (2) MPHT (Chh) 110: 2009 (4) East CriC 493 (Chhat).

**94. Precedent – Significance of –** Every case has to be dealt with on its own facts and no set principle or straight jacket formula can be applied, especially while dealing with bail matters; *Sanchita Gupta @ Shilpi* v. *State of Rajasthan*, 2014 (1) Crimes 26: 2014 (1) Raj LW 340 (Raj).

**95. Provision – Applicability of –** In view of section 2(k), 2(i) and section 7A read with section 20 of the 'Act 2000', the provisions of Act would be applicable to the case of accused as he was juvenile on the date of occurrence; *Balwant Singh* v. *State of Uttar Pradesh*, 2014 (2) ADJ 378: 2014 (1) All CriR 656 (All).

**96. Unreasonable – Meaning of –** The word "unreasonable" necessarily connotes a consideration of all the circumstances including the conduct of parties in order to find out what is unreasonable; *P.J. Irani* v. *State of Madras*, AIR 1961 SC 1731: 1962 (1) Mad LJ 92: 1962 (1) SCJ 194.

**97. Weak Accused – Bail for –** Both the accused are employees of main accused and neither of them are in a position to either influence or tamper with the evidence or threat to complainant in any manner unlike the main accused; *Sharad @ Sharad Chandra* v. *State of Rajasthan*, 2014 (2) Crimes 159 (Raj).

**98. Writ of *Certiorari* – Meaning of –** Professor De Smith gives an interesting historical background of this writ. Initially, it was essentially a royal demand for information. The King would wish to be certified of some matter and direct that necessary information be provided to him. The King issued numerous such writs. The people frustrated with the judicial process in the courts increasingly sought remedy from the King himself in the form of a royal writ. This resulted in interventions in the judicial process and, in due course, the remedy by way of writ was issued by the King's Court rather than the King himself. Eventually, writs came to be issued in standard forms. Prof. De Smith points out that the writ system has a "hint of paradox" since *certiorari* which was initially an executive command aimed at avoiding judicial proceedings became the central mechanism for judicial control of executive action. '*Certiorari*' is a Latin word being the passive form of the word '*certiorare*' meaning 'informed' and occurred in the original Latin words of the writ which translated read 'we being desirous for certain reasons, that the said record should by you be certified to us'. '*Certiorari*' was essentially a royal demand for information; the King wishing to be certified of some matter, orders that the necessary information be provided for him. A *certiorari* is an original writ issuing out of a Chancery or King's Bench, directed in the King's name, to the Judges or officers of inferior courts, commanding them to return the record of a cause pending before them, with a view to provide the party speedy justice or such other justice as he shall assign to determine the cause; *Gujarat State Road Transport Corporation* v. *Firoze M. Mogal*, 2014 (1) GLH 1: AIR 2014 Guj 33: 2014 (2) GLR 1373 (Guj) (LB) [Hon'ble Judges: Ravi R. Tripathi, Jayant Patel, M.R. Shah, J.B. Pardiwala, A.G. Uraizee].

**13. Information to parent, guardian or probation officer.**—Where a juvenile is arrested, the officer incharge of the police station or the special juvenile police unit to which the juvenile is brought shall, as soon as may be after the arrest, inform—

(a) the parent or guardian of the juvenile, if he can be found of such arrest and direct him to be present at the Board before which the juvenile will appear; and

(b) the probation officer of such arrest to enable him to obtain information regarding the antecedents and family background of the juvenile and other material circumstances likely to be of assistance to the Board for making the inquiry.

**SYNOPSIS**

1. Police Officer – Role of
2. Pursis – Comments on

**COMMENTS**

**1. Police Officer – Role of** – Section 13(b) of the Act says that where a juvenile is arrested, the officer-in-charge of the police station shall inform the Probation Officer of such arrest to enable him (Probation Officer) to obtain information regarding the antecedents and family backgrounds of the juvenile and other material circumstances likely to be of assistance to the Board for making inquiry; *Dushyant* v. *State of Uttar Pradesh*, 2011 (3) Crimes 41 (All): 2011 (4) ADJ 25: 2011 (73) ACC 482.

**2. Pursis – Comments on** – The pursis is in a pre-conceived printed format where the case number, name of the Juvenile and date are kept blank. The same are filled in by hand. In the printed format, spaces are marked for the signatures of the Juvenile in conflict with law and of the parents of the Juvenile in conflict 'with law. The pursis is to the effect that the parent of the Juvenile in conflict with law accepts that the offence has been inadvertently committed by the Juvenile for which he is repenting and that the Juvenile has voluntarily pleaded guilty. An assurance is recorded that the Juvenile will not commit any such offence in future. The procedure of taking such a pursis is not contemplated by the Act and the said Rules; *High Court on its Own Motion* v. *State of Maharashtra*, 2013 (3) AIR BomR 119: 2013 (8) RCR (Cri) 892 (Bom) (DB).

**14. Inquiry by Board regarding juvenile.**—[1][(1)] Where a juvenile having been charged with the offence is produced before a Board, the Board shall hold the inquiry in accordance with the provisions of this Act and may make such order in relation to the juvenile as it deems fit:

Provided that an inquiry under this section shall be completed within a period of four months from the date of its commencement, unless the period is

1. Section 14 renumbered as sub-section (1) thereof by Act 33 of 2006, sec. 11 (w.e.f. 22-8-2006).

extended by the Board having regard to the circumstances of the case and in special cases after recording the reasons in writing for such extension.

[1][(2) The Chief Judicial Magistrate or the Chief Metropolitan Magistrate shall review the pendency of cases of the Board at every six months, and shall direct the Board to increase the frequency of its sittings or may cause the constitution of additional Boards.]

**SYNOPSIS**



**COMMENTS**

**1. Provision – Comments on –** Section 14 is of utmost importance as this relates to an enquiry by the Board regarding a juvenile which precedes the examination of section 12 in the context of a benefit of bail to be granted. Upon a finding recorded by the Board regarding a person in conflict with law being a juvenile, a right would be conferred in his favour to be released on bail ordinarily unless such a right is circumscribed by inhibitive factors of bringing him into association with any known criminal or expose him to moral, physical or psychological danger or that his release would defeat the ends of justice. It is now imperative to understand how a person in conflict with law can be determined to be a juvenile so as to avail himself of the benefit of section 12, as also other intended benefits flowing from the statute. Where the Court is dealing with a child or a juvenile in conflict with law, the benefit of the protection of the Act would be afforded to him without even ascertaining these factors mentioned in section 2(d)(iii), (iv), (v), (vi), (viii) and the Board would proceed to determine this question solely on the basis of a person attaining the age of 18 years giving primacy only to the biological aspects; *Shimil Kumar* v. *State of Haryana,* 2013 (4) RCR (Cri) 16 (P&H): 2014 (1) Crimes 74 (528) (P&H).

**2. Benefit to Child or Juvenile – Law on –** Rule 12 of the Juvenile Justice (Care & Protection of Children) Rules, 2007 speaks that where the assessment of the age is not possible, the Court or the Board or as the case may be, the Committee, for the reasons to be recorded by them, may, if considered necessary, give benefit to the child or the juvenile by considering his/her age on lower side within the margin of one year and while passing orders in such cases shall after taking into consideration such evidence as

1. Ins. by Act 33 of 2006, sec. 11 (w.e.f. 22-8-2006).

may be available or the medical opinion as the case may be, record a finding in respect of his age; *Thakat Singh* v. *State of Madhya Pradesh*, 2012 (5) RCR (Cri) 284: 2012 (2) Crimes 425 (MP): 2012 Cr LJ 2573 (MP) (Gwalior Bench).

**3. Competent Authority – Duties of –** A duty is cast upon the competent authority to make due enquiry as to the age of the person brought before it under any of the provisions of the Act otherwise than for the purpose of evidence; *Asha Tamang* v. *State of West Bengal*, 2012 (1) Cal HN 465 (Cal) (DB).

**4. Benefit for Juvenile – Law on –** This is apparent from a reading of the provisions of sections 15 and 16 of the Act. By virtue of section 7A of the Act, the benefit has to be given to the juvenile in conflict with law at any stage of the matter; *Jitender @ Jitu* v. *State*, 2011 (124) DRJ 1 (Del) (DB).

**5. Board – Bounden Duty of –** Under section 14 of the Act, the Board is bound to conduct an enquiry. section 15 of the Act categorically states that in such enquiry the Board must consider whether "the juvenile has committed an offence". Undoubtedly, the thrust of the enquiry under section 14 of the Act is to ascertain whether the juvenile has committed an offence. He would be entitled for all the protections under the due process provisions of the Constitution in such enquiry under section 14 in which it is to be decided whether he has committed an offence or not; *Selvi* v. *State of Kerala*, 2009 (3) Crimes 662 (Ker): 2008 (4) Ker LT 329 (Ker).

**6. Board – Powers & Functions of –** Section 14 of the Act stipulates that wherever a juvenile is charged with an offence and is produced before a Board, the Board shall hold the inquiry in accordance with the provisions of the said Act and may make such order in relation to the juvenile as it deems fit. Section 15 of the Act provides for the orders that may be passed by the Board regarding a juvenile. Section 15(1) clearly stipulates that where a Board is satisfied on inquiry that a juvenile has committed an offence, then notwithstanding anything to the contrary contained in any other law for the time being in force, the Board may, if it so thinks fit, pass any order of the nature specified in clauses (a) to (g). Section 15(1)(g) contemplates an order directing the juvenile to be sent to a special home for a period of three years; *Chatpal @ Satpal* v. *State*, 2011 (123) DRJ 131 (Del) (DB).

**7. Claim of Juvenility – Law on –** Whenever a claim of juvenility is raised, before any court, the same is bound to hold an enquiry, takes such evidence as may be necessary (but not an affidavit) so as to determine the age of such person. It is also provided that claim of juvenility may be raised before any court at any stage. According to rule 12(3) of the Rules 2007, the age of an accused shall be determined by seeking evidence by obtaining the matriculation or equivalent certificate in the absence thereof, on the basis of date of birth recorded in the school first attended and in the absence thereof, on the basis of birth certificate if given by Corporation or Municipal authority or a Panchayat and in the absence of all three options mentioned above, the medical opinion shall be sought from a duly constituted Medical Board; *Ram Singh* v. *State of Uttar Pradesh*, 2013 (7) ADJ 50: 2013 (5) ALJ 537: 2013 (3) ACR 3210.

**8. Computation of Age – Law on –** If date of birth of a person is found registered as required by the Registration of Births and Deaths Act, 1969, soon after his birth then, that entry amounts to be admissible under section 76 of the Indian Evidence Act and it is a conclusive proof to that fact but, if registration of birth was done after sometime then, the Court has to consider the reasons of such delay and genuineness of the entry. *Secondly*, when a person continues with his shown date of birth for a longer period then, he is estopped to say contrary to that fact and therefore, he could be believed for that entry because when the date of birth was informed to a particular authority and it continues for a longer period then, it cannot be said that a particular date of birth was mentioned due to a particular reason but, such a principle is not acceptable in case of the prosecutrix of any case. The reason behind the principle is that the computation of age should be done in a manner that if any doubt is created then, benefit of doubt should be given to the accused. Therefore, when a date of birth of the accused is to be counted then, his entry relating to date of birth given to the school, which continues till his high school examination then, that entry of date of birth shall be considered in favour of the accused, if no cognate evidence is submitted by him contrary to that entry, whereas in case of a prosecutrix, it is to be considered as to whether the entry given to the school authorities was given on the basis of any document and what was the source of that entry. Otherwise, that entry becomes doubtful and benefit of doubt is to be given to the accused. Similarly, in ossification test, if age of the accused is computed then, variation of two years may be considered on the lower side to assess as to whether he is a juvenile or not, whereas, age of the prosecutrix assessed by the ossification test, may be added by two years on upper side, so that the benefit of doubt may be given to the accused. However, age of any person, if it is computed by the ossification test then, two years may be added or deleted, according to the other symptoms of that person and factual position of the case and therefore, it cannot be said that it is a hard and fast rule, by which age may be computed; *Subham* v. *State of Madhya Pradesh*, 2013 Cr LJ 1716: 2013 ILR 961 (MP).

**9. Expression "Trial" – Meaning of –** The expression "trial" has been generally understood as the examination by court of issues of fact and law in a case for the purpose of rendering the judgment relating some offences committed. Courts find in very many cases that the Court/the J.J. Board while determining the claim of juvenility forget that what they are expected to do is not to conduct an inquiry under section 2(g) of the Code of Criminal Procedure, but an inquiry under the J.J. Act, following the procedure laid under rule 12 and not following the procedure laid down under the Code; *Ashwani Kumar Saxena* v. *State of Madhya Pradesh*, 2012 AIR SCW 5377: 2012 (10) SCR 540: AIR 2013 SC 553.

**10. Finding in Respect of Age – Law on –** Court has to take evidence as may be necessary so as to determine the age of such person and shall record a finding whether the person is a Juvenile or a child or not, stating his age as nearly as may be. As per rule 12(3), the Court is required to first seek evidence by obtaining the specified certificate in sub-clauses (i) to (iii) of clause (a) and in absence thereof seek medical opinion from a duly constituted Medical Board. Further, if exact assessment of the age cannot be done, the Court for the reasons to be recorded, May, if considered necessary, give benefit to the child or juvenile by considering his/her age on lower side within the margin of one year. Furthermore, while passing order in such cases, the Court is expected to record a finding in respect of the age of the person. Finding so recorded by the Court alone can be conclusive proof of the age as regards such child or juvenile in conflict with law; *Vijay Gokul Mhaske* v. *State of Maharashtra*, 2012 All MR (Cri) 1184: 2012 (3) BCR (Cri) 429 (Bom) (DB).

**11. Inquiry – Law on –** A plain reading of the provisions makes it clear that insofar as a juvenile in conflict with law is concerned, the Juvenile Justice Board has exclusive power to deal with such a juvenile in respect of the proceedings under the said Act. Furthermore, by virtue of section 7 if a Magistrate who is not empowered to exercise the powers of the Juvenile Justice Board, is of the opinion that a person brought before him is a juvenile then he is required to record such an opinion without delay and forward the juvenile and the record of the proceedings to the competent authority having jurisdiction under the Act. The meaning of this is clear that where any Magistrate who is not functioning as a Juvenile Justice Board feels that a person brought before him is a juvenile he has to record such an opinion and send such juvenile to be dealt with by the competent authority. Before a person can be sent to the competent authority for being dealt with in accordance with the said Act, the Magistrate has to record an opinion that such person is a juvenile as defined in section 2(k) of the said Act. Section 7(2) provides that after the juvenile has been sent to the competent authority, the latter shall hold the 'inquiry' as if the juvenile or the child had originally been brought before it. This 'inquiry' has reference to the inquiry to be conducted by the Board under section 14 of the Act and does not have reference to the inquiry for determination of age of a person under section 49 of the said Act; *Sakir Mewati* v. *State of Madhya Pradesh*, 2011 Cr LJ 4469: 2011 (2) Jab LJ 245 (MP) (Gwalior Bench).

**12. Inquiry – Procedure for –** The Code lays down the procedure to be followed in every investigation, inquiry or trial for every offence, whether under the Indian Penal Code or under other Penal laws. The Code makes provisions for not only investigation, inquiry into or trial for offences but also inquiries into certain specific matters. The procedure laid down for inquiring into the specific matters under the Code naturally cannot be applied in inquiring into other matters like the claim of juvenility under section 7A read with rule 12 of the 2007 Rules. In other words, the law regarding the procedure to be followed in such inquiry must be found in the enactment conferring jurisdiction to hold inquiry. Consequently, the procedure to be followed under the J.J. Act in conducting an inquiry is the procedure laid down in that statute itself *i.e.*, rule 12 of the 2007 Rules. Courts cannot import other procedures laid down in the Code of Criminal Procedure or any other enactment while making an inquiry with regard to the juvenility of a person, when the claim of juvenility is raised before the court exercising powers under section 7A of the Act; *Ashwani Kumar Saxena* v. *State of Madhya Pradesh*, 2012 (10) SCR 540: AIR 2013 SC 553: 2012 Cr LJ 4731.

**13. Inquiry and Evidence – Comments on –** Section 7A obliges the court only to make an inquiry, not an investigation or a trial, an inquiry not under the Code of Criminal Procedure, but under the Act. Statute requires the Court or the Board only to make an 'inquiry' and in what manner that inquiry has to be conducted is provided in JJ Rules. Few of the expressions used in section 7A and rule 12 are of considerable importance and a reference to them is necessary to understand the true scope and content of those provisions. Section 7A has used the expression "court shall make an inquiry", "take such evidence as may be necessary" and "but not an affidavit". The Court or the Board can accept as evidence something more than an affidavit *i.e.*, the Court or the Board can accept documents, certificates etc., as evidence need not be oral evidence; *Ashwani Kumar Saxena* v. *State of Madhya Pradesh*, 2012 (10) SCR 540: AIR 2013 SC 553: 2012 Cr LJ 4731.

**14. Jurisdictional Issue – Disposal of –** The jurisdictional issue based on purported age of the accused needs consideration first; *Bikau Pandey* v. *State of Bihar*, 2003 (10) SCALE 173: 2003 (8) Supreme 429: AIR 2004 SC 997.

**15. Juvenile – Rights of –** Under section 14, whenever a juvenile charged with an offence is brought before the JJ Board, the latter must conduct an 'inquiry' under the JJ Act. A juvenile cannot be tried with an adult. Determination of the age of the juvenile is required to be made on the basis of documentary evidence (such as birth certificate, matriculation certificate, or Medical Board examination). The Board is expected to conclude the inquiry as soon as possible under rule 13. Further, the Board is required to satisfy itself that the juvenile has not been tortured by the police or any other person and to take steps if ill-treatment has occurred. Proceedings must be conducted in the simplest manner and a child-friendly atmosphere must be maintained [Rule 13(2)(b)], and the juvenile must be given a right to be heard [Clause (c)]. The inquiry is not to be conducted in the spirit of adversarial proceedings, a fact that the Board is expected to keep in mind even in the examination of witnesses [Rule 13(3)]. Rule 13(4) provides that the Board must try to put the juvenile at ease while examining him and recording his statement; the Board must encourage him to speak without fear not only of the circumstances of the alleged offence but also his home and social surroundings. Since the ultimate object of the Act is the rehabilitation of the juvenile, the Board is not merely concerned with the allegations of the crime but also the underlying social causes for the same in order to effectively deal with such causes. The Board may dispense with the attendance of the juvenile during the inquiry, if thought fit (Section 47). Before the Board concludes on the juvenile's involvement, it must consider the social investigation report prepared by the Welfare Officer [Rule 15(2)]. The inquiry must not prolong beyond four months unless the Board extends the period for special reasons due to the circumstances of the case. In all non-serious crimes, delay of more than 6 months will terminate the trial [Rule 13(7)]; *Subramanian Swamy* v. *Raju*, JT 2014 (4) SC 328: 2014 (4) SCALE 305: AIR 2014 SC 1649 *Nirbhaya* case [Hon'ble Judges: P. Sathasivam, Ranjan Gogoi, Shiva Kirti Singh].

**16. Juvenile 'Inquiry' – Law on –** The JJ Board conducts a child-friendly "inquiry" and not an adversarial trial. This is not to say that the nature of the inquiry is non-adversarial, since both prosecution and defence submit their cases. Instead, the nature of the proceedings acquires a child-friendly colour. The emphasis of criminal trials is to record a finding on the guilt or innocence of the accused. In case of established guilt, the prime object of sentencing is to punish a guilty offender. The emphasis of juvenile 'inquiry' is to find the guilt/innocence of the juvenile and to investigate the underlying social or familial causes of the alleged crime. Thus, the aim of juvenile sentencing is to reform and rehabilitate the errant juvenile. The adult criminal system does not regulate the activities of the offender once s/he has served the sentence. Since the JJ system seeks to reform and rehabilitate the juvenile, it establishes post- trial avenues for the juvenile to make an honest living; *Subramanian Swamy* v. *Raju*, JT 2014 (4) SC 328: 2014 (4) SCALE 305: AIR 2014 SC 1649, *Nirbhaya* case [Hon'ble Judges: P. Sathasivam, Ranjan Gogoi, Shiva Kirti Singh].

**17. Juvenility of Person – Law on –** One point is well established that the juvenility of a person in conflict with law has to be reckoned from the date of the incident and not from the date on which cognizance was taken by the Magistrate. The law as now crystallized on a conjoint reading of sections 2(k), 2(1), 7A, 20 and 49 read with rules 12 and 98, places beyond all doubt that all persons who were below the age of 18 years on the date of commission of the offence even prior to 1st April, 2001, would be treated as juveniles, even if the claim of juvenility was raised after they had attained the age of 18 years on or before the date of commencement of the Act and were undergoing sentence upon being convicted; *Hari Ram* v. *State of Rajasthan*, 2009 (13) SCC 211: 2009 (6) SCALE 695: 2009 SCR 1381.

**18. Knowingly or Willfully Given False Evidence – Law on –** Section 344, Cr.P.C. provides that at the time of delivery of any judgment the Court of Session or Magistrate of the first class expresses an opinion to the effect that any witness appearing in such proceeding had knowingly or willfully given false evidence or had fabricated false evidence with the intention that such evidence should be used in such proceeding, it or he may, if satisfied that it is necessary and expedient in the interest of justice that the witness should be tried summarily for giving or fabricating, as the case may be, false evidence, take cognizance of the offence and may, after giving the offender a reasonable opportunity of showing cause why he should not be punished for such offence, try such offender summarily and sentence him to imprisonment for a term which may extend to three months, or to fine which may extend to five hundred rupees, or with both; *Kallu* v. *State of Uttar Pradesh*, 2013 (82) ACC 637 (All).

**19. Medical Evidence – Significance of –** It is well settled that it is neither feasible nor desirable to lay down an abstract formula to determine the age of a person. The date of birth is to be determined on the basis of material on record and on appreciation of evidence adduced by the parties. The Medical evidence as to the age of a person, though a very useful guiding factor, is not conclusive and has to be considered along with other cogent evidence; *Babloo Pasi* v. *State of Jharkhand*, AIR 2009 SC 314: 2008 (13) SCC 133: 2008 (13) SCALE 137.

**20. Medical Opinion of Duly Constituted Medical Board – Significance of –** Rules stipulate that in every case concerning a child or juvenile in conflict with law, the age determination inquiry shall be conducted by the Court or the Board or, as the case may be, the Committee by seeking evidence by obtaining the documents specified in clause (a), namely, (i) the matriculation or equivalent certificates, if available; and in the absence whereof; (ii) the date of birth certificate from the school (other than a play school) first attended; and in the absence whereof; (iii) the birth certificate given by a corporation or a municipal authority or a panchayat; and in the absence of either (i), (ii) and (iii) of clause (a), the medical opinion of a duly constituted Medical Board. There is no evidence concerning the three types of documents mentioned in clause (a) of rule 12(3) of the said Rules. Consequently, it is the medical opinion of a duly constituted Medical Board, which will have to be considered for the purposes of declaration of the age of the accused. No further medical opinion is necessary; *Surender Khare* v. *State*, 2011 (10) AD 24 (Del): 2012 Cr LJ 1: 2012 (3) RCR (Cri) 456.

**21. Minor Represented by Guardian – Law on –** Our international obligations as laid down in the Convention on the Rights of the Child and the Beijing Rules require the involvement of the parents or legal guardians in the legal process concerning a juvenile in conflict with law. For example, a reference may be made to article 40 of the Convention and Principles 7, 10 and 15 of the Beijing Rules. That this is not unusual is clear from the fact that in civil disputes, our domestic law requires a minor to be represented by a guardian; *Jitendra Singh @ Babboo Singh* v. *State of Uttar Pradesh*, 2013 (11) SCC 193: JT 2013 (11) SC 152: 2013 (9) SCALE 18.

**22. Opinion of District Probation Officer – Law on –** If opinion of District Probation Officer is that the parents have got no control over the accused is based on no material placed before it then such report is bad. Giving an opinion against an juvenile without any background facts was not a fair exercise by Probation Officer. Such a opinion by the Officer definitely polluted the thinking process of the Board/court; *Shiva @ Suryakant* v. *State of Uttar Pradesh*, 2011 (7) ADJ 384: 2011 (74) ACC 538: 2011 (7) RCR (Cri) 2290 (All).

**23. Opportunity – Law on –** Trial Court will hold an inquiry for the purpose of ascertaining the age of the accused after providing an opportunity to both the parties to adduce their evidence and thereafter will pass order afresh; *Ummed Singh* v. *State of Madhya Pradesh*, 2007 (4) Crimes 16: 2007 (5) MPHT 227: 2007 (3) MPLJ 214.

**24. Ossification and Radiological Examination – Significance of –** Even if an accused is clearly below the age of 18 years on the date of commission of offence, should not be granted protection or treatment available to a juvenile under the Juvenile Justice Act if a dispute regarding his age had been raised but was finally resolved on scrutiny of evidence. What is meant to be emphasized is that where the courts cannot clearly infer in spite of available evidence on record that the accused is a juvenile or the said plea appear to have been raised merely to create a mist or a smokescreen so as to hide his real age in order to shield the accused on the plea of his minority, the attempt cannot be allowed to succeed so as to subvert or dupe the cause of justice. Drawing parallel between the plea of minority and the plea of alibi, it may be worthwhile to state that it is not uncommon to come across criminal cases wherein an accused makes an effort to take shelter under the plea of alibi which has to be raised at the first instance but has to be subjected to strict proof of evidence by the court trying the offence and cannot be allowed lightly in spite of lack of evidence merely with the aid of salutary principle that an innocent man may not have to suffer injustice by recording an order of conviction in spite of his plea of alibi. Similarly, if the conduct of an accused or the method and manner of commission of the offence indicates an evil and a well planned design of the accused committing the offence which indicates more towards the matured skill of an accused than that of an innocent child, then in the absence of reliable documentary evidence in support of the age of the accused, medical evidence indicating that the accused was a major cannot be allowed to be ignored taking shelter of the principle of benevolent legislation like the Juvenile Justice Act, subverting the course of justice as statutory protection of the Juvenile Justice Act is meant for minors who are innocent law breakers and not accused of matured mind who use the plea of minority as a ploy or shield to protect themselves from the sentence of the offence committed by them. The benefit of benevolent legislation under the Juvenile Justice Act obviously will offer protection to a genuine child accused/juvenile who does not put the court into any dilemma as to whether he is a juvenile or not by adducing evidence in support of his plea of minority but in absence of the same, reliance placed merely on shaky evidence like the school admission register which is not proved or oral evidence based on conjectures leading to further ambiguity, cannot be relied upon in preference to the medical evidence for assessing the age of the accused. While considering the relevance and value of the medical evidence, the doctor's estimation of age although is not a sturdy substance for proof as it is only an opinion, such opinion based on scientific medical test like ossification and radiological examination will have to be treated as a strong evidence having corroborative value while determining the age of the alleged juvenile accused; *Om Prakash* v. *State of Rajasthan,* AIR 2012 SC 1608: 2012 (4) SCALE 348: 2012 (5) SCC 201.

**25. Probation Officer – Duties of –** Section 14 deals with inquiry of Board regarding juveniles. In this regard rule 51 of the Uttar Pradesh Juvenile Justice (Care and Protection of Children) Rules, 2004 has got its own importance. It casts a duty upon the Probation Officer that he shall enquire into the antecedents and family history of the juvenile or the child and such other material circumstances, as may be necessary, and thereafter he will submit a report either to the investigator or to the Board in prescribed Form No. VIII; *Dushyant* v. *State of Uttar Pradesh,* 2011 (3) Crimes 41 (All): 2011 (4) ADJ 25: 2011 (73) ACC 482.

**26. Procedure for Trials – Law on –** There is no provision for convicting a Juvenile in conflict with law for any offence. Various categories of the orders which can be passed against the Juvenile have been specified in sub-section (1) of section 15 of the Act. However, the said orders can be passed only when the Board is satisfied on inquiry that a Juvenile has committed an offence alleged against him. In view of section 54(1) of the said Act, subject to the procedure as may be prescribed. While holding an inquiry as contemplated under section 14 and sub-section (1) of section 15 of the Act, the procedure laid down in the Code for trial in summons cases is required to be followed. As there is no prescribed procedure which makes a departure from, the procedure contemplated by the Code for trial of the summons cases, the Board is under obligation to follow the procedure for trials in summons cases for holding an inquiry under sub-section (1) of section 15 of the said Act; *High Court on its Own Motion* v. *State of Maharashtra,* 2013 (3) AIR BomR 119: 2013 (8) RCR (Cri) 892 (Bom) (DB).

**27. Proceedings Conducted in Chamber – Validity of –** The object of the said rule is to provide child friendly atmosphere for the juvenile so that without any fear he can participate in the enquiry. Further, the object is only to rehabilitate the juvenile and not to punish him for the offence committed by him. Rule 7 of the Tamil Nadu Rules states that the Board shall hold its sitting in the premises of the Observation Home or at any place as may be specified by the State Government in this behalf. The proceedings conducted in the Chamber of the Magistrate cannot be stated to be child friendly. The Juvenile Justice Board ought not to have held its sitting in the Magistrate Court premises at all. When the Rule mandates that the place where the proceedings are conducted shall not look like a Court room in any manner, it is unfortunate that the entire proceedings were conducted in the Court premises itself. This is yet another illegality that may be committed by the Juvenile Justice Board; *Idukkan* v. *Inspector of Police,* 2012 (4) CTC 718 (Mad).

**28. Protective Custody – Law on –** Under section 14 of the Juvenile Act, it is only the Juvenile Justice Board which can conduct an inquiry as to whether a juvenile has committed the offence or not. Even if the Board comes to the conclusion that a juvenile has committed an offence, he cannot be sentenced and sent to a prison. Section of 15 of the Juvenile Act states what orders can be passed regarding a juvenile who has committed an offence. Under section 15(g), the Board may direct the juvenile to be sent to a special home for a period of three years. Under the proviso, the Board may, for reasons to be recorded, reduce the period of stay to such period as it thinks fit. Section 16 forbids the court from sentencing a juvenile and committing him to prison. Proviso to section 16 states that where a juvenile who has attained the age of 16 years has committed an offence and the Board is satisfied that the offence committed is so serious in nature or that his conduct and behaviour have been such that it would not be in his interest or in the interest of other juvenile in a special home to send him to such special home and that none of the other measures provided under the Juvenile Act is suitable or sufficient, the Board may order such a juvenile to be kept in such place of safety and in such manner as it thinks fit and shall report the case for the order of the State Government. Under sub-section (2) of section 16 on a report received from the Board under sub-section (1), the State Government may order that such juvenile may be kept under protective custody at such place and on such conditions as it thinks fit. However, the period of detention shall not exceed in any case the maximum period provided under section 15 *i.e.,* the period of 3 years; *Kalu @ Amit* v. *State of Haryana,* AIR 2012 SC 3212: 2012 Cr LJ 4244: 2012 (8) SCC 34.

**29. Question of Juvenility – Law on –** As per the provisions of section 7A of the Act, when an application claiming juvenility is moved before the Court, the Court is bound to hold an inquiry and to take such evidence, as may be necessary (but not an affidavit) so as to determine the age of such person, and to record a finding whether the person is a juvenile or a child or not. It is the duty of the Court to hold a proper inquiry and to decide the question of juvenility of the accused in accordance with section 7A of the Act and rule 12(3) of the Rules 2007; *Sanjay* v. *State of Uttar Pradesh,* 2011 (7) ADJ 801 (All).

**30. Relaxation – Law on –** It is apparent from the rule 12(3)(b) that the relaxation of one year is not automatic but it should be granted after considering all the evidence available on record; *Mohd. Wasim* v. *State,* 2012 Cr LJ 3883: 2012 (3) JCC 1552: 2013 (7) RCR (Cri) 810 (Del) (DB).

**31. Sentence – Effect of –** The provisions connotes an idea that when the matter of juvenility would be raised by any court, the court shall make an enquiry and take such evidence as may be necessary (but not an affidavit) so as to determine the age of such person and shall record a finding whether the person is a juvenile or a child or not, stating his age as nearly as may be. And if the court finds a person to be juvenile on the date of commission of the offence under sub-section (1), it shall forward the juvenile to the Board for passing appropriate order, and the sentence if any passed by a court, shall be deemed to have no effect; *Nasaruddin @ Raja* v. *State of Uttar Pradesh,* 2013 (1) ACrR 797 (All).

**32. Court – Powers of –** When the high school marks-sheet was filed and if the trial Court had any doubt, it could have summoned the relevant school records or the records of the High School Board. The Principal of the school could also have been summoned to establish the correct date of birth of the revisionist. An inquiry into juvenility of an accused is not a game of chess between the accused, the complainant and the State. Heavy responsibility rests on the shoulders of the Court to find out the truth irrespective of the fact whether a party is being represented properly or incompetently. The powers of the Court to inquire into the juvenility of an accused are unlimited. On one side; a person should not be permitted to take a false plea of juvenility to escape punishment and on the other hand, a juvenile: should not suffer on account of lack of proper representation or lack of means. When an inquiry is being held by the Court, it can summon any person as a witness at the expense of the State to find out the truth. Such an inquiry is not a mere formality; *Neelu Chaurasia @ Arvind Kumar Chaurasia* v. *State of Uttar Pradesh*, 2013 (3) All CriR 3125: 2013 (5) ADJ 69: 2013 (6) ALJ 54.

**33. Determination of Age – Discussion on –** The appellant was tried and convicted for the offences punishable under section 376 and 202 of IPC for committing rape on a 7 year old girl and thereafter killing her by crushing her head with a stone. When the contention was raised that at the time of commission of the offence the accused was a juvenile , the Supreme Court held that the general rule about age determination is that the age as determined can vary plus minus two years but the Board constituted to determine the age of the accused has in the case at hand spread over a period of 6 years and taken a mean to fix the age of the appellant at 33 years. The court observed that it was not sure whether that was the correct way of estimating the age of the appellant and what assured the court about the estimate of age is the fact that the same is determined by a medical Board comprising Professors of Anatomy, Radiodiagnosis and Forensic Medicine whose opinion must get the respect it deserves. Even if the age of the appellant was determined by the upper extremity limit *i.e.*, 36 years the same would have been subject to variation of plus minus 2 years meaning thereby that he could as well be 34 years on the date of the examination. Taking his age as 34 years on the date of the examination he would have been 18 years, 2 months and 7 days on the date of the occurrence but such an estimate would be only an estimate and the appellant may be entitled to additional benefit of one year in terms of lowering his age by one year in terms of rule 12(3)(b) of the Juvenile Justice (Care and Protection of Children) Rules, 2007 which would bring him to be 17 years and 2 months old, therefore, a juvenile and the sentence awarded to him under section 302 and 376 of IPC is liable to be set aside; *Darga Ram @ Gunga* v. *State of Rajasthan*, (2015) 2 SCC 775.

Declaration of the age of the child who is in conflict with law by mere reliance upon a School Leaving Certificate or even a positive proof of the certificate of registration of birth *ipso facto* should not be the foundational basis to declare a person juvenile more particularly, when such a juvenile is accused of having committed a heinous offence particularly when days or few months separated him from adulthood. One necessarily has to understand that in a country like ours and especially in a strata which is ignorant of even the basic requirement of getting a birth registered, there would be no conclusive proof of age and the age given in the school certificate or the records of the school would only speak of an age imaginatively conjured by the parents at the time of admission of such a child. Even though it may form a persuasive piece of material, but certainly no credence and outright acceptability should be afforded to it. One may also keep in mind that quite a few births will take place in homes and not in hospitals. If the birth takes place in the hospital, there would possibly be a record and a consequent registration establishing a correct date of birth but not in other cases. Factors such as ossification tests etc., may also be considered but they themselves are in determinative and not reliable and can form only collateral material in an enquiry. But in the cases of aggravated offences, what is of importance to establish whether a person is a child or not, is his ability to comprehend what is right and what is wrong, what is lawful and what is unlawful and whether he understands the consequences of his actions. It is the advancement of his mental faculty that would suggest whether he is an adult or a juvenile and for this purpose, there has to be a specialized examination of the child at the hands of experts who can evaluate the ability of such a child to segregate good and bad, the lawful and unlawful and the consequences ensuing therefrom and this would show his maturity or immaturity to answer for his deeds. It is the factors related to growth and maturity psychologically and socially, but not entirely biologically, which would give an insight as to whether a person is a child or an adult and merely because the age of 18 years would confer a lot of social and political privileges in a civil society, would not certainly mean that a person before attainment of such an age continues to remain a child and eluding adulthood, while he in his conduct otherwise demonstrates the capability of correct comprehension. It is, therefore, the competence of a juvenile which has to be established before the Board and the Board and the courts ought not to automatically assume that the statutory definition would confer the halo of a juvenile and give him an undeserving protection and benefits. Apart from determining such abilities, an enquiry should also establish the social factors surrounding such a person in conflict with law, as they also possibly may reveal the cause of a distorted or a perverted mind set, which may eventually lead to an appreciation of the ability of correct comprehension. After the Juvenile Justice Board and the court concerned have addressed the afore-expressed concern which can be achieved by involving a professional psychologist/psychiatrist and sociologists, the Board can then proceed to determine the second aspect as to whether to release a juvenile on bail which would now be dependent upon the first question because if a person is found capable of comprehending what is right and wrong, and is enabled to understand sufficiently his actions, then as an automatic corollary it should follow that release of such a person on bail would defeat the ends of justice and the remaining aspects of the likelihood of a child coming into contact with any known criminal or exposing him to moral, physical or psychological danger, would be questions dependent solely on factors and inferences which such facts may throw up; *Shimil Kumar* v. *State of Haryana,* 2013 (4) RCR (Cri) 16: 2014 (1) Crimes 74 (528) (P&H).

**34. Enquiry – Condition for –** Mandate of rule 12(3) of the Rules warrants basing an opinion on the matriculation or equivalent certificate for determining the date of birth of a juvenile or the date of birth certificate from a school first attended (other than a play school) and it is only in the absence of this material that the Court is required to proceed to enquire and look into some other material; *Harpreet Singh* v. *State of Haryana,* 2011 (1) ILR 155 (P&H).

**35. High Court – Powers of –** Section 6(2) of the Act clearly and unambiguously declares that when the proceedings are before the High Court or the Court of Session "in appeal, revision or otherwise", such Courts are entitled to exercise the powers conferred on the Board; *Selvi* v. *State of Kerala,* 2009 (3) Crimes 662 (Ker): 2008 (4) Ker LT 329 (Ker).

**36. Natural Justice – Comments on –** The extent and application of the doctrine of natural justice cannot be imprisoned within the strait-jacket of a rigid formula. The application of the doctrine depends upon the nature of the jurisdiction conferred on the Administrative Authority, upon the character of the rights of the persons affected, the scheme and policy of the statute and other relevant circumstances disclosed in the particular case; *Union of India* v. *P.K. Roy,* AIR 1968 SC 850.

**37. Precedents – Theory of –** According to the well-settled theory of precedents, every decision contains three basic postulates (i) findings of material facts, direct and inferential. An inferential finding of facts is the inference which the Judge draws from the direct, or perceptible facts; (ii) statements of the principles of law applicable to the legal problems disclosed by the facts; and (iii) judgment based on the combined effect of the above. A decision is only an authority for what it actually decides. What is of the essence in a decision is its ratio and not every observation found therein nor what logically follows from the various observations made in the judgment. Every judgment must be read as applicable to the particular facts proved, or assumed to be proved, since the generality of the expressions which may be found there is not intended to be exposition of the whole law, but governed and qualified by the particular facts of the case in which such expressions are to be found. It would, therefore, be not profitable to extract a sentence here and there from the judgment and to build upon it because the essence of the decision is its ratio and not every observation found therein. The enunciation of the reason or principle on which a question before a court has been decided is alone binding as a precedent; *Union of India* v. *Dhanwanti Devi,* JT 1996 (8) SC 306: 1996 (6) SCALE 431: 1996 (6) SCC 44.

**38. Trials – Law on –** The trials are traditionally open which an indispensable attribute of the criminal justice is. This characteristic flowed not merely from the public interest is seeing fairness and proper conduct in the administration of criminal trials, but, more important, the "therapeutic value" to the public of seeing its criminal laws in operation, purging the society of the outrage felt with the commission of many crimes, convincingly demonstrated why the tradition developed and is maintained. This is the accepted practice of guaranteeing a public trial to an accused as having its roots in the English Common Law heritage. But, however, though it is an indispensable attribute of the criminal justice, in exceptional circumstances there cannot be any legal ban in having the trial in camera. Though the criminal justice prevailing in our country recognises and accepts the practice of only open trial, there is an exception to such trial as contemplated under section 237(2) of the Code of Criminal Procedure falling under Chapter XVIII with caption "Trial Before a Court of Session" which provides an exemption to the general practice; *Kartar Singh; Kripa Shankar Rai* v. *State of Punjab*, 1994 Cr LJ 3139: 1994 (3) SCC 569: 1994 (2) SCR 375.

**15. Order that may be passed regarding juvenile.**—(1) Where a Board is satisfied on inquiry that a juvenile has committed an offence, then, notwithstanding anything to the contrary contained in any other law for the time being in force, the Board may, if it so thinks fit,—

(a) allow the juvenile to go home after advice or admonition following appropriate inquiry against and counselling to the parent or the guardian and the juvenile;

(b) direct the juvenile to participate in group counselling and similar activities;

(c) order the juvenile to perform community service;

(d) order the parent of the juvenile or the juvenile himself to pay a fine, if he is over fourteen years of age and earns money;

(e) direct the juvenile to be released on probation of good conduct and placed under the care of any parent, guardian or other fit person, on such parent, guardian or other fit person executing a bond, with or without surety, as the Board may require, for the good behaviour and well-being of the juvenile for any period not exceeding three years;

(f) direct the juvenile to be released on probation of good conduct and placed under the care of any fit institution for the good behaviour and well-being of the juvenile for any period not exceeding three years;

[1][(g) make an order directing the juvenile to be sent to a special home for a period of three years:

Provided that the Board may, if it is satisfied that having regard to the nature of the offence and the circumstances of the case, it is expedient so to do, for reasons to be recorded, reduce the period of stay to such period as it thinks fit.]

(2) The Board shall obtain the social investigation report on juvenile either through a probation officer or a recognised voluntary organisation or otherwise, and shall take into consideration the findings of such report before passing an order.

(3) Where an order under clause (d), clause (e) or clause (f) of sub-section (1) is made, the Board may, if it is of opinion that in the interests of the juvenile and of the public, it is expedient so to do, in addition make an order that the juvenile in conflict with law shall remain under the supervision of a probation officer named in the order during such period, not exceeding three years as may

---

1. Subs. by Act 33 of 2006, sec. 12, for clause (g) (w.e.f. 22-8-2006). Clause (g), before substitution, stood as under:

"(g) make an order directing the juvenile to be sent to a special home,—

(i) in the case of juvenile, over seventeen years but less than eighteen years of age for a period of not less than two years;

(ii) in case of any other juvenile for the period until he ceases to be a juvenile:

Provided that the Board may, if it is satisfied that having regard to the nature of the offence and the circumstances of the case it is expedient so to do, for reasons to be recorded, reduce the period of stay to such period as it thinks fit.".

be specified therein, and may in such supervision order impose such conditions as it deems necessary for the due supervision of the juvenile in conflict with law:

Provided that if at any time afterwards it appears to the Board on receiving a report from the probation officer or otherwise, that the juvenile in conflict with law has not been of good behaviour during the period of supervision or that the fit institution under whose care the juvenile was placed is no longer able or willing to ensure the good behaviour and well-being of the juvenile it may, after making such inquiry as it deems fit, order the juvenile in conflict with law to be sent to a special home.

(4) The Board shall while making a supervision order under sub-section (3), explain to the juvenile and the parent, guardian or other fit person or fit institution, as the case may be, under whose care the juvenile has been placed, the terms and conditions of the order and shall forthwith furnish one copy of the supervision order to the juvenile, the parent, guardian or other fit person or fit institution, as the case may be, the sureties, if any, and the probation officer.

**SYNOPSIS**



**COMMENTS**

**1. Object of Act – Comments on –** The object of the Act appears to be for rehabilitation of a Juvenile in conflict with law. Therefore, there is no specific provision for convicting a Juvenile in conflict with law even if, on inquiry, the Board finds that the Juvenile has committed an offence. There are various actions contemplated under sub-section (1) of section 15 of the said Act. The Juvenile can be ordered to go home after advice or admonition. He can be directed to perform community service; he can be directed to pay fine and he can be sent to a special home for a period of three years. Under the proviso to sub-section (1) of section 16, there is a power vested in the Board not to send Juvenile to a special home but he can be kept in such place of safety and in such manner as the Board thinks fit. Such power can be exercised where a Juvenile who has attained the age of 16 years has committed an offence and the Board is satisfied that the offence committed by him is of such a serious nature, or that his conduct and behaviour have been such that it would not be in his interest or in the interest of other Juveniles in a special home to send him to such special home. Sub-rules 11 to 13 of rule 15 of the said Rules refer to the said power. Even assuming that the Board was of the view that the plea of guilty deserves to be accepted, before passing an order of payment of fine and releasing him on probation, obviously some application of mind was necessary as to why other courses provided in by sub-section (1) of section 15 of the said Act should not be followed. The Board is expected to record reasons as to why a particular option under sub-section (1) of section 15 of the said Act has peen exercised; *High Court on its Own Motion* v. *State of Maharashtra,* 2013 (3) AIR BomR 119: 2013 (8) RCR (Cri) 892 (Bom) (DB).

**2. Provision – Non-attraction of –** Under section 15 of the said Act of 2000 the most stringent action which can be taken against a juvenile is of directing the juvenile to be sent to a Special Home for a period of three years. The offence was committed more than 20 years back. The present age of the accused is 37 years. The accused has already suffered in the sense that it is an admitted position that the accused has undergone sentence in terms of the order of High Court passed in Appeal for more than three years. Accused is 37 years, now no purpose will be served by adopting any of the options open under sub-section 1 section 15 of the Act of 2000. This view is required to be taken in the light of the peculiar facts of the case in as much as the accused has already undergone sentence for more than three years; *Balu Bapusaheb Gade* v. *State of Maharashtra,* 2010 All MR (Cri) 167: 2010 (2) Crimes 724 (Bom): 2011 (8) RCR (Cri) 1425.

**3. Board – Powers of –** It is provided that the Board on being satisfied on an inquiry that the juvenile had committed offence, then notwithstanding to the contrary the Board may make an order directing the juvenile to be sent to special home for the period of three years. The Juvenile Justice Board has already directed the revisionist to be sent to special home as stated above. In view of proviso to section 16 of the Juvenile Justice (Care and Protection of Children) Act, 2000, the period of detention so ordered shall not exceed in any case the maximum period of three years; *Kamlesh Kumar* alias *Ankush* v. *State of Uttar Pradesh,* 2012 (7) ADJ 78: 2012 (3) ACrR 2614 (All).

**4. Board – Functions of –** Section 15 of the Act, 2000 provides about the order that may be passed regarding a juvenile. Under section 15(1)(g), it has been provided that the Board may make an order directing the juvenile to be sent to a special home for a period of three years. Under the proviso, the Board has power, for the reasons to be recorded, to reduce the period of stay to such period as it thinks fit; *Santosh Kumar Vishvakarma* v. *State of Chhattisgarh,* 2013 (5) MPHT 37 (Chh): 2014 (1) Cg LJ 193 (Chh) (DB).

**5. Board – Role of –** Section 16 Act sets out the orders that may not be passed against a juvenile. Section 16(1) provides that notwithstanding anything to the contrary contained in any other law for the time being in force, no juvenile in conflict with law, shall be sentenced to death or imprisonment for any term which may extend to imprisonment for life or be committed to prison in default of payment of fine or any default in furnishing a security. The proviso to section 16(1), however, permits the Board to direct that a juvenile in conflict with law, be kept in a place of safety or in a special home as it may deem fit in certain cases. The proviso to section 16(2) clearly stipulates that the period of detention, which may be ordered under section 16(1), shall not exceed, in any case, the maximum period provided under section 15 of the said Act; *Chatpal @ Satpal* v. *State,* 2011 (123) DRJ 131 (Del) (DB).

**6. Special Home – Comments on –** It appears from section 15 of the Act, 2000 and sub-rule (13) of rule 15 of the Rules 2007 that the law makers prescribed that a juvenile in conflict with law will remain under supervision of Probation Officer for a period of not exceeding 3 years for commission of an offence in a special home; *Dipak Nama* v. *State of Tripura,* 2013 (4) Crimes 79 (Gau): 2012 Cr LJ 4356: 2013 (7) RCR (Cri) 2320 (Gau) (Agartala Bench) (DB).

**7. Tender Age – Law on –** Section 15(g) is very important. It states that where a Board is satisfied that a juvenile has committed an offence then notwithstanding anything to the contrary contained in any other law for the time being in force, the Board may make an order directing the juvenile to be sent to a special home for a period of three years. The provisions make it clear that a juvenile in conflict with law cannot be tried by an ordinary criminal court. He cannot be sentenced. Even if it is found that he has committed an offence he can be sent to a special home for a period of three years only. These provisions are beneficent provisions. The object of these provisions is obviously to ensure that the juvenile is not treated like an ordinary criminal. Special treatment is introduced to prevent him from becoming a confirmed offender. Considering the tender age of the juvenile in conflict with law, the provisions seek to rehabilitate him rather than sending him to prison where there will no scope for his reformation; *Gangaram*

*Dushanna Dandil* v. *State of Maharashtra*, 2009 (4) Crimes 697 (Bom): 2009 (2) BCR (Cri) 277: 2009 (5) AIR BomR 45.

**8. Words 'Detention' and 'Sentence' – Comments on –** Upon going through clause (g) of sub-section (1) of section 15 of the Act, 2000 it appears that a Board of inquiry can send a juvenile to a special home for a period of three years and sub-rule (13) of rule 15 of the Rules, 2007 speaks, in any case the period of detention shall not exceed beyond the maximum period provided in clause (g) of sub-section (1) of section 15 of the Act, 2000, it can be observed that a juvenile cannot be sentenced for committing an offence either under the Penal Code or any other penal provision of the statute. In this pretext it would be proper on our part of examine the words 'sentence' and 'detention' and what is the difference between these two words. As per *Black's Law Dictionary*, 9th Edn., the word 'detention' means confinement or fact of holding a person in custody and the word 'sentence' means the punishment imposed on a criminal wrong doer. As per the *Major Law Lexicon by P. Ramanatha Aiyar*, 4th Edn., the word, 'detention' means the keeping in confinement or custody and the word 'sentence' means a direction by which punishment is prescribed and meted out. In view of the above, it can be said that a juvenile in conflict with law cannot be sentenced either by Juvenile Board or by a Court if the commission of offence is proved rather he can only be sent for detention in a special home for his care and protection, so that he can get a chance for his rectification. But in this case admittedly the Court in absence of plea of juvenility after conviction sentenced him, which requires to be examined by us; *Dipak Nama* v. *State of Tripura*, 2013 (4) Crimes 79 (Gau): 2012 Cr LJ 4356: 2013 (7) RCR (Cri) 2320 (Gau) (Agartala Bench) (DB).

**9. Custody for Over Four Years – Law on –** Juvenile has already been in custody for over four years, which is more than the maximum period of detention of three years prescribed under the said Act, he is entitled to be released forthwith; *Mukesh Kumar Yadav* v. *State*, 2012 (1) Crimes 645 (Del): 2011 (185) DLT 714: 2012 (1) RCR (Cri) 915.

**10. Detention – Law on –** Section 15(1)(g) of the Act and rule 15(13) of the Rules 2007, when read together, give rise to the only conclusion that a juvenile in conflict with law cannot be held in detention for a period exceeding 3 years; *Salim Mohammad* v. *State of Uttar Pradesh*, 2011 (9) ADJ 811: 2012 (1) ACrR 245: 2013 (6) RCR (Cri) 2527 (All).

**11. Determination of Juvenility – Comments on –** Under section 15 of the Act, the maximum period prescribed for detaining in a special home or in a fit institution is only 3 years. Therefore, if any person claims juvenility at any stage even after final disposal of the case, the juvenility will be determined on an enquiry and if it is found that he was a juvenile as per section 2(k) & (1) of the Act 2000 at the time committing the offence and if he is undergoing a sentence, section 64 has to be applied and if it is found that he has already undergone the maximum period of 3 years he must be set at liberty; *Latha w/o Kundumani @ Pilchai Kani* v. *Inspector of Police*, 2012 (4) CTC 158 (Mad) (Madurai Bench) (DB).

**12. Different Types of Orders – Comments on –** Under section 15 of the Juvenile Justice Act, it is provided that if the Board is satisfied on inquiry that a juvenile has committed an offence, then the Board may pass different types of orders as mentioned in sub-section (1) of section 15 of the Juvenile Justice Act. One of the orders that is contemplated under the said provisions is to make an order directing the juvenile to be sent to a special home for a period of three years. That appears to be the maximum period for which the juvenile could be kept in a special home; *Ajay Kumar* v. *State of Madhya Pradesh*, 2013 (2) SCC (Cri) 128: 2010 (15) SCC 83 (SC).

**13. Enquiry – Time Period for –** As per section 14 of the Juvenile Justice (Care and Protection of Children) Act, 2000, the Juvenile Board is required to complete the enquiry within four months from the date of its commencement. As per section 15 of the said Act, the maximum sentence that can be awarded is by sending the juvenile to special home for a period of three years besides of course even releasing the juvenile on probation of good conduct; *Chander Mohan @ Bunti* v. *State of Haryana*, 2011 Cr LJ 898: 2011 (161) Punj LR 237: 2011 (5) RCR (Cri) 233 (P&H).

**14. Illegal Detention – Law on –** Section 7A of the Act provides that the juvenility can be raised before any Court at any stage *i.e.*, even after disposal of the case. Section 64 deals with a situation where a juvenile in conflict with law is already undergoing the sentence at the time of commencement of the Act. There is no corresponding Rule under the Tamil Nadu Juvenile Justice (Care and Protection of Children) Rules, 2001 dated 17-1-2012. Under rule 98 of the Juvenile Justice (Care and Protection of Children) Rules, 2007, the State Government or Board either *suo motu* or on an Application made for the purpose, review the case and pass appropriate order under section 64 of the Act. In other words, section 7A empowers any person or a juvenile to raise a claim of juvenility before 'any Court' and at 'any stage', even after final disposal of the case which includes invoking the Writ jurisdiction under article 226 of the Constitution of India by way of filing *Habeas Corpus* Petition. This view is fortified by the word mentioned in section 7A "any Court" which necessarily be a "Court other than the Board". Moreover any contravention of section 15 of the Act, namely, detention beyond three years is to be treated as illegal detention. High Court has ample powers under article 226 of the Constitution of India to exercise implementation of the provisions of The Juvenile Justice (Care and Protection of Children) Act, 2000 and the Rules thereon. It is to be remembered that Writ jurisdiction is exercised also in cases where the remedy otherwise is not efficacious. Efficacy would also include not requiring a different body to pass orders upon decisions already arrived at by High Court. Once High Court has arrived at a decision, it may by itself pass suitable orders rather than require a different body to pass such order; *Latha w/o Kundumani @ Pilchai Kani* v. *Inspector of Police*, 2012 (4) CTC 158 (Mad) (Madurai Bench) (DB).

**15. Inquiry Report – Importance of –** If the inquiry report, which inspires confidence, unquestionably establishes that as on the date of occurrence, the accused was below the age of eighteen years; was thus, a "juvenile" in terms of the Juvenile Justice Act and cannot be denied the benefit of the provisions of the said Act. Therefore, having been found to have committed the offence, for the purpose of sentencing, he has to be dealt with in accordance with the provisions contained in section 15 thereof. As per clause (g) of sub-section (1) of section 15 of the Juvenile Justice Act, the maximum period for which the appellant could be sent to a special home is a period of three years; *Vaneet Kumar Gupta @ Dharminder* v. *State of Punjab*, 2009 (17) SCC 587: 2011 (1) SCC (Cri) 1092: 2011 (8) RCR (Cri) 1315 (SC).

**16. Period of Detention – Law on –** Section 15 of the Act of 2000 provides for various orders which the Juvenile Justice Board may pass against a juvenile when it is satisfied that the juvenile has committed an offence, which includes an order directing the juvenile to be sent to a special home for a period of three years. Section 16 of the Act of 2000 stipulates that where a juvenile who has attained the age of sixteen years has committed an offence and the Board is satisfied that the offence committed is so serious in nature that it would not be in his interest or in the interest of other juvenile in a special home to send him to such special home and that none of the other measures provided under the Act is suitable or sufficient, the Board may order the juvenile in conflict with law to be kept in such place of safety and in such manner as it thinks fit and shall report the case for the order of the State Government. Proviso to sub-section (2) of section 16 of the Act of 2000 provides that the period of detention so ordered shall not exceed in any case the maximum period provided under section 15 of the said Act, *i.e.*, for three years. The Accused has undergone an actual period of sentence of 2 years, 4 months and 4 days and is now aged about thirty five years; *Dharamdir* v. *State (NCT of Delhi)*, AIR 2010 SC 1801: 2010 (4) SCALE 316: 2010 (5) SCC 344.

**17. Question of Sentence – Comments on –** The milder offences and deviant behaviour requiring the minimum correctional approach is adequately addressed by the provisions of section 15 and it is only those cases where diabolic and monstrous acts are committed by a child in conflict with law that hackles of concerns are raised. Apprehensions as to whether a release of a juvenile would be detrimental to him and bring him in association with moral or physical danger would depend upon the facts of each case. But in cases where a juvenile has been accused of aggravated offences which shock the conscience of the society, it would be safer to protect him from collective wrath of a community or a society, on account of retribution such a dastardly act may possibly invite. Factors preceding the commission of an offence, his collaborators and accomplices would be the indices for a person being endangered by evil influence, and likewise the Board and the Court have to imaginatively conceive of succeeding consequences to the offence, to conclude regarding the safety of a juvenile. All these aspects are extremely significant for they would reflect and play upon the mind of the Court, when it considers the question of sentence to be visited upon a juvenile in conflict with law; *Shimil Kumar* v. *State of Haryana*, 2013 (4) RCR (Cri) 16: 2014 (1) Crimes 74 (528) (P&H).

**18. Reception and Rehabilitation – Law on –** The provision dealing with bail places the burden for denying bail on the prosecution. Ordinarily, a juvenile in conflict with law shall be released on bail, but he may not be so released if there appear reasonable grounds for believing that the release is likely to bring him into association with any known criminal or expose him to moral, physical or psychological danger or that his release would defeat the ends of justice. Orders that may be passed by a Juvenile Justice Board against a juvenile, if it is satisfied that he has committed an offence, are mentioned in section 15 of the Act. One of the orders that may be passed is for his reception and rehabilitation in a Special Home for a period of three years, as a measure of last resort; *Jitendra Singh @ Babboo Singh* v. *State of Uttar Pradesh*, 2013 (11) SCC 193: 2013 (9) SCALE 18: 2013 (83) All CriC 651.

**19. Special Home – Law on –** Section 15(g) of the Juvenile Justice Act, 2000 prescribes that where the Juvenile Justice Board is satisfied on inquiry that a juvenile has committed an offence, the Board may if it thinks fit make an order directing the juvenile to be sent to a special home for a period of 3 years and the Board may, for the reasons to be recorded reduce the period of stay to such period depending upon the nature of offence and circumstances of the case as it thinks fit; *Alok @ Jitendra Pani* v. *State of Orissa*, 2011 (2) ILR (Cut) 707 (Ori).

**20. Time Spent in Prison – Law on –** Accused has been in custody for 2 years 6 months and 21 days and has spent this time in prison whereas in view of the provisions of the said Act, he ought not to have spent a single day in prison but could have been directed to be detained in a Special Home or in a Place of Safety in view of the provisions of section 15 and 16 of the said Act. Section 15(1)(g) of the said Act clearly indicates that the Courts exercising these powers may make an order directing the juvenile to be sent to a Special Home for a period of 3 years. The proviso to the provision stipulates that the Court may, if it is satisfied that having regard to the nature of the offence and the circumstances of the case, it is expedient so to do, for reasons to be recorded, reduce the period of stay to such period as it thinks fit; *Mukesh* v. *State of Delhi*, 2012 (1) AD (Del) 737: 2012 (2) Crimes 171 (Del): 2012 (2) RCR (Cri) 102.

**21. Board – Special Powers of –** Section 16 of the Act indicates the orders that may not be passed against a juvenile. Section 16(1) clearly stipulates that notwithstanding anything to the contrary contained in any other law for the time being in force, no juvenile in conflict with law shall be sentenced to death or imprisonment for any term which may extend to imprisonment for life, or committed to prison in default of payment of fine or in default of furnishing security. The proviso to section 16(1) further stipulates that where a juvenile who has attained the age of sixteen years has committed an offence and the Board is satisfied that the offence committed is of so serious in nature or that his conduct and behaviour have been such that it would not be in his interest or in the interest of other juveniles in a special home to send him to such special home and that none of the other measures provided under the Act would be suitable or sufficient, the Board may order the juvenile in conflict with law to be kept in such place of safety and in such manner as it thinks fit and shall report the case for the order of the State Government. The proviso to section 16(2) is also material inasmuch as it clearly mandates that the period of detention so ordered shall not exceed in any case the maximum period provided under section 15 of the said Act; *Anil* v. *State (Govt. of NCT of Delhi)*, 2009 (111) DRJ 102: 2009 (3) Crimes 443 (Del) (DB).

**22. Liberty of Detenu – Law on –** While considering the relief sought for by the accused for setting the detenu at liberty, as he is now aged 34 years and is in jail for more than 11 years, as per section 2(1) of the Act, as he was a "juvenile in conflict with law" at the time of commission of offence, he cannot be sentenced to life and as per section 15 of the Act, at the most, he could be kept in Special Home for three years and following the mandate of law and the decisions rendered by the Apex Court, Courts consider it appropriate that the detenu has to be set at liberty forthwith, as he was "a juvenile in conflict with law" as per section 2(1) of the Act, the date of commission of offence and his age was 17 years, 9 months and 28 days on the date of commission of offence, which has been confirmed by a roving enquiry conducted by the District Judge, who submitted the enquiry report, as quoted above; *Kalai Selvi* v. *State Represented by Inspector of Police*, 2013 (4) Mad LJ (Cri) 101 (Mad) (DB).

**23. Stay in Special Home – Law on –** Section 15(1) (g) of the Act clearly indicates that the Courts exercising these powers may make an order directing the juvenile to be sent to a Special Home for a period of 3 years. The proviso to the provision stipulates that the Court may, if it is satisfied that having regard to the nature of the offence and the circumstances of the case, it is expedient to do so, for reasons to be recorded, reduce the period of stay to such period as it thinks fit; *Mukesh* v. *State of Delhi*, 2012 (1) AD (Del) 737: 2012 (2) Crimes 171: 2012 (2) RCR (Cri) 102 (Del).

**24. Jail Custody Certificate –** produced by the accused suggests that he has undergone the actual period of sentence of more than three years out of the maximum period prescribed under section 15 of the Act. So he is liable to be released; *Babla @ Dinesh* v. *State of Uttarakhand*, 2012 (8) SCALE 447: 2012 (8) SCC 800: 2012 (7) SCR 477.

**16. Order that may not be passed against juvenile.**—(1) Notwithstanding anything to the contrary contained in any other law for the time being in force, no juvenile in conflict with law shall be sentenced to death [1][or imprisonment for any term which may extend to imprisonment for life], or committed to prison in default of payment of fine or in default of furnishing security:

Provided that where a juvenile who has attained the age of sixteen years has committed an offence and the Board is satisfied that the offence committed is so serious in nature or that his conduct and behaviour have been such that it would not be in his interest or in the interest of other juvenile in a special home to send him to such special home and that none of the other measures provided under this Act is suitable or sufficient, the Board may order the juvenile in conflict with law to be kept in such place of safety and in such manner as it thinks fit and shall report the case for the order of the State Government.

(2) On receipt of a report from a Board under sub-section (1), the State Government may make such arrangement in respect of the juvenile as it deems

1. Subs. by Act 33 of 2006, sec. 13, for "or life imprisonment" (w.e.f. 22-8-2006).

proper and may order such juvenile to be kept under protective custody at such place and on such conditions as it thinks fit:

[1][Provided that the period of detention so ordered shall not exceed in any case the maximum period provided under section 15 of this Act.]

**SYNOPSIS**



**COMMENTS**

**1. Provision – Comments on –** Section 16 of the Act provides that no juvenile shall be sentenced to death or life imprisonment, or committed to prison in default of payment of fine or in default of furnishing security. A juvenile, under the provisions of the Act, can be referred to the Juvenile Board for such orders to be passed by the Board as it thinks fit in terms of section 15 of the Act. Section 20 provides for special provision in respect of pending cases. It provides that notwithstanding anything containing in the Act, all proceedings in respect of a juvenile pending in any court in any area on the date on which the Act came into force in that area shall be continued in that court as if the act had not been passed and if the court finds that the juvenile has committed an offence, it shall record such finding and instead of passing any sentence in respect of the juvenile, forward the juvenile to the Board which shall pass orders in respect of that juvenile in accordance with the provisions of the Act as if it had been satisfied on inquiry under this Act that a juvenile has committed the offence. The Act came into force on 1-4-2001; *Upendra Kumar* v. *State of Bihar*, 2005 (3) SCC 592: 2005 (4) PLJR 54 (SC): 2005 SCC (Cri) 778 (SC).

**2. Provision – Stipulation of –** Section 16(1) also stipulates that notwithstanding anything to the contrary contained in any other law for the time being in force, no juvenile in conflict with law shall be sentenced to death or imprisonment for any terms which may extend to imprisonment for life, or committed to prison in default of payment of fine or in default of furnishing security. The proviso to section 16(1) stipulates that where a juvenile who has attained the age of sixteen years has committed an offence and the Board is satisfied that the offence committed is so serious in nature or that his conduct and behaviour have been such that it would not be in his interest or in the interest of other juveniles in a special home to send him to such special home and that none of the other measures provided under this Act is suitable or sufficient, the Board may order the juvenile in conflict with law to be kept in such 'place of safety' and in such manner as it thinks fit and shall report the case for the order of the State Government. Section 16(2) provides that on the receipt of a report from a Board under sub-section (1) of section 16, the State Government may make such arrangement in respect of the juvenile as it

1. Subs. by Act 33 of 2006, sec. 13, for the proviso (w.e.f. 22-8-2006). The proviso, before substitution, stood as under:

   "Provided that the period of detention so ordered shall not exceed the maximum period of imprisonment to which the juvenile could have been sentenced for the offence committed.".

deems proper and may order such juvenile to be kept under protective custody at such place and on such conditions as it thinks fit. The proviso to section 16(2) of the said Act is very material as it stipulates that the period of detention so ordered shall not exceed, in any case, the maximum period provided under section 15 of the said Act; *Surender Khare* v. *State*, 2011 (10) AD (Del) 24: 2012 Cr LJ 1: 2012 (3) RCR (Cri) 456.

**3. State Government – Functions of** – Section 64 which deals with juvenile in conflict with law undergoing sentence at the commencement of the Act *i.e.* 1-4-2001, enjoins that the State Government shall direct such juvenile in lieu of undergoing such sentence be sent to special home or be kept in a fit institution in such manner as it would think fit for the remainder of the period of the sentence and that the provisions of the Act would apply to him/her as if he/she had been ordered by the Board to be sent to such special home or institution or as the case may be ordered to be kept under protective care under section 16(2) of the Act. The *Explanation* to this section clarifies in clear terms that in all cases where a juvenile in conflict with law is undergoing a sentence of imprisonment at any stage on the date of the commencement of the Act, his/her case including the issue of juvenility should be decided in terms of section 2(1) and other provisions of the Act and the Rules made thereunder irrespective of the fact that he/she had ceased to be a juvenile on or before such date and be sent to the special home or a fit institution as the case may be for the remainder of the period of the sentence subject to the maximum term as provided in section 15; *State of Assam (in re:)*, 2012 Cr LJ 471: 2011 (4) Gau LR 235: 2013 (6) RCR( Cri) 2190 (Gau) (DB).

**4. State Government – Duties of** – Section 64 which deals with juvenile in conflict with law undergoing sentence at the commencement of the Act *i.e.* 1-4-2001, enjoins that the State Government shall direct such juvenile in lieu of undergoing such sentence be sent to special home or be kept in a fit institution in such manner as it would think fit for the remainder of the period of the sentence and that the provisions of the Act would apply to him/her as if he/she had been ordered by the Board to be sent to such special home or institution or as the case may be ordered to be kept under protective care under section 16(2) of the Act. The *Explanation* to this section clarifies in clear terms that in all cases where a juvenile in conflict with law is undergoing a sentence of imprisonment at any stage on the date of the commencement of the Act, his/her case including the issue of juvenility should be decided in terms of section 2(1) and other provisions of the Act and the Rules made thereunder irrespective of the fact that he/she had ceased to be a juvenile on or before such date and be sent to the special home or a fit institution as the case may be for the remainder of the period of the sentence subject to the maximum term as provided in section 15; *State of Assam (in re:)*, 2012 Cr LJ 471: 2011 (4) Gau LR 235: 2013 (6) RCR (Cri) 2190 (Gau) (DB).

**5. Bar on Juvenile – Law on** – Under section 16 of the Act of 2000, there is a bar on a juvenile being sentenced to death or life imprisonment. Section 20 of the Act mandates that proceedings in respect of a juvenile pending in the Court on the date on which the Act came into force namely 1st April, 2001 should be continued in a Court as if the Act had not been passed. Further if the Court finds the juvenile has committed an offence, it could record such finding but instead of passing any sentence in respect of same, forward the juvenile to the Board to pass orders in respect of juvenile in accordance with provisions of the Act; *Sayyed Mirazuddin Alis Miraz* v. *State (NCT of Delhi)*, 2006 Cr LJ 2403: 2006 (4) RCR (Cri) 364 (Del) (DB).

**6. Computation of Period of Detention – Law on** – In view of the fact that sentence of imprisonment cannot be passed against juvenile in conflict with law but the period already undergone by him in judicial custody before declaration of his juvenility cannot be ignored while computing the total period of three years. The provisions of the aforesaid Act are part of beneficial legislation. It is incumbent upon the courts before proceeding with the trial or committing the accused in judicial custody in a prison to ensure that the person before court is not a juvenile. During investigation, inquiry or trial the accused may apply to the court for declaring him juvenile. In this process if he is in judicial custody and not allowed to be released on bail, will deemed to be in judicial custody for the purpose of computing a period of three years as provided in sections 15 and 16 of the Act. The provisions of section 428 of Cr.P.C. can be applied in computing the period of detention under section 16 of the Act; *Sunil Kumar* v. *State of Uttar Pradesh*, 2013 (4) ALJ 632: 2013 (8) RCR (Cri) 1330 (All) (Lucknow Bench).

**7. Default in Payment of Fine or in Default of Furnishing Security – Law on –** The 'delinquency' of a Juvenile is to be enquired into by a specially constituted 'Juvenile Justice Board' composed of persons having expertise in child welfare and child psychology. Whatever might be the nature of the offence, whether bailable or non-bailable, bail is the rule and detention in an Observation Home is the exception. No death sentence or life sentence could be awarded to a Juvenile in conflict with law; he cannot be kept in a prison for default in payment of fine or in default of furnishing security; *Jayavel* v. *State*, 2013 (1) LW (Cri) 643: 2013 (2) Mad LJ 889 (Cri): 2013 (8) RCR (Cri) 1812 (Mad) (DB).

**8. Default to Payment of Fine – Law on –** If the accused are to be treated as the 'juvenile in conflict with law' on the date of commission of the alleged offence, even if they are found to have committed an offence but in view of the mandate of section 16 of the Act, imprisonment for any term which may extend to imprisonment for life or committed to prison in default to payment of fine is absolutely illegal and without jurisdiction; *Sajal Barui* v. *State of West Bengal*, 2012 (2) Cal HN 788: 2011 (4) Cal LT 355: 2012 Cr LJ 1763 (Cal) (DB).

**9. Default to Payment of Fine – Comments on –** In view of the mandate of section 16 of the Act, imprisonment for any term which may extend to imprisonment for life or committed to prison in default to payment of fine is absolutely illegal and without jurisdiction; *Sajal Barui* v. *State of West Bengal*, 2012 (2) Cal HN 788: 2011 (4) Cal LT 355: 2012 Cr LJ 1763 (Cal) (DB).

**10. Prison in Default of Payment of Fine – Law on –** It has been provided in section 16 of the Juvenile Justice (Care and Protection of Children) Act, 2000 that notwithstanding anything to the contrary contained in any other law for the time being in force, no juvenile in conflict with law shall be sentenced to death or life imprisonment, or committed to prison in default of payment of fine or in default of furnishing security; *Biswajit Biswas* v. *State of Tripura*, 2012 (3) GLD 574: 2012 Cr LJ 3688: 2013 (7) RCR (Cri) 2731 (Gau) (Agartala Bench).

**11. Detention – Law on –** As per section 16 of the Juvenile Justice Act, 2000, no death sentence or life sentence could be awarded to a 'juvenile in conflict with law'. As per its section 15, at the most, a juvenile in conflict with law can be detained in a Special Home up to three years; *S. Madheswaran* v. *State of Tamil Nadu*, 2012 Cr LJ 4398 (Mad) (DB).

**12. Gravity of Offence – Law on –** It is significant to note that gravity of offence or its seriousness alone, divorced from above exceptional reasons, and has not been taken as a rider by the Legislature to deny bail to a juvenile in conflict with law. It is only danger to his moral, physical and psychological qualities and likely hood of his attaching himself with criminals or his release defeating ends of justice that Board or the courts may not exercise discretion in his favour and enlarge him on bail. For such a determination no hard and fast rule of inflexible nature can be laid down as it depends on facts and circumstances peculiar to each case; *Kushagra Mokhriwale* v. *State of Uttar Pradesh*, 2012 (1) Crimes 69 (All): 2012 Cr LJ 164: 2011 (7) ADJ 363.

**13. Juvenile – Relief for –** The new Juvenile Justice Act, 2000, contains many benevolent provisions for the benefit of the Juveniles, who becomes a 'Juveniles in conflict with law', since he is alleged to have exhibited a 'deviant behaviour' and committed a 'delinquent act'. A Juvenile in conflict with law cannot be charged. He shall not be mixed with adult accused persons. He shall be kept in a Government observation Home.

The children are National Wealth and are hopes of future of this Nation. The idea of the Juvenile law is not to punish them, but to reform and rehabilitate them and bring them back to the main stream of life; *Master Jithu* v. *State of Tamil Nadu,* 2013 (4) Mad LJ (Cri) 311 (Mad).

**14. Mis-Carriage of Justice – Law on –** Apex Court dealt with the issue of the liberal approach adopted by the court to grant an unwarranted acquittal, and held that while dealing with a criminal case, it is a matter of paramount importance for any court to ensure that the mis-carriage of justice be avoided in all circumstances; *Ramesh Harijan* v. *State of Uttar Pradesh,* 2012 AIR SC 1979; *See* also: *Sucha Singh* v. *State of Punjab,* AIR 2003 SC 3617 and *S. Ganesan* v. *Rama Raghuraman,* (2011) 2 SCC 83.

**15. Sentence – Law on –** Proviso to sub-section (1) and sub-section (2) of section 16 of the Act are important. Section 16 of the said Act provides that notwithstanding anything to the contrary contained in any other law for the time being in force, no Juvenile in conflict with law shall be sentenced to death or imprisonment for any term which may extend to imprisonment for life, or committed to prison in default of payment of fine or in default of furnishing security; *High Court on its Own Motion* v. *State of Maharashtra,* 2013 (3) AIR BomR 119: 2013 (8) RCR (Cri) 892 (Bom) (DB).

**16. Sentence Passed by Court – Law on –** As per provisions of sections 15 and 16 of the Act of 2000, a juvenile can be sent to a special home for a period of three years. As per section 7A(2) of the Act of 2000, the sentence passed by a Court shall be deemed to have no effect with regard to a juvenile. Thus, normally when a convict is held to be a juvenile, the case has to be remitted to the Juvenile Justice Board (JJB) for an inquiry whether the juvenile has committed any offence and for passing appropriate orders; *Chand Babu* v. *State (Govt. of NCT of Delhi),* 2013 (4) AD 125 (Del).

**17. Set Off – Law on –** In view of section 16 of the Act juvenile is conflict with law cannot be sentenced to death or imprisonment for any term or committed to prison in default of payment of fine or in default of furnishing the security. Proviso to sub-section 2 of section 16 of the Act clearly provides that period of detention so ordered shall not exceed the maximum period provides under section 15 of the Act. Clause (e), (f), and (g) of sub-section (1) of section 15 and sub-section (3) of section 15 provide that in any case the period of supervision or detention in some protective home or any other place cannot in any case exceed more than three years. Section 428 of the Criminal Procedure Code provides that period of detention undergone by the accused to be set off against the sentence of imprisonment; *Sunil Kumar* v. *State of Uttar Pradesh,* 2013 (4) ALJ 632: 2013 (8) RCR (Cri) 1330 (All) (Lucknow Bench).

**18. Board – Role of –** Section 16(1) of the Act, 2000 provides that notwithstanding anything to the contrary contained in any other law for the time being in force, no juvenile in conflict with law shall be sentenced to death or imprisonment for any term which may extend to imprisonment for life, or committed to prison in default of payment of fine or in default of furnishing security. According to the proviso, where a juvenile who has attained the age of sixteen years has committed an offence and the Board is satisfied that the offence committed is so serious in nature or that his conduct and behavior have been such that it would not be in his interest or in the interest of other juvenile in a special home to send him to such special home and that none of the other measures provided under this Act is suitable or sufficient, the Board may order the juvenile in conflict with law to be kept in such place of safety and in such manner as it thinks fit and shall report the case for the order of the State Government. Sub-section (2) of section 16 further provides that on receipt of a report from a Board under sub-section (1), the State Government may make such arrangement in respect of the juvenile as it deems proper and may order such juvenile to be kept under protective custody at such place and on such conditions as it thinks fit; *Santosh Kumar Vishvakarma* v. *State of Chhattisgarh,* 2013 (5) MPHT 37 (Chh): 2014 (1) Cg LJ 193 (Chh) (DB).

**17. Proceeding under Chapter VIII of the Code of Criminal Procedure not competent against juvenile.**—Notwithstanding anything to the contrary contained in the Code of Criminal Procedure, 1973 (2 of 1974) no proceeding shall be instituted and no order shall be passed against the juvenile under Chapter VIII of the said Code.

**SYNOPSIS**

1. Arresting Authority – Duties of
2. Arrest – Comments on
3. Different Scheme for Trial – Law on
4. Joint Trial of Juvenile – Law on
5. Security Bond – Law on

**COMMENTS**

**1. Arresting Authority – Duties of** – When any person is arrested, it is obligatory for the arresting authority to ensure that he is got examined by a medical officer in the service of the Central or the State Government or by a registered medical practitioner. The medical officer or registered medical practitioner is mandated to prepare a record of such examination including any injury or mark of violence on the person arrested; *Jitendra Singh @ Babboo Singh* v. *State of Uttar Pradesh,* 2013 (11) SCC 193: JT 2013 (11) SC 152: 2013 (9) SCALE 18.

**2. Arrest – Comments on** – Provisions of the Criminal Procedure Code relating to arrest and the provisions of the Juvenile Justice (Care and Protection of Children) Act, 2000 being the law of the land, should be scrupulously followed by the concerned authorities in respect of juveniles in conflict with law; *Jitendra Singh @ Babboo Singh* v. *State of Uttar Pradesh,* 2013 (11) SCC 193: JT 2013 (11) SC 152: 2013 (9) SCALE 18.

**3. Different Scheme for Trial – Law on** – If the provisions of the Act clearly indicate the legislative intent in the light of the country's international commitments and the same is in conformity with the constitutional requirements, it is not necessary for the Court to understand the legislation in any other manner. If the Legislature has adopted the age of 18 as the dividing line between juveniles and adults and such a decision is constitutionally permissible the enquiry by the Courts must come to an end. Even otherwise there is a considerable body of world opinion that all under 18 of age ought to be treated as juveniles and separate treatment ought to be meted out to them so far as offences committed by such persons are concerned. The avowed object is to ensure their rehabilitation in society and to enable the young offenders to become useful members of the society in later years. India has accepted the above position and legislative wisdom has led to the enactment of the JJ Act in its present form. If the Act has treated all less than 18 as a separate category for the purposes of differential treatment so far as the commission of offences is concerned, The Act does not do away or obliterate the enforcement of the law insofar as juvenile offenders are concerned. The same penal law *i.e.* Indian Penal Code apply to all juveniles. The only difference is that a different scheme for trial and punishment is introduced by the Act in place of the regular provisions under the Code of Criminal Procedure for trial of offenders and the punishments under the Indian Penal Code; *Subramanian Swamy* v. *Raju,* JT 2014 (4) SC 328: 2014 (4) SCALE 305: AIR 2014 SC 1649- *Nirbhaya* case [Hon'ble Judges: P. Sathasivam, Ranjan Gogoi, Shiva Kirti Singh].

**4. Joint Trial of Juvenile – Law on** – Section 17 says that no proceeding can be instituted and no order shall be passed against a juvenile under Chapter VIII of the Criminal Procedure Code. Section 18 forbids a joint trial of a juvenile and a person who is not a juvenile. Section 19 makes it clear that a juvenile who has committed an offence and has been dealt with under the provisions of the Juvenile Act shall not suffer disqualification, if any, attached to a conviction of an offence. Sub-section (2) of section 19 goes a step further. It states that in case of conviction, the Board shall make an order directing that the records of such conviction shall be removed after the expiry of the period of appeal or a reasonable period as prescribed under the rules, as the case may be; *Kalu @ Amit* v. *State of Haryana,* AIR 2012 SC 3212: 2012 (7) SCALE 404: 2012 (8) SCC 34.

**5. Security Bond – Law on –** No security bond for keeping good behaviour and peace shall be obtained from him. At the most, he can be detained in a Special Home up to three years. In no case he shall be jailed along adult accused. Instead of awarding him punishment various kinds of rehabilitative measures also have been prescribed in the Act. Conviction under J.J. Act is not a disqualification. Details of juvenile shall not be published in any media. Injuring a juvenile is punishable. J.J. Act is a child oriented, child-friendly and a piece of Welfare Legislation containing various beneficial measures for the rehabilitation of young persons having deviant behaviour and it completely prohibits awarding them death sentence, life sentence and detention beyond 3 years; *Jayavel* v. *State,* 2013 (1) LW 643 (Cri): 2013 (2) Mad LJ 889 (Cri): 2013 (8) RCR (Cri) 1812 (Mad) (DB).

**18. No joint proceeding of juvenile and person not a juvenile.**—(1) Notwithstanding anything contained in section 223 of the Code of Criminal Procedure, 1973 (2 of 1974) or in any other law for the time being in force, no juvenile shall be charged with or tried for any offence together with a person who is not a juvenile.

(2) If a juvenile is accused of an offence for which under section 223 of the Code of Criminal Procedure, 1973 (2 of 1974) or any other law for the time being in force, such juvenile and any person who is not a juvenile would, but for the prohibition contained in sub-section (1), have been charged and tried together, the Board taking cognizance of that offence shall direct separate trials of the juvenile and the other person.

**SYNOPSIS**

1. Human Right Violation – Comments on
2. Prejudice Caused to Accused – Law on
3. Rehabilitative Process – Law on
4. Courts – Role of
5. Trial before Regular Court – Law on
6. Vitiated Trial – Law on

**COMMENTS**

**1. Human Right Violation – Comments on –** Keeping a Juvenile in conflict with law along with adult accused person is a very serious matter. In fact, the Sessions Judges and the Chief Judicial Magistrates, have the power to make surprise visit to the jails and verify whether any Juvenile in conflict with law is kept along with adult accused persons and if a Juvenile is there, immediately they have to take action as per law because it is a human right violation; *Master Jithu* v. *State of Tamil Nadu,* 2013 (4) Mad LJ (Cri) 311 (Mad).

**2. Prejudice Caused to Accused – Law on –** Failure of justice is an extremely pliable or facile expression, which can be made to fit into any situation in any case. The court must endeavour to find the truth. There would be "failure of justice"; not only by unjust conviction, but also by acquittal of the guilty, as a result of unjust failure to produce requisite evidence. Of course, the rights of the accused have to be kept in mind and also safeguarded, but they should not be over emphasised to the extent of forgetting that the victims also have rights. It has to be shown that the accused has suffered some disability or detriment in respect of the protections available to him under the Indian criminal jurisprudence. "Prejudice" is incapable of being interpreted in its generic sense and applied to criminal jurisprudence. The plea of prejudice has to be in relation to investigation or trial, and not with respect to matters falling outside their scope. Once the accused is able to show that there has been serious prejudice caused to him, with respect to either of these aspects, and that the same has defeated the rights available to him under criminal jurisprudence, then the accused can seek benefit under the orders of the court; *Darbara Singh* v. *State of Punjab,* AIR 2013 SC 840; *See* also, *Shivaji Sahebrao*

*Bobade* v. *State of Maharashtra,* AIR 1973 SC 2622; *Rafiq Ahmed @ Rafi* v. *State of Uttar Pradesh,* AIR 2011 SC 3114; *Rattiram* v. *State of Madhya Pradesh,* AIR 2012 SC 1485 and *Bhimanna* v. *State of Karnataka,* AIR 2012 SC 3026.

**3. Rehabilitative Process – Law on –** There can be no denial of the fact that lodging juveniles along with hardened adult criminals can have drastic implications on the physical and mental well being of a juvenile offender. Trying minor in adult courts and sentencing them in adult prison is totally against the object and purpose of the JJ Act. Even for hardened career criminals, jail can be a dangerous place, but for youth it can be especially dangerous as they are often vulnerable to prison victimization because of their size and age. It cannot be overlooked that youth offenders often have psychological or social issues that need to be addressed as part of the rehabilitative process. Adult facilities/prison often lack the staff to address the needs of young incarcerated persons. In effect, what will happen is that if the youth is sent to an adult prison, then it is more likely for him to re-offend and escalate into violent behaviour than their peers who go to juvenile system, where rehabilitative services are far more extensive. Juveniles confined within an adult prison may not have social services they need but with constant access to criminal minds, there are more chances of them becoming a recidivist; *Court on its Own Motion* v. *Deptt. of Women and Child Development,* 2012 (4) AD 641 (Del): 2013 (3) RCR (Cri) 382 (Del) (DB).

**4. Courts – Role of –** Section 7A(2) speaks that if the court finds a person to be a juvenile on the date of commission of the offence under sub-section (1), it shall forward the juvenile to the Board for passing appropriate order, and the sentence, if any, passed by a Court shall be deemed to have no effect, meaning thereby in order to commence the proceeding of a juvenile case after declaration of juvenility, it shall be sent to the Board of Juvenile Justice for appropriate order. This term does not confine only to pass a final order by the Juvenile Justice Board; it having the extensive scope permits the proceeding of the case also from that very stage to be proceeded by the special court; *Indra Pal* v. *State of Uttar Pradesh,* 2011 (2) ALJ 707: 2011 (8) RCR (Cri) 2078: 2011 (3) ADJ 751.

**5. Trial before Regular Court – Law on –** A child, juvenile and a young person, who commits a crime, should not be treated on par with adult offenders. The mental frame of a juvenile, who commits a 'delinquent act', is different from the mental element of an adult accused. So, necessarily they have to be treated differently. As per section 2(l) of the New J.J. Act, 2000, a Juvenile when commits a crime becomes a 'Juvenile in conflict with law'. A Juvenile with a 'deviant behaviour', namely, a delinquent Juvenile, under the New J.J. Act, 2000 is a 'juvenile in conflict with law'. Whatever might be the nature of the offence committed by a Juvenile, he cannot be tried before a regular Court. He cannot be tried along with adult accused; *Jayavel* v. *State,* 2013 (1) LW (Cri) 643: 2013 (2) Mad LJ (Cri) 889: 2013 (8) RCR (Cri) 1812 (Mad) (DB).

**6. Vitiated Trial – Law on –** If the accused was a 'juvenile in conflict with law' on the date of the alleged occurrence and as such he being tried along with the persons who are not juvenile and are adult, so far as the trial of the accused is concerned, the same is vitiated; *Sk Ismail* v. *State of West Bengal,* 2012 (3) Cal HN 72 (Cal) (DB).

**19. Removal of disqualification attaching to conviction.**—(1) Notwithstanding anything contained in any other law, a juvenile who has committed an offence and has been dealt with under the provisions of this Act shall not suffer disqualification, if any, attaching to a conviction of an offence under such law.

(2) The Board shall make an order directing that the relevant records of such conviction shall be removed after the expiry of the period of appeal or a reasonable period as prescribed under the rules, as the case may be.

**SYNOPSIS**

1. Provision – Comments on
2. Disqualification – Comments on
3. Removal of Disqualification – Law on

**COMMENTS**

**1. Provision – Comments on** – Section 15 deals with the orders that may be passed regarding juvenile. Section 16 deals with the orders that may not be passed against the juvenile. Section 18 envisages that notwithstanding anything contained in section 223 of the Code of Criminal Procedure, 1973 or in any other law for the time being in force, no juvenile shall be charged with or tried for any offence together with a person who is not a juvenile. Section 19 of the 2000 Act envisages that notwithstanding anything contained in any other law, a juvenile who has committed an offence and has been dealt with under the provisions of this Act shall not suffer disqualification, if any, attaching to a conviction of an offence under such law; *Chagalamarri Subbaiah* v. *State rep. by its Public Prosecutor*, 2010 Cr LJ 655: 2009 (2) ALD (Cri) 121: 2009 (3) ALT (Cri) 36.

**2. Disqualification – Comments on** – By virtue of the provisions of section 19(1) of the said Act, notwithstanding anything contained in any other law, a juvenile who has committed an offence and has been dealt with under the provisions of the Act shall not suffer disqualification, if any, attaching to a conviction of an offence under such law; *Government of NCT of Delhi* v. *Sumit Kumar*, 2012 (190) DLT 551 (Del) (DB).

**3. Removal of Disqualification – Law on** – Section 19 of the Act, 2000 provides for removal of disqualification attaching to conviction. It provides that notwithstanding anything contained in any other law, a juvenile, who has committed an offence and has been dealt with under the provisions of this Act, shall not suffer disqualification, if any, attaching to a conviction of an offence under such law; *Santosh Kumar Vishvakarma* v. *State of Chhattisgarh*, 2013 (5) MPHT 37 (Chh): 2014 (1) Cg LJ 193 (Chh) (DB).

**20. Special provision in respect of pending cases.**—Notwithstanding anything contained in this Act, all proceedings in respect of a juvenile pending in any court in any area on the date on which this Act comes into force in that area, shall be continued in that court as if this Act had not been passed and if the court finds that the juvenile has committed an offence, it shall record such finding and instead of passing any sentence in respect of the juvenile, forward the juvenile to the Board which shall pass orders in respect of that juvenile in accordance with the provisions of this Act as if it had been satisfied on inquiry under this Act that a juvenile has committed the offence:

[1][Provided that the Board may, for any adequate and special reason to be mentioned in the order, review the case and pass appropriate order in the interest of such juvenile.

*Explanation.*—In all pending cases including trial, revision, appeal or any other criminal proceedings in respect of a juvenile in conflict with law, in any court, the determination of juvenility of such a juvenile shall be in terms of clause (l) of section 2, even if the juvenile ceases to be so on or before the date of commencement of this Act and the provisions of this Act shall apply as if the said provisions had been in force, for all purposes and at all material times when the alleged offence was committed.]

**SYNOPSIS**

1. Provision – Attraction of
2. Provision – Purpose of
3. Provision – View on
4. Provision – Comments on

1. Ins. by Act 33 of 2006, sec. 14 (w.e.f. 22-8-2006).

## COMMENTS

**1. Provision – Attraction of –** Section 20 of the 2000 Act would apply only to cases in which the accused was below 18 years of age on April 1, 2001, the date on which the 2000 Act came into force but it would have no application in case the accused had crossed the age of 18 years on the date of coming into force of the 2000 Act; *Daya Nand* v. *State of Haryana,* 2011 Cr LJ 1157: 2011 (1) SCALE 143: 2011 (2) SCC 224.

**2. Provision – Purpose of –** Section 20 of the 2000 Act deals with the special provision in respect of pending cases and begins with a *non obstante* clause. The sentence "notwithstanding anything contained in this Act, all proceedings in respect of a juvenile pending in any court in any area on the date on which this Act came into force" has great significance. The proceedings in respect of a juvenile pending in any court referred to in section 20 of the Act are relatable to proceedings initiated before the 2000 Act came into force and which are pending when the 2000 Act came into force. The term "any court" would include even ordinary criminal courts. If the person was a "juvenile" under the 1986 Act the proceedings would not be pending in criminal courts. They would be pending in criminal courts only if the boy had crossed 16 years or the girl had crossed 18 years. This shows that section 20 refer to cases where a person had ceased to be a juvenile under the 1986 Act but had not yet crossed the age of 18 years then the pending case shall continue in that court as if the 2000 Act has not been passed and if the court finds that the juvenile has committed an offence it shall record such finding and instead of passing any sentence in respect of the juvenile shall forward the juvenile to the Board which shall pass orders in respect of that juvenile. Such an interpretation does not offend article 20(1) of the Constitution and the juvenile is not subjected to any penalty greater than that which might have been inflicted on him under the 1986 Act; *Gaurav Pradip Verma* v. *State of Gujarat,* 2008 Cr LJ 4009: 2008 (1) GLH 724: 2008 (19) GHJ 496.

**3. Provision – View on –** Section 20, make it obligatory for the Court concerned to proceed with the matter and record its conclusion as to the guilt or otherwise of the juvenile. The prohibition is against the Court passing an order of sentence against the juvenile, for which purpose the juvenile has to be forwarded to the Board for appropriate orders. That is precisely the view which Apex Court has taken in a line of decisions; *Jitendra Singh @ Babboo Singh* v. *State of Uttar Pradesh,* 2013 (11) SCC 193: JT 2013 (11) SC 152: 2013 (9) SCALE 18.

**4. Provision – Comments on –** The effect is that once a person is found to be a juvenile in conflict with law as defined by section 12(1) of the Juvenile Justice Act, 2000, then irrespective of his age at the time when this matter is considered in any pending proceeding when the Act came into force, he would continue to be treated as juvenile in conflict with law and be entitled to the benefits in relation thereto. Section 20 enables the court to consider and determine the juvenility of a person even after conviction by the regular court and also empowers the court, while maintaining the conviction, to set aside the sentence imposed and forward the case to the Juvenile Justice Board concerned for passing sentence in accordance with the provisions of the Juvenile Justice Act, 2000; *Sudhakar Dwivedi* v. *State of Uttar Pradesh,* 2012 (6) ADJ 649: 2012 (2) ACrR 2250 (All).

**5. Provision – Requirements of –** Section 20 of the Juvenile Justice (Care and Protection of Children) Act, 2000 requires that if the court has upheld the judgment of conviction, which was passed in respect of the juvenile then it could not pass any order of sentence. The said Act requires that in such a case the whole records of the case shall be transmitted to the concerned Juvenile Justice Board for passing appropriate order of sentence upon such convicted juvenile in the light of sections 15 and 16 of the said Act; *Daya Ram* v. *State of Uttar Pradesh,* 2014 (1) ALJ 173: 2013 (82) ACC 869 (All) (DB).

**6. Provision in Respect of Pending Cases – Law on –** Section 20 deals with the special provision in respect of pending cases and begins with *non-obstante* clause. The sentence "notwithstanding anything contained in this Act, all proceedings in respect of a juvenile pending in any Court in any area on date of which this Act came into force" has great significance. The proceedings in respect of a juvenile pending in any court referred to in section 20 of the Act is relatable to proceedings initiated before the 2000 Act came into force and which are pending when the 2000 Act came into force. The term "any court" would include even ordinary criminal courts. If the person was a "juvenile" under the 1986 Act the proceedings would not be pending in criminal courts. They would be pending in criminal courts only if the boy had crossed 16 years or girl had crossed 18 years. This shows that section 20 refers to cases where a person had ceased to be a juvenile under the 1986 Act but had not yet crossed the age of 18 years then the pending case shall continue in that Court as if the 2000 Act has not been passed and if the Court finds that the juvenile has committed an offence, it shall record such finding and instead of passing any sentence in respect of the juvenile, shall forward the juvenile to the Board which shall pass orders in respect of that juvenile; *Pratap Singh* v. *State of Jharkhand,* AIR 2005 SC 2731: 2005 (1) SCALE 763: 2005 (3) SCC 551.

**7. Determination of Juvenility – Law on –** A juvenile who had not completed eighteen years on the date of commission of the offence was also entitled to the benefits of the Juvenile Justice Act, 2000, as if the provisions of section 2(k) had always been in existence even during the operation of the 1986 Act. Even the said position was re-emphasised by virtue of the amendments introduced in section 20 of the 2000 Act, whereby the Proviso and *Explanation* were added to section 20, which made it even more explicit that in all pending cases, including trial, revision, appeal and any other criminal proceedings in respect of a juvenile in conflict with law, the determination of juvenility of such a juvenile would be in terms of clause (l) of section 2 of the 2000 Act, and the provisions of the Act would apply as if the said provisions had been in force when the alleged offence was committed; *Ravindra Singh Bisht @ Dheerendra Singh* v. *State,* 2011 Cr LJ 21: 2011 (74) ACC 432 (Uttra).

**8. Past Juvenility – Law on –** So, the New J.J. Act, 2000 covers cases under the Old J.J. Act, 1986 even subsequent to the date of the offence when the juvenile in conflict with law had crossed 18 years of his age. If a Juvenile, who has committed an offence, when he was below 18 years of his age, even after disposal of his case, even after crossing his 18 years of age, as per section 7A and *Explanation* to section 20, can claim juvenility at any stage of the case, trial, revision, appeal or in any other criminal proceedings. So, even if the case is over in the Trial Court or in the next Appellate Court or Revisional Court or even in the Honourable Supreme Court, subsequently in an independent proceedings, for the first time, the ex-juvenile in conflict with law can claim benefit under the New J.J. Act, 2000 based on his past juvenility on the date of his commission of the offence; *Jayavel* v. *State,* 2013 (1) LW (Cri) 643: 2013 (2) Mad LJ (Cri) 889: 2013 (8) RCR (Cri) 1812 (Mad) (DB).

**9. Pending Cases – Comments on –** By virtue of *Explanation* added to section 20 of the Amended Act 2006, it may be made clear that in all pending cases the determination of juvenile has to be in terms of clause (l) of section 2 even if the juvenile ceases to be a juvenile on or before the date on which the Act 2000 came into force *i.e.* 1-4-2001; *Bijendra Kumar* v. *State of Uttar Pradesh,* 2013 (3) DMC 389: 2013 (3) ADJ 619: 2013 (2) ACrR 1616 (All).

**10. Punishment – Law on –** As per section 20 *Explanations,* the date of the offence though important, the definition in clause (1) and section (2) is important. In view of the amended provision juvenile means the person who is below the age of 18 years or who has not completed the age of 18 years on the date of commission of offence. If the Act is made retrospective and the age of the applicant is considered below 17 years and therefore, no punishment can be imposed on the applicant; *Basavraj Sangramappa Thonte* v. *State of Maharashtra,* 2009 Cr LJ 1360: 2010 (2) BCR (Cri) 183: 2009 (2) AIR BomR 265.

**11. Restriction – Comments on –** Section 18 of the Act, 2000 begins with the *non-obstante* clause with regard to section 223 of Code of Criminal Procedure, 1973, while section 20 begins with *non-obstante* clause with regard to anything contained in this Act. Section 18 provides that no juvenile shall be charged with or tried for any offence together with a person who is not a juvenile. Whereas provisions of section 20 are special provisions in respect of pending cases which clearly mandates that all proceedings in respect of juvenile pending in any court in any area on the date of which this Act comes into force in that area, shall be continued in that court as if this Act had not been passed. The only restriction is that if the court finds that the juvenile has committed an offence, it shall not pass any sentence but shall forward the case to the Juvenile Board which shall pass the orders in accordance with the provisions of this Act; *Zafar Iqbal* v. *State of Uttar Pradesh,* 2012 (10) ADJ 259: 2013 (1) ACrR 501 (All).

**12. Revisional Court – Functions of –** Moreover law is well settled that revisional Court is not required to re-appreciate and reappraise the evidence as a Court of appeal and come to a different finding as recorded by trial Court on the basis of the same evidence. High Court in revision can interfere only if any illegality or material irregularity has been committed by trial Court in passing in the impugned order. Hence, in view of this legal preposition, High Court is to see as to whether any illegality or material irregularity has been committed by trial Court in passing the impugned order; *Rajbir* v. *State of Haryana,* 2011 (3) RCR (Cri) 222 (P&H).

**13. Trial Court – Powers of –** Trial Court shall be free to summon the concerned School, Panchayat or the Electoral office record or any other record from any other source which it considers necessary for a proper determination of the age. Trial Court shall be free to constitute a Medical Board comprising at least three experts on the subject for determination of the age, based on medical tests and examination; *Jitendra Singh @ Babboo Singh* v. *State of Uttar Pradesh,* 2011 Cr LJ 1004: 2010 (12) SCALE 171: 2010 (13) SCC 523.

**14. Benefit of Act – Comments on –** Accused would get the benefit of the JJ Act since he did not complete 18 years on the date of the commission of the offence. The effect of the insertion of the *Explanation* to section 20 is that as long as the accused was a juvenile on the date of the offence he will get the benefit of the JJ Act, even during the pendency of his appeal, notwithstanding that may have ceased to be a juvenile as on the date of the coming into force of the JJ Act; *Imran* v. *State,* 2009 (3) Crimes 549 (Del).

**15. Conviction – Law on –** Section 20 also enables the Court to consider and determine the juvenility of a person even after conviction by the regular Court and also empowers the Court, while maintaining the conviction to set aside the sentence imposed and forward the case to the J.J. Board concerned for passing sentence in accordance with the provisions of the 2000 Act; *Santosh Kumar Vishvakarma* v. *State of Chhattisgarh,* 2013 (5) MPHT 37 (Chh): 2014 (1) CgLJ 193 (Chh) (DB).

**16. Court – Duties of** – Section 20 enables the Court to consider and determine the juvenility of a person even after conviction by the regular court and also empowers the court, while maintaining the conviction, to set aside the sentence imposed and forward the case to the Board concerned for passing sentence in accordance with the provision of the Act. Provision of section 7A also makes it clear that the claim of juvenility can be raised before any court at any stage, even after final disposal of the case and sets out the procedure which the court is required to adopt, when such claim of juvenility is raised; *Brijesh Awasthi* v. *State of Uttar Pradesh,* 2013 (1) ADJ 292: 2013 (1) ACrR 779 (All).

**17. Court – Role of** – More importantly section 20 obliges the Court concerned to record a finding whether the juvenile has committed any offence. If the Court finds the juvenile guilty, it is required to forward the juvenile to the Board which would then pass an order in accordance with the provisions of the Act as if it had been satisfied on enquiry under the Act that the juvenile had committed an offence; *Bharat Bhushan* v. *State of Himachal Pradesh,* 2013 (11) SCC 274: AIR 2013 SC 2018: 2013 Cr LJ 2932.

**18. Determination of Juvenility – Law on** – Section 20 in clear terms makes the provisions of the Act applicable to the cases pending on the date of its commencement. The *Explanation* incorporated in this section ordains that in all pending cases including trial, revision, appeal or any other criminal proceedings in respect of a juvenile in conflict with law in any court, the determination of juvenility has to be in terms of section 2(1), even if a juvenile has ceased to be so on or before the date of commencement of the Act and the provisions thereof would apply as if it had been in force for all purposes at all material times when the alleged offence had been committed; *State of Assam (in re:),* 2012 Cr LJ 471: 2011 (4) Gau LR 235: 2013 (6) RCR (Cri) 2190 (Gau) (DB).

**19. Determination of Juvenility – View on** – Section 7 (A) contemplates that a claim of juvenility can be raised before any court and has to be considered at any stage even after disposal of the case. The claim so raised is required to be determined in accordance with the provisions of the Act 2000 and the rules framed thereunder. The necessary implication of the amended Act is that it is immaterial that the juvenile has ceased to be so on or before on 1-4-2001, which is date of commencement of the Act 2000. From a punctilious reading of the language of the *Explanation* to section 20, it is obvious that in all pending cases which would include not only trials but even subsequent proceedings for determination of juvenility of a juvenile has to be in terms of clause (l) to section 2 even if the juvenile ceases to be a juvenile on or before 1-4-2001. Thus, from a conjoint reading of sections 2(l), 7(A) and 20 read with rule 12 of Rules 2007, it is manifest that a person, who was below 18 years on the date of commission of the offence even prior to 1-4-2001 would be entitled to get the benefits accruing from the amended Act 2000 as juvenile. It is meaningless that the claim of juvenility is raised after attaining the age of 18 years on or before the date when the Act came into force; *Bijendra Kumar* v. *State of Uttar Pradesh,* 2013 (3) DMC 389: 2013 (3) ADJ 619: 2013 (2) ACrR 1616 (All).

**20. Evidence – Law on** – The entire evidence should be recorded in accordance with section 326 Cr.P.C. read with section 20 of the Juvenile Justice Act; *Union of India* v. *Ram Kumar Mehta,* 2013 (83) ACC 872 (All) (Lucknow Bench).

**21. Explanation – Inference from** – Section 20 in clear terms makes the provisions of the Act applicable to the cases pending on the date of its commencement. The *Explanation* incorporated in this section ordains that in all pending cases including trial, revision, appeal or any other criminal proceedings in respect of a juvenile in conflict with law in any court, the determination of juvenility has to be in terms of section 2(1), even if a juvenile has ceased to be so on or before the date of commencement of the Act and the provisions thereof would apply as if it had been in force for all purposes at all material times when the alleged offence had been committed; *In State of Assam (in re:),* 2012 Cr LJ 471: 2011 (4) Gau LR 235: 2013 (6) RCR (Cri) 2190 (Gau) (DB).

**22. Finding of Guilt in Respect of Juvenile – Law on –** If a juvenile has committed an offence and if the court finds him having done so then the court may record a finding of guilt in respect of the juvenile, but will refrain from passing a sentence upon the juvenile in the light of the provision and, in turn, shall forward the juvenile to the Board which shall be passing orders in respect of that juvenile in accordance with the provisions of the act. Orders which could be passed by the Board may be covered by section 15 and 16 of the Act. 'Board' means as per definition of the term in section 2(c) the Juvenile Justice Board constituted under section 4; *Jhaman Yadav* v. *State of Bihar,* 2010 Cr LJ 3000: 2010 (58) BLJR 449: 2010 (2) PLJR 507 (Pat) (DB).

**23. High Court – Role of –** Section 20 ordains High Court to scrutinize the order of conviction and if it finds the same correctly passed then it prohibits the court to uphold and affirm the order of sentence rather it makes it imperative for the court to set aside the order of sentence and to direct the Juvenile Justice Board to proceed under section 15 read with section 16 of the Act; *Iqbal Ahmad* v. *State,* 2013 (3) ACrR 2514: 2013 (82) ACC 587 (All) (DB).

**24. Judgment of Conviction – Comments on –** Section 20 of the Act of 2000 takes care of such a situation stating that despite the same the trial shall continue in that court as if that act has not been passed and in the event, he is found to be guilty of commission of an offence, a finding to that effect shall be recorded in the judgment of conviction, if any, but instead of passing any sentence in relation to the juvenile, he would be forwarded to the board which shall pass orders in accordance with the provisions of the Act as if he has been satisfied on inquiry that a juvenile has committed the offence. A legal fiction has, thus, been created in the said provision. A legal fiction as is well-known must be given its full effect although it has its limitations. Section 20 of the Act of 2000 would, therefore, be applicable when a person is below the age of 18 years as on 1-4-2001. For the purpose of attracting section 20 of the Act, it must be established that: (i) on the date of coming into force the proceedings in which the petitioner was accused was pending; and (ii) on that day he was below the age of 18 years. For the purpose of the said Act, both the aforementioned conditions are required to be fulfilled. By reason of the provisions of the said Act of 2000, the protection granted to a juvenile has only been extended but such extension is not absolute but only a limited one. It would apply strictly when the conditions precedent therefor as contained in section 20 or section 64 are fulfilled. The said provisions repeatedly refer to the words 'juvenile' or 'delinquent juveniles' specifically. This appears to be the object of the Act and for ascertaining the true intent of the Parliament, the rule of purposive construction must be adopted. The purpose of the Act would stand defeated if a child continues to be in the company of an adult. Thus, the Act of 2000 intends to give the protection only to a juvenile within the meaning of the said Act and not an adult. In other words, although it would apply to a person who is still a juvenile having not attained the age of 18 years but shall not apply to a person who has already attained the age of 18 years on the date of coming into force thereof or who had not attained the age of 18 years on the date of commission of the offence but has since ceased to be a juvenile; *Pratap Singh* v. *State of Jharkhand,* AIR 2005 SC 2731: 2005 (1) SCALE 763: 2005 (3) SCC 551; *Vide* also, *Bhavnagar University* v. *Palitana Sugar Mill (P) Ltd.,* (2003) 2 SCC 111; *I.T.W. Signode India Ltd.* v. *Collector of Central Excise,* 2003 (9) SCALE 720 and see *Ashok Leyland Ltd.* v. *State of Tamil Nadu,* (2004) 3 SCC 1.

**25. Juvenile Ceased to be Juvenile – Law on –** Section 20 makes a special provision in respect of pending cases. It states that notwithstanding anything contained in the Juvenile Act, all proceedings in respect of a juvenile pending in any court in any area on the date on which Juvenile Act comes into force in that area shall be continued in that court as if the Juvenile Act had not been passed and if the court finds that the juvenile has committed an offence, it shall record such finding and instead of passing any sentence in respect of the juvenile forward the juvenile to the Board which shall pass orders in respect of that juvenile in accordance with the provisions of the Juvenile Act as if it had been satisfied on inquiry under the Juvenile Act that the juvenile has committed the offence. The *Explanation* to section 20 makes it clear that in all pending cases, which would include not only trials but even subsequent proceedings by way of revision or appeal, the determination of juvenility of a juvenile would be in terms of clause (l) of section 2, even if the juvenile ceased to be a juvenile on or before 1-4-2001, when the Juvenile Act came into force, and the provisions of the Juvenile Act would apply as if the said provision had been in force for all purposes and for all material times when the alleged offence was committed; *Kalu @ Amit* v. *State of Haryana,* AIR 2012 SC 3212: 2012 Cr LJ 4244: 2012 (7) SCALE 404.

**26. Law of Review – Comments on –** A close and patient reading of the provisions, embodied under section 20 of the new Act, shows that if a proceeding is pending in any Court on the date of coming into force of the new Act, the proceeding shall be continued as if the new Act had not been passed and if the Court finds that a juvenile had committed an offence, it shall record such a finding and, instead of passing any sentence in respect of the juvenile, forward the juvenile to the Board constituted under section 4 of the new Act, and, then, the Board shall pass appropriate order in respect of the juvenile in accordance with the provisions of the new Act as if it had not been satisfied, on enquiry, that the juvenile had committed the offence. It is also extremely important to bear in mind, with regard to the above, that if an accused is found to be a juvenile in conflict with law and if the case against the juvenile was pending in the Court on the date of coming into force of the Juvenile Justice Act, then such a juvenile cannot be convicted by the Court and it is on the basis of the finding of guilt that the juvenile is required to be convicted by the Juvenile Justice Board. The proviso to section 20 of the Juvenile Justice Act, 2000, however, empowers the Board to review the case for adequate and special reasons to be mentioned in their order and, then, to pass appropriate order in the interest of the juvenile; *Halla Dhar Das* v. *State of Assam,* 2012 (4) Gau LT 583 (Gau).

**27. Legal Fiction – Law on –** In terms of the 1986 Act, a person who was not juvenile could be tried in any court. section 20 of 2000 Act takes care of such a situation stating that despite the same the trial shall continue in that court as if that act has not been passed and in the event, he is found to be guilty of commission of an offence, a finding to that effect shall be recorded in the judgment of conviction, if any, but instead of passing any sentence in relation to the juvenile, he would be forwarded to the Juvenile justice Board (in short the 'board') which shall pass orders in accordance with the provisions of the Act as if it has been satisfied on inquiry that a juvenile has committed the offence. A legal fiction has, thus, been created in the said provision. A legal fiction as is well- known must be given its full effect although it has its limitations. In interpreting a provision creating a legal fiction, the Court has to ascertain for what purpose the fiction is created; *Bijender Singh* v. *State of Haryana,* AIR 2005 SC 2262: 2005 (3) SCALE 467: 2005 (3) SCC 685; See *Bhaunagar University* v. *Palitana Sugar Mill (P) Ltd.,* JT 2002 (10) SC 55, *I.T.W. Signode India Ltd.* v. *Collecror of Central Excise,* JT 2004 (6) SC 456 and *Ashok Leyland Ltd.* v. *State of Tamil Nadu,* JT 2004 (1) SC 289.

**28. Plea of Being Juvenile – Law on –** Section 20 provided a special provision in respect of pending cases as on 1-4-2001. It was common knowledge that on the date of commencement of the new Act *i.e.,* on 1-4-2001, the cases against the juvenile in conflict with law were pending as initiated under the old Act, 1986. Therefore, to deal with those cases, pending under 1986 Act when the Act 2000 came into operation, a special provision was incorporated. According to this provision, if any proceeding was pending on the date of the Act 2000, the same has to be concluded under the provisions of the Old Act. However, it has been further provided that if the finding is recorded that the concerned Juvenile committed the alleged offence, no sentence is to be passed, instead the concerned Juvenile along with that finding is to be sent to the Juvenile Board and the Board then pass appropriate order under the new Act. Therefore, at that time, when the new Act came into force, it did not take effect retrospectively. However, a question was raised whether the plea of being a Juvenile to be taken at a later stage. The Supreme Court and all the High Courts have held the juvenility may be claimed at any stage of the trial even in the appellate stage. Therefore, section 7A of the Act was inserted by the amendment Act 33 of 2006 with effect from 22-8-2006; *Latha, w/o Kundumani @ Pilchai Kani* v. *Inspector of Police,* 2012 (4) CTC 158 (Mad) (Madurai Bench) (DB).

**29. Punishment for Juvenile – Comments on –** It is clear that the case of the juvenile has to be examined on merits. If it found that the juvenile is guilty of the offence alleged to have been committed, he simply cannot go unpunished. However, as the law stands, the punishment to be awarded to him or her must be left to the Juvenile Justice Board constituted under the Juvenile Justice (Care and Protection of Children) Act, 2000. This is the plain requirement of section 20 of the Juvenile Justice (Care and Protection of Children) Act, 2000; *Jitendra Singh @ Babboo Singh* v. *State of Uttar Pradesh,* 2013 (11) SCC 193: JT 2013 (11) SC 152: 2013 (9) SCALE 18.

**30. Retrospective Effect – Comments on –** Sub-section (1) of the section 7A provides for an inquiry to determine the juvenility of the accused on the date of commission of the offence as and when any such question is raised before the Court or the Court is of the opinion that the accused person was juvenile on the date of commission of offence. Proviso to sub-section 1 further empowers the Court to recognize the factum of juvenility at any stage, even after final disposal of the case and to determine such claim in accordance with the provisions of the Act and the Rules even if the juvenile ceased to be so on or before the commencement of the act. This Act came into force on the date of its publication in the Central Government Gazette *i.e.* 1-4-2001 *vide* S.O. 177(E). Section 20 of the Act further applies the provisions of this Act even on pending cases. Thus, from the conjoint reading of proviso to section 7A and section 20, it can be conveniently gathered that the provisions of this Act will be attracted even if, the commission of offence had taken place prior to the operation of this Act; *Sunil Kumar* v. *State of Haryana,* 2010 (4) RCR (Cri) 414 (P&H).

**31. Rights and Privileges – Law on –** No doubt the purpose of the Act of 2000 is benevolent and the juvenile is entitled to the benefits of the Act but that does not mean that process of law can be misused by such juvenile in the garb of benefits provided under the Act of 2000. Section 20 of the Act of 2000 is a special provision in respect of pending cases and it take cares of all the rights and privileges available to the juvenile. Provisions of section 20 of the Act of 2000 have over-riding effect over all the provisions of this Act of 2000 which provides that all the proceedings in respect of juvenile pending in any court shall be continued in that court as if this Act had not been passed; *Zafar Iqbal* v. *State of Uttar Pradesh,* 2012 (10) ADJ 259: 2013 (1) ACrR 501 (All).

**32. Sentence – Law on –** Section 20 deals with the special provision in respect of pending cases. It starts with a *non-obstante* clause and states that notwithstanding anything contained in the Act, all proceedings in respect of a juvenile pending in any court, in any area on the date on which the Act comes into force in that area, shall be continued in that court as if the Act had not been passed. If the court finds that the juvenile has committed an offence, it shall record such a finding and instead of passing any sentence in respect of the juvenile, forward him to the Juvenile Justice Board which shall pass orders in respect of him in accordance with the provisions of the Act. *Explanation* to section 20 of the Act makes it clear that in all pending cases including trial, revision, appeal or any other criminal proceedings in respect of a juvenile in conflict with law, in any court, the determination of juvenility shall be in terms of clause (1) of section 2 of the Act; *A. Kabeer* v. *State of Kerala,* 2013 (2) Ker LJ 107 (Ker).

**33. Court – Duties of –** From a plain reading of the language of section 20 of Act 2000, it is implicit that all proceedings in respect of juvenile pending in any court on the date on which the Act comes into force, shall be continued in that court as if the Act 2000 had not been passed. If the court finds that juvenile has committed an offence, it shall record such finding but pass no sentence against him. Instead of passing any sentence, the court shall forward the juvenile along with the records of the proceedings to the Board. It is the Board, which shall pass orders in respect of the juvenile so forwarded by the trial court in accordance with the provisions of the Act 2000, as if the Board had been satisfied on the enquiry under this Act that a juvenile has committed offence. The Board may, for any adequate and special reason to be mentioned in the order, review the case and pass an appropriate order in the case of the juvenile. Thus, section 20 contemplates special provisions in respect of pending cases; *Bijendra Kumar* v. *State of Uttar Pradesh*, 2013 (3) DMC 389: 2013 (3) ADJ 619: 2013 (2) ACrR 1616 (All).

**34. Satisfaction – Law on –** Section 20 provides for special provision in respect of pending cases. It provides that notwithstanding anything containing in the Act, all proceedings in respect of a juvenile pending in any Court in any area on the date on which the Act came into force in that area shall be continued in that Court as if the Act had not been passed and if the Court finds that the juvenile has committed an offence, it shall record such finding and instead of passing any sentence in respect of the juvenile, forward the juvenile to the Board which shall pass orders in respect of that juvenile in accordance with the provisions of the Act as if it had been satisfied on inquiry under this Act that a juvenile has committed the offence. Section 16 of the Juvenile Justice (Care & Protection of Children) Act, 2000 provides that no juvenile shall be sentenced to death or life imprisonment, or committed to prison in default of payment of fine or in default of furnishing security. A juvenile, under the provisions of the Act, can be referred to the Juvenile Board for such orders to be passed by the Board as it thinks fit in terms of section 15 of the Act; *Chiddu* v. *State of Uttaranchal*, 2005 Cr LJ 4251: 2006 (1) RCR (Cri) 361 (Uttra).

[1][**21. Prohibition of publication of name, etc., of juvenile in conflict with law or child in need of care and protection involved in any proceeding under the Act.**—(1) No report in any newspaper, magazine, news-sheet or visual media of any inquiry regarding a juvenile in conflict with law or a child in need of care and protection under this Act shall disclose the name, address or school or any other particulars calculated to lead to the identification of the juvenile or child nor shall any picture of any such juvenile or child be published:

Provided that for reasons to be recorded in writing, the authority holding the inquiry may permit such disclosure, if in its opinion such disclosure is in the interest of the juvenile or the child.

(2) Any person who contravenes the provisions of sub-section (1), shall be liable to a penalty which may extend to twenty five thousand rupees.]

---

1. Subs. by Act 33 of 2006, sec. 15, for section 21 (w.e.f. 22-8-2006). Section 21, before substitution, stood as under:

"21. *Prohibition of publication of name, etc., of juvenile involved in any proceeding under the Act.*—(1) No report in any newspaper, magazine, news-sheet or visual media of any inquiry regarding a juvenile in conflict with law under this Act shall disclose the name, address or school or any other particulars calculated to lead to the identification of the juvenile nor shall any picture of any such juvenile be published:

Provided that for reasons to be recorded in writing the authority holding the inquiry may permit such disclosure, if in its opinion such disclosure is in the interest of the juvenile.

(2) Any person contravening the provisions of sub-section (1) shall be punishable with fine, which may extend to one thousand rupees.".

**SYNOPSIS**

1. Confidentiality – Comments on
2. Prohibition of Publication – Law on

**COMMENTS**

**1. Confidentiality – Comments on** – Article 39 of the Constitution of India, the International Convention and the provisions of the Act thus clearly provide that maintaining confidentiality of the proceedings in matters involving juveniles in conflict with law has an overriding public interest. However, it may be noted that while providing for utmost confidentiality and privacy and minimizing the judicial intervention, the Conventions and the JJ Act did not take away the right of appeal/revision permitted to an aggrieved person under the JJ Act; *X Minor Thr. Father Natural Guardian* v. *State*, 2012 (5) RCR (Cri) 191: 2012 Cr LJ 4482 (Del).

**2. Prohibition of Publication – Law on** – Section 21 of the Act clearly prohibits publication, and this provision has to be scrupulously followed by the media and all concerned. It is hence, made clear that no picture or other details of any of the children involved in this case or any "child in need of care and protection" shall, hereinafter, be published in any newspaper, magazine, news-sheet or visual media etc., except to the extent, if any, permitted by the appropriate authority concerned. The authority holding the enquiry is empowered to permit such disclosure, in the interest of juvenile or the child. But, while granting permission, the authority has to record the reasons in writing. As per section 21 of the Act, no report in any newspaper, magazine, news-sheet or visual media of any enquiry regarding a "child in need of care and protection" under the Act shall disclose the name, address or school or any other particulars calculated to lead to the identification of the juvenile or child, except in cases where the authority holding the enquiry specifically permit, for reasons to be recorded in writing, in the best interest of the child. No picture of any such juvenile or child shall also be published. It is also relevant to mention here that as per section 21(2) of the Act, any person contravenes the provisions in sub-section 91) shall be liable to a penalty which may extent to Rs. 25,000; *Jose Maveli* v. *State of Kerala*, 2007 Cr LJ 2709: 2007 (2) Ker LT 761 (Ker).

**22. Provision in respect of escaped juvenile.**—Notwithstanding anything to the contrary contained in any other law for the time being in force, any police officer may take charge without warrant of a juvenile in conflict with law who has escaped from a special home or an observation home or from the care of a person under whom he was placed under this Act, and shall be sent back to the special home or the observation home or that person, as the case may be; and no proceeding shall be instituted in respect of the juvenile by reason of such escape, but the special home, or the observation home or the person may, after giving the information to the Board which passed the order in respect of the juvenile, take such steps in respect of the juvenile as may be deemed necessary under the provisions of this Act.

**COMMENTS**

**Police Officer – Comments on** – There is no exhaustive definition of the expression 'Police Officer' in any of our statutes. In the absence of a statutory definition, and, apart from all authority, one would be tempted to say that a police officer is a person whom any statute or other provision of law calls such, or, on whom it confers all or substantially all the powers and imposes the duties of a police officer. If he is expressly called a police officer there is no difficulty whatsoever. If he is not so called then the next step is to ask: what does the law require him to do ? What are the duties imposed on him ? and what are the powers conferred on him ? If these are substantially those of a police officer there need be no qualms in regarding him as one. If his powers and duties are confined to a particular extent of territory or to a particular subject-matter he will be a police officer only in respect of that territory or that subject-matter. The material thing to consider would be not the name given to him, nor the colour of the uniform he is required to wear, but his functions, powers and duties. A police officer does not cease to be such merely because he is put into a white khadder uniform instead of one in khaki drill; a medicine will be just the same whether it is packaged in a glass jar or a plastic container"; *State of Punjab* v. *Barkat Ram,* AIR 1962 SC 276: 1962 Cr LJ 217: 1962 (3) SCR 338.

**23. Punishment for cruelty to juvenile or child.**— Whoever, having the actual charge of, or control over, a juvenile or the child, assaults, abandons, exposes or wilfully neglects the juvenile or causes or procures him to be assaulted, abandoned, exposed or neglected in a manner likely to cause such juvenile or the child unnecessary mental or physical suffering shall be punishable with imprisonment for a term which may extend to six months, or fine, or with both.

**SYNOPSIS**

**1.** Bail to Influenced Person – Law on **2.** High Court – Powers of

**COMMENTS**

**1. Bail to Influenced Person – Law on –** If apprehension is expressed by the State and the counsel for the complainant that the accused, who has both the backing of a large followers and money power, is likely to use the same to win over the witnesses and tamper with evidence then bail application should; *Saint Shri Asharam Bapu* v. *State of Rajasthan,* 2014 (2) Crimes 162 (Raj).

**2. High Court – Powers of –** It is true that Juvenile Justice (Care and Protection of Children) Act, 2000 has been enacted to protect the interest of juvenile or child, who requires care and protection and also to reform the juvenile, who is in conflict with law. It is settled law, if High Court is satisfied that, even if the entire allegations made against the accused was admitted to be true and if, those allegations will not attract or constitute the ingredients of the offence alleged against them, then High Court can invoke the power under section 482 of the 'Code', to quash the proceedings; *Joseph* v. *State of Kerala,* 2014 (2) ILR 259 (Ker): 2014 (2) Ker LT 91: 2014 (2) Ker LJ 215.

**24. Employment of juvenile or child for begging.**—(1) Whoever employs or uses any juvenile or the child for the purpose or causes any juvenile to beg shall be punishable with imprisonment for a term which may extend to three years and shall also be liable to fine.

(2) Whoever, having the actual charge of, or control over, a juvenile or the child abets the commission of the offence punishable under sub-section (1), shall be punishable with imprisonment for a term which may extend to one year and shall also be liable to fine.

**COMMENTS**

**Fundamental Rights – Comments on –** Article 32(1) confers the right to move Apex Court by appropriate proceedings for enforcement of the fundamental rights guaranteed under the Constitution. Article 32(2) makes provision for the powers of Apex court in the matter of granting relief in any proceeding in Apex Court for enforcement of the fundamental rights guaranteed by the Constitution; *Bandhua Mukti Morcha* v. *Union of India,* AIR 1984 SC 802: 1984 (3) SCC 161: 1984 (2) SCR 67.

**25. Penalty for giving intoxicating liquor or narcotic drug or psychotropic substance to juvenile or child.**—Whoever gives, or causes to be given, to any juvenile or the child any intoxicating liquor in a public place or any narcotic drug or psychotropic substance except upon the order of duly qualified medical practitioner or in case of sickness shall be punishable with imprisonment for a term which may extend to three years and shall also be liable to fine.

### COMMENTS

**"Narcotic Drug" and "Psychotropic Substance" – Meaning of –** The definition of Narcotic drug and Psychotropic substance is given in section 2(xiv) and (xxiii) of the Narcotic Drugs and Psychotropic Substances Act, 1985 which is as follows:

(xiv) "Narcotic drug" means coca leaf, cannabis (hemp), opium, poppy straw and includes all manufactured drugs;

(xxiii) "Psychotropic substance" means any substance, natural or synthetic, or any natural material or any salt or preparation of such substance or materials included in the list of psychotropic substances specified in the Schedule.

**26. Exploitation of juvenile or child employee.**—Whoever ostensibly procures a juvenile or the child for the purpose of any hazardous employment keeps him in bondage and withholds his earnings or uses such earning for his own purposes shall be punishable with imprisonment for a term which may extend to three years and shall also be liable to fine.

### SYNOPSIS

1. Legislature – Intention of
2. Allegations against God Man – Comments on
3. Child above Age of 14 years Forced to Work – Law on
4. Compensation – Law on
5. Child Labour – Comments on
6. Employment of Juvenile – Law on

### COMMENTS

**1. Legislature – Intention of –** The legislative intendment underlying sections 3 and 26 read with the preamble, aims and objects of the Act is clearly discernible. A conjoint reading of the sections, preamble, aims and objects of the Act leaves no matter of doubt that the Legislature intended to provide protection, treatment, development and rehabilitation of neglected or delinquent juveniles and for the adjudication thereof; *Pratap Singh* v. *State of Jharkhand,* AIR 2005 SC 2731: 2005 (1) SCALE 763: 2005 (3) SCC 551.

**2. Allegations against God Man – Comments on –** The allegations made by the prosecutrix against the accused are serious and punishable with life imprisonment. The offence becomes more severe and invites more serious repercussion if it is committed by a person whose public image is of a God Man, a saint, who is worshiped by the victim's own family and committed the same under the garb of giving 'treatment' and that too upon a minor. The stand of the prosecutrix is consistent. Thus it cannot be said that the allegations are false or motivated; *Saint Shri Asharam Bapu* v. *State of Rajasthan,* 2013 (4) Raj LW 3361 (Raj).

**3. Child above Age of 14 years Forced to Work – Law on –** Whenever a child above the age of 14 years is forced to work, it has to be treated as an offence under section 374, IPC and it is to be dealt with sternly. The problem, however, may arise when a child between 14 and 18 years of age is committed to labour by the parents willingly and with their consent. It may be difficult to prohibit the same. The task of this Commission is akin to that of Human Rights Commission with the only difference that the State Commissions, established under the Commissions for Protection of Child Rights Act, 2005, would be dealing with the human rights of children. We, thus, hold that as and when any matter is brought to the notice of the State Commission (or for that matter *suo motu* cognizance taken by the State Commission) involving violation of child rights even where a child above the age of 14 year is employed, the State Commission under the CPCR Act will have the jurisdiction to deal with the same and pass necessary directions; *Court on its Own Motion* v. *State of Punjab,* 2013 (3) RCR (Cri) 298 (P&H) (DB).

**4. Compensation – Law on –** The interim relief awarded, can always be reduced or enhanced by the trial court. In the given circumstances, to ensure that such an interim compensation awarded is not misused, way can be evolved for return of the amount, if it is held by the trial court that the case has been falsely instituted. In that case, the amount can be recovered along with damages from the person, who, on the basis of false allegations has set the criminal law into motion; *Shiva @ Savaram* v. *State of Rajasthan,* 2014 (1) Crimes 102 (Raj).

**5. Child Labour – Comments on –** Under the J.J. Act of 2000, a person up to the age of 18 years is treated as 'child'. Same age is prescribed under the Commissions for Protection of Child Rights Act, 2005 as well. However when it comes to prohibition of Child Labour Act of 1986, the definition of child means a person who has not completed his fourteenth year of age. Thus, virtually there is no prohibition of child labour in case of children who are more than 14 years but less than 18 years of age. Furthermore, this Act focuses on the prohibition of employment of children in certain specified work places, which are harmful for the children, and there is no absolute prohibition. At the same time, now, RTE Act creates an obligation on the part of State to provide free and compulsory education to all children aged between 6 to 14 years. This is now the constitutional obligation as well. As right to education is made fundamental, it would, therefore, follow that as far as children up to the age of 14 years are concerned, since they are to be provided free education, there would be absolute ban/bar and prohibition from child labour; *Court on its Own Motion* v. *State of Punjab,* 2013 (3) RCR (Cri) 298 (P&H) (DB).

**6. Employment of Juvenile – Law on –** The section 26 is analogous to section 44 of the Juvenile Justice Act, 1986. A reading of the section clearly spells out that the employment of juvenile or child to constitute an offence must be one which by its nature is hazardous. Over and above the nature of hazardous employment the section also contemplates of keeping the juvenile or child in bondage and withholding his earnings or using of such earnings by his employer; *Vinod S. Panicker* v. *Sub-Inspector of Police,* 2013 (2) RCR (Cri) 1054: 2013 Cr LJ 833: 2012 (4) Ker LJ 384 (Ker).

**27. Special offences.**—The offences punishable under sections 23, 24, 25 and 26 shall be cognizable.

**COMMENTS**

**Expression "Ends of Justice" – Comments on –** Ends of justice has not been defined in any statute, however, this expression "ends of justice" has been used in the Constitution of India under article 139A(2) that the Supreme Court may, if it deems it expedient so to do for the ends of justice, transfer any case, appeal or other proceedings pending before any High Court to any other High Court. Article 142 of the Constitution empowers this Court to pass an order which may be necessary for doing complete justice in any case or matter pending. Section 151 of the Code of Civil Procedure, 1908 confers unlimited inherent powers on the court to make such orders as may be necessary for the ends of justice. Section 482 of the Code confers inherent power upon the High Court to pass an order as may be necessary to secure the ends of justice. The words in section 151 of CPC to "secure the" seems to be more powerful then the term to meet the ends of justice as the former is of unfathomable limits. It has always been the subject-matter of debate as what does the words "the ends of justice" mean, for the reason "that it is one of those questions to which the resigned wisdom applies that man cannot find a definitive answer, but can only try to improve the question"; *Essa @ Anjum Abdul Razak Memon* v. *State of Maharashtra,* 2013 (3) Supreme 195: 2013 (2) Mad LJ (Cri) 401: 2013 (3) SCALE 1; *Vide* also, *Vijay Kumar* v. *Public Prosecutor, A.P.,* AIR 1978 SC 1485.

**28. Alternative punishment.**—Where an act or omission constitute an offence punishable under this Act and also under any other Central or State Act, then, notwithstanding anything contained in any law for the time being in force, the offender found guilty of such offences shall be liable to punishment only under such Act as provides for punishment which is greater in degree.

**SYNOPSIS**



**COMMENTS**

**1. Children – Relaxation for –** As per section 82 of the Penal Code nothing is an offence which is done by a child under seven years of age and as per section 83 of the Penal Code nothing is an offence which is done by a child above seven years of age and under twelve years, who has not attained sufficient maturity of understanding to judge of the nature and consequences of his conduct on that occasion; *Vinod Singh* v. *State of Uttar Pradesh,* 2014 (85) ACC 156 (All) (DB).

**2. Two Statutes Provide for Overriding Effect – Law on –** Where two statutes provide for overriding effect on the other law for the time being in force and the court has to examine which one of them must prevail, the court has to examine the issue considering the following two basic principles of statutory interpretation:

1. *leges posteriores priores conterarias abrogant* (later laws abrogate earlier contrary laws).
2. *generalia specialibus non derogant* (a general provision does not derogate from a special one.)

The principle that the latter Act would prevail the earlier Act has consistently been held to be subject to the exception that a general provision does not derogate from a special one. It means that where the literal meaning of the general enactment covers a situation for which specific provision is made by another enactment contained in the earlier Act, it would be presumed that the situation was intended to continue to be dealt with by the specific provision rather than the later general one. The basic rule that general provisions should yield to the specific provisions is based on the principle that if two directions are issued by the competent authority, one covering a large number of matters in general and another to only some of them, his intention is that these latter directions should prevail as regards these while as regards all the rest the earlier directions must be given effect to. It is a settled legal proposition that while passing a special Act, the Legislature devotes its entire consideration to a peculiar subject. Therefore, when a general Act is subsequently passed, it is logical to presume that the Legislature has not repealed or modified the former special Act unless an inference may be drawn from the language of the special Act itself. In order to determine whether a statute is special or general one, the court has to take into consideration the principal subject-matter of the statute and the particular perspective for the reason that for certain purposes an Act may be general and for certain other purposes it may be special and such a distinction cannot be blurred. Thus, where there is inconsistency between the provisions of two statutes and both can be regarded as special in nature, the conflict has to be resolved by reference to the purpose and policy underlying the two enactments and the clear intendment of the Legislature conveyed by the language of the relevant provisions therein; *Essa @ Anjum Abdul Razak Memon* v. *State of Maharashtra,* 2013 (3) Supreme 195: JT 2013 (6) SC 1: 2013 (3) SCALE 1; *Vide* also, *Shri Ram Narain* v. *The Simla Banking and Industrial Co. Ltd.,* AIR 1956 SC 614; *J.K. Cotton Spinning & Weaving Mills Co. Ltd.* v. *State of Uttar Pradesh,* AIR 1961 SC 1170; *Kumaon Motor Owners Union Ltd.* v. *State of Uttar Pradesh,* AIR 1966 SC 785; *Shri Sarwan Singh* v. *Shri Kasturi Lal,* (1977) 1 SCC 750; *The U.P. State Electricity Board* v. *Hari Shanker Jain,* (1978) 4 SCC 16; *The Life Insurance Corporation of India* v. *D.J. Bahadur,* AIR 1980 SC 2181; *Ashoka Marketing Ltd.* v. *Punjab National Bank,* AIR 1991 SC 855 and *T.M.A. Pai Foundation* v. *State of Karnataka,* AIR 2003 SC 355.

**3. Interpretation – Law on –** A statute must be interpreted having regard to the purpose and object of the Act. The doctrine of purposive construction must be resorted to. It would not be permissible for the court to construe the provisions in such a manner which would destroy the very purpose for which the same was enacted. The principles in regard to the approach of the Court in interpreting the provisions of a statute with the change in the societal condition must also be borne in mind. The rules of purposive construction have to be resorted to which would require the construction of the Act in such a manner so as to see that the object of the Act fulfilled; which in turn would lead the beneficiary under the statutory scheme to fulfill its constitutional obligations. It is the duty of the court to adopt a harmonious construction by which both the provisions remain operative; *Essa @ Anjum Abdul Razak Memon* v. *State of Maharashtra,* 2013 (3) Supreme 195: JT 2013 (6) SC 1: 2013 (3) SCALE 1; Vide *Cantonment Board, Mhow* v. *Madhya Pradesh State Road Transport Corporation,* AIR 1997 SC 2013; *Bharat Petroleum Corporation Ltd.* v. *Maddula Ratnavalli,* (2007) 6 SCC 81; and *Krishna Kumar Birla* v. *Rajendra Singh Lodha,* (2008) 4 SCC 300.

## *CHAPTER III*

## CHILD IN NEED OF CARE AND PROTECTION

**29. Child Welfare Committee.**—(1) The State Government may, [1][within a period of one year from the date of commencement of the Juvenile Justice (Care and Protection of Children) Amendment Act, 2006, by notification in the Official Gazette, constitute for every district], one or more Child Welfare Committees for exercising the powers and discharge the duties conferred on such Committees in relation to child in need of care and protection under this Act.

(2) The Committee shall consist of a Chairperson and four other members as the State Government may think fit to appoint, of whom at least one shall be a woman and another, an expert on matters concerning children.

(3) The qualifications of the Chairperson and the members, and the tenure for which they may be appointed shall be such as may be prescribed.

(4) The appointment of any member of the Committee may be terminated, after holding inquiry, by the State Government, if—

(i) he has been found guilty of misuse of power vested under this Act;

(ii) he has been convicted of an offence involving moral turpitude, and such conviction has not been reversed or he has not been granted full pardon in respect of such offence;

(iii) he fails to attend the proceedings of the Committee for consecutive three months without any valid reason or he fails to attend less than three-fourth of the sittings in a year.

(5) The Committee shall function as a Bench of Magistrates and shall have the powers conferred by the Code of Criminal Procedure, 1973 (2 of 1974) on a Metropolitan Magistrate or, as the case may be, a Judicial Magistrate of the first class.

**SYNOPSIS**

**1.** Chapter III – Comments on

**2.** Chapter III – View on

**3.** Committee – Role of

1. Subs. by Act 33 of 2006, sec. 16, for "by notification in Official Gazette, constitute for every district or group of districts specified in the notification" (w.e.f. 22-8-2006).

**COMMENTS**

**1. Chapter III – Comments on** – Chapter III of the Act deals with the general subject titled "Child in Need of Care and Protection". As per section 29(1) of the Act, the State Government may, within one year from the date of commencement of the Juvenile Justice (Care and Protection of Children) Amendment Act, 2006, constitute for every district, one or more Child Welfare Committees for exercising the powers and discharge the duties conferred on such Committees in relation to child in need of care and protection under the Act. The powers of the Child Welfare Committee hereinafter referred to as 'the Committee, are conferred under section 31 of the Act; *Vidya* v. *Government of India*, 2010 Cr LJ 1387: 2010 (3) AICLR 308: 2009 (4) Ker LT 937 (Ker).

**2. Chapter III – View on** – Chapter 3 of the Act deals with the protection in respect of the child in need of care and protection. section 29 of the Act speaks about the constitution of the Child Welfare Committee and it is specifically stated that the State Government, by notification in the Official Gazette, shall constitute one or more Child Welfare Committee for exercising powers and discharge the duties conferred on such committees in relation to the Child in need of care and protection under the Act; *Seva Chakkara Samajam* v. *Chairman, Child Welfare Committee*, 2012 (5) LW 293 (Mad).

**3. Committee – Role of** – The Committee/Magistrate has to act as a true guardian of the "child in need of care and protection" and ensure that the provisions of the Act and Rules are scrupulously followed by all concerned and everything is done in the best interest of the welfare of the children. Neither Institution nor any person shall be allowed to violate the express provisions of the Act and Rules. The violations, if any noticed, shall be viewed seriously especially since such violations are likely to affect the children's welfare adversely. The Committee/Magistrate shall also be more alert in matters relating to children who are in need of care and protection. Learned Magistrate, however, did not advert his attention to any of the above facts before entrusting the children to the Institution. This appears to be the same state of affair in the case of other Committees across the State, which are dealing with children under section 2(d) of the Act, may be because, no guide lines were so far laid down; *Jose Maveli* v. *State of Kerala*, 2007 Cr LJ 2709: 2007 (2) Ker LT 761 (Ker).

**30. Procedure, etc., in relation to Committee.**—(1) The Committee shall meet at such times and shall observe such rules of procedure in regard to the transaction of business at its meetings, as may be prescribed.

(2) A child in need of care and protection may be produced before an individual member for being placed in safe custody or otherwise when the Committee is not in session.

(3) In the event of any difference of opinion among the members of the Committee at the time of any interim decision, the opinion of the majority shall prevail but where there is no such majority the opinion of the Chairperson shall prevail.

(4) Subject to the provisions of sub-section (1), the Committee may act, notwithstanding the absence of any member of the Committee, and no order made by the Committee shall be invalid by reason only of the absence of any member during any stage of the proceeding.

**SYNOPSIS**

1. Provision – Comments on
2. Committee – Comments on
3. Committees – Powers of

**COMMENTS**

**1. Provision – Comments on** – Therefore, the Child Welfare Committee has to be constituted only in relation to the child in need of care and protection under this Act,

This has also been made clear in section 30 of the Act, which deals with the procedure in relation to Committee and as per section 30(2), a child in need of care and protection, may be produced before an individual member for being placed in safe custody, or otherwise, when the Committee is not in Session. Section 32 says that, any child in need of care and protection may be produced before the Committee by the persons named in that section. Section 33 says that an enquiry has to be conducted, on receipt of the report under section 32. Section 34 authorizes the Government to recognize the Children's Homes and as per section 34(3) all Institutions run by voluntary organizations for children in need of care and protection, shall register themselves under the provisions of the Act; *Seva Chakkara Samajam* v. *Chairman, Child Welfare Committee,* 2012 (5) LW 293 (Mad).

**2. Committee – Comments on –** Take a case where a juvenile in need of care and protection is picked up by the authorities under the Act. As provided under rule 27 of the Rules, 2011, such a juvenile in need of care and protection shall be produced before the Committee within 24 hours by any of the persons enumerated under the Rules. As provided under the rule 27(4) of the Rules, if the Committee is not sitting, then such a juvenile will be produced before the single member of the Committee as per the provisions laid down under sub-section (2) of section 30 of the Act for being placed in a safe custody of parent or guardian or fit person or fit institutions, as the case may be, till such time that the child can be produced before the Committee. The rule 27(5) further provides that in case even if the single member is not available, or that the hours are odd, the juvenile would be taken by the non-governmental organization or Childline or Police to an appropriate institution for children registered under the Act with all the necessary documents, and would be placed in such institution till the time of production before the Committee. If the juvenile is kept at an observation/remand home, where he may mingle with juveniles in conflict with law, then the very object and the purpose with which the Act has been enacted would get frustrated; *Rohit Sitapatikumar Verma* v. *State of Gujarat,* 2013 (1) GLR 766 Guj (DB).

**3. Committees – Powers of –** A reading of the various provisions of Chapter III of the Act, makes it clear that the Child Welfare Committee is constituted to exercise powers and to discharge duties only in relation to child in need of care and protection and in respect of other child, as defined under section 2(k), the Committees shall have a final Authority to dispose of all the cases for care, treatment, education, training, development and rehabilitation of the children as well as to provide the basic needs and protection of Human Rights. Further, section 31(2) of the Act also makes it clear that the Child Welfare Committee shall have the power to deal exclusively with all proceedings under this Act relating to children in need of care and protection; *Seva Chakkara Samajam* v. *Chairman, Child Welfare Committee,* 2012 (5) LW 293 (Mad).

**31. Powers of Committee.**—(1) The Committee shall have the final authority to dispose of cases for the care, protection, treatment, development and rehabilitation of the children as well as to provide for their basic needs and protection of human rights.

(2) Where a Committee has been constituted for any area, such Committee shall, notwithstanding anything contained in any other law for the time being in force but save as otherwise expressly provided in this Act, have the power to deal exclusively with all proceedings under this Act relating to children in need of care and protection.

## COMMENTS

**Power of Child Welfare Committee – Law on –** Section 31 of the Act speaks about the power of the Committee in general. However, sub-section (3) of section 39 of the Act confers power on the Child Welfare Committee to restore any child in need of care and protection to his parent, guardian, and fit person or fit institution, as the case may be, and give them suitable directions; *Sebati Padhi* v. *Child Welfare Committee, Cuttack,* 2013 Cr LJ 3500: 2013 (2) Ori LR 171: 2013 (8) RCR (Cri) 2340 (Ori).

**32. Production before Committee.**—(1) Any child in need of care and protection may be produced before the Committee by one of the following persons:—

(i) any police officer or special juvenile police unit or a designated police officer;

(ii) any public servant;

(iii) childline, a registered voluntary organisation or by such other voluntary organisation or an agency as may be recognised by the State Government;

(iv) any social worker or a public spirited citizen [1][***]; or

(v) by the child himself:

[2][Provided that the child shall be produced before the Committee without any loss of time but within a period of twenty-four hours excluding the time necessary for the journey.]

(2) The State Government may make rules consistent with this Act to provide for the manner of making the report [3][***] to the Committee and the manner of sending and entrusting the child to children's home pending the inquiry.

**SYNOPSIS**

1. Additional Sessions Judge – Powers of
2. Committee – Object and Aim of
3. Committee – Role of
4. Enquiry – Law on
5. Judicial Magistrate – Role of
6. Kerala Rules in Case of Child in Need of Care and Protection – Law on
7. State Government – Duties of
8. Production of Child – Law on

**COMMENTS**

**1. Additional Sessions Judge – Powers of –** There is no doubt that the Additional Sessions Judge had the power and it was well within his jurisdiction to determine the age of the accused. Even in the absence of an enquiry under the Act, the Sessions Court, after the case is committed to it has the power to make an enquiry and determine the age of the accused if it considers it necessary in the interests of justice or a prayer is made in that behalf. Even if the opinion of the Sessions Court is that, a person before it, is a juvenile and the juvenile is sent to the Juvenile Justice Board, it would still be incumbent upon the Juvenile Justice Board to hold an inquiry under section 32(1) of the Juvenile Justice Act which is similar to section 49 of the said Act; *Sakir Mewati* v. *State of Madhya Pradesh,* 2011 Cr LJ 4469: 2011 (2) Jab LJ 245 (MP) (Gwalior Bench).

**2. Committee – Object and Aim of –** The object and aim of the Committee at that stage must be to arrive at a *prima facie* satisfaction: (i) that the child comes under section 2(d) of the Act (ii) that the report filed under rule 11 contains the truth (iii) that the person who produces the child is such person specified in section 32 or rule 10(iv) that the parent/guardian/person/institution to whom the child may be released and the surety or sureties, if any, are fit enough of releasing the child (v) that the child hails from a place lying within the jurisdiction of the Committee or other place outside its jurisdiction, for

1. The words "authorised by the State Government" omitted by Act 33 of 2006, sec. 17 (w.e.f. 22-8-2006).
2. Ins. by Act 33 of 2006, sec. 17 (w.e.f. 22-8-2006).
3. The words "to the Police and" omitted by Act 33 of 2006, sec. 17 (w.e.f. 22-8-2006).

the purpose of deciding whether the child shall be transferred under section 38 of the Act (vi) that the child the child has not been subjected to any ill-treatment or harassment either by police or any other person who takes charge of the child for the purpose of bringing before the Committee and (vii) such other factors which the Committee may deem it necessary to ascertain, to pass an interim order in respect of the child. This may be done as per a 'preliminary enquiry' by questioning the child, the alleged parent/ guardian is available, the person who produces the child or such other person which the Committee may deem fit and proper. It shall also peruse the report and may insist, if necessary to file an affidavit by such person as the Committee may direct so as to act upon a *'prima facie'* satisfaction for exercising jurisdiction over the child. No detailed enquiry, following any of the provisions under the code of criminal procedure can be conducted at that stage. There may not be time or opportunity also to do this. Because, the child needs to be released or sent to appropriate shelter at the earliest, as the Committee may deem fit and proper, pending a detailed enquiry under the provision. The second part of the inquiry under section 33 of the Act is a detailed inquiry, in the manner prescribed under section 33 read with rule 11 of the Rules. Rule 11 of the Rules slays down how the enquiry is to be conducted. The enquiry contemplated under section 33 of the Act after sending a child to the Children's home etc., is not an enquiry as provided under the Code of Criminal Procedure. I cannot agree with the argument advanced by learned counsel for the revision petitioner that the Committee is bound to follow the procedure laid down in the Code for trial in summons cases, as laid down by section 54 of the Act; *Jose Maveli* v. *State of Kerala,* 2007 Cr LJ 2709: 2007 (2) Ker LT 761 (Ker).

**3. Committee – Role of –** It is for the Committee to decide, on facts and circumstances of each case, whether a parent is "unfit" and whether financial incapacity of his parent has, in any way, contributed to his unfitness, so as to bring the child within the purview of section 2(d). I make it clear that I do not mean to mention that under no circumstance a financially poor parent can be stated to be "unfit". There may be cases where burning poverty may be a basic factor which would lead to undesirable situation in the family and the children may be forced for anti-social activities etc. The Committee will examine the relevant facts and decide, on the facts and circumstances of each case, whether the parent is "unfit" or not. But, the financial unfitness of the parent alone may not be sufficient to deprive the child of parental care, if the parent is other wise fit. If the Committee finds that a parent goes wrong in any manner and does anything detrimental to the child's welfare, it may issue suitable direction to the parent, to prevent any harm being caused to him. But such wrongs committed by the parent alone may not be sufficient in all cases to deny parental care to the child. In fit cases, as erring parent may be punished for his illegal acts, as per the provisions of the Act itself. But before depriving child of his parental care and environment, on the ground of unfitness or any other disqualifications of his biological parent, the Committee/Magistrate must be extremely cautious. It is always better that a parent is corrected and the probable harm be prevented, by issuing directions, as the Committee may deem fit an proper. But, in no case, the child shall be lightly denied his right to live with his parents in a family atmosphere. It is better for the courts to think twice, as to what would happen, if a child in need of care and protection (who is released to an Institution or Children's home) attains 18 years of age; *Jose Maveli* v. *State of Kerala,* 2007 Cr LJ 2709: 2007 (2) Ker LT 761 (Ker).

**4. Enquiry – Law on –** Section 8(1) of the Juvenile Justice Act reflects the proper spirit and principle which also applies to any case before any Magistrate or Court not empowered to deal with a juvenile delinquent under the Juvenile Justice Act where any question or doubt is raised about the age of the accused. Going by that principle, if during the trial of a case in a Criminal Court any question of juvenility of any accused is raised before the Court it becomes incumbent upon the court to make a preliminary enquiry in the matter and form an opinion as to whether the person concerned is a juvenile and if the opinion is affirmative in that event the case has to be referred to the Juvenile

Court for being dealt with under the Juvenile Justice Act, in which case the Juvenile Court shall yet make due enquiry under section 32(1) of the Juvenile Justice Act about age of the person and record a finding whether the person concerned is a juvenile or not. However, if the opinion of the Criminal Court is otherwise, namely, that the person concerned was not a juvenile on the date of the occurrence, then the matter need not be referred to the Juvenile Court, but such opinion of court will be subject to revision by a superior Court; *Sakir Mewati* v. *State of Madhya Pradesh,* 2011 Cr LJ 4469: 2011 (2) Jab LJ 245 (MP) (Gwalior Bench).

**5. Judicial Magistrate – Role of –** The victim of crime who happens to be a child, who has not completed 18th year of age, when produced or appears before any Magistrate, an enquiry has to be conducted by the Magistrate and if it expresses willingness to join the parents or the guardian and the parents/lawful guardian are willing to take the child, the custody has to be given to them. In the event of the child expressing apprehension about the parents/lawful guardian and refuse to go with them, the child becomes a child in need of care and protection contemplated under section 2(d) of the Act. In such an event, the Judicial Magistrate shall immediately forward the child to the Child Welfare Committee through any one of the persons mentioned in section 32 of the Act. The same shall apply in a case in which the parents/lawful guardian are disinclined to take the child with them or none of them is available to take the child. Thereafter, it is for the Child Welfare Committee to deal with the child in accordance with the provisions of the Act; *Jyothi w/o S. Babu* v. *Director General of Police, Police Head Quarters, Chennai,* 2013 (6) RCR (Cri) 2219 (Mad) (DB).

**6. Kerala Rules in Case of Child in Need of Care and Protection – Law on –** A perusal of rule 32 would show that any child in need of care and protection should be produced by any one of the persons mentioned therein and the Committee or any Police officer or special juvenile police unit or the designated police shall hold an enquiry in the prescribed manner and the Committee may, on its own, or on the representation of any person mentioned in section 32(1), pass an order to send the child to the Children's Home. There is, therefore, a well laid down procedure, in the matter of production of a child in need of care and protection before the Child Welfare Committee. Rule 37 of the Kerala Rules has imbibed the spirit of the plenary statute. Kerala Rules provide for a procedure to be adopted, while producing a child in need of care and protection, before the Child Welfare Committee and the nature of the enquiry to be conducted and the steps that have to be taken thereafter by the Committee. In other words, rule 33(4)(c) of the Central Rules deals essentially with a step, in the procedure, that is comprehensively provided for by the State Rules. Consequently, it has to be concluded that the rule operates in an area which is already occupied comprehensively by a provision in the State Rules. Rule 33(4)(c) of the Central Rules has no application to the State of Kerala; *Vidya* v. *Government of India,* 2010 Cr LJ 1387: 2010 (3) AICLR 308: 2009 (4) Ker LT 937 (Ker).

**7. State Government – Duties of –** As per sub-section (2) of section 32, the State Government is to make Rules consistent with the Act to provide for the manner of making a report to the Committee and the manner of sending and entrusting the child/children home, pending enquiry; *Vidya* v. *Government of India,* 2010 Cr LJ 1387: 2010 (3) AICLR 308: 2009 (4) Ker LT 937 (Ker).

**8. Production of Child – Law on –** As per section 32 and rule 10(1) of the Rules, "child in need of care and protection" shall be produced before the Committee by certain persons specified therein. Under section 32(iii) of the Act, (as the provision stood at the relevant time, prior to amendment) a "child in need of care and protection" shall be produced by a registered organization or agency as may be recognized by State Government. As per section 32(iv) of the Act, the child shall be produced before the Committee by a social worker or a public spirited citizen authorized by the State Government. Recognition or authorization is essential for the organization for the social worker/public spirited citizen, as the case may be, under section 32 and rule 10 of the Rules, for producing a child in need of care and protection before him Committee as on the relevant date. In the absence of such recognition or authorization, the production of the children before the Committee by an organization/person who is not recognized or authorized by government also is not in accordance with the provisions of the Act and Rules. (It has to be mentioned here that the above provision was subsequently amended); *Jose Maveli* v. *State of Kerala,* 2007 Cr LJ 2709: 2007 (2) Ker LT 761 (Ker).

**33. Inquiry.**—(1) On receipt of a report under section 32, the Committee [1][***] shall hold an inquiry in the prescribed manner and the Committee, on its own or on the report from any person or agency as mentioned in sub-section (1) of section 32, may pass an order to send the child to the children's home for speedy inquiry by a social worker or child welfare officer.

(2) The inquiry under this section shall be completed within four months of the receipt of the order or within such shorter period as may be fixed by the Committee:

Provided that the time for the submission of the inquiry report may be extended by such period as the Committee may, having regard to the circumstances and for the reasons recorded in writing, determine.

[2][(3) The State Government shall review the pendency of cases of the Committee at every six months, and shall direct the Committee to increase the frequency of its sittings or may cause the constitution of additional Committees.

(4) After the completion of the inquiry, if, the Committee is of the opinion that the said child has no family or ostensible support or is in continued need of care and protection, it may allow the child to remain in the children's home or shelter home till suitable rehabilitation is found for him or till he attains the age of eighteen years.]

**SYNOPSIS**

1. Enquiry – Law on
2. Expression 'Parent', 'Guardian' or 'Child' – Law on
3. Parental Environment – Comments on
4. Retention of Child – Law on
5. Rights of Children – Comments on
6. Social Enquiry – Law on
7. Social Investigation – Law on
8. Child in Need of Care and Protection – Law on

**COMMENTS**

**1. Enquiry – Law on** – A close look at section 33 of the Act and rule 11 of the Rules reveal that there are mainly tow stages of enquiry envisaged under section 33 of the Act. The first stage of enquiry is on production of the children before the Committee. It may be called 'preliminary enquiry' for convenience. As per section 33, on the report from any person referred to in section 32(1) or its own, the Committee shall hold an inquiry in the prescribed manner etc., and may pass an order to send the child to the Children's home. It is not, however, specifically stated in the provision as to how an enquiry under

1. The words "or any police officer or special juvenile police unit or the designated police officer" omitted by Act 33 of 2006, sec. 18 (w.e.f. 22-8-2006).
2. Subs. by Act 33 of 2006, sec. 18, for sub-section (3) (w.e.f. 22-8-2006). Sub-section (3), before substitution, stood as under:

 "(3) After the completion of the inquiry if the Committee is of the opinion that the said child has no family or ostensible support, it may allow the child to remain in the children's home or shelter home till suitable rehabilitation is found for him or till he attains the age of eighteen years.".

sub-section (1) of section 33 of the Act is to be conducted, before sending the child to Children's Home, a fit person, Institution etc. The main purpose of the enquiry at the initial stage is for taking a decision as to how a child can be dealt with, on its production. An immediate decision will have to be taken at that stage and hence a detailed enquiry may not be possible. A *prima facie* satisfaction of the relevant facts has to be arrived at to pass an appropriate order. As per rule 11 of the Rules, the Committee may release the child to the care of parent/guardian/fit/person/fit institution with or without sureties, till such time the final disposition is made; *Jose Maveli* v. *State of Kerala,* 2007 Cr LJ 2709: 2007 (2) Ker LT 761 (Ker).

**2. Expression 'Parent', 'Guardian' or `Child` – Law on –** The object of the Act is mainly to restore and children to their parents and parental environment. The very object being so, it is unreasonable to think that a child who has a parent has to be treated as a "child in need of care and protection", for the sake of sending him/her back to the same parent. Since the object of the Act itself is to bring the child who is deprived of parental care back to the family environment, it will be meaningless to say that a child having a parent has to be deemed to be a "child in need of care and protection" so as to send him back to the same parent, especially when such parent is not disqualified under any of the sub-clauses of section 2(d) of the Act. The case of a child who has a parent/guardian has been specifically and distinctly dealt with under sub-clauses (ii), (iv) and (v) of section 2(d) of the Act. So, if a child has a parent, only those provisions may be made applicable to him/her. Further, there is nothing in the language in sub-clause (i) of section 2(d) of the Act to show that the said provision applies to a child who is having a parent who is homeless, penniless etc. The very expression 'parent' or 'guardian' is missing in the provision and hence going by the plain language used therein; it may not apply to a child who has a parent or guardian. While certain other sub-clauses in the same provision *viz.,* section 2(d) specifically refers to a child having a parent or guardian, the omission to refer to a parent/guardian in sub-clause (1) of section 2(d) must be taken note of, while interpreting the relevant provision. It is also relevant to note that it is not laid down in any of the sub-clauses in section 2(d) that if a parent" is without home, settled place or abode or means, a child born to such parent will be a "child in need of care and protection". On the other hand, if the parent is unfit or is having any of the disqualifications as stated in the relevant sub-clauses, his/her child can be stated to be a "child in need of care and protection". But, in none of such sub-clauses, financial incapacity, poverty and the consequential lack of means of a parent, absence of a house, settled place or abode have been made disqualifications of a parent, so as to bring his/her child within the sweep of section 2(d) of the Act. Under section 2(d)(i), it is the means of the "child what is made relevant and not that of the "parent". Sub-clause (i) of section 2(d) deals with a homeless 'child" who has no settled place or abode and who is without ostensible means. It does not specifically refer to a "child" who has a parent without home, ostensible means etc. In such circumstances section 2(d)(i) would apply to "child" who is homeless, without a settled place or abode and without any ostensible means. The said provision does not refer specifically to a homeless "parent", without settled place or abode and without ostensible means. Had Legislature intended that the means, residence etc., of the parent must be made relevant under section 2(d)(i) of the Act, there would have been no difficulty to draft the said provision accordingly, by including the relevant expression in the provision. So long as a provision does not refer to particular expression, [in this case, "parent" in section 2(d)(i)], it may not be proper or legal for the court to inset any expression which is found missing in the provision so as to give it a particular meaning, as the court may desire, unless such insertion can be justified, as consistent with the legislative object or intention. As long as there is nothing in the particular provision to indicate that refers to or include a homeless, penniless parent also, in my view, court shall not go beyond what is expressly laid down in the provision, particularly if, it is likely to defeat the object of the Act. If a child who has a parent also is to be included in section 2(d)(i), the court will be forced to introduce the word, "parent" or similar expression in section 2(d)(i), wherever applicable. However, such an alteration is not permissible, while interpreting a provision in a Statute, unless it is necessary to achieve the object of the Act. The court cannot, therefore, read into section 2(d)(i), the word "parent" or any other word to bring within its purview, a child who is born to a financially poor parent; *Jose Maveli* v. *State of Kerala,* 2007 Cr LJ 2709: 2007 (2) Ker LT 761 (Ker).

**3. Parental Environment – Comments on –** The Committee also has power under section 33 of the Act to restore the "child in need of care and protection" to his parent, guardian etc., and give them suitable direction. As per *Explanation* to section 39, "restoration of child" means restoration to a parents; (b) adopted parents; (c) foster parents. But, neither the Institution nor the Committee/Magistrate took any steps for "restoration" of the children as laid down in section 39 of the Act, except by observing that the children are entrusted to the Institution for 'rehabilitation etc. Nothing more was done, though much is to be one under the Act. The failure to comply section 39 of the Act resulted in the children being kept away from their home, close relatives and parental environment for about three long years, which is not at all intended by the Act. As per the relevant provisions of law, the organization who receives a 'child in need of care and protection' is bound to take all necessary steps to trace out the family of the 'child in need of care and protection' to his/her parent. The Institution to which the child is sent by the Committee shall also take all steps for restoration of the children to the parents, foster parents or adopted parents. Rehabilitation shall also be effected, as stated in the act. But, the Institution did not care to take any step in these lines; *Jose Maveli* v. *State of Kerala,* 2007 Cr LJ 2709: 2007 (2) Ker LT 761 (Ker).

**4. Retention of Child – Law on –** As per section 33(3) of the Act and rule 11(14) of the Rules, the Committee can order retention of a "child in need of care and protection" in Children's Home, till he attains eighteen years of age. The child can be retained in an Institution only till 18 years of age. Thereafter, it is unthinkable as to where, to which place, land, home, hell or heaven the child has to go. The child, in all probabilities, will be forced to join his family, once he/she attains 18 years of age after the institutional care. It is needless to say that the Institution will have no right to keep the children in its custody after they attain 18 years of age. The Committee will also be powerless to issue orders to allow such retention in the Institution. So, if the children are kept away from biological parents or guardian, who have no disqualification, as referred to in sub-clauses (ii)(iv) or (v) of section 2(d) of the Act, that too for such long period, there can be no doubt that the children may be total strangers in their family and even at their own native land. Having been maintained under the institutional care, away from the home and family for such a long period, the parents, guardian, home and relatives with whom the child has to ultimately land up, on his/her attaining 18 years of age, will be totally alien to him/her. It is likely that the child may normally; find it difficult to adjust with the atmosphere in the poor family, particularly in their teenage. Back home, in his teenage, the child may find a world of difference between his life at the Institution and that in the family. It is likely that he may face severe adjustment problems in his own home and he may even turn out to be psychological wreck, finding it difficult to get along with his own kith and kin and the strange atmosphere in his own house. Thus, the child may, in reality, feel totally unprotected, rather than well-protected, contrary to the dreams of the law-makers; *Jose Maveli* v. *State of Kerala,* 2007 Cr LJ 2709: 2007 (2) Ker LT 761 (Ker).

**5. Rights of Children – Comments on –** The Constitution of India, has, in several provisions including clause (3) of article 15, clause (e) and (f) of article 39, articles 45 and 47 imposed on the State, the primary responsibility of ensuring that all the needs of children are met and their prescribed human rights are fully protected. Further, rights of children have been protected in the national conventions and treaties. The United Nations adopted a convention on the rights of child and prescribed a set of standards to be adhered to by all the State authorities in securing the interest of the child. Further, it emphasized the social re-integration of child victims to the extent possible without resorting to judicial proceedings. On the above stated principles, the Juvenile Justice (Care and Protection of Children) Act, 2000 has been enacted and accordingly, it has brought certain rights from the earlier Act, namely, Juvenile Justice Act, 1986. The Juvenile Justice (Care and Protection of Children) Act, 2000, was brought into force on 1-4-2001. The Act was aimed at providing a juvenile justice system for juveniles in conflict with law and children in need of care and protection by adopting a child friendly approach in the adjudication and disposition of matters in the best interests of children and for their rehabilitation keeping in view the developmental needs of the children; *Kalai Selvi* v. *State Represented by Inspector of Police,* 2013 (4) Mad LJ (Cri) 101 (Mad) (DB).

**6. Social Enquiry – Law on –** A reference to rule 11 also makes the position quite clear. Sub-clause (5) of rule 11 provides that the Committee shall direct the Probation Officers or any other person/organization empowered to conduct "social enquiry" including the prospects of rehabilitation and to furnish the report to the Committee. The procedure for enquiry referred to in section 33 is laid down in rule 11 wherein specific provisions are made referring to a "social enquiry" and "social investigation' etc. A "social enquiry" can be ordered to be conducted in Form No. 1 in sub-rule (5). Even a form is prescribed for giving a direction for the enquiry to be conducted in the case of a "child in need of care and protection" produced before the committee. (The above rule comes under Chapter III which relates to the "child in need of care and protection"); *Jose Maveli* v. *State of Kerala,* 2007 Cr LJ 2709: 2007 (2) Ker LT 761 (Ker).

**7. Social Investigation – Law on –** The enquiry under section 33 read with rule 11() shall be completed within four months of receipt of the order or within such a shortest period as may be fixed by the Committee etc, provided that the period of submission of report may be extended by the Committee having regard to the circumstances and for reasons to be recorded in writing. There can also be social investigation report as provide in Form No. 2. It is depending upon the contents of such reports referred to in section 33 and rule 11 that the Committee shall take a final decision on conclusion of the inquiry under section 33(3) read with rule 11(14) of the Rules; *Jose Maveli* v. *State of Kerala,* 2007 Cr LJ 2709: 2007 (2) Ker LT 761 (Ker).

**8. Child in Need of Care and Protection – Law on –** A close reading of section 2(d) of the Act shows that a child who is having a parent or guardian cannot, strictly speaking, be said to be a "child in need of care and protection", unless such parent/guardian is possessed for such disqualifications as are specifically laid down in sub-clauses (ii), (iv) or (v) of section 2(d) of the Act. Sub-clauses (ii), (iv) and (v) specifically refer to a child who has a parent or guardian. As per sub-clause (iv), if the child has a parent, only if such parent is unfit or incapacitated to exercise control over the child that his child becomes a "child in need of care and protection". (May be, the parent is mentally deranged or so). Under sub-clause (v), if the child has parents, they must have abandoned him/her so that such child can be treated as a "child in need of care and protection". If it is case of a 'missing and run away child', the child can be treated as a 'child in need of care and protection" under section 2(d)(v), only if the parent cannot be found, even after a reasonable enquiry. It is also clear from section 2(d)(v) that a child can be stated to be a "child in need of care and protection", if no one is willing to take care of him/her, though he has no parent. The corollary that follows from the above clause is that even in cases where the child is parentless; he does not become a "child in need of care and protection", unless no one is willing to take care of him/her. As per section 2(d)(ii)(a) or (b) of the Act, in case the child is residing with a parent or guardian (*vide* definition of guardian), such person must have threatened to kill or injure the child and there is a reasonable likelihood of the threat carried out or the parent must have killed, abused or neglected some other child or children and there is likelihood of the child in question being killed, abused or neglected by such person for treating a child to be a "child in need of care and protection". It is only under the above circumstances that a child who has a parent can be stated to be a child coming under section 2(d) of the Act. A child who is having a parent, cannot ordinarily be brought under the definition of section 2(d) of the Act, unless such parent is having such disqualifications or incapacities as are specifically referred to in sub-clauses (ii)(a) or (b) or sub-clauses (iv) or (v) of section 2(d) of the Act or that he is to be "unfit" by the Committee. It must be noted that it is not all and every disqualification of a parent which is brought within the sweep of section 2(d) of the Act. The disqualifications of a parent/guardian are as specified in the provision. The petitioner has no case that the children produced in this case have parent or guardian or that such person is unfit or has any such disqualifications as are referred to in the relevant sub-clauses in section 2(d) of the Act; *Jose Maveli* v. *State of Kerala,* 2007 Cr LJ 2709: 2007 (2) Ker LT 761 (Ker).

**34. Children's homes.**—(1) The State Government may establish and maintain either by itself or in association with the voluntary organisations, children's homes, in every district or group of districts, as the case may be, for the reception of child in need of care and protection during the pendency of any inquiry and subsequently for their care, treatment, education, training, development and rehabilitation.

(2) The State Government may, by rules made under this Act, provide for the management of children's homes including the standards and the nature of services to be provided by them, and the circumstances under which, and the manner in which, the certification of a children's home or recognition to a voluntary organisation may be granted or withdrawn.

[1][(3) Without prejudice to anything contained in any other law for the time being in force, all institutions, whether State Government run or those run by voluntary organizations for children in need of care and protection shall, within a period of six months from the date of commencement of the Juvenile Justice (Care and Protection of Children) Amendment Act, 2006, be registered under this Act in such manner as may be prescribed.]

**COMMENTS**

**Juvenile in Place of Safety – Law on –** Where a juvenile commits a serious offence, the Board must report the matter to the State Government who may keep the juvenile in a place of safety for not more than 3 years. A juvenile cannot be sentenced to death or life imprisonment; *Subramanian Swamy* v. *Raju,* 2014 (4) SCALE 305: AIR 2014 SC 1649: 2014 (2) Crimes 307 (SC)-*Nirbhaya* case [Hon'ble Judges: P. Sathasivam, Ranjan Gogoi, Shiva Kirti Singh]

**35. Inspection.**—(1) The State Government may appoint inspection committees for the children's homes (hereinafter referred to as the inspection committees) for the State, a district and city, as the case may be, for such period and for such purposes as may be prescribed.

(2) The inspection committee of a State, district or of a city shall consist of such number of representatives from the State Government, [2][***], Committee,

1. Ins. by Act 33 of 2006, sec. 19 (w.e.f. 22-8-2006).
2. The words "local authority" omitted by Act 33 of 2006, sec. 5 (w.e.f. 22-8-2006).

voluntary organisations and such other medical experts and social workers as may be prescribed.

**COMMENTS**

**Citizen – Rights of –** The Preamble, an integral part of the Constitution, pledges to secure 'socio-economic justice' to all its citizens with stated liberties, 'equality of status and of opportunity', assuring 'fraternity' and 'dignity' of the individual in a united and integrated Bharat; *Gaurav Jain* v. *Union of India*, AIR 1997 SC 3021: 1997 (4) SCALE 657: 1997 (8) SCC 114.

**36. Social auditing.**—The Central Government or State Government may monitor and evaluate the functioning of the Children's homes at such period and through such persons and institutions as may be specified by that Government.

**COMMENTS**

**Social Audit – Comments on –** Democracy is government by the people. It is a continual participative operation, not a cataclysmic, periodic exercise. The little man, in his multitude, marking his vote at the poll does a social audit of his Parliament plus political choice of this proxy. Although the full flower of participative government rarely blossoms, the minimum credential of popular government is appeal to the people after every term for a renewal of confidence. So we have adult franchise and general elections as constitutional compulsions. "The right of election is the very essence of the Constitution. It needs little argument to hold that the heart of the Parliamentary system is free and fair elections periodically held, based on adult franchise, although social and economic democracy may demand much more; *Mohinder Singh Gill* v. *Chief Election Commissioner, New Delhi*, 1978 (1) SCC 405: 1978 (2) SCR 272: AIR 1978 SC 851.

**37. Shelter homes.**—(1) The State Government may recognise, reputed and capable voluntary organisations and provide them assistance to set up and administer as many shelter homes for juveniles or children as may be required.

(2) The shelter homes referred in sub-section (1) shall function as drop-in-centres for the children in the need of urgent support who have been brought to such homes through such persons as are referred to in sub-section (1) of section 32.

(3) As far as possible, the shelter homes shall have such facilities as may be prescribed by the rules.

**SYNOPSIS**

1. Parental Care – Comments on
2. Right to Privacy and Confidentiality of Juvenile – Law on

**COMMENTS**

**1. Parental Care – Comments on –** A child would learn a lot in his life from the bed-time fairly tales, under the parental care, whether he or she be, in a hut or a palace. The sweet and sour- family environment may cool down, the heat of his thirst and hunger. Though poverty may taste bitter to him, the parental care and affection may be sweet and soothing. Nothing can substitute it. The silky bed or velvet clothes, sweet bread or honey, a golden bowl or silver spoon at an Institution, may not replace the warmth of a family environment. The poor financial condition of a parent alone is not at all sufficient to deprive the child of a family environment, which is to be ensured by the provisions of the special enactment. Unfitness of the parent referred to in sub-clause (iv) of section 2(d) of the Act has also, therefore, no reference to the financial incapacity alone. A parent who is not of an acceptable standard or not suitable to be a parent can be said to be 'unfit'. A child of such a parent is a child in need of care and protection' as per section 2(d)(iv). But, poverty of the parent by itself may not make a parent 'unfit" to be a parent and bring his child under any of the sub-clauses of section 2(d) of the Act. That may not be sufficient to bring a child born to a financially poor parent under sub-clause (i) of section 2(d) of the Act also; *Jose Maveli* v. *State of Kerala,* 2007 Cr LJ 2709: 2007 (2) Ker LT 761 (Ker).

**2. Right to Privacy and Confidentiality of Juvenile – Law on –** The Rules, particularly rule 3, provide that in all decisions taken within the context of administration of justice, the principle of best interests of a juvenile shall be the primary consideration. What this means is that "the traditional objectives of criminal justice, that is retribution and repression, must give way to rehabilitative and restorative objectives of juvenile justice". The right to privacy and confidentiality of a juvenile is required to be protected by all means and through all the stages of the proceedings, and this is one of the reasons why the identity of a juvenile in conflict with law is not disclosed. Following the requirements of the Convention on the Rights of the Child, rule 3 provides that institutionalization of a child or a juvenile in conflict with law shall be the last resort after a reasonable inquiry and that too for the minimum possible duration; *Jitendra Singh @ Babboo Singh* v. *State of Uttar Pradesh,* 2013 (11) SCC 193: JT 2013 (11) SC 152: 2013 (9) SCALE 18.

**38. Transfer.**—(1) If during the inquiry it is found that the child hails from the place outside the jurisdiction of the Committee, the Committee shall order the transfer of the child to the competent authority having jurisdiction over the place of residence of the child.

(2) Such juvenile or the child shall be escorted by the staff of the home in which he is lodged originally.

(3) The State Government may make rules to provide for the travelling allowance to be paid to the child.

**SYNOPSIS**

1. Provision – Comments on
2. Jurisdiction – Law on

**COMMENTS**

**1. Provision – Comments on –** Section 38 of the Act lays down that if the child is found to be hailing from a place outside jurisdiction of the Committee, the Committee shall order the transfer of the child to the competent authority having jurisdiction over the place of residence of the child. The Committee shall also, under rule 11(3) satisfy itself that the child has not been subjected to any ill-treatment or harassment either by police or any other person who takes charge of the child for the purpose of bringing before the Committee. If any such ill-treatment or harassment is noticed by the Committee or it is caused to be brought to the notice of the Committee, it shall initiate appropriate action against the offenders by filing a complaint before the Magistrate having jurisdiction, as referred to in rule 11(3) of the Rules; *Jose Maveli* v. *State of Kerala,* 2007 Cr LJ 2709: 2007 (2) Ker LT 761 (Ker).

**2. Jurisdiction – Law on –** Section 38 of the Act and rule 36 of the rules lay down that if during inquiry, it is found that the child hails from the place outside the jurisdiction of the Committee, the Committee shall order transfer of the child to the competent authority having jurisdiction over the place of residence of he child, having regard to the best interest and safety either absolutely or on conditions as it deems fit. Arrangement shall be made to escort the child to the Committee to which the child is transferred. The case file and records relating to the child shall also be sent along with the child, as per rule 36(4) of the Rules. It is better to keep in mind, the purpose behind the provision. A Child hailing from another State may not feel comfortable in a State where people around him speak a totally different language, which may be unknown to him. The child may find it difficult to communicate and speak out his difficulties or ventilate his tress and strain, to his satisfaction because of communication problems. Hence, it shall be the duty of the Committee/Magistrate to ensure that such child is transferred to its native place at the earliest; *Jose Maveli* v. *State of Kerala,* 2007 Cr LJ 2709: 2007 (2) Ker LT 761 (Ker).

**39. Restoration.**—(1) Restoration of and protection to a child shall be the prime objective of any children's home or the shelter home.

(2) The children's home or a shelter home, as the case may be, shall take such steps as are considered necessary for the restoration of and protection to a child deprived of his family environment temporarily or permanently where such child is under the care and protection of a children's home or a shelter home, as the case may be.

(3) The Committee shall have the powers to restore any child in need of care and protection to his parent, guardian, fit person or fit institution, as the case may be, and give them suitable directions.

[1][*Explanation.*—For the purposes of this section "restoration of and protection of a child" means restoration to—

(a) parents;
(b) adopted parents;
(c) foster parents;
(d) guardian;
(e) fit person;
(f) fit institution.]

**COMMENTS**

**Absence of Children's Home – Law on** – As per section 39 of the Act, in the case of a child who has a parent of guardian, the Children's Home to which the child is sent (vide also section 33 of the act), shall take such steps as are necessary for the restoration and protection of a child, who is deprived of his family environment, temporarily or permanently. In the absence of Children's Home, if the child is sent to a person/ institution, naturally, such person/Institution shall also have the same statutory duties and liabilities to restore the child, as stated in section 39 of the Act; *Jose Maveli* v. *State of Kerala,* 2007 Cr LJ 2709: 2007 (2) Ker LT 761 (Ker).

## *CHAPTER IV*

## REHABILITATION AND SOCIAL REINTEGRATION

**40. Process of rehabilitation and social reintegration.**—The rehabilitation and social reintegration of a child shall begin during the stay of the child in a children's home or special home and the rehabilitation and social reintegration of children shall be carried out alternatively by (i) adoption, (ii) foster care, (iii) sponsorship, and (iv) sending the child to an after-care organisation.

1. Subs. by Act 33 of 2006, sec. 20, for *Explanation* (w.e.f. 22-8-2006). *Explanation,* before substitution, stood as under:

"*Explanation.*—For the purposes of this section "restoration of child" means restoration to—

(a) parents;
(b) adopted parents;
(c) foster parents.".

### COMMENTS

**Opportunity to Children – Law on –** The provisions of the Juvenile Justice Act, 2000, as amended by the Amendment Act, 2006 and the Juvenile Justice Rules, 2007 aim at providing an opportunity to the children, who have, for some reasons or the other, gone astray, to realize their mistakes, rehabilitate themselves and rebuild their lives and become useful citizens of society instead of degenerating into hardened criminals; *Subash Sahu* v. *State of Orissa*, 2012 Cr LJ 4607: 2013 (7) RCR (Cri) 2646 (Ori) (DB).

**41. Adoption.**—(1) The primary responsibility for providing care and protection to children shall be that of his family.

[1][(2) Adoption shall be resorted to for the rehabilitation of the children who are orphan, abandoned or surrendered through such mechanism as may be prescribed.

(3) In keeping with the provisions of the various guidelines for adoption issued from time to time, by the State Government, or the Central Adoption Resource Agency and notified by the Central Government, children may be given in adoption by a court after satisfying itself regarding the investigations having been carried out as are required for giving such children in adoption.

(4) The State Government shall recognise one or more of its institutions or voluntary organisations in each district as specialised adoption agencies in such manner as may be prescribed for the placement of orphan, abandoned or surrendered children for adoption in accordance with the guidelines notified under sub-section (3):

Provided that the children's homes and the institutions run by the State Government or a voluntary organisation for children in need of care and protection, who are orphan, abandoned or surrendered, shall ensure that these children are declared free for adoption by the Committee and all such cases shall be referred to the adoption agency in that district for placement of such children in adoption in accordance with the guidelines notified under sub-section (3).]

(5) No child shall be offered for adoption—

(a) until two members of the Committee declare the child legally free for placement in the case of abandoned children,

(b) till the two months period for reconsideration by the parent is over in the case of surrendered children, and

(c) without his consent in the case of a child who can understand and express his consent.

---

1. Subs. by Act 33 of 2006, sec. 21, for sub-sections (2), (3) and (4) (w.e.f. 22-8-2006). Sub-section (2), (3) and (4), before substitution, stood as under:

"(2) Adoption shall be resorted to for the rehabilitation of such children as are orphaned, abandoned, neglected and abused through institutional and non-institutional methods.

(3) In keeping with the provisions of the various guidelines for adoption issued from time to time by the State Government, the Board shall be empowered to give children in adoption and carry out such investigations as are required for giving children in adoption in accordance with the guidelines issued by the State Government from time to time in this regard.

(4) The childern's homes or the State Government run institutions for orphans shall be recognised as an adoption agencies both for scrutiny and placement of such children for adoption in accordance with the guidelines issued under sub-section (3).".

[1][(6) The Court may allow a child to be given in adoption—

(a) to a person irrespective of marital status or;

(b) to parents to adopt a child of same sex irrespective of the number of living biological sons or daughters; or

(c) to childless couples.]

**SYNOPSIS**

1. Adoptive Child of Same Sex – Law on
2. Adoption – Law on
3. Jurisdiction in Matters of Adoption and Guardianship – Law on
4. Procedural Irregularities – Law on
5. Court – Comments on
6. Courts should be Vigil in Safeguarding Interest of Child – Article 21 of the Constitution

**COMMENTS**

**1. Adoptive Child of Same Sex – Law on –** Clause (b) of sub-section (6) of section 41 of the Juvenile Justice Act is permissive and not restrictive. It permits parents to adopt a child of the same sex even if they have a living biological child of the same sex. It is often thought that a subtle differentiation may be made by the parents between a biological child and an adoptive child of the same sex. The Legislature has therefore expressly permitted adoption of a child of the same sex even if the parents have a biological child or children of the same sex living on the date of adoption. Section 6(b) or any other provision of the Juvenile Justice Act does not prevent adoption of a child where the adoptive parents have another living adopted child of the same sex; *Indian Association for Promotion of Adoption & Child Welfare* v. *Christopher Drury, Shenaz Drury*, 2012 (2) All MR 316: 2013 (1) BCR 161: 2012 (2) Mh LJ 811 (Bom).

**2. Adoption – Law on –** Under section 41(5)(a), no child shall be offered for adoption until two members of the Committee declare the child legally free for placement in case of abandoned children. Rule 25 speaks about the functions and powers of the Committee. Rule 25(m) envisages that the Committee shall declare a child legally free for adoption. Under rule 33(3)(b), a child becomes eligible for adoption when the Committee has completed its enquiry and declares the child legally free for adoption. Therefore, a conjoint reading of section 41(5) and rules 25(m) and rule 33(3)(b) makes it crystal clear that when an abandoned child is offered for adoption, the Child Welfare Committee, which is a quasi judicial authority has to declare the child free for adoption, where-after the competent court has to pass necessary orders under section 41 allowing a child to be given in adoption. It is only the Child Welfare Committee under the J.J. Act, who is authorized to declare a child free for adoption and law does not require any other agency, be it the State Council for Child Welfare or any other body, to have any say in regard to adoption. Section 41(6)(b) of the J.J. Act specifically provides that the court may allow a child to be given in adoption to a person irrespective of marital status. Clause 44(5) of the CARA (Central Adoption Resources Agency) Guidelines prescribes that siblings of different ages shall, as far as possible, be placed in adoption in the same family and such children shall also be categorized as special need children; *Secretary, Subhadra Mahatab Seva Saces of Kolathia* v. *State of Orissa*, 2013 (116) Cut LT 181: 2013 (1) Ori LR 455: AIR 2013 Ori 110.

**3. Jurisdiction in Matters of Adoption and Guardianship – Law on –** From the amended provisions of the Act it is amply clear that the Court may allow a child to be

---

1. Subs. by Act 33 of 2006, sec. 21, for sub-section (6) (w.e.f. 22-8-2006). Sub-section (6), before substitution, stood as under:

"(6) The Board may allow a child to be given in adoption—

(a) to a single parent, and

(b) to parents to adopt a child of same sex irrespective of the number of living biological sons or daughters.".

given in adoption. Consequently, after the amendment, the Board has no jurisdiction to allow the child to be adopted under the Act. Rule 33(5) of the Central Rules, 2007 specifies that for the purpose of section 41 of the Act, the Court implies the Civil Court and may include a Court of the District Judge, Family Court and the City Civil Court. So also, rule 35(12) of the Karnataka Rules, 2010 also specifies that for the purpose of section 41 of the Act, the Court implies Civil Court which has the jurisdiction in the matters of adoption and guardianship, including the Court of District Judge, Family Court, City Civil Court and the High Court. Hence, it is more than clear that it is the Court which has got jurisdiction to decide as to whether the child should be permitted to be adopted or not. The Board has no jurisdiction to decide such matters; *Krishnanugraha* v. *Commissioner Registrar of Birth and Death Udupi Municipality,* 2013 (1) KCCR 870: AIR 2013 Karn 62: 2013 (2) AIR Kar R 1.

**4. Procedural Irregularities – Law on –** There is another principle of law. A Court would legitimately refuse to issue a writ of *certiorari* or *mandamus* where procedural irregularities are found; *Chhatravas Chandra Arya Vidya Mandir* v. *Govt. of NCT of Delhi,* 2012 (188) DLT 455 (Del) (DB).

**5. Court – Comments on –** Section 3 of the Indian Evidence Act defines courts to include all Judges and Magistrates and all persons except arbitrators legally authorized to take evidence. The definition is also of no crucial help to this court in understanding the concept of the court for the purpose of section 41(6). In order to decode the intention of the Legislature and to decipher the purpose for which the expression 'Board' which was there earlier in section 41(6) was amended to bring in the expression "court". It is in exercise of powers of the Central Government that the model rules relations to Adoptions have been formulated now under rule 33 in Chapter 5. The relevant sub-rule is sub-rule 5 of rule 33 which reads as follows:

> "For the purpose of section 41 of the Act, 'court' implies a civil court, which has jurisdiction in matters of adoption and guardianship and may include the court of the district judge, family courts and city civil court"; *Andrew Mendez* v. *State of Kerala,* 2008 Cr LJ 2368: 2008 (1) KerLJ 647: 2008 (1) Ker LT 1000 (Ker).

**6. Courts should be Vigil in Safeguarding Interest of Child – Article 21 of the Constitution –** The Constitutional guarantee for life and personal liberty under Article 21 of the Constitution shall also be safeguarded in following the adoption procedure under section 41(6) of the Act and the relevant Rules. The court has to maintain uniformity and be vigil in safeguarding the interest of child under section 41(6) of the Act when the child is being adopted by persons residing outside the country or by foreign national; *Arjun Neelakantan* v. *NIL,* AIR 2015 (NOC) 112 (Mad).

**42. Foster care.**—(1) The foster care may be used for temporary placement of those infants who are ultimately to be given for adoption.

(2) In foster care, the child may be placed in another family for a short or extended period of time, depending upon the circumstances where the child's own parent usually visit regularly and eventually after the rehabilitation, where the children may return to their own homes.

(3) The State Government may make rules for the purposes of carrying out the scheme of foster care programme of children.

**SYNOPSIS**

1. Journey Time – Law on
2. Poor Financial Background – Comments on

**COMMENTS**

**1. Journey Time – Law on –** It is laid down in rule 10(2)(i) of the Act that when a person/organization receives a "child in need and care of protection", and if such child is above the age of five years, it shall be produced before the Committee, within shortest possible time, but not later than twelve hours of such reception, excluding the journey time, as per rule 10(2)(i). For children under five years of age, the person/organization shall send a written report, along with the photograph of the child, within twenty four hours of reception excluding the journey time after admitting the child in a nearby Foundling Home/Placement Agency; *Jose Maveli* v. *State of Kerala,* 2007 Cr LJ 2709: 2007 (2) Ker LT 761 (Ker).

**2. Poor Financial Background – Comments on** – In a country like India, poverty is quite common. It will therefore, be unjust and even cruel, if poor financial condition of a parent or guardian ALONE is made the basis for disqualifying a biological parent to be 'unit', so as to treat his child as a "child in need of care and protection". A child may not be treated as a "child in need of care and protection", and nipped him off from the care of his/her own biological parents, only because his parent if financially poor, homeless or penniless. Even if the parents are poor and their purses are empty to feed the children or provide to them a hut to live in, it is needless to say that a conducive family atmosphere is ensured by most of the parents. Majority of Indian children are born, not with a silver spoon. The poor financial background of a parent of family alone has not spoiled their welfare in many cases. On other hand, this is a country where children are educated and taken to great heights, though many of them are, without even a roof under which, they can comfortably sleep. They may not even have sufficient food to satiate or quench their hunger or thirst. Still, they may study under the dim glow of a street light or a neighbour's candle to reach glorious heights. The poverty of their parents alone has never been a hurdle for a Indian child to come up in his life in many a case; *Jose Maveli* v. *State of Kerala,* 2007 Cr LJ 2709: 2007 (2) Ker LT 761 (Ker).

**43. Sponsorship.**—(1) The sponsorship programme may provide supplementary support to families, to children's homes and to special homes to meet medical, nutritional, educational and other needs of the children with a view to improving their quality of life.

(2) The State Government may make rules for the purposes of carrying out various schemes of sponsorship of children, such as individual to individual sponsorship, group sponsorship or community sponsorship.

**44. After-care organisation.**—The Sate Government may, by rules made under this Act, provide—

(a) for the establishment or recognition of after-care organisations and the functions that may be performed by them under this Act;

(b) for a scheme of after-care programme to be followed by such after-care organisations for the purpose of taking care of juveniles or the children after they leave special homes, children homes and for the purpose of enabling them to lead an honest, industrious and useful life;

(c) for the preparation or submission of a report by the probation officer or any other officer appointed by that Government in respect of each juvenile or the child prior to his discharge from a special home, children's home, regarding the necessity and nature of after-care of such juvenile or of a child, the period of such after-care, supervision thereof and for the submission of report by the probation officer or any other officer appointed for the purpose, on the progress of each juvenile or the child;

(d) for the standards and the nature of services to be maintained by such after care organisations;

(e) for such other matters as may be necessary for the purpose of carrying out the scheme of after-care programme for the juvenile or the child:

Provided that any rule made under this section shall not provide for such juvenile or child to stay in the after-care organisation for more than three years:

Provided further that a juvenile or child over seventeen years of age but less than eighteen years of age would stay in the after-care organisation till he attains the age of twenty years.

**45. Linkages and co-ordination.**—The State Government may make rules to ensure effective linkages between various governmental, non-governmental, corporate and other community agencies for facilitating the rehabilitation and social reintegration of the child.

## *CHAPTER V*

## MISCELLANEOUS

**46. Attendance of parent or guardian of juvenile or child.**—Any competent authority before which a juvenile or the child is brought under any of the provisions of this Act, may, whenever it so thinks fit, require any parent or guardian having the actual charge of or control over the juvenile or the child to be present at any proceeding in respect of the juvenile or the child.

### COMMENTS

**Adoption – Comments on –** There is no common law of adoption. The Customary Hindu law as modified and codified by the Hindu Adoptions and Maintenance Act recognizes the rights of Hindu parents and Hindu children to adopt and be adopted. Except when customary law permits adoption those of other faiths had no legal option of adopting a child and conferring on such child all rights of a biological legitimate child. The Juvenile Justice Act, 2000 made it possible for Indian children to be adopted and Indian parents to adopt. Initially it was stipulated that the Juvenile Justice Board may allow the child to be adopted. Later by Act 33/06, the Act was amended to clarify what adoption meant. It was further declared that the 'court' and not the Board have powers under section 46 of the Act to allow adoption. What the Parliament did not or could not do overtly by introducing the Adoption Bills in 1972 and 1980 was sought to be achieved covertly by making stipulations in Chapter IV of the Juvenile justice Act; *Andrew Mendez* v. *State of Kerala,* 2008 Cr LJ 2368: 2008 (1) Ker LJ 647: 2008 (1) Ker LT 1000 (Ker).

**47. Dispensing with attendance of juvenile or child.**—If, at any stage during the course of an inquiry, a competent authority is satisfied that the attendance of the juvenile or the child is not essential for the purpose of inquiry, the competent authority may dispense with his attendance and proceed with the inquiry in the absence of the juvenile or the child.

**48. Committal to approved place of juvenile or child suffering from dangerous diseases and his future disposal.**—(1) When a juvenile or the child who has been brought before a competent authority under this Act, is found to be suffering from a disease requiring prolonged medical treatment or physical or mental complaint that will respond to treatment, the competent authority may send the juvenile or the child to any place recognised to be an approved place in accordance with the rules made under this Act for such period as it may think necessary for the required treatment.

[1][***]

---

1. Sub-section (2) omitted by Act 12 of 2011, sec. 2 (w.e.f. 1-1-2012). Sub-section (2), before omission, stood as under:

   "(2) Where a juvenile or the child is found to be suffering from leprosy, sexually transmitted disease, Hepatitis B, open cases of Tuberculosis and such other diseases or is of unsound mind, he shall be dealt with separately through various specialised referral services or under the relevant laws as such.".

**49. Presumption and determination of age.**—(1) Where it appears to a competent authority that person brought before it under any of the provisions of this Act (otherwise than for the purpose of giving evidence) is a juvenile or the child, the competent authority shall make due inquiry so as to the age of that person and for that purpose shall take such evidence as may be necessary (but not an affidavit) and shall record a finding whether the person is a juvenile or the child or not, stating his age as nearly as may be.

(2) No order of a competent authority shall be deemed to have become invalid merely by any subsequent proof that the person in respect of whom the order has been made is not a juvenile or the child, and the age recorded by the competent authority to be the age of person so brought before it, shall for the purpose of this Act, be deemed to be the true age of that person.

**SYNOPSIS**

1. Provision – Law on
2. Provision – Attraction of
3. Provision – Mandate of
4. Certificate Issued by Village Chowkidar – Law on
5. Date of Birth – Law on
6. Evidence for Determination of Age – Law on
7. Medical Opinion – Conditions for
8. Primary School Leaving Certificate – Comments on
9. Sequence of Birth Certificates – Law on
10. Absence of Evidence – Law on
11. Admission Register – Law on
12. Assessment of Age – Law on
13. Benefit to Child – Law on
14. Birth Certificate – Ambit of
15. Case Remanded by High Court – Comments on
16. Certificate Issued by Corporation or Nagar Panchayat – Law on
17. Child's Statements – Law on
18. Claim of Juvenility – Law on
19. Competent Authority – Duties of
20. Competent Authority – Powers of
21. Competent Authority – Restriction for
22. Conclusive Proof of Age – Law on
23. Indian Majority Act – Provision of
24. Court – Powers of
25. Court, Board, Child Welfare Committee or Competent Authority – Solemn Statutory Duty of
26. Date of Birth under U.P.Rules – Discussion on
27. Delinquent in Borderline Cases – Law on
28. Detailed Probe – Law on
29. Determination of Age – Discussion on
30. Determination of Date of Birth – Law on
31. Discretion of Court – Law on
32. Discretionary Powers – Law on
33. Entry Regarding Age in School Register – Law on
34. Exact Assessment of Age – Law on
35. Fusion of Iliac Bone – Law on
36. Gram Panchayat – Status of
37. Guiding Factor for Determining Age – Law on
38. Inquiry for Claim of Juvenility – Law on
39. Magistrate – Duties of
40. Magistrate – Functions of
41. Margin of One Year – Law on
42. Matriculation Certificate – Importance of
43. Medical Board's Opinion based on Radiological Examination – Law on
44. Medical Evidence – Law on
45. Medical Evidence Based on Scientific Investigation – Law on
46. Medical Opinion by Duly Constituted Medical Board – Comments on
47. Order of Competent Authority – Law on
48. Ossification Report – Law on
49. Ossification Test – Comments on
50. Overwritten and Interpolated Entry in School Register – Law on
51. Physical Appearance – Law on
52. Physical Appearance – Comments on
53. Registration Certificate – Law on
54. School Record with Ambiguity – Law on
55. Subsequent Proof – Law on
56. Transfer Certificate Issued by School First Attended – Significance of
57. U.P. Rules – Comments on
58. Voters List – Law on
59. X-Ray Ossification Test – Law on
60. Courts – Role of
61. Determinative Factors of Juvenility – Comments on
62. Inquiry – Time Period for
63. No Exact Assessment – Law on

**COMMENTS**

**1. Provision – Law on –** The opening words of sub-section (1) of section 49, above, shows that only when a person is "brought before the competent authority" under any of the provisions of the Act, the competent authority is required to make due enquiry as to the age of that person and for that purpose take such evidence as may be necessary and record a finding whether the person is a juvenile or not. Section 49 is, therefore, attracted when a person is brought before the competent authority and not otherwise; *Yuv Raj* v. *State of Himachal Pradesh*, 2011 (2) Shim LC 373 (HP).

**2. Provision – Attraction of –** The opening words of sub-section (1) of section 49 shows that only when a person is "brought before the competent authority" under any of the provisions of the Act, the competent authority is required to make due enquiry as to the age of that person and for that purpose take such evidence as may be necessary and record a finding whether the person is a juvenile or not. Section 49 is, therefore, attracted when a person is brought before the competent authority and not otherwise; *Jabar Singh* v. *Dinesh*, 2010 (2) SCALE 856: 2010 (3) SCC 757: 2010 (3) SCR 353.

**3. Provision – Mandate of –** If a person is produced before the competent authority and if he appears to be a juvenile then the competent authority is mandated by law to hold an inquiry to determine as to whether the person is a juvenile or not and will determine his age. The competent authority is also mandated to take such evidence as may be necessary for determination of age of that person who has been brought before it. However, the filing of the affidavit in the said inquiry for determination of age has not been countenanced by the statute as the words "but not an affidavit" used under that section prohibits relying upon affidavits and taking it as a piece of evidence in such an inquiry. The section also mandated that the age of a person be determined "as nearly as may be". This indicates that the age of the accused be determined as far as possible to be his real age. Sub-section (2) of section 49, however, provides that no order passed by the competent authority under sub-section (1) will become invalid "merely by any subsequent proof that the person in respect of whom the order has been made is not a juvenile or a child." The said sub-section further provides that the age of a person determined by the competent authority for the purpose of this Act "be deemed to be a true age of that person." Applicability of sub-section (2) of section 49 of the Act will arise when there has already been a determination of age by a competent authority and the said determination of age cannot be set aside by a subsequent proof. The words "subsequent proof" used under this sub-section (2) indicate the proof, which was not available with the competent authority at the time of determination of the age during the said proceeding. Those words "subsequent proof" indicate those proofs, which were discovered subsequently after age of the person has already been determined by the competent authority. Thus it is clear from the above analytical analysis that if the person has been declared to be a juvenile by the competent authority then he cannot be declared otherwise on the basis of subsequent material which was not available during the conducting of inquiry by the competent authority and was not produced before him. Such new material will not make the order passed by competent authority illegal and the age which has already been determined by him will be the true age of the person concerned; *Vineet Kumar* v. *State of Uttar Pradesh*, 2007 (5) ALJ 302: 2007 Cr LJ 3891 (All).

**4. Certificate Issued by Village Chowkidar – Law on –** When the law gives prime importance to the date of birth certificate issued by the school first attended, the genuineness of which is not disputed, there is no question of placing reliance on the certificate issued by the village Chowkidar; *Jodhbir Singh* v. *State of Punjab*, 2012 (11) SCR 230: AIR 2013 SC 1: 2012 (11) SCALE 595.

**5. Date of Birth – Law on –** Sub-rule 3 of rule 12 of Rules of 2007 envisages that in every case concerning a child or juvenile, in conflict with law, the age determination inquiry shall be conducted by the Court or the Board, as the case may be, or the Committee by seeking evidence by obtaining the matriculation or equivalent certificates, if available, and in the absence whereof; the date of birth certificate from the school and in the absence whereof, the birth certificate given by a corporation or a municipal authority or a panchayat. The medical opinion with regard to the age of the delinquent child shall be sought only when a birth certificate or school certificate or matriculation certificate is not available with him. Rule 12 of the Rules 2007 categorically envisages that the medical opinion from the Medical Board should be sought only when the matriculation certificate or school certificate or any birth certificate issued by a Corporation or by any Panchayat or Municipality is not available; *Vikram Saini* v. *State of Rajasthan,* 2011 (2) Raj LW 1455: 2013 (7) RCR (Cri) 3527 (Raj).

**6. Evidence for Determination of Age – Law on –** Rule 12 of the Rules categorically envisages that the medical opinion from the medical board should be sought only when the matriculation certificate or school certificate or any birth certificate issued by a corporation or by any Panchayat or municipality is not available. Entry relating to date of birth entered in the mark sheet is one of the valid proofs of evidence for determination of age of an accused person. The School Leaving Certificate is also a valid proof in determining the age of the accused person. Rule 12 of the Rules which were brought in pursuance of the Act describes four categories of evidence which have been provided in which preference has been given to school certificate over the medical report; *Shah Nawaz* v. *State of Uttar Pradesh,* AIR 2011 SC 3107: 2011 (8) SCALE 423: 2011 (13) SCC 751.

**7. Medical Opinion – Conditions for –** A perusal of sub-rule (3) of rule 12 shows that the Court or the Board which is required to determine the age shall conduct the enquiry for determining the age and for the aforesaid purpose, seek evidence by obtaining the matriculation or equivalent certificates if available. Clause (a)(i) of sub-rule (3) further provides that only in the absence of the matriculation or equivalent certificate, the date of birth certificate from the school (other than a play school) first attended can be looked into as per clause (ii) and in the absence of both, the third category of evidence as mentioned in clause (iii) by way of birth certificate given by the Corporation or Municipality or a Panchayat can be looked into. The words in clause (i), (ii) and (iii) of clause (a) of sub-rule (3) of rule 12 in the absence cannot be lost sight of and the Legislature while framing rule 12 has specifically given a mandate that the availability of the first of the documents would exclude the taking into consideration of all the remaining documents in clause (ii) and (iii). It is further reiterated by the provisions of rule 12(3)(b) which makes it further clear that while enabling the Board/Court for seeking the medical opinion with regard to the age that the opinion can be sought only in the absence of the material mentioned in either clause (i)(ii) or (iii) of clause (a); *Lekhram* v. *State of Rajasthan,* 2013 (3) Raj LW 2123: 2013 (3) Raj LW 2545: 2012 Cr LJ 4258 (Raj) (Jaipur Bench) (DB).

**8. Primary School Leaving Certificate – Comments on –** Section 7A confers jurisdiction whenever a claim of juvenility is raised before any Court. The Court shall make an enquiry so as to determine the age of the applicant and shall record a finding whether the person was juvenile on the date of commission of the offence or not. Court/ Board while determining the age, shall at first instance consider the birth certificate issued by a competent authority. In case, it is not filed a date of birth certificate from School first attended or matriculation or equivalent certificate. In the absence of aforementioned, the medical opinion of the duly constituted Medical Board regarding his age to be obtained. If the applicant has filed his primary School leaving certificate, wherein his date of birth and other relevant particulars have been noted and being the School first attended, this document alone must have been taken into considered to decide whether the applicant is juvenile or not; *Amol Singh @ Bade @ Rajesh* v. *State of Uttar Pradesh,* 2013 (4) Crimes 24 (All): 2012 (10) ADJ 111: 2012 (3) JIC 723.

**9. Sequence of Birth Certificates – Law on –** A perusal of the rule 12(3) of the Central Rules shows that it gives precedence to matriculation or equivalent certificates with regard to entry of date of birth over certificates issued by the school (other than a play school) first attended or the date-of-birth certificate given by a Corporation or a Municipal Authority or a Panchayat. Rule 22(5) of the U.P. Rules on the other hand gives the sequence of certificates to be considered and in the sequence, the birth certificate given by a Corporation or Municipal Authority is placed first and date of birth certificate from school first attended is placed above the matriculation or equivalent certificates, if available, which is placed in the last but before the medical opinion by a duly constituted Medical Board; *Jai Prakash Tiwari* v. *State of Uttar Pradesh,* 2012 (10) ADJ 478: 2013 (2) ACrR 1383 (All).

**10. Absence of Evidence – Law on –** The 2000 Act is indisputably a beneficial legislation. Principles of beneficial legislation, however, are to be applied only for the purpose of interpretation of the statute and not for arriving at a conclusion as to whether a person is juvenile or not. Whether an offender was a juvenile on the date of commission of the offence or not is essentially a question of fact which is required to be determined on the basis of the materials brought on records by the parties. In absence of any evidence which is relevant for the said purpose as envisaged under section 35 of the Indian Evidence Act, the same must be determined keeping in view the factual matrix involved in each case. For the said purpose, not only relevant materials are required to be considered, the orders passed by the court on earlier occasions would also be relevant; *Jyoti Prakash Rai* v. *State of Bihar,* AIR 2008 SC 1696: 2008 (15) SCC 223: 2008 (3) SCALE 348.

**11. Admission Register – Law on –** Admission register in the school in which the candidate first attended is a relevant piece of evidence of the date of birth; *Ashwani Kumar Saxena* v. *State of Madhya Pradesh,* 2012 (10) SCR 540: AIR 2013 SC 553: 2012 (9) SCALE 90.

**12. Assessment of Age – Law on –** In case exact assessment of the age cannot be done, the Court or the Board or, as the case may be, the Committee, for the reasons to be recorded by them, may, if considered necessary, give benefit to the child or juvenile by considering his/her age on lower side within the margin of one year. It would thus be seen that under the rules, the age of the person claiming to be a juvenile, is to be determined on the basis of the matriculation or equivalent certificate, if such a certificate is available. In case the matriculation or equivalent certificate is not available, the age of the juvenile is to be determined on the basis of the birth certificate issued from the school, other than the play school first attended by him. If neither the certificate of the first nature nor the certificate of the second nature is available, the age is to be determined on the basis of the birth certificate given by the corporation or municipal authorities or Panchayat. It is only in the absence of matriculation or equivalent certificate, the date of birth certificate from school first attended and the birth certificate given by the corporation or a municipal authority or Panchayat that the medical opinion can be sought with respect to the age of a person claiming to be a juvenile in conflict with law. The obvious reason behind giving preference to certificates over the medical opinion appears to be that, the documents, if found to be genuine, would reflect the precise age of the person claiming to be a juvenile whereas the medical opinion, cannot be said to be absolutely error free; *Yash Sehrawat* v. *Board of Control for Cricket in India,* 2014 (141) DRJ 518.

**13. Benefit to Child – Law on –** Rule 12(3)(b) of Juvenile Justice (Care and Protection of Children) Rules, 2007 requires that only in the absence of any of the above forms of evidence/proof, medical opinion would be sought from a duly constituted Medical Board which will declare the age of the juvenile or the child. It is provided as well that in case the exact assessment cannot be done, the Court or the Board or as the case be, the Committee, for reasons to be recorded by them, may, if considered necessary, give benefit to the child or the juvenile by considering his/her age on lower side within the margin of one year; *State of Assam (in re:),* 2012 Cr LJ 471: 2011 (4) Gau LR 235: 2013 (6) RCR (Cri) 2190 (Gau) (DB).

**14. Birth Certificate – Ambit of –** Even otherwise, the entry in the registration register is not a document in terms of rule 12(3)(a)(iii), since it is not a birth certificate given by a corporation or a municipality or a panchayat. It is trite to say that a birth certificate normally comes into existence at the time of birth of the incumbent and it is therefore, a contemporaneous record of the date of birth of the said incumbent. The aforesaid entries in the registration register are not contemporaneous. Therefore, it would be improper to rely upon and take into consideration the entries in the registration register regarding the date of birth. Therefore, the resort to the ossification test conducted for determination of the age of the accused is justified and proper; *Nazir* v. *State*, 2013 Cr LJ 1891 (Del) (DB).

**15. Case Remanded by High Court – Comments on –** A close look at rule 12 reveals that this rule itself provides a complete code in which "inquiry" referred to in section 7A of the Act about determination as the age of a juvenile is to be conducted and if any of the documents referred to in this rule is available on record then no further evidence is required to be taken and the Court on the basis of the document referred to in the rule itself shall determine the age of the person. According to rule 12(3)(a)(i) first of all the age determination inquiry shall be conducted by seeking evidence by obtaining the matriculation or equivalent certificate. Once the matriculation certificate or any other equivalent certificate is available on record, no further evidence is required to be taken by the reason that by obtaining the matriculation certificate or equivalent certificate the inquiry is complete. If in a case the matriculation certificate or equivalent certificate is available that shall be the conclusive proof of age of the person by whom the claim of juvenility was made. If the secondary school certificate issued by the Board of Secondary Education was produced on behalf of the accused to prove his date of birth, no further evidence was required to be taken by the Court even if High Court while remanding the matter back, directed the Court below to conduct inquiry in the matter in accordance with rule 12 of the Rules of 2007. The production of secondary school certificate by the accused by itself amounts an inquiry that was to be conducted by the Court below as directed by this Court; *Madan Lal* v. *State of Rajasthan*, 2011 Cr LJ 4001: 2012 (1) Raj LW 639: 2012 (1) RCR (Cri) 392 (Raj) (Jaipur Bench).

**16. Certificate Issued by Corporation or Nagar Panchayat – Law on –** Now third preference evidence is certificate issued by the Corporation or Nagar Panchayat but it has also not been proved by the accused as to who entered the date of birth in the Nagar Panchayat or on whose instance the date of birth has been entered in Nagar Panchayat. The original record of Nagar Panchayat has not been brought before the court. This certificate is based on the date of birth shown in the school, which was not found to be proved. Therefore, this third category of evidence cannot be taken into consideration; *Shahid Ali Beg* v. *State of Uttar Pradesh*, 2013 (3) ACrR 3068 (All) (Lucknow Bench).

**17. Child's Statements – Law on –** The child's appearance, while it should be given due consideration in determining his or her age, should not be permitted to outweigh or overcome positive testimony, facts, and circumstances tending to show him or her to be under the given age. The child's statements or admissions as to his or her age, although admissible on that issue, are not controlling as against positive evidence; *Ishtikhar* v. *State of Uttar Pradesh*, 2012 (5) SCALE 47: 2012 (12) SCC 307 (SC).

**18. Claim of Juvenility – Law on –** Section 7A of the Act states that when a claim of juvenility is raised before a Court or the Court is of the opinion that the accused person was juvenile, on the date of the commission of the offence, the Court shall make an enquiry and take such evidence as may be necessary. The claim of juvenility has to be determined as per provisions of the Act and the Rules made thereunder; *Nazir* v. *State*, 2013 Cr LJ 1891 (Del) (DB).

**19. Competent Authority – Duties of –** When any Magistrate not empowered to exercise the powers of the Board under this Act is of opinion that a person brought before him under any provisions of this Act (other than for purpose of giving evidence) is juvenile or the child, he shall without delay record such opinion and forward the juvenile or the child and record of the proceeding to the competent authority having jurisdiction over the proceeding. Then the competent authority shall hold the inquiry as if the juvenile or the child has been brought before it. It clearly indicates as soon as the trial court not having jurisdiction under the Act found *prima facie* that the accused present before the court is juvenile, it shall forward the juvenile or the child along with the record of the proceeding to the Board having jurisdiction under the Act for making an inquiry under section 49 of the Act; *Narayan Sharma* v. *State of Madhya Pradesh*, 2012 Cr LJ 736: 2013 (6) RCR (Cri) 1672 (MP) (Gwalior Bench).

**20. Competent Authority – Powers of –** Sub-section (1) of section 49 empowers the competent authority to make due inquiry as to the age of a person brought before it and for the said purpose to take such evidence as may be necessary and shall record a finding as to whether the person is a juvenile or a child or not, stating his age as nearly as may be; *Subash Sahu* v. *State of Orissa*, 2012 Cr LJ 4607: 2013 (7) RCR (Cri) 2646 (Ori) (DB).

**21. Competent Authority – Restriction for –** Under section 49, the competent authority as defined in section 2(g) is to make due enquiry as to the age of a person brought before it, if he/she appears to be a juvenile or a child and for that purpose, take such evidence as may be necessary and record a finding whether the person is a juvenile or child or not and state his age as nearly as may be; *State of Assam (in re:),* 2012 Cr LJ 471: 2011 (4) Gau LR 235: 2013 (6) RCR (Cri) 2190 (Gau) (DB).

**22. Conclusive Proof of Age – Law on –** Section 7A of Juvenile Justice (Care and Protection of Children) Act, 2000, thus, makes it clear that a claim as to the juvenility of the accused shall be determined by the courts only in terms the provisions of the said Act or the Rules made thereunder. Rule 12 of the Delhi Juvenile Justice (Care and Protection of Children) Rules, 2009 is similar to rule 12 of the Juvenile Justice (Care and Protection of Children) Rules, 2007 except the order of priority set out under sub-clause (3)(a) of the rule 12 of 2007. Rule 12 of Delhi Juvenile Justice (Care and Protection of Children) Rules, 2009 envisages the age determination inquiry concerning a juvenile in conflict with law to be conducted by the court or the Juvenile Justice Board, as the case may be. In the order of priority, the first precedence has been given to the date of birth certificate from the school (other than a play school) first attended, if available; and if such a certificate is duly proved on record in accordance with law then such a certificate may itself be sufficient to determine the age of the offender. In the absence of the date of birth certificate from the school (other than a play school) first attended, the second priority has been given to the birth certificate given by a corporation, municipal authority or a Panchayat; and in the absence of these two certificates, the third priority has been given to matriculation or equivalent certificates. Under rule 12(3)(b), in the absence of the said three documentary evidence of clause (a), the Court or the Board can seek medical opinion from any duly constituted Medical Board in order to determine the age of offender by conducting an ossification test. This rule 12(3)(b) further envisages that in case the exact assessment of the age cannot be done by the Court or the Board then for the reasons to be recorded by the court it may give benefit to the offender by considering his/her age on lower side within the margin of one year and while passing such order the court may take into consideration such evidence as may be available on record or the medical opinion as the case may be and record a finding in respect of his age based on either of the evidences produced before the court as specified in any of the clause (a)(i), (ii), (iii) or in the absence whereof, the medical evidence in terms of clause (b) which shall be a conclusive proof of the age as regards such a Juvenile in conflict with law; *State* v. *Vinod @ Pandit*, 2013 (4) Crimes 27 (Del): 2013 (7) AD 161 (Del): 2013 (3) JCC 1767.

**23. Indian Majority Act – Provision of –** Section 3 of the Indian Majority Act, 1875 provides for age of majority of persons domiciled in India and the criteria for computation of age of majority. It reads as under:

"3. Age of majority of persons domiciled in India.—(1) Every person domiciled in India shall attain the age of majority on his completing the age of eighteen years and not before.

(2) In computing the age of any person, the day on which he was born is to be included as a whole day and he shall be deemed to have attained majority at the beginning of the eighteenth anniversary of that day."

12. Three Contingencies – Comments on – A bare reading of section 12 of the Act provides that there are three contingencies in which bail could be refused to juvenile.

(1) If there appear reasonable grounds for believing that the release is likely to bring him into association with any known criminal or

(2) expose him to moral, physical or psychological danger or

(3) that his release would defeat the ends Justice; *Shiv Kumar @ Sadhu* v. *State of Uttar Pradesh,* 2010 (2) Crimes 521 (All): 2011 (8) RCR (Cri) 1346: 2010 (1) ADJ 718: 2010 (3) Cri CC 459.

**24. Court – Powers of –** Court is empowered to determine the age of the juvenile or a child. Sub-rule 3(b) of rule 12 of the Rules can be pressed into service in case of there being no date of birth certificate from the School or any other document; *Pilli Mangaiah* v. *State of Andhra Pradesh,* 2010 (2) Crimes 696 (AP): 2011 (8) RCR (Cri) 1408.

**25. Court, Board, Child Welfare Committee or Competent Authority – Solemn Statutory Duty of –** Provisions of the Act and the Rules evinces a solemn statutory duty of a Court, a Board, a Child Welfare Committee or the competent authority as the case may be to examine the issue of juvenility of a person claiming to be a child or a juvenile in conflict with law on the date of commission of an offence and ascertain his/her age by taking such evidence as may be considered necessary and thereafter pass appropriate orders or issue necessary directions as enjoined by the Act and/or the Rules. That the provisions of the Act and the Rules, bearing on the aspect of juvenility are applicable to a person who is a juvenile in conflict with law as defined, even if he/she has ceased to be so on or before the date of commencement of the Act *i.e.* 1-4-2001; *State of Assam (in re:),* 2012 Cr LJ 471: 2011 (4) Gau LR 235: 2013 (6) RCR (Cri) 2190 (Gau) (DB).

**26. Date of Birth under U.P. Rules – Discussion on –** No doubt, under rule 12 of the Rules of 2007 the primacy has been given to the matriculation certificate in the process of determining the age of the accused. The other sources cited under the Rules follow and take effect when the matriculation certificate is not available. But in the U.P. Rules, 2004 such primacy has not been mandated. Rules 2004 have simply given the list of certificates to be followed and in this list, birth certificate by a Corporation or a Municipal authority has been placed first, the date of birth certificate from School first attended comes later and still later comes the matriculation or equivalent certificate if available. Rule 22 of the U.P. Rules, 2004 does not exclude the consideration of one certificate over the other. As the U.P. Rules, 2004 have been framed under section 68 of the Act, they apply to the matters in Uttar Pradesh and in such view of the matter, High School Certificate does not have any primacy if other certificates are available. Rule 22 of the U.P. Rules, 2004 allows discretion to the Court to take into consideration the birth certificate issued from any Corporation or from any municipal authority or certificate from the School first attended or the matriculation certificate. The practical approach will require consistency in the date of birth maintained in the School certificates from the institution first attended upto the school from which matriculation or higher qualification is completed. The date of birth so maintained at different levels of educational progress must be accepted. The certificate from the School first attended may be as much precarious and may require to be proved as genuine as the matriculation certificate obtained after abrupt admission in that class or a class before, and date of birth propelled on an affidavit. Certificate from the school first attended is more reliable with regard to age than the High School or matriculation certificate introducing date of birth on an affidavit of the student himself fancying his own date of birth or of either of the parents who can hardly remember the same at such a late stage. It will not be impertinent to assume that guardian of a minor ward or student of mature understanding is conscious that minimum age would bring in maximum service benefits and therefore tendency to reducing age at every possible occasion must be taken into account in the process of determining the age of the delinquent; *Amit Kumar* v. *State of Uttar Pradesh,* 2013 (5) ALJ 672: 2013 (6) ADJ 21: 2013 (3) ACrR 3146: 2013 (81) ACC 899 (All).

**27. Delinquent in Borderline Cases – Law on** – Determination of age of a delinquent, particularly in borderline cases, is rather a complex exercise. Hence, before considering the rival contentions of the parties it would be profitable to set out the material provisions of the Juvenile Justice (Care & Protection) Act, 2000; *Hariom Soni* v. *State of Madhya Pradesh,* 2012 (6) RCR (Cri) 1269: 2012 (1) Crimes (MP) 111 (MP).

**28. Detailed Probe – Law on** – Age determination inquiry contemplated under the JJ Act and Rules has nothing to do with an enquiry under other legislations, like entry in service, retirement, promotion etc. There may be situations where the entry made in the matriculation or equivalent certificates, date of birth certificate from the school first attended and even the birth certificate given by a Corporation or a Municipal Authority or a Panchayat may not be correct. But Court, J.J. Board or a Committee functioning under the J.J. Act is not expected to conduct such a roving enquiry and to go behind those certificates to examine the correctness of those documents, kept during the normal course of business. Only in cases where those documents or certificates are found to be fabricated or manipulated, the Court, the J.J. Board or the Committee needs to go for medical report for age determination. To carry on detailed probe is totally unwarranted; *Ashwani Kumar Saxena* v. *State of Madhya Pradesh,* 2012 (10) SCR 540: AIR 2013 SC 553: 2012 Cr LJ 4731.

**29. Determination of Age – Discussion on** – Discussing the need for the court to act cautiously while examining the documents as envisaged under rule 12(3)(a)(i), (ii), (iii) so as to determine the age of the offender, the Juvenile Justice (Care and Protection) Act, 2000 is a piece of social welfare legislation aimed at handling the children below the age of 18 years of age accused of committing crimes so as to draw a line of distinction between them and the adults in terms of treatment and consequences of the offences committed. The germination of the said Act is based on the premise that the children of an impressionable age are unaware of the import of their actions as compared to adults and to brand them as criminals meting out harsh punishment would scar them for life vandalizing their outlook towards life and their future. The determination of the age of a person accused, whether juvenile or not can sway and change his fate as the punishment awarded to a juvenile *vis-a-vis* an adult for the same offence varies considerably. In other words, an offender who may be accused of a serious crime like death or rape, who otherwise deserves harshest punishment under the ordinary penal law might be simply sent to a correction home for a period of three years if found to be less than 18 years of age under the Act. Such difference in treatment of juvenile is based on the rationale that the age factor plays a vital role in behavior of a person. There is a greater chance of a young criminal, a minor succeeding in transforming his life and becoming a more responsible person once he gets an opportunity of reformation, than a person who is a major. Hence, the application of the yardsticks to determine the age of an offender is at times an arduous task enjoined upon the courts of law and therefore the responsibility sacrosanct. In the eventuality of the fact that a mere decision as to the age of the offender at the time of the offence, of either being less or more than 18 years, can seal the fate of a person, the courts are therefore expected to decide the issue with utmost care and sensitivity, involving meticulous deliberation and diligence. It is an unfortunate but a bitter reality, that a seemingly large number of provisions on the statute book that are enacted to serve an honorable and equitable purpose are arm twisted for ulterior motives, and this provision is no different. The courts thus have to be vigilant to prevent its misuse by those trying to evade punishment under the garb of juvenility. The courts must carefully scrutinize the documentary evidence in support of the offender's claim of juvenility, placed on record by him, more so, when the ossification test has been held to be a non-conclusive test. The court is not to act as a mute spectator to blindly trust the matriculation or school certificates produced by the offender but must make every endeavour to ascertain the genuineness of such documents by directing the offender to lead evidence in support of it. The courts must not act obliviously and overlook the practical realities prevailing in our country with respect to the poor school administration, especially in schools located in the rural areas and also the aspect that rackets of engineering fake certificates are not uncommon in our country. Due consideration must be given to ascertain as to whether the manner in which the certificates are prepared by the school authority is trustworthy; whether the officer of the admission department, who may be illiterate/ semi-literate in most of the cases and literate in few, has made the entries in the record book meticulously; whether the record books have been kept and retained by the school authority in a safe and secure custody immune from any kind of manipulation or tampering. Such degree of care and caution to be exercised by the courts may vary from case to case, not to dwell so as to threadbare examine every document but also not to let the offender take a blanket protection under the said Act; *Mor Pal* v. *State*, 2013 (198) DLT 487 (Del).

**30. Determination of Date of Birth – Law on –** Rule 12(3) of the Juvenile Justice (Care and Protection of Children) Rules, 2007 contemplates three type of evidence, namely, matriculation or equivalent certificate, if that is not available, birth certificate from school (other than play school) first attended, if that is also not available, then birth certificate issued by Corporation or Municipality or Panchayat. If the said three certificates are not available then only medical evidence has to be sought for to determine the age of the person; *Jayavel* v. *State*, 2013 (1) LW (Cri) 643: 2013 (2) Mad LJ (Cri) 889: 2013 (8) RCR (Cri) 1812 (Mad) (DB).

**31. Discretion of Court – Law on –** Resort to Medical Board in each and every case is not the mandate of law; rather it comes into play only when the documents as mentioned in the Rules are not available. It may further be noted that once a finding of juvenility is given in terms of sections 7A, 14 and 49 of the Juvenile Justice Act of 2000, by virtue of section 49 and in particular sub-section (2) thereof no subsequent proof is at all admissible to deny the benefit of juvenility and the declaration once made is final. Thus seen, there is no discretion on the Court but in the said circumstances as mentioned above to hold an enquiry and give a finding in the manner prescribed; *Ranjeet Kumar Jha, Sushil Kumar Jha* v. *State of Bihar*, 2011 (59) BLJR 3227: 2012 Cr LJ 759: 2011 (4) PLJR 265.

**32. Discretionary Powers – Law on –** Section 49 of the Act grants the competent authority, namely, the Board/court below absolute discretion to call for such evidence as may be necessary (excluding the evidence on affidavit) while conducting the enquiry to determine the age of the juvenile/person produced before it and record finding about the age of the person/juvenile produced before it considering the value of the evidence so produced. Such absolute discretion vested in the competent authority/Board/court below appears to have been eroded and restricted by providing in sub-rule (3) of rule 12 of the Central Rules that the date of birth entry in the matriculation or equivalent certificate, if available, in absence thereof such entry in the birth certificate from the school first attended and in absence thereof the date of birth entry in the birth certificate given by the Corporation or municipal authority or Panchayat shall be conclusive. It is thus evident that the discretion granted to the competent authority/Board/court to take such evidence as may be necessary in its opinion to determine the age of the juvenile under section 49 of the Act is eroded and restricted as no sooner either of the aforesaid three certificates is produced the date of birth entry recorded therein is taken as conclusive proof of the age of the person produced and thereby the discretion of the competent authority/Board/court below to take such evidence as may be necessary and to consider its value and to record a finding on the basis of the value of the evidence produced is eroded and restricted. It is thus obvious that the provisions contained in sub-rule (3) of rule 12 of the Central Rules override, erode/restrict and denude the discretion of the competent authority under section 49 of the Act to take such evidence which may be necessary to determine the age of the juvenile, in the circumstances, sub-rule (3) of rule 12 of the Central Rules, whereunder the date of birth entry in either of the three certificates is made conclusive has to be read down so as to make sub-rule (3) of rule 12 of the Central Rules in tune with section 49 of the Act whereunder the age of the juvenile/person produced has to be determined with reference to the evidence taken by the competent authority/Board/court below as per its absolute discretion applying the norms of section 4 of the Evidence Act which *inter alia* provides that presumption about correctness of fact in issue can always be rebutted by producing evidence in rebuttal. Conclusive presumption of law can only be drawn with regard to the matters covered by sections 41, 112 and 113 of the Evidence Act and not with regard to questions of fact. Any entry in public or other official book, register or record about the fact in issue is a relevant fact as per section 35 of the Evidence Act which can always be rebutted by producing evidence in rebuttal. No sooner evidence in rebuttal disputing the date of birth entry in the certificate is produced, it is within the discretion of the Board/Court concerned to weigh the date of birth entry in the certificate with the evidence produced in rebuttal disputing such entry and to place reliance on either of the two certificates or to place reliance on the report of the Medical Board or any other evidence produced in rebuttal; *Chandan Kumar Gandhi* v. *State of Bihar,* 2010 (88) AIC 856: 2010 Cr LJ 1814: 2010 (1) PLJR 533 (Pat).

**33. Entry Regarding Age in School Register – Law on –** the three documentary evidences as envisaged under rule 12(3)(a)(i)(ii)(iii) of the Juvenile Justice (Care and Protection of Children) Rules, 2007 are the relevant facts to determine the age of the offender but before they are admitted in evidence they must be proved in accordance with law. Section 35 of the Indian Evidence Act, 1872 lays down that entry in any public, official book, register, record stating a fact in issue or relevant fact and made by a public servant in the discharge of his official duty specially enjoined by the law of the country is itself the relevant fact. To render a document admissible under section 35 of the Indian Evidence Act, three conditions must be satisfied, *firstly,* entry that is relied on must be one in a public or other official book, register or record; *secondly,* it must be an entry stating a fact in issue or relevant fact; and *thirdly,* it must be made by a public servant in discharge of his official duty, or any other person in performance of a duty especially enjoined by law. An entry relating to a date of birth made in the school register is relevant and admissible under section 35 of the Act but the entry regarding the age of a person in a school register is of not much evidentiary value to prove the age of the person in the absence of the material on which the age was recorded; *Mor Pal* v. *State,* 2013 (198) DLT 487 (Del).

**34. Exact Assessment of Age – Law on –** Rule 12(3) clearly stipulates the procedure to conduct the enquiry by the court or the Board, as the case may be. Sub-rule (3)(a) of rule 12 further prescribes the nature of documents which can be taken as evidence for determination of the date of birth. Sub-rule (3)(b) provides that in the absence of such evidence, the medical opinion will be sought for from a duly constituted Medical Board which will declare the age of the juvenile or child. Even it provides that in case the exact assessment of the age cannot be done, the court for the reasons to be recorded by it may, if considered necessary, give benefit to the child or juvenile by considering his/her age on lower side within the margin of one year. The court is also required to record a finding in respect of the age after taking into consideration the medical opinion where evidence of the nature prescribed in sub-rule (3)(a) is not available and the medical report shall be the conclusive proof of the age as regards such child or juvenile in conflict with law; *Simanchal Behera @ Kuna @ Rowdy* v. *State of Orissa*, 2012 (1) ILR 493 (Cut).

**35. Fusion of Iliac Bone – Law on –** Accused was subjected to the radiological examination, where a categorical finding has been recorded by the Medical Board that when the X-ray plates of right elbow joint and right iliac bone were obtained and examined, it was found that there was a clear fusion of the joints and the iliac fusion was on the verge of its completion, which demonstrates that the Accused must be bordering in between 19 to 21 years of age. Therefore, there remains no doubt about the correctness of the conclusion arrived at by the Court that the accused was certainly above the age of 18 years and was not a juvenile on the date of incident, in terms of the provisions of the Juvenile Justice (Care & Protection of Children) Act, 2000. The ossification test and the exact opinion of the Medical Board in relation to the fusion of the iliac bone, gives a conclusive evidence of the fact. The ossification test and the exact opinion of the Medical Board in relation to the fusion of the iliac bone, gives a conclusive evidence of the fact; *Banti @ Santosh* v. *State of Madhya Pradesh*, 2010 (1) MPHT 309: 2010 (1) MPWN 96: 2010 (1) Crimes 663 (MP).

**36. Gram Panchayat – Status of –** In view of the provisions of sub-rule 5 of rule 22 of Uttar Pradesh Juvenile Justice (Care and Protection of Children) Rules, 2004, the Gram Panchayat cannot be said to be a Corporation or a Municipal Authority; *Satya Pal Singh; S.P. Singh* v. *State of Uttar Pradesh*, 2013 (5) ADJ 79: 2013 (6) ALJ 231: 2013 (3) ACrR 3313.

**37. Guiding Factor for Determining Age – Law on –** As per rule 22 of Jharkhand Juvenile Justice (Care and Protection of Children) Rules, 2003 in the absence of birth or matriculation certificates, in order to record a finding in respect of age of a person, the Board is required to obtain the opinion of a duly constituted Medical Board. It is clear from a bare reading of the rule that although the Board is bound to obtain the opinion of the Medical Board but the opinion *per se* is not a conclusive proof of age of the person concerned. It is no more than an opinion. Moreso, when even the Medico-Legal opinion is that owing to the variation in climatic, dietic, hereditary and other factors, affecting the people of different States in the country, it would be imprudent to formulate a uniform standard for the determination of the age. True, that a Medical Board's opinion based on the radiological examination is a useful guiding factor for determining the age of a person but is not incontrovertible; *Narayan Sharma* v. *State of Madhya Pradesh*, 2012 Cr LJ 736: 2013 (6) RCR (Cri) 1672 (MP) (Gwalior Bench).

**38. Inquiry for Claim of Juvenility – Law on –** Sub-section (1) of section 7A of the Act provides that whenever a claim of juvenility is raised before any Court, the Court shall make an inquiry, take such evidence as may be necessary so as to determine the age of such person and shall record a finding whether the person is a juvenile stating his age as nearly as may be. The proviso to this sub-section provides that if a claim of juvenility is raised then such claim shall be determined in terms of the provisions contained in the Act and the Rules made thereunder. This provision clearly shows that although an inquiry is required to be made if a claim of juvenility is raised before any Court, but evidence is required to be taken only when the Court feels that it is necessary to take evidence. The provision also indicates that the claim of juvenility shall be determined in terms of the provisions contained in the Act and Rules made thereunder. It is an admitted fact that the Central Government has framed Rules of 2007 under the Act. The procedure of inquiry for the determination of the juvenility is provided in rule 12 of the Rules of 2007 which has already been quoted in entirety as above; *Madan Lal* v. *State of Rajasthan*, 2011 Cr LJ 4001: 2012 (1) Raj LW 639: 2012 (1) RCR(Cri) 392.

**39. Magistrate – Duties of –** As and when a juvenile delinquent is shown as an Accused and produced before a Magistrate and his age is shown by the police as 18 or

19 years, then the Magistrate should observe the accused and try to ascertain his age and form an opinion regarding his age, as he would have the opportunity to see and observe the accused or juvenile delinquent. If necessary he must send the accused for examination by the Medical Board and ascertain his age. It may result in doing great injustice or defeating the provisions of the legislation if the Magistrate does not exercise his discretion and power at the stage when the accused is produced before him. The Magistrate need not accept the age mentioned by the Investigating Officer as gospel truth. As and when the accused takes a plea that he is a child or it appears to the Magistrate that the accused may be a child, he must make an enquiry and ascertain the age of the accused. If such accused is mixed with the ordinary adult criminals, it will defeat the provisions of the Beneficial Legislation and also cause bad effect on such juvenile delinquent; *Chagalamarri Subbaiah* v. *State Rep by its Public Prosecutor*, 2010 Cr LJ 655: 2009 (2) ALD (Cri) 121: 2009 (3) ALT (Cri) 36.

**40. Magistrate – Functions of –** When any Magistrate not empowered to exercise the powers of the Board under Act is of opinion that a person brought before him under any provisions of Act (other than for purpose of giving evidence) is juvenile or the child, he shall without delay record such opinion and forward the juvenile or the child and record of the proceeding to the competent authority having jurisdiction over the proceeding. Then the competent authority shall hold the inquiry as if the juvenile or the child has been brought before it. It clearly indicates as soon as the trial court not having jurisdiction under the Act found *prima facie* that the accused present before the court is juvenile, it shall forward the juvenile or the child alongwith the record of the proceeding to the Board having jurisdiction under the Act for making an inquiry under section 49 of the Act; *Thakat Singh* v. *State of Madhya Pradesh*, 2012 (5) RCR (Cri) 284: 2012 (2) Crimes 425 (MP): 2012 Cr LJ 2573 (MP) (Gwalior Bench).

**41. Margin of One Year – Law on –** The rules provides that for determination of age of a juvenile, the Juvenile Justice Board, has to first rely upon the birth certificate issued by the Corporation or Municipal Authority or a date of birth certificate from the school first attended, matriculation or equivalent certificate and in absence of the aforesaid certificate/certificates, the medical opinion of a duly constituted Medical Board may be called for subject to a margin of one year; *Deepak Kumar Singh* v. *State of Jharkhand*, 2012 (1) Crimes 485 (Jhar).

**42. Matriculation Certificate – Importance of –** A plain reading of rule 12(3) clearly shows that the opinion of the Medical Board is to be sought only in absence of any matriculation or other such certificates detailed in the rule. If there was already a matriculation certificate showing the date of birth of the accused then there was no requirement at all for constituting a Medical Board for getting the age of the accused determined; *Sanjay Kumar Mandal @ Sanjay Mandal* v. *State of Jharkhand*, 2013 (3) JLJR 77 (Jhar).

**43. Medical Board's Opinion based on Radiological Examination – Law on –** As per rule 22, in the absence of birth or matriculation certificates, in order to record a finding in respect of age of a person, the Board is required to obtain the opinion of a duly constituted Medical Board. It is clear from a bare reading of the rule that although the Board is bound to obtain the opinion of the Medical Board but the opinion *per se* is not a conclusive proof of age of the person concerned. It is no more than an opinion. More so, when even the Medico-Legal opinion is that owing to the variation in climatic, dietic, hereditary and other factors, affecting the people of different States in the country, it would be imprudent to formulate a uniform standard for the determination of the age. True, that a Medical Board's opinion based on the radiological examination is a useful guiding factor for determining the age of a person but is not incontrovertible. An entry relating to date of birth made in the school register is relevant and admissible under section 35 of the Act but the entry regarding the age of a person in a school register is of not much evidentiary value to prove the age of the person in the absence of the material on which the age was recorded; *Thakat Singh* v. *State of Madhya Pradesh*, 2012 (5) RCR (Cri) 284: 2012 (2) Crimes 425 (MP): 2012 Cr LJ 2573 (MP) (Gwalior Bench).

**44. Medical Evidence – Law on –** If a Matriculation certificate is available the date of birth mentioned in any other certificate cannot be gone into. If a Matriculation certificate is not available then date of birth as mentioned in the birth certificate from the school first attended is to be taken into consideration. If the said certificate is also not available then the date of birth certificate given by the Corporation or a Municipal Authority or Panchayat has to be considered. Clause (b) of rule 12(3) of the Rules of 2007 regarding medical evidence comes into operation only when the three certificates as mentioned in rule 12(3)(a) are not available; *Chand Babu* v. *State (Govt. of NCT of Delhi)*, 2013 (4) AD 125 (Del).

**45. Medical Evidence Based on Scientific Investigation – Law on –** If there is a clear and unambiguous case in favour of the juvenile accused that he was a minor below the age of 18 years on the date of the incident and the documentary evidence at least *prima facie* proves the same, he would be entitled for this special protection under the Juvenile Justice Act. But when an accused commits a grave and heinous offence and thereafter attempts to take statutory shelter under the guise of being a minor, a casual or cavalier approach while recording as to whether an accused is a juvenile or not cannot be permitted as the courts are enjoined upon to perform their duties with the object of protecting the confidence of common man in the institution entrusted with the administration of justice. Hence, while the courts must be sensitive in dealing with the juvenile who is involved in cases of serious nature like sexual molestation, rape, gang rape, murder and host of other offences, the accused cannot be allowed to abuse the statutory protection by attempting to prove himself as a minor when the documentary evidence to prove his minority gives rise to a reasonable doubt about his assertion of minority. Under such circumstance, the medical evidence based on scientific investigation will have to be given due weight and precedence over the evidence based on school administration records which give rise to hypothesis and speculation about the age of the accused. The matter however would stand on a different footing if the academic certificates ad school records are alleged to have been with held deliberately with ulterior motive and authenticity of the medical evidence is under challenge by the prosecution; *Om Prakash* v. *State of Rajasthan*, AIR 2012 SC 1608: 2012 Cr LJ 2266: 2012 (5) SCC 201.

**46. Medical Opinion by Duly Constituted Medical Board – Comments on –** In view of rule 22 of U.P. Juvenile Justice (Care and Protection of Children) Rules, 2004, the Board is required to obtain a birth certificate given by a Corporation or Municipal Authority at the first instance and if that is not available then the date of birth certificate from the School first attended. In the third instance the matriculation or equivalent certificate is to be obtained and in the last and in absence of above, the medical opinion by a duly constituted Medical Board subject to margin of one year may be taken into consideration; *Satya Pal Singh; S.P. Singh* v. *State of Uttar Pradesh*, 2013 (5) ADJ 79: 2013 (6) ALJ 231: 2013 (3) ACrR 3313.

**47. Order of Competent Authority – Law on –** Sub-section (1) of section 49 vests the Competent Authority with power to make due inquiry as to the age of a person brought before it and for the said purpose to take such evidence as may be necessary (but not an affidavit) and shall record a finding as to whether the person is a juvenile or a child or not, stating his age as nearly as may be. Sub-section (2) is of equal importance as it provides that no order of a Competent Authority would be deemed to have become invalid merely on account of any subsequent proof that the person, in respect of whom an order is made, is not a juvenile or a child, and the age recorded by the Competent Authority to be the age of the person brought before it, would, for the purpose of the Act, be deemed to be the true age of a child or a juvenile in conflict with law; *Hari Ram* v. *State of Rajasthan*, 2009 (13) SCC 211: 2009 (6) SCALE 695: 2009 SCR 1381.

**48. Ossification Report – Law on** – It is settled law that medical opinion as to age of an individual is not an exact science, but the same is susceptible to a variation of 2 years on either side. That apart, ossification report in view of rule 12(3) of the Juvenile Justice (Care and Protection of Children) Rules, 2007 (hereinafter referred to as the said Rules), is subject to the date of birth as transpiring from the certificate from the school which the accused person first attended; *Utpal Roy* v. *State of West Bengal*, 2014 Cr LJ 620 (Cal).

**49. Ossification Test – Comments on** – Determination of age on the basis of ossification test is merely the opinion of the radiologist and not conclusive proof of age. Two years margin can be given in either side; *Narendra Yadav* alias *Mantoo* v. *State of Madhya Pradesh*, 2009 (2) MPLJ 369: 2009 ILR 2450 (MP).

**50. Overwritten and Interpolated Entry in School Register – Law on** – The rule 12 of Juvenile Justices (Care and Protection of Children) Rules, 2007 prescribed the procedure for determination of the age of a juvenile in conflict with law, the court has to seek evidence by obtaining matriculation certificate or equivalent certificate in absence whereof; the date of birth certificate from the school first attended and in absence whereof the birth certificate given by corporation or municipal authority or a panchayat. In absence of above three documents the court is to obtain a medical opinion from a duly constituted Medical Board. If neither there was any matriculation certificate or equivalent certificate nor the birth certificate issued either by the corporation or a municipal authority or a panchayat. In such a situation, the investigating authority obtained the birth certificate from the school. If it is apparent from the admission register that date of birth of the accused noted therein was overwritten and interpolated, therefore, it cannot be said the Magistrate without following the first option laid down in the rule has illegally directed ossification test. It cannot be said that the Magistrate has exceeded his jurisdiction; *Ramesh Maity* v. *State of West Bengal*, 2014 Cr LJ 691 (Cal).

**51. Physical Appearance – Law on** – In every case concerning a child or a juvenile in conflict with law, the Court or the Board or as the case may be, the Committee referred to in rule 19 of the Rules, shall determine the age of such juvenile or child or a juvenile conflict with law within a period of thirty days from the date of making of the application for that purpose. Sub-rule (2) of rule 12 further provides that while doing so, *prima facie* on the basis of physical appearance or documents, if available, the Court or the Board or the Committee can decide the question of juvenility while sub-rule (3) lays down that the evidence to be considered for the purpose of determining the juvenility of an incumbent will be sought in the form of matriculation or equivalent certificates, if available and in the absence whereof, the date of birth certificate from the school, other than a play school, first attended and in the absence whereof, the birth certificate given by corporation or a municipal authority or a Panchayat and if none of these are available, then the medical opinion is to be sought from a duly constituted Medical Board which will declare the age of such juvenile. Sub-rule (4) contemplates the passing of and order after such an enquiry. The first and foremost requirement is that initially a satisfaction has to be recorded by the Court on the *prima facie* appearance of the juvenile and thereafter, further enquiry on the basis of certificates or medical opinion has to be undertaken; *Harpreet Singh* v. *State of Haryana*, 2011 (1) ILR 155 (P&H).

**52. Physical Appearance – Comments on** – Rule 22 of Uttar Pradesh Juvenile Justice (Care and Protection of Children) Rules, 2004 nowhere provides any option to the Juvenile Justice Board to assess the age of the person on the basis of physical appearance; *Satya Pal Singh; S.P. Singh* v. *State of Uttar Pradesh*, 2013 (5) ADJ 79: 2013 (6) ALJ 231: 2013 (3) ACrR 3313.

**53. Registration Certificate – Law on** – It is the settled law that as between the School Certificate issued by the Board of Secondary Education and the report of Radiological Examination it is the former that should prevail because the age ascertained on medical examination is not necessarily the exact age of a person. Magistrate was not legally justified in discarding the Registration Certificate and the Final School Leaving Certificate and in relying on the Radiological Examination report which is not at all a conclusive one, the same being leaving margin of 2 years in either side; *Rejuanul Hoque* alias *Mithun* v. *State of West Bengal,* 2008 (1) Cal Cri LR 880: 2008 Cr LJ 3468: 2008 (4) AICLR 585 (Cal).

**54. School Record with Ambiguity – Law on –** Age of the accused could not be proved merely on the basis of the school record as the courts below in spite of its scrutiny could not record a finding of fact that the accused, in fact, was a minor on the date of the incident. Hence, in a situation when the school record itself is not free from ambiguity and conclusively prove the minority of the accused, medical opinion cannot be allowed to be overlooked or treated to be of no consequence; *Om Prakash* v. *State of Rajasthan,* AIR 2012 SC 1608: 2012 (4) SCALE 348: 2012 (5) SCC 201.

**55. Subsequent Proof – Law on –** Once age of a person claiming to be juvenile is determined then such order passed by a competent authority shall not be deemed to have become invalid merely by any subsequent proof that the person in respect of whom an order has been passed is not a juvenile. When once the question of juvenility of an accused, on an application filed by him with proof, has been decided against him by the Court and held that he was not a juvenile then the question cannot be re-agitated by such person and the order cannot be amended by any authority/Court; *Sheo Narayan* v. *State of Rajasthan,* 2011 Cr LJ 3878: 2011 (4) Raj LW 3465: 2012 (6) RCR (Cri) 757.

**56. Transfer Certificate Issued by School First Attended – Significance of –** Court can place reliance on the School Register and Transfer Certificate Form issued by the school first attended by the accused (other than the play school) in accordance with rule 12 of the Delhi Juvenile Justice (Care and Protection of Children) Rules, 2009 so as to determine the age of the accused; *State* v. *Vinod @ Pandit,* 2013 (4) Crimes 27 (Del): 2013 (7) AD 161 (Del): 2013 (3) JCC 1767.

**57. U.P. Rules – Comments on –** If Central Rules were required to be placed before both the houses of Parliament [section 68 (3)], the State Rules were also required to be placed before the Legislature of the State [section 68 (4)]. No inconsistency has been shown in the Rules with regard to the determination of age except that the model Rules give precedence to the entry of date of birth in the matriculation or equivalent certificates over any other certificate, whereas the U.P. Rules lay open choice of the Board to take into account the birth certificate given by a Corporation or a Municipal Authority or date of birth certificate from the school first attended or a matriculation or equivalent certificates. The Central Rules are exclusive in nature. They obligate the Board or Court to necessarily accept preferential documents or evidence leaving little room for the Board or Court to determine consistency. The U.P. Rules on the contrary are inclusive and allow the Board or Court enough opportunity of evaluating facts in their consistency and corroboration. Besides, regarded from pragmatic stand-point the U.P. Rules are better poised to carry out the purposes of the Act; *Jai Prakash Tiwari* v. *State of Uttar Pradesh,* 2012 (10) ADJ 478: 2013 (2) ACrR 1383 (All).

**58. Voters List – Law on –** Mere Production of a copy of the Voters List, though a public document, in terms of section 35, was not sufficient to prove the age of the accused; *Babloo Pasi* v. *State of Jharkhand,* AIR 2009 SC 314: 2008 (13) SCC 133: 2008 (13) SCALE 137.

**59. X-Ray Ossification Test – Law on –** R.P. Sethi, J., speaking for the majority in a three-Judge Bench, had observed that an X-ray ossification test may provide a surer basis for determining the age of an individual than the opinion of a medical expert but it can by no means be so infallible and accurate a test as to indicate the exact date of birth of the person concerned. Too much of reliance cannot be placed upon text books, on medical jurisprudence and toxicology while determining the age of an accused. In this vast country with varied latitudes, heights, environment, vegetation and nutrition, the height and weight cannot be expected to be uniform. It is well settled that it is neither feasible nor desirable to lay down an abstract formula to determine the age of a person. The date of birth is to be determined on the basis of material on record and on appreciation of evidence adduced by the parties. The Medical evidence as to the age of a person, though a very useful guiding factor, is not conclusive and has to be considered along with other cogent evidence; *Ramdeo Chauhan* alias *Raj Nath* v. *State of Assam*, (2001) 5 SCC 714.

**60. Courts – Role of –** It must be remembered that in the case of juvenile, the Trial Court is not a mute spectator between the prosecution and the defence but the Trial Judge must take active part in the enquiry. Such evidence or witnesses must be summoned who are relevant for the question regarding date of birth of an accused. In the absence of documentary evidence, the medical opinion has to be obtained from duly constituted Board and only thereafter an appropriate finding regarding juvenility of an accused can be recorded by the Trial Court; *Waseem* v. *State of Uttar Pradesh*, 2013 (5) ALJ 563: 2013 (6) ADJ 47: 2013 (82) ACC 510 (All).

**61. Determinative Factors of Juvenility – Comments on –** As per the rule, date of birth, as mentioned in the matriculation or equivalent certificate, is to be treated as binding and final in the enquiry to be conducted on the question of juvenility. In the absence of matriculation or equivalent certificate, the date of birth certificate from the school, other than a play school first attended, is determinative. In the absence thereof, the date of birth certificate given by a corporation or a municipal authority or a Panchayat is the determinative factor. It is only in the absence of any of the certificates mentioned above that opinion of Medical Board can be sought and thereafter the Court can determine the age and if necessary, benefit of one year can be given; *Asrar @ Loveloo @ Lovely* v. *State*, 2013 (197) DLT 6: 2013 (1) JCC 67: 2013 (7) RCR (Cri) 2493 (Del) (DB).

**62. Inquiry – Time Period for –** A look at section 14(1) and its proviso would make this abundantly clear. The said proviso requires that the inquiry shall be completed within a period of four months from the date of its commencement unless the period is extended by the Board having regard to the circumstances of the case and special cases, after recording the reasons in writing for such extension. This gives an indication that under normal circumstances, a juvenile, who does not have the benefit of having been released on bail under section 12(1), but is sent to a Special Home or a Place of Safety under section 12(3) during the pendency of inquiry regarding him, shall not have to remain in such a limbo for more than four months. The maximum period of sending a person to a Special Home, now prescribed under the amended section 15(1)(g) is three years. Reference may also be made to the provisions of section 65 of the Act which also indicate that the sentence shall not exceed the maximum period provided under section 15 of the Act even in respect of those juveniles who were undergoing sentence at the time of introduction of the said Act; *Sunil Ojha* v. *State of NCT of Delhi*, 2007 (4) Crimes 596: 2007 (4) AICLR 56: 2007 Cr LJ 3068.

**63. No Exact Assessment – Law on –** Rule 12(3) specifically stipulates that in case the exact assessment of the age cannot be done, the Court may, if necessary, give the benefit to the child or juvenile by considering his/her age on the lower side within the margin of one year; *Mukesh* v. *State of Delhi*, 2012 (1) AD (Del) 737: 2012 (2) Crimes 171: 2012 (2) RCR (Cri) 102.

**50. Sending a juvenile or child outside jurisdiction.**—In the case of a juvenile or the child, whose ordinary place of residence lies outside the jurisdiction of the competent authority before which he is brought, the competent authority may, if satisfied after due inquiry that it is expedient so to do, send the juvenile or the child back to a relative or other person who is fit and willing to receive him at his ordinary place of residence and exercise proper care and control over him, notwithstanding that such place of residence is outside the jurisdiction of the competent authority; and the competent authority exercising jurisdiction over the place to which the juvenile or the child is sent shall in respect of any matter arising subsequently have the same powers in relation to the juvenile or the child as if the original order had been passed by itself.

**51. Reports to be treated as confidential.**—The report of the probation officer or social worker considered by the competent authority shall be treated as confidential:

Provided that the competent authority may, if it so thinks fit, communicate the substance thereof to the juvenile or the child or his parent or guardian and may give such juvenile or the child, parent or guardian an opportunity of producing such evidence as may be relevant to the matter stated in the report.

### COMMENTS

**Criminal Record of Juvenile – Law on –** Even where a juvenile is found to have committed an offence, he shall not suffer any disqualification and even the records are to be obliterated after a specified period of time. The intention of the Legislature is absolutely clear that insofar as juveniles are concerned; their criminal record is not to stand in their way in their future life; *Government of NCT of Delhi* v. *Pradeep Hooda*, 2012 (192) DLT 356: 2012 (9) AD 650 (Del) (DB).

**52. Appeals.**—(1) Subject to the provisions of this section, any person aggrieved by an order made by a competent authority under this Act may, within thirty days from the date of such order, prefer an appeal to the Court of Session:

Provided that the Court of Session may entertain the appeal after the expiry of the said period of thirty days if it is satisfied that the appellant was prevented by sufficient cause from filing the appeal in time.

(2) No appeal shall lie from—

(a) any order of acquittal made by the Board in respect of a juvenile alleged to have committed an offence; or

(b) any order made by a Committee in respect of a finding that a person is not a neglected juvenile.

(3) No second appeal shall lie from any order of the Court of Session passed in appeal under this section.

### SYNOPSIS

**1.** Appeal – Law on
**2.** Maintainability of Appeal – Law on
**3.** Appeal – Maintainability
**4.** Appeal – Maintainability of
**5.** Admission of Appeals – Effect of
**6.** Claim of Juvenility – Law on
**7.** Plea of Juvenility – Law on
**8.** Alternate Remedy – Law on
**9.** Appeal from Order of Acquittal – Law on
**10.** Claim of Juvenility – Law on
**11.** Claim of Juvenility – Sustainability of
**12.** Condonation of Delay – Law on
**13.** Judicial Intervention – Law on
**14.** Order Passed by Sessions Court – Effect of
**15.** Plea of Juvenile – Law on
**16.** Presumption of Innocence of Accused – Law on
**17.** Presumption of Innocence of Accused – View on
**18.** Re-trial – Law on
**19.** Sentence in Respect of Juvenile – Law on
**20.** Reduction of Sentence – Law on
**21.** Sentence – Appeal against

**COMMENTS**

**1. Appeal – Law on –** A bare reading of provision makes it clear that no appeal shall lie from any order of acquittal made by the Board in respect of a juvenile and therefore, an acquittal appeal under proviso to section 372 of the Cr. P.C. against the order of acquittal passed by the Board in respect of a juvenile alleged to have committed an offence would not be maintainable; *S.L. Warkare* v. *State of Chhattisgarh,* 2012 Cr LJ 4368 (Chha) (DB).

**2. Maintainability of Appeal – Law on –** When an application is moved before the competent authority under section 49 of the Act for determination of juvenality, against the order of Competent Authority appeal would be maintainable under section 52 of the Act before the Sessions Judge. While mentioning about the word 'finding of the Court', the Apex Court virtually meant the finding of the trial Court and in reference to trial Court's order that observation was made that appeal was not maintainable and it was only that revision was maintainable as appeal was maintainable against the order of the competent authority; *Irfan @ Saddam* v. *State of Uttar Pradesh,* 2012 (3) Crimes 454 (All): 2011 (7) ADJ 511: 2011 (75) ACC 6.

**3. Appeal – Maintainability –** When an application is moved before the competent authority under section 49 of the Act for determination of juvenility, then appeal would be maintainable under section 52 of the Act before the Sessions Judge. While mentioning about the word 'finding of the Court', the Apex Court virtually meant the finding of the trial Court and in reference to trial Court's order that observation was made that appeal was not maintainable and it was only that revision was maintainable as appeal was maintainable against the order of the competent authority; *Irfan @ Saddam* v. *State of Uttar Pradesh,* 2012 (3) Crimes 454 (All): 2012 (2) RCR (Cri) 748: 2011 (7) ADJ 511.

**4. Appeal – Maintainability of –** On a careful reading of the above provisions of law, it is found that there is a clear bar to prefer any appeal as against any order of acquittal passed by the Board in respect of a juvenile, who has allegedly committed an offence section 378 of the Code which governs the field of general procedure to prefer an appeal as against the acquittal passed by the Court below would not apply to this case when the said Act specifically debarred the aggrieved party to prefer any appeal as against the order of acquittal passed by the Board. The special enactment has overriding effect over the general procedure contemplated under the procedural law. The Legislature in its wisdom has incorporated a revisional power for the High Court under section 53 of the Act with a sole purpose of testing the legality and propriety of any order that may be passed by the Board or the Court of Sessions in connection with a case launched as against a juvenile. Therefore, it is always open to the aggrieved party to knock at the doors of the High Court invoking the revisional power under section 53 of the Act to call for the record of the proceedings before the Board or the Court of Sessions to satisfy itself to the legality and propriety of the order passed by it; *State of Haryana* v. *Mohan* alias *Monu,* 2011 (3) RCR (Cri) 433 (P&H) (DB).

**5. Admission of Appeals – Effect of –** Appellate Court while admitting any appeal for hearing suspends the execution of the sentence and orders for release of the appellant on bail but in such a position, the order of conviction remains intact until it is set aside by the final verdict of the Appellate Court. Thus, the status of the applicant despite the admission of appeals and his release on bail was that of convict and he cannot be exonerated of the consequences provided under section 437(ii) Cr.P.C; *Rajendra Nishad* v. *State of Uttar Pradesh,* 2013 (2) ACrR 1605: 2013 (81) ACC 759 (All).

**6. Claim of Juvenility – Law on –** It is crystal clear that the claim of the juvenility can be raised before any court and if the court is of the opinion that an accused person was a juvenile on the date of commission of the offence, the court shall make an enquiry, take such evidence as may be necessary (but not an affidavit) for the purpose of determining the age of such person, and shall record a finding whether the person is a juvenile or a child or not, stating his age as nearly as may be. The claim of juvenility can be raised before any court and it shall be recognised at any stage even after final disposal of the case and such claim shall be determined according to provisions contained in this Act and rules made thereunder. Even if the juvenile has ceased to be juvenile on or before the date of commencement of this Amendment Act and if the court finds the person to be juvenile on the date of commission of offence under sub-section (1), it shall forward the juvenile to the Board for passing appropriate order, and the sentence if any, passed by a court shall be deemed to have no effect; *Sudhakar Dwivedi* v. *State of Uttar Pradesh*, 2012 (6) ADJ 649: 2012 (2) ACrR 2250 (All).

**7. Plea of Juvenility – Law on –** By virtue of section 7A of the Act The plea of juvenility could be agitated by any person at any stage of proceeding, even in revision and appeal and that plea has to be considered by the higher courts. As per the definition of 'juvenile in conflict with law' as contained in section 2(l) of the Act, a juvenile is a person who is alleged to have committed an offence and has not completed 18 years of age on the date of commission of such offence. Thus, this amendment on the definition of 'juvenile in conflict with law' has made the definition retrospective and the date from which the juvenility has to be reckoned is the date of occurrence; *Sashi Mandal* alias *Shashi Kumar, Son of Devendra Mandal* v. *State of Bihar*, 2011 Cr LJ 3885: 2012 (6) RCR (Cri) 753: 2012 (1) PLJR 298 (Pat).

**8. Alternate Remedy – Law on –** It is a well settled position in law that in the event an order passed by the concerned authority is without jurisdiction, though an alternate remedy of appeal is available; it is open for the Aggrieved to approach High Court directly, under articles 226 and 227 of the Constitution of India; *Ashwin Jayantibhai Parmar* v. *State of Maharashtra*, 2012 All MR (Cri) 2545: 2012 (2) Mh LJ (Cri) 559 (Bom) (DB).

**9. Appeal from Order of Acquittal – Law on –** No appeal shall lie from any order of acquittal made by the Board in respect of a Juvenile alleged to have committed an offence as per section 52(2) of the Juvenile Justice (Care and Protection of Children) Act, 2000. Of course under section 53 of the Act, 2000 *suo moto* revision or a revision based on the application received in that behalf can be entertained by the High Court to satisfy itself as to the legality or propriety of any such order passed by the Juvenile Justice Board; *State of Punjab* v. *Rajesh* alias *Tilak Ram*, 2012 (1) Crimes 437 (P&H): 2011 (4) RCR (Cri) 621 (P&H) (DB).

**10. Claim of Juvenility – Law on –** If Courts apply sections 2(k), 2(l), 7A, 20 and 49 of the 2000 Act read with rules 12 and 98 of the Juvenile Justice (Care and Protection of Children) Rules, 2007 all persons who were below the age of 18 years on the date of commission of the offence even prior to 1-4-2001, would be treated as juveniles even if the claim of juvenility is raised after they have attained the age of 18 years on or before the date of the commencement of the 2000 Act and were undergoing sentences upon being convicted; *Ketankumar Gopalbhai Tandel* v. *State of Gujarat*, 2013 (5) Supreme 582: JT 2013 (9) SC 554: 2013 (9) SCALE 487.

**11. Claim of Juvenility – Sustainability of –** It is settled proposition that if a person accused of committing an offence was below the age of 18 years as on the date of commission of the offence, such person shall be entitled to the benefits of the Juvenile Justice (Care and Protection of Children) Act, 2000 as amended by Act 33 of 2006, even though he might have completed the age of 18 years on the date of commencement of the said Act. It is also crystal clear that the plea of juvenility can be taken before any court at any stage of the proceedings and that such a claim can be made even after the disposal of the case. If the claim is made during inquiry or trial before a court, such court can take evidence and decide the sustainability of the claim of juvenility. If such a claim is raised in an appeal or revision, then the appellate court or the court of revision, as the case may be, can decide the question of sustainability of the claim of juvenility and grant the relief in accordance with the Act; *A. Chinnaponnu W/o Annamalai* v. *State of Tamil Nadu*, 2011 (3) Mad LJ 433 (Cri): 2011 (8) RCR (Cri) 663 (Mad) (DB).

**12. Condonation of Delay – Law on –** Normally, the Courts take a lenient and liberal view in the matters regarding condonation of delay. To be hyper technical and punishing a client for the fault of his counsel has never been the job of the Courts. The Courts must act in a manner so that justice may be done to the parties irrespective of the fault of the counsel; *Sonu (In Jail)* v. *State of Uttar Pradesh*, 2011 (8) ADJ 662: 2011 (3) ACrR 3368: 2011 (6) AWC 2415 (All).

**13. Judicial Intervention – Law on –** Though the JJ Act and the Conventions provide for minimum possible judicial intervention, however at the same time it cannot be said that an order passed by the Juvenile Justice Board shall be final and no appeal or revision against it would lie before the superior Courts. This would be contrary to the fundamental principle of right of access to justice. A perusal of section 52 of the JJ Act shows that any person aggrieved by an order made by a competent authority under the JJ Act can prefer an appeal to the Court of Session within 30 days. However, no such appeal shall lie from an order of acquittal made by the Board in respect of a juvenile alleged to have committed an offence. Thereby meaning that except in the case of an order of acquittal, an appeal by any aggrieved person would lie before a Court of Sessions. A restrictive meaning to the words "aggrieved person" cannot be given. If the Legislature had so intended, it would have then used the words "juvenile in conflict with law" and not "any person aggrieved". However, at the same time it may be noted that the right of appeal is limited as no appeal against an acquittal lies. Thus, the other orders on which the victim or the State may have the grievance like an order declaring a person juvenile, the aggrieved person would be entitled to copy of the order for challenge before the Superior Court; *X Minor Thr. Father Natural Guardian* v. *State*, 2012 (5) RCR (Cri) 191: 2012 Cr LJ 4482 (Del).

**14. Order Passed by Sessions Court – Effect of –** Under section 52 of the Act Sessions Judge is the appellate authority of any order passed by the Board. Thus in an appeal a Sessions Court has got the power to set aside the order of the Board. With such a power conferred on the Sessions Court it surpasses all suppositions that Board can sit over the order passed by its appellate Court, when every order is passed by the Sessions Court is binding on the Board. The Act or the Rules framed thereunder no where provides that if a plea of being a juvenile is raised by an accused before the Sessions Court or the High Court then for determination of such a plea the matter has to be referred to the Board or that the matter should be transferred to the Board for its adjudication. If the Statute does not provide such a course, the Board while interpreting the Act can not legislate such a duty on High Court or Court of Session. Further the power conferred under section 6(2) of the Act is concurrent both for Sessions Court and High Court; *Manish Tyagi* v. *State of Uttar Pradesh*, 2007 (5) ADJ 102: 2007 (4) ALJ 103: 2007 Cr LJ 3165.

**15. Plea of Juvenile – Law on –** As per the provision of section 7A of the Act, plea of juvenile can be raised at any stage and before any court and it shall be recognized as such by the court; *Satveer Valmiki* v. *State of Uttaranchal*, 2013 Cr LJ 81 (Uttar) (Nainital Bench).

**16. Presumption of Innocence of Accused – Law on –** The trial of an accused under the criminal justice system is governed by a well laid down procedure the essence of which is clarity of the charge brought against the accused; the duty of the prosecution to prove the charge by reliable and legal evidence and the presumption of innocence of the accused. Culpability is to be determined on the touchstone of proof beyond reasonable doubt but if convicted, punishment as provided for is required to be inflicted with little or no exception. The accused is entitled to seek an exoneration from the charge(s) levelled *i.e.*, discharge (amounting to an acquittal) mid course; *Subramanian Swamy* v. *Raju*, 2014 (4)

SCALE 305: AIR 2014 SC 1649: 2014 (2) Crimes 307 (SC), *Nirbhaya* case [Hon'ble Judges: P. Sathasivam, Ranjan Gogoi, Shiva Kirti Singh].

**17. Presumption of Innocence of Accused – View on –** The trial of an accused under the criminal justice system is governed by a well laid down procedure the essence of which is clarity of the charge brought against the accused; the duty of the prosecution to prove the charge by reliable and legal evidence and the presumption of innocence of the accused. Culpability is to be determined on the touchstone of proof beyond reasonable doubt but if convicted, punishment as provided for is required to be inflicted with little or no exception. The accused is entitled to seek an exoneration from the charge(s) levelled *i.e.,* discharge (amounting to an acquittal) mid course; *Subramanian Swamy* v. *Raju,* 2014 (4) SCALE 305: AIR 2014 SC 1649: 2014 (2) Crimes 307 (SC), *Nirbhaya* case [Hon'ble Judges: P. Sathasivam, Ranjan Gogoi, Shiva Kirti Singh].

**18. Re-trial – Law on –** It goes without saying that the provisions of section 386 Cr.P.C. is clear enough to empower the Appellate Court in an appeal from a conviction to commit a criminal case for re-trial. However, order of re-trial cannot be made as a matter of course and merely because both the Counsels appearing on behalf of the accused and the State had agreed on that score. As the law stands such power has to be exercised sparingly and in very exceptional cases and that too for ends of justice. While making such order the Court must always be on guard and must be sure that such order would not enable the prosecution to lead evidence which it could but has not cared to lead; *State of West Bengal* v. *Sanjiv @ Sanjit Pan,* 2012 (4) Cal HN 302 (Cal) (DB).

**19. Sentence in Respect of Juvenile – Law on –** It is clear that in cases which are pending, which includes pending appeals, as would be apparent from a reading of the *Explanation,* the same would be continued in the Court before which they are pending as if the Act has not been passed. It is further provided that if the Court finds that the juvenile has committed an offence it shall record such finding and instead of passing any sentence in respect of the juvenile, forward the juvenile to the Board, which shall pass orders in respect of the juvenile in accordance with the provisions of the said Act, as if it had been satisfied, on inquiry, under the Act that the juvenile had committed the offence; *Chatpal @ Satpal* v. *State,* 2011 (123) DRJ 131 (Del) (DB).

**20. Reduction of Sentence – Law on –** In order to enable a Court to impose a reduced sentence, the statutory requirement is that the Court has to record not only adequate, but also reasons, which are special to the case, warranting sentence, which is less than the prescribed minimum. Thus, the reasons assigned must be adequate and also special. What is adequate and/or special reason will depend on the facts of a given case. The criminal law adheres to the principle of proportionality of punishment and this principle of proportionality depends on the nature of culpability". No doubt, criminal law allows some discretion to a Judge in deciding the sentence in each case; but the sentence imposed must be commensurate with the gravity of the offence and this would obviously include the impact of the sentence on the society. When the legislative intent in prescribing minimum punishment for an offence is aimed at making the sentence work as deterrent, imperative it is that the Court respects such legislative policy and intent. Sometimes, it is, as a measure of correctional needs, that perpetrator of an offence may be required to be given a reduced sentence. The minimum sentence can be reduced only for such reasons, which serves the legislative purpose. It is the legislature, which with the help of a piece of penal legislation, tries to remove a mischief in the society. Such minimum prescribed sentence reflects social anxiety, tension and concern over the impact of the offence, which is sought to be penalized by prescribing minimum punishment; *Tamok Komut* v. *State of Arunachal Pradesh,* 2008 Cr LJ 3961 (Gau) (DB).

**21. Sentence – Appeal against –** section 377 enables only the State Government or the Central Government, as the case may be, to direct the Public Prosecutor to prefer appeal against the sentence on the ground of its inadequacy. It is also of immense importance to note that section 377(3) puts an embargo on the High Court not to enhance the sentence without giving to the accused a reasonable opportunity of showing cause against such an enhancement and while showing cause, the accused may plead for his acquittal or for reduction of the sentence. This shows that when the High Court considers a case for enhancement of sentence, it is within the powers of the High Court to determine if the charge has been brought home, particularly, when the accused pleads for his acquittal; *Tamok Komut* v. *State of Arunachal Pradesh,* 2008 Cr LJ 3961 (Gau) (DB).

**53. Revision.**—The High Court may, at any time, either of its own motion or on an application received in this behalf, call for the record of any proceeding in which any competent authority or Court of Session has passed an order for the purpose of satisfying itself as to the legality or propriety of any such order and may pass such order in relation thereto as it thinks fit:

Provided that the High Court shall not pass an order under this section prejudicial to any person without giving him a reasonable opportunity of being heard.

**SYNOPSIS**



**COMMENTS**

**1. Revision – Law on –** On a careful reading of the above provisions of law, it is found that there is a clear bar to prefer any appeal as against any order of acquittal passed by the Board in respect of a juvenile, who has allegedly committed an offence section 378 of the Code which governs the field of general procedure to prefer an appeal as against the acquittal passed by the Court below would not apply to this case when the said Act specifically debarred the aggrieved party to prefer any appeal as against the order of acquittal passed by the Board. The special enactment has overriding effect over the general procedure contemplated under the procedural law. The Legislature in its wisdom has incorporated a revisional power for the High Court under section 53 of the Act with a sole purpose of testing the legality and propriety of any order that may be passed by the Board or the Court of Sessions in connection with a case launched as against a juvenile. Therefore, it is always open to the aggrieved party to knock at the doors of the High Court invoking the revisional power under section 53 of the Act to call for the record of the proceedings before the Board or the Court of Sessions to satisfy itself to the legality and propriety of the order passed by it; *State of Haryana* v. *Mohan* alias *Monu,* 2011 (3) RCR (Cri) 433 (P&H) (DB).

**2. Revisional Powers – Comments on –** No doubt revisional powers of this court are *vide* enough to judge correctness, legality or propriety of any finding, sentence or order or regularity of any proceeding, but this does not mean that revisional court should be transformed as a second appeal court; *Atin Jaiswal* v. *State of Uttar Pradesh,* 2012 (6) RCR (Cri) 2011: 2012 (2) ACrR 1228

**3. Revisional Powers – Law on –** A careful reading of section 397 read with section 401 shows that the High Court may call for and examine the record of any proceeding before any inferior criminal Courts within its jurisdiction for the purpose of satisfying itself as to the correctness, legality or propriety of any finding, sentence or order, recorded or passed, and as to the regularity of any proceedings of such inferior Court. Thus, section 397(1) not only vests the High Court with the power to examine the correctness, legality and propriety of any finding of guilt or otherwise, but also of the sentence or order, which may have been passed by any inferior criminal Court. There is nothing in the provisions of section 397 to show that the High Court's exercise of its revisional jurisdiction would be only *suo motu* and not on the basis of a petition made by a person aggrieved by the finding, which an inferior criminal Court may have recorded, or by sentence or order, which an inferior criminal Court may have passed; *Tamok Komut* v. *State of Arunachal Pradesh,* 2008 Cr LJ 3961 (Gau) (DB).

**4. Appeal against Single Judge – Law on** – It is well settled that an appeal under clause 15 of the Letters Patent would lie only against an order passed by a Single Judge in exercise of powers under article 226 of the Constitution of India, whereas no appeal is maintainable if the order passed by the learned Single Judge is in exercise of his supervisory jurisdiction as conferred under article 227 of the Constitution of India; *Gujarat State Road Transport Corporation* v. *Firoze M. Mogal,* 2014 (1) GLH 1: AIR 2014 Guj 33: 2014 (2) GLR 1373 (Guj) (LB) [Hon'ble Judges: Ravi R. Tripathi, Jayant Patel, M.R. Shah, J.B. Pardiwala, A.G. Uraizee].

**5. Question of Juvenility – Law on** – The *Explanation* to section 20 of the new Act makes it clear that, in all cases, including trial, revision, appeal or any other criminal proceedings in respect of a juvenile in conflict with law, in any Court, the determination of juvenility of such a juvenile shall be in terms of clause (l) of section 2, even if the juvenile ceases to be a juvenile on or before the commencement of the new Act and the provisions of the new Act shall apply as if the said provisions had been in force, for all purposes and at all material times, when the alleged offence was committed. Section 20 of the new Act has, however, brought revolutionary changes making special provisions in respect of all cases, which were pending against persons. To put it a little differently, when a male person, older than 16 years, happens to face trial for commission of an offence, he has to be treated as a juvenile in conflict with law under the new Act, if he had not crossed the age of 18 years on the date of the commission of the offence, when the new Act came into force and, in such circumstances, the procedure, as prescribed by section 20 of the new Act, has to be followed, which allows the trial, as against such person, to proceed in the trial Court but by treating the person concerned as a juvenile in conflict with law within the meaning of section 2(l) of the new Act and, if the criminal Court arrives at the finding of guilt against such a person, then, instead of convicting such a person of the offence, which the person has been found guilty of, the criminal Court is required to record its finding and, then, instead of convicting and sentencing him accordingly, make over such a person to the Juvenile Justice Board for passing appropriate order. Section 20 also makes it clear that even in the revision or appeal, arisen against a person conviction and sentence by a criminal Court, the convicted person can raise question of his juvenility for receiving the benefit of section 20, if he can show that though he had, as a male person, ceased to be juvenile by having crossed the age of 16 years, he was, nevertheless, less than 18 years, when the new Act came into force; *Halla Dhar Das* v. *State of Assam,* 2012 (4) Gau LT 583 (Gau).

**6. Constitutional Proceedings – Law on** – The constitutional proceedings under article 226 and article 227 are mutually exclusive of one another and collectively exhaustive of the High Court's powers under the Constitution of India and not let thereby made interchangeable, inter-convertible, inter-substitutable; *Gujarat State Road Transport Corporation* v. *Firoze M. Mogal,* 2014 (1) GLH 1: AIR 2014 Guj 33: 2014 (2) GLR 1373 (Guj) (LB) [Hon'ble Judges: Ravi R. Tripathi, Jayant Patel, M.R. Shah, J.B. Pardiwala, A.G. Uraizee].

**7. Determination of Juvenility – Law on** – In all pending cases including trial, revision, appeal or any other criminal proceedings in respect of a juvenile in conflict with law, in any court, the determination of juvenility of such a juvenile shall be in terms of clause (1) of section 2, even if the juvenile ceases to be so on or before the date of commencement of this Act and the provisions of this Act shall apply as if the said provisions had been in force, for all purposes and at all material times when the alleged offence was committed; *Bijendra Kumar* v. *State of Uttar Pradesh,* 2013 (3) DMC 389: 2013 (3) ADJ 619: 2013 (2) ACrR 1616 (All).

**8. Ends of Justice – Meaning of –** While dealing with such an issue, the court must not lose sight of the fact that meaning of "ends of justice" essentially refers to justice to all the parties. This phrase refers to the best interest of the public within the four corners of the statute. In fact, it means preservation of proper balance between the Constitutional/Statutory rights of an individual and rights of the people at large to have the law enforced. The "ends of justice" does not mean vague and indeterminate notions of justice, but justice according to the law of the land; *Essa @ Anjum Abdul Razak Memon* v. *State of Maharashtra,* 2013 (3) Supreme 195: 2013 (2) Mad LJ (Cri) 401: 2013 (3) SCALE 1; *Vide* also: *State Bank of Patiala* v. *S.K. Sharma,* AIR 1996 SC 1669; and *Mahadev Govind Gharge* v. *The Special Land Acquisition Officer, Upper Krishna Project, Jamkhandi, Karnataka,* (2011) 6 SCC 321.

**9. Inadequate Sentence – Law on –** The revisional jurisdiction can be invoked by an informant of a case if the sentence passed against a person found guilty of an offence is inadequate or if no sentence is passed treating such a person as juvenile, though he may not, under law, be a juvenile or though he ought not to have been treated as juvenile under the law; *Tamok Komut* v. *State of Arunachal Pradesh,* 2008 Cr LJ 3961 (Gau) (DB).

**10. Opportunity of Being Heard – Law on –** In exercise of its revisional jurisdiction the High Court cannot pass an order, prejudicial to any person without affording him a reasonable opportunity of being heard. At this juncture, it would be profitable to note that section 54 of the Act also prescribes the procedure to be followed while dealing with inquiries, appeals and revisions under the Act. Sub-section (2) thereof stipulates that save as otherwise expressly provided under the Act, the procedure to be followed in hearing, revisions under the Act, shall be as far as practicable in accordance with the provisions of the Code of Criminal Procedure, 1973 (for short 'the Code'). Sub-section (2) of section 401 of the Code contemplates that no order under the said section shall be made to the prejudice of the accused or other person unless he has had an opportunity of being heard either personally or by pleader in his own defence. It is well settled that save in certain exceptional situations, the principle of *audi alteram partem* mandates that no one shall be condemned unheard. It is a part of rules of natural justice and the soul of natural justice is fair play in action', which demands that before any prejudicial or adverse order is passed or action is taken against a person, he must be given an opportunity to be heard; *Babloo Pasi* v. *State of Jharkhand,* AIR 2009 SC 314: 2008 (13) SCC 133: 2008 (13) SCALE 137.

**11. Sentence – Law on –** As per proviso (1) to section 7A thereof the claim of juvenility can be raised before a Court at any stage even after final disposal of the case and even if the juvenile had ceased to be so on or before the date of this Act. Sub-section (2) of section 7A states that if the Court finds a person to be a juvenile on the date of commission of the offence under sub-section (1), it shall forward the juvenile to the Board for passing appropriate order and the sentence, if any passed by a Court shall be deemed to have no effect; *Gangaram Dushanna Dandil* v. *State of Maharashtra,* 2009 (4) Crimes 697 (Bom): 2009 (2) BCR (Cri) 277: 2009 (5) AIR BomR 45.

**12. High Court – Powers of –** A plain reading of section 52 of the Act shows that no statutory appeal is available against any finding of the court that a person was not a juvenile at the time of commission of the offence. Section 53 of the Act which is titled "Revision", however, provides that the High Court may at any time, either of its own motion or on an application received on that behalf, call for the record of any proceeding in which any competent authority or court of session has passed an order for the purpose of satisfying itself as to the legality or propriety of any such order, and may pass such order in relation thereto as it thinks fit. While exercising such revisional powers, the High Court cannot convert itself to an appellate court and reverse the findings of fact arrived at by the trial court on the basis of evidence or material on record, except where the High Court is not satisfied as to the legality or propriety of the order passed by the trial court; *Jabar Singh* v. *Dinesh*, 2010 Cr LJ 2043: 2010 (2) SCALE 856: 2010 (3) SCC 757.

**13. Writ – Meaning of –** A Plain Dictionary meaning of the word "writ" is as under:—

> "a form of written command to act or not act in some way" As per Law Lexicon "writ" is explained as under:-
>
> > "in general is the king's precept, in writing under seal, issuing out of some court, to the sheriff, or other person, and commanding something to be done touching a suit or action, or giving commission to have it done. A writ is said to be a formal letter of king's sealed with a seal, directed to some judge, officer, or minister, etc., at the suit or plaint of a subject, requiring to have a thing done, for cause briefly expressed, which is to be discussed in the proper court, according to law (*Tomlins Law Dic.*) a written command, precept, or formal order issued by a court, directing or enjoying the person or persons to whom it is addressed to do or refrain from doing some act specified therein." While as per the *Black's Law Dictionary*, the term "writ" has been explained as under:—
> >
> > "a court's written order, in the name of a state or other competent legal authority, commanding the addressee to do or refrain from doing some specified act"; *Gujarat State Road Transport Corporation* v. *Firoze M. Mogal*, 2014 (1) GLH 1: AIR 2014 Guj 33: 2014 (2) GLR 1373 (Guj) (LB) [Hon'ble Judges: Ravi R. Tripathi, Jayant Patel, M.R. Shah, J.B. Pardiwala, A.G. Uraizee].

**54. Procedure in inquiries, appeals and revision proceedings.**—(1) Save as otherwise expressly provided by this Act, a competent authority while holding any inquiry under any of the provisions of this Act, shall follow such procedure as may be prescribed and subject thereto, shall follow, as far as may be, the procedure laid down in the Code of Criminal Procedure, 1973 (2 of 1974) for trials in summons cases.

(2) Save as otherwise expressly provided by or under this Act, the procedure to be followed in hearing appeals or revision proceedings under this Act shall be, as far as practicable, in accordance with the provisions of the Code of Criminal Procedure, 1973 (2 of 1974).

**COMMENTS**

**Nature of Enquiry – Law on –** section 54 of the Act lays down that save as otherwise expressly provided by this Act, a competent authority while holding any inquiry under any of the provision of this Act, shall follow such procedure as may be prescribed and subject thereto, shall follow, as far as may be, the procedure laid down in the Code of Criminal Procedure, 1973 (2 of 1974) for trails in summons cases. The nature of enquiry to be conducted in section 33 has been specifically laid down in the provisions of the Act and rules. Section 33(1) of the Act provides that the child may be sent to a Children's Home for "speedy enquiry" by a social worker or Chief Welfare Officer. The enquiry referred to in sub-section (1) of section 33 (after the child is ordered to be sent to Children's Home) is thus, a "speedy enquiry". Such an enquiry has to be conducted by a social worker or a Child Welfare Officer and not by the Committee. Thus, there is no enquiry which has to be personally conducted by the Committee itself, as per section 33(1) of the Act, after the child is ordered to be sent to the Children's Home etc. As per section 54 of the Act, competent authority shall follow such procedure as may be prescribed and subject thereto, shall follow, as far as may be, the procedure laid down in the Code of Criminal

Procedure, 1973 (2 of 1974) for trails in summons cases, only if the Committee itself is holding any inquiry under any of the provisions of this Act. But, there is no such enquiry to be conducted by the Committee itself as per section 33 and rule 11, and hence, there is no question of the Committee following any provision in the code for trials in the summons cases for the detailed enquiry; *Jose Maveli* v. *State of Kerala,* 2007 Cr LJ 2709: 2007 (2) Ker LT 761 (Ker).

**55. Power to amend orders.**—(1) Without prejudice to the provisions for appeal and revision under this Act, any competent authority may, on an application received in this behalf, amend any order as to the institution to which a juvenile or the child is to be sent or as to the person under whose care or supervision a juvenile or the child is to be placed under this Act:

Provided that there shall be at least two members and the parties or its defence present during the course of hearing for passing an amendment in relation to any of its order.

(2) Clerical mistakes in orders passed by a competent authority or errors arising therein from any accidental slip or omission may, at any time, be corrected by the competent authority either on its own motion or on an application received in this behalf.

### COMMENTS

**Safeguard of Rights of Child – Comments on –** It is quite clear from the above that the purpose of the Act is to rehabilitate a juvenile in conflict with law with a view to reintegrate him into society. This is by no means an easy task and it is worth researching how successful the implementation of the Act has been in its avowed purpose in this respect. As regards procedurally dealing with a juvenile in conflict with law, the Rules require the concerned State Government to set up in every District a Special Juvenile Police Unit to handle the cases of juveniles or children in terms of the provisions of the Act (Rule 84). This Unit shall consist of a juvenile or child welfare officer of the rank of Police Inspector having an aptitude and appropriate training and orientation to handle such cases. He will be assisted by two paid social workers having experience of working in the field of child welfare of which one of them shall be a woman. Rule 75 of the Rules requires that while dealing with a juvenile or a child, except at the time of arrest, a police officer shall wear plain clothes and not his uniform. The Act and the Model Rules clearly constitute an independent code for issues concerning a child or a juvenile, particularly a juvenile in conflict with law. This code is intended to safeguard the rights of the child and a juvenile in conflict with law and to put him in a category separate and distinct from an adult accused of a crime; *Jitendra Singh @ Babboo Singh* v. *State of Uttar Pradesh,* 2013 (11) SCC 193: JT 2013 (11) SC 152: 2013 (9) SCALE 18.

**56. Power of competent authority to discharge and transfer juvenile or child.**—The competent authority [1][***] may, notwithstanding anything contained in this Act, at any time, order a child in need of care and protection or a juvenile in conflict with law to be discharged or transferred from one children's home or special home to another, as the case may be, keeping in view the best interest of the child or the juvenile, and his natural place of stay, either absolutely or on such conditions as it may think fit to impose:

Provided that the total period of stay of the juvenile or the child in a childern's home or a special home or a fit institution or under a fit person shall not be increased by such transfer.

---

1. The words "or the local authority" omitted by Act 33 of 2006, sec. 5 (w.e.f. 22-8-2006).

[1][**57. Transfer between children's homes, under the Act, and juvenile homes of like nature in different parts of India.**—The State Government may direct any child or the juvenile to be transferred from any children's home or special home within the State to any other children's home, special home or institution of a like nature or to such institutions outside the state in consultation with the concerned State Government and with the prior intimation to the Committee or the Board, as the case may be, and such order shall be deemed to be operative for the competent authority of the area to which the child or the juvenile is sent.]

[2][**58. Transfer of juvenile or child as are mentally ill or addicted to alcohol or other drugs.**—(1) Where it appears to the competent authority that any juvenile or child kept in a special home or an observation home or a children's home or a shelter home or in an institution in pursuance of this Act, is a mentally ill person or addicted to alcohol or other drugs which lead to behavioural changes in a person, the competent authority may order his removal to a psychiatric hospital or psychiatric nursing home in accordance with the provisions of the Mental Health Act, 1987 (14 of 1987) or the rules made thereunder.

(2) In case the juvenile or child had been removed to a psychiatric hospital or psychiatric nursing home under sub-section (1), the competent authority may, on the basis of the advice given in the certificate of discharge of the psychiatric hospital or psychiatric nursing home, order to remove such juvenile or child to an Integrated Rehabilitation Centre for Addicts or similar centres maintained by the State Government for mentally ill persons (including the persons addicted to any narcotic drug or psychotropic substance) and such removal shall be only for the period required for the in-patient treatment of such juvenile or child.

*Explanation.*—For the purposes of this sub-section,—

(a) "Integrated Rehabilitation Centre for Addicts" shall have the meaning assigned to it under the scheme called "Central Sector Scheme of

---

1. Subs. by Act 33 of 2006, sec. 22, for section 57 (w.e.f. 22-8-2006). Section 57, before substitution, stood as under:

   "57. *Transfer between children's homes, under the Act, and juvenile homes, of like nature in different parts of India.*—The State Government or the local authority may direct any child or the juvenile to be transferred from any children's home or special home outside the State to any other children's home, special home or institution of a like nature with the prior intimation to the local Committee or the Board, as the case may be, and such order shall be deemed to be operative for the competent authority of the area to which the child or the juvenile is sent.".

2. Subs. by Act 12 of 2011, sec. 3, for section 58 (w.e.f. 1-1-2012). Section 58, before substitution, stood as under:

   "58. *Transfer of juvenile or child of unsound mind or suffering from leprosy or addicted to drugs.*—Where it appears to the competent authority that any juvenile or the child kept in a special home or a children's home or shelter home or in an institution in pursuance of this Act, is suffering from leprosy or is of unsound mind or is addicted to any narcotic drug or psychotropic substance, the competent authority may order his removal to a leper asylum or mental hospital or treatment centre for drug addicts or to a place of safety for being kept there for such period not exceeding the period for which he is required to be kept under the order of the competent authority or for such further period as may be certified by the medical officer necessary for the proper treatment of the juvenile or the child.".

Assistance for Prevention of Alcoholism and Substance (Drugs) Abuse and for Social Defence Services" made by the Government of India in the Ministry of Social Justice and Empowerment or any other corresponding scheme for the time being in force;

(b) "mentally ill person" shall have the meaning assigned to it in clause (l) of section 2 of the Mental Health Act, 1987 (14 of 1987);

(c) "psychiatric hospital" or "psychiatric nursing home" shall have the meaning assigned to it in clause (q) of section 2 of the Mental Health Act, 1987 (14 of 1987).]

**59. Release and absence of juvenile or child on placement.**—(1) When a juvenile or the child is kept in a children's home or special home and on a report of a probation officer or social worker or of Government or a voluntary organisation, as the case may be, the competent authority may consider, the release of such juvenile or the child permitting him to live with his parent or guardian or under the supervision of any authorised person named in the order, willing to receive and take charge of the juvenile or the child to educate and train him for some useful trade or calling or to look after him for rehabilitation.

(2) The competent authority may also permit leave of absence to any juvenile or the child, to allow him, on special occasions like examination, marriage of relatives, death of kith and kin or the accident or serious illness of parent or any emergency of like nature, to go on leave under supervision, [1][for a period generally not exceeding seven days], excluding the time taken in journey.

(3) Where a permission has been revoked or forfeited and the juvenile or the child refuses or fails to return to the home concerned or juvenile to which he was directed so to return, the Board may, if necessary, cause him to be taken charge of and to be taken back to the concerned home.

(4) The time during which a juvenile or the child is absent from a concerned home in pursuance of such permission granted under this section shall be deemed to be part of the time for which he is liable to be kept in the special home:

Provided that when a juvenile has failed to return to the special home on the permission being revoked or forfeited, the time which elapses after his failure so to return shall be excluded in computing the time during which he is liable to be kept in the institution.

**60. Contribution by parents.**—(1) The competent authority which makes an order for sending a juvenile or the child to a children's home or to a special home or placing the juvenile under the care of a fit person or fit institution may make an order requiring the parent or other person liable to maintain the juvenile or the child to contribute to his maintenance, if able to do so, in the prescribed manner according to income.

(2) The competent authority may direct, if necessary, the payment to be made to poor parent or guardian by the Superintendent or the Project Manager of the home to pay such expenses for the journey of the inmate or parent or guardian or both, from the home to his ordinary place of residence at the time of sending the juvenile as may be prescribed.

1. Subs. by Act 33 of 2006, sec. 23, for "for maximum seven days" (w.e.f. 22-8-2006).

**61. Fund.**—(1) The State Government [1][***] may create a Fund under such name as it thinks fit for the welfare and rehabilitation of the juvenile or the child dealt with under this Act.

(2) There shall be credited to the Fund such voluntary donations, contributions or subscriptions as may be made by any individual or organisation.

(3) The Fund created under sub-section (1) shall be administered by the State advisory board in such manner and for such purposes as may be prescribed.

**COMMENTS**

**Administration of Criminal Justice – Law on –** The administration of criminal justice in India can be divided into two broad stages at which the machinery operates. The first is the investigation of an alleged offence leading to prosecution and the second is the actual prosecution of the offender in a Court of Law. The jurisprudence that has evolved over the decades has assigned the primary role and responsibility at both stages to the State though Courts must hasten to add that in certain exceptional situations there is recognition of a limited right in a victim or his family members to take part in the process, particularly, at the stage of the trial. The law, however, frowns upon and prohibits any abdication by the State of its role in the matter at each of the stages and, in fact, does not recognize the right of a third party/stranger to participate or even to come to the aid of the State at any of the stages; *Subramanian Swamy* v. *Raju*, 2013 (10) SCC 465: 2013 (10) SCALE 365: 2013 (5) CTC 106.

**62. Central, State, district and city advisory boards.**—(1) The Central Government or a State Government may constitute a Central or a State advisory board, as the case may be, to advise that Government on matter relating to the establishment and maintenance of the homes, mobilisation of resources, provision of facilities for education, training and rehabilitation of child in need of care and protection and juvenile in conflict with law and co-ordination among the various official and non-official agencies concerned.

(2) The Central or State advisory board shall consist of such persons as the Central Government or the State Government, as the case may be, may think fit and shall include eminent social workers, representatives of voluntary organisation in the field of child welfare corporate sector, academicians, medical professionals and the concerned Department of the State Government.

(3) The district or city level inspection committee constituted under section 35 of this Act shall also function as the district or city advisory board.

[2][**62A. Constitution of Child Protection Unit responsible for implementation of the Act.**—Every State Government shall constitute a Child Protection Unit for the State and, such Units for every District, consisting of such officers and other employees as may be appointed by that Government, to take up matters relating to children in need of care and protection and juveniles in conflict with law with a view to ensure the implementation of this Act including the establishment and maintenance of homes, notification of competent authorities in relation to these children and their rehabilitation and co-ordination with various official and non-official agencies concerned.]

**63. Special juvenile police unit.**—(1) In order to enable the police officers who frequently or exclusively deal with juveniles or are primarily engaged in the

1. The words "or local authority" omitted by Act 33 of 2006, sec. 5 (w.e.f. 22-8-2006).
2. Ins. by Act 33 of 2006, sec. 24 (w.e.f. 22-8-2006).

prevention of juvenile crime or handling of the juveniles or children under this Act to perform their functions more effectively, they shall be specially instructed and trained.

(2) In every police station at least one officer with aptitude and appropriate training and orientation may be designated as the 'juvenile or the child welfare officer' who will handle the juvenile or the child in co-ordination with the police.

(3) Special juvenile police unit, of which all police officers designated as above, to handle juveniles or children will be members, may be created in every district and city to co-ordinate and to upgrade the police treatment of the juveniles and the children.

**COMMENTS**

**Child Welfare Officer – Appointment of –** The Home Departments and the Director Generals of Police of the States/Union Territories will ensure that at least one police officer in every police station with aptitude is given appropriate training and orientation and designated as Juvenile or Child Welfare Officer, who will handle the juvenile or child in coordination with the police as provided under sub-section (2) of section 63 of the Act. The required training will be provided by the District Legal Services Authorities under the guidance of the State Legal Services Authorities and Secretary, National Legal Services Authority will issue appropriate guidelines to the State Legal Services Authorities for training and orientation of police officers, who are designated as the Juvenile or Child Welfare Officers. The training and orientation may be done in phases over a period of six months to one year in every State and Union Territory. The Home Departments and the Director Generals of Police of the States/Union Territories will also ensure that Special Juvenile Police Unit comprising of all police officers designated as Juvenile or Child Welfare Officer be created in every district and city to coordinate and to upgrade the police treatment to juveniles and the children as provided in sub-section (3) of section 63 of the Act; *Sampurna Behura* v. *Union of India*, 2011 (7) Supreme 84: 2011 (11) SCALE 512: 2011 (9) SCC 801.

**64. Juvenile in conflict with law undergoing sentence at commencement of this Act.**—In any area in which this Act is brought into force, the State Government [1][***] [2][shall direct] that a juvenile in conflict with law who is undergoing any sentence of imprisonment at the commencement of this Act, shall, in lieu of undergoing such sentence, be sent to a special home or be kept in fit institution in such manner as the State Government [1][***] thinks fit for the remainder of the period of the sentence; and the provisions of this Act shall apply to the juvenile as if he had been ordered by the Board to be sent to such special home or institution or, as the case may be, ordered to be kept under protective care under sub-section (2) of section 16 of this Act:

[3][Provided that the State Government or as the case may be the Board, may, for any adequate and special reason to be recorded in writing, review the case of a juvenile in conflict with law undergoing sentence of imprisonment, who has ceased to be so on or before the commencement of this Act, and pass appropriate order in the interest of such juvenile.

1. The words "or the local authority" omitted by Act 33 of 2006, sec. 5 (w.e.f. 22-8-2006).
2. Subs. by Act 33 of 2006, sec. 25, for "may direct" (w.e.f. 22-8-2006).
3. Ins. by Act 33 of 2006, sec. 25 (w.e.f. 22-8-2006).

*Explanation.*—In all cases where a juvenile in conflict with law is undergoing a sentence of imprisonment at any stage on the date of commencement of this Act, his case including the issue of juvenility, shall be deemed to be decided in terms of clause (l) of section 2 and other provisions contained this Act and the rules made thereunder, irrespective of the fact that he ceases to be a juvenile on or before such date and accordingly he shall be sent to the special home or a fit institution, as the case may be, for the remainder of the period of the sentence but such sentence shall not in any case exceed the maximum period provided in section 15 of this Act.]

**65. Procedure in respect of bonds.**—Provisions of Chapter XXXIII of the Code of Criminal Procedure, 1973 (2 of 1974) shall, as far as may be, apply to bonds taken under this Act.

**66. Delegation of powers.**—The State Government may, by the general order, direct that any power exercisable by it under this Act shall, in such circumstances and under such conditions, if any, as may be prescribed in the order, be exercisable also by an officer subordinate to that Government [1][***].

**SYNOPSIS**

1. Provision – Comments on
2. Transfer of Juveniles in Conflict with Law – Law on
3. Age Determination of Juvenile – Law on
4. Claim of Juvenility – Law on
5. Immaturity of Juvenile – Law on
6. Indication of Nature of Order – Law on
7. Medical Opinion – Law on
8. Obligation upon Government – Comments on
9. Provisions of 2000 Act – Attraction of
10. Review Case of Juvenile in Conflict with Law – Law on
11. Review – Law on
12. Review Case of Juvenile – Law on
13. State Government – Duties of
14. Review – Law on

**COMMENTS**

**1. Provision – Comments on –** Section 64 of the Act 2000 deals with a situation where a juvenile in conflict with law is already undergoing the sentence at the time of commencement of the Act. The commutative effect of section 2(k), 2(1), 7A & 20 is that the benefit under the Act 2000 is retrospective and the Juvenility is to be reckoned as per section 2(k) & 2(1) of the Act even prior to the commencement of the Act 2000. In other words, if a person was considered as adult *i.e.,* completed 17 years of age and not completed 18 years of age under the old Act, and if he is undergoing an imprisonment the Juvenility has to be considered only in accordance with the Act 2000 *i.e.,* he has to be considered only as Juvenile as he has not completed the age of 18 and section 64 of the Act has to be pressed into service. However, the *Explanation* to section 64 would provide that in all cases where a Juvenile in conflict with law is undergoing sentence of imprisonment at any stage on the date of commencement of this Act, his case including the issue of juvenility shall be deemed to be decided in terms of section 2(1) and accordingly, he shall be sent to the special home or a reputed institution for the remainder of the period of the sentence but such sentence shall not in any case exceed the maximum period provided in section 15 of the Act; *Latha W/o Kundumani @ Pilchai Kani* v. *Inspector of Police,* 2012 (4) CTC 158 (Mad) (Madurai Bench) (DB).

**2. Transfer of Juveniles in Conflict with Law – Law on –** Though the proviso to section 7A(1) states that a claim of juvenility can be raised even after final disposal of the case, it has been further provided therein that such a claim shall be determined in terms of the provisions contained in the Act and the rules made there under. Section 20 of the Act provides the procedure to be adopted in pending cases. There is no specific provision

1. The words "or the local authority" omitted by Act 33 of 2006, sec. 5 (w.e.f. 22-8-2006).

in the Act as to which forum is to be approached for making the claim of juvenility after the disposal of the case. Section 64 of the Act provides for the transfer of juveniles in conflict with law who are undergoing any sentence of imprisonment to special homes or fit institutions and restrict such internment for a total period of three years as stipulated in section 15 of the Act. The said section also does not refer to a forum which is to be approached for making the plea of juvenility. Therefore, we have to necessarily look to the Juvenile Justice (Care and Protection of Children) Rules, 2007. The relevant rules are rule 97 and 98; *A. Chinnaponnu w/o Annamalai* v. *State of Tamil Nadu,* 2011 (3) Mad LJ (Cri) 433: 2011 (8) RCR (Cri) 663 (Mad) (DB).

**3. Age Determination of Juvenile – Law on –** In enquiry for age determination of a juvenile in conflict with law the matriculation or equivalent certificate if available is to be given preference and if the same is not available the date of birth certificate from the school other than the play school is to be given preference and it is only in the absence whereof, the medical opinion would be sought from the duly constituted Medical Board; *Rajbir* v. *State of Haryana,* 2011 (3) RCR (Cri) 222 (P&H).

**4. Claim of Juvenility – Law on –** The accused is entitled to the claim of juvenility at any stage even after the final disposal of the case and such claim of juvenility should be determined only in terms of the provisions contained in Juvenile Justice (Care and Protection of Children) Act, 2000. In other words, though the accused has crossed 16 years and was a major as per the old Juvenile Justice Act, 1986, he can very well make a claim of juvenility as per the provisions of the new Act which defines a juvenile as a person who has not completed 18 years of age; *Ishaq* v. *State of Haryana,* 2011 (2) RCR (Cri) 485 (P&H).

**5. Immaturity of Juvenile – Law on –** It is true that there is no bar in raising the plea at any stage and the reason is that it is a beneficial legislation, which targets a very important segment of our population, who are the future foundation stones of our country. A mere act which might have been defined as an offence, if committed in the immaturity of a juvenile, is sought to be condoned so much so that it could not have an indelible effect on the future life of a person who could be found committing that particular act. As such, the application of the provision of the Act was made applicable to all Juveniles, even after the judgment had reached its finality on account of being confirmed or affirmed by the Supreme Court of India that it could be agitated and considered in the light of section 64 of the said Act; *Dilip Kumar Paswan, Son of Sri Nago Paswan* v. *State of Bihar,* 2011 (59) BLJR 1456 (Pat).

**6. Indication of Nature of Order – Law on –** Section 15 of the Act enumerates the orders that can be passed by the Board. Section 16 of the Act enumerates the orders that cannot be passed by the Board. Under the proviso to section 64 of the Act appropriate order has to be passed. The *Explanation* to section 64 of the Act gives an indication of the nature of the order that can be passed as also the worst order that can be passed against a juvenile. The *Explanation* states that the juvenile can be sent to a special home or a fit institution for the remainder period of sentence. But it is clarified that such sentence shall not in any case exceed the "maximum period provided in section 15 of the Act." Under section 15(l)(g), he can be sent to the special home for a period of 3 years; *Selvi* v. *State of Kerala,* 2009 (3) Crimes 662 (Ker): 2008 (4) Ker LT 329 (Ker).

**7. Medical Opinion – Law on –** Rule 12(3)(b) requires that only in the absence of any of the required forms of evidence/proof, medical opinion would be sought from a duly constituted Medical Board which will declare the age of the juvenile or the child. It is provided as well that in case the exact assessment cannot be done, the Court or the Board or as the case be, the Committee, for reasons to be recorded by them, may, if considered necessary, give benefit to the child or the juvenile by considering his/her age on lower side within the margin of one year; *State of Assam (in re:),* 2012 Cr LJ 471: 2011 (4) Gau LR 235: 2013 (6) RCR (Cri) 2190 (Gau) (DB).

**8. Obligation upon Government – Comments on –** section 64 of the Juvenile Act provides that, "in any area in which this Act is brought into force, the State Government shall direct that a juvenile in conflict with law who is undergoing any sentence of imprisonment at the commencement of this Act, shall, in lieu of undergoing such sentence, be sent to a special home or be kept in fit institution in such manner as the State Government thinks fit for the remainder of the period of the sentence; and the provisions of this Act shall apply to the juvenile as if he had been ordered by the Board to be sent to such special home or institution or, as the case may be, ordered to be kept under protective care under sub-section (2) of section 16 of the Juvenile Act, provided that the State Government, or as the case may be the Board, may, for any adequate and special reason to be recorded in writing, review the case of a juvenile in conflict with law undergoing a sentence of imprisonment, who has ceased to be so, on or before the commencement of this Act, and pass appropriate order in the interest of such juvenile." *Explanation* clause to section 64 specifically provides that "in all cases where a juvenile in conflict with law is undergoing a sentence of imprisonment at any stage on the date of commencement of this Act, his case including the issue of juvenility, shall be deemed to be decided in terms of clause (1) of section 2 and other provisions contained in this Act and the rules made thereunder, irrespective of the fact that he ceases to be a juvenile on or before such date and accordingly he shall be sent to the special home or a fit institution, as the case may be, for the remainder of the period of the sentence but such sentence shall not in any case exceed the maximum period provided in section 15 of this Act". Section 15 of the Juvenile Act prescribes maximum sentence of 3 years. Undoubtedly section 64 casts an obligation upon the Government to take appropriate steps in relation to a person who falls in the category of juvenile in conflict with law"; *Saheb Sopan Kale* v. *State of Maharashtra,* 2008 (3) Crimes 469 (Bom): 2008 Cr LJ 2115: 2008 (2) Mah LJ 614 (Cri).

**9. Provisions of 2000 Act – Attraction of –** Under section 64 where a juvenile is undergoing a sentence of imprisonment at the commencement of the 2000 Act he would, in lieu of undergoing such sentence, be sent to a special home or be kept in a fit institution. These provisions show that even in cases where a mere inquiry has commenced or even where a juvenile has been sentenced the provisions of the 2000 Act would apply. Therefore, section 20 is to be appreciated in the context of the provisions; *Pratap Singh* v. *State of Jharkhand,* AIR 2005 SC 2731: 2005 (1) SCALE 763: 2005 (3) SCC 551.

**10. Review Case of Juvenile in Conflict with Law – Law on –** Section 7A of the Juvenile Justice (Care and Protection of Children) Act, 2000, has been inserted by the Juvenile Justice (Care and Protection of Children) Amendment Act, 2006, which deals with the procedure to be followed when juvenility is claimed before any court even after final disposal of the case but this provision does not provide as to where the petition for determining the juvenility would be filed by such person, who is serving out the sentence after final disposal of the case in appeal even by the Hon'ble Apex Court. The provision of section 64 of the Juvenile Justice (Care and Protection of Children) Act, 2000, provides that the State Government, or as the case may be the Board, may, pass appropriate order and review the case of a juvenile in conflict with law undergoing a sentence by giving the adequate and special reason. Rule 98 of the Juvenile Justice (Care and Protection of Children) Rules, 2007, supplements the provision of section 64 of the Juvenile Justice (Care and Protection of Children) Act, 2000. The aforesaid Rule provides that the State Government or as the case may be the Board may, either *suo motu* or on an application made for the purpose, review the case of a person or a juvenile in conflict with law, determine his juvenility in terms of the Act and pass appropriate order in the interest of juvenile in conflict with law under section 64 of the Act; *Majbul Hoda; Izharul Haque* v. *State of Bihar,* 2013 Cr LJ 3167: 2013 (8) RCR (Cri) 851 (Pat).

**11. Review – Law on –** Even in disposed of cases of juveniles in conflict with law, the State Government or the Board could, either *suo motu* or on an application made for the purpose, review the case of a juvenile, determine the juvenility and pass an appropriate order under section 64 of the Act for the immediate release of the juvenile whose period of detention had exceeded the maximum period provided in section 15 of the Act *i.e.* 3 years; *Subash Sahu* v. *State of Orissa*, 2012 Cr LJ 4607: 2013 (7) RCR (Cri) 2646 (Ori) (DB).

**12. Review Case of Juvenile – Law on –** It is clear from the section 7A the claim of juvenility to be raised before any court at any stage, even after final disposal of the case and sets out the procedure which the court is required to adopt, when such claim of juvenility is raised. Apart from the aforesaid provisions of the Act as amended, and the Juvenile Justice (Care and Protection of Children) Rules, 2007, (in short 'the Rules') rule 98, in particular, has to be read along with section 20 of the Act as amended by the Amendment Act, 2006 which provides that even after disposal of cases of juveniles in conflict with law, the State Government or the Board could, either *suo motu* or on an application made for the purpose, review the case of juvenile, determine the juvenility and pass an appropriate order under section 64 of the Act for immediate release of the juvenile whose period of detention had exceeded the maximum period provided in section 15 of the Act *i.e.* 3 years; *Amit Singh* v. *State of Maharashtra*, 2011 (8) SCALE 439: 2011 (13) SCC 744: 2011 (9) SCR 890.

**13. State Government – Duties of –** Once accused raises plea of juvenile, then the State Government in terms of section 64 of the Act is obliged to inquire into the matter and get the matter inquired into and then, take appropriate steps. It must be kept in mind that this Act, as Supreme Court has repeatedly held, is a beneficial piece of legislation for the protection of juveniles. It gives certain protections to juveniles who are in conflict with law. The date of juvenility, which is material, is the date when the occurrence took place, however old he may be now. The benefit, if they are found to be juvenile has to be given to them; *Arshad Alam Chhotu Irshad* v. *State of Bihar*, 2012 Cr LJ 256: 2011 (4) PLJR 256: 2013 (6) RCR (Cri) 270 (Pat) (DB).

**14. Review – Law on –** The proviso makes it clear that the case of such a juvenile in conflict with law undergoing a sentence of imprisonment can be reviewed even when such juvenile has ceased to be a juvenile on or before the commencement of the Act. On such review appropriate orders are to be passed "in the interests of such juvenile". The review is to be undertaken only if there are special and adequate reasons as per the proviso to section 64. The fact that the juvenile was a juvenile under the age of 18 years on the date of the offence is the first reason. The second reason is that the juvenile has remained in custody for a long period of time. *Explanation* to section 64 of the Act which along with the proviso was introduced after 'the amendment in 2006 reiterates that while undertaking such review also the issue of juvenility must be decided in terms of the amended section 2(1) of the Act. Of course, in the *Explanation* the Legislature has used the words "shall be deemed to be decided" and not that the issue "shall be decided"; *Selvi* v. *State of Kerala*, 2009 (3) Crimes 662 (Ker): 2008 (4) Ker LT 329 (Ker).

**67. Protection of action taken in good faith.**—No suit or legal proceedings shall lie against the State Government or voluntary organisation running the home or any officer and the staff appointed in pursuance of this Act in respect of anything which is in good faith done or intended to be done in pursuance of this Act or of any rules or order made thereunder.

**SYNOPSIS**

1. Expression "Good Faith" – Comprehension of
2. Expression "Good Faith" – Law on
3. Term 'Good Faith' – Comments on
4. Element of Honesty – Law on
5. Mistake – Law on
6. Good faith
7. Good Faith – Meaning of

## COMMENTS

**1. Expression "Good Faith" – Comprehension of –** The expression "good faith" has several sets of meaning, however, in popular sense, it simply means honestly, without fraud, collusion or deceit, really, actually, without pretence and without intent to assist or act in furtherance of a fraudulent or otherwise unlawful scheme. The quality and quantity of honesty requisite for constituting good faith is conditioned by the context and object of the statute in which the term is employed. As per the provisions of section 3 of the General Clauses Act, 1897, a thing shall be deemed to have been done in good faith where it is, in fact, done honestly though might have been done negligently. Section 52 of the Indian Penal Code defines the term "negatively" that nothing is said to be done or believed in good faith which is done or believed without due care and attention. Therefore, the question of good faith requires consideration with reference to the position of the accused and the circumstances under which he has acted. In insolvency mailers, for deciding good faith, the test of honesty is more appropriate than the test of due care and attention. Good faith includes a due inquiry. A person is entitled for excuse for committing an error of judgment only if he exercised due care and attention and his conduct shows that there has been no negligence on his part; *Raman Lal* v. *State of Rajasthan,* 2001 (1) Raj LW 342: 2001 Cr LJ 800 (Raj).

**2. Expression "Good Faith" – Law on –** The expression "good faith" in criminal jurisprudence has a definite connotation. Its import is totally different from saying that the person concerned has honestly believed the truth of what is said. *See* the language of the law in this regard. It starts in the negative tone excluding all except what is allowed to be within its amplitude. Insistence sought to be achieved through the commencing words of the definition "nothing is said to be done or believed in good faith" is that the solitary item included within the purview of the expression "good faith" is what is done with "due care and attention." Due care denotes the degree of reasonableness in the care sought to be exercised. In *Black's Law Dictionary,* "reasonable care" is explained as "such a degree of care, precaution, or diligence as may fairly and properly be expected or required, having regard to the nature of the action, or of the subject-matter and the circumstances surrounding the transaction. It is such care as an ordinary prudent person would exercise under the conditions existing at the time he is called upon to act." So before a person proposes to make an imputation on another the author must first make an enquiry into the factum of the imputation which he proposes to make. It is not enough that he does just a make-believe show for an enquiry. The enquiry expected of him is of such a depth as a reasonable and prudent man would make with the genuine intention in knowing the real truth of the imputation which is up in his sleeves. If he does not do so he cannot claim that what he did was *bona fide i.e.* done in good faith; *(In Re:) S.K. Sundaram,* AIR 2001 SC 2374: 2001 Cr LJ 2932: 2001 (2) SCC 171.

**3. Term 'Good Faith' – Comments on –** The term 'good faith' is not attempted to be defined there but all that is stated is that if an act is not done with due care and attention it would not be said to be done in 'good faith'. This definition comes into conflict with the definition in the General Clauses Act to this extent only that if a thing has been done negligently, though honestly, it would not be deemed to have been done in "good faith'. The definition of the term in the General Clauses Act lays stress on one aspect only, but, that in the Penal Code places emphasis on two aspects, namely the honesty of intention along with due care and attention. Thus section 52 excludes the element or negligence from the purview of 'good faith'. Both the definitions retain the realty essence of 'good faith', which is that a thing is lone 'honestly'. This is a Feature common to both definitions without which the term 'good faith' will lose its real meaning. 'Good faith' therefore implies not only an upright mental attitude, and clear conscience of a person, but also the doing an act, showing, that ordinary prudence has been exercised according to the standards of a reasonable person. 'Good faith' contemplates an honest effort to ascertain the facts upon which exercise of the power must rest. It must, therefore, be summed as 'an honest determination from ascertained facts.' 'Good faith' precludes pretence or deceit and also negligence and recklessness. A lack of diligence, which an honest man of ordinary prudence is accustomed to exercise, is, in law, a want of good faith. Once this is shown, good faith does not require a sound judgment; *Harbhajan Singh* v. *State of Punjab*, AIR 1961 P&H 215: 1961 Cr LJ 710: 1961 (63) Pun LR 794 (P&H).

**4. Element of Honesty – Law on** – Good faith is defined by section 52 of the Code. Nothing says section 52, is said to be done or believed in 'good faith' which is done or believed without due care and attention. It will be recalled that under the General Clauses Act, "A thing shall be deemed to be done in good faith where it is in fact done honestly whether it is done negligently or not". The element of honesty which is introduced by the definition prescribed by the General Clauses Act is not introduced by the definition of the Code; *Harbhajan Singh* v. *State of Punjab*, AIR 1966 SC 97: 1965 (3) SCR 235: 1966 Cr LJ 82.

**5. Mistake – Law on** – 'Mistake' is not mere forgetfulness. It is a slip 'made, not by design, but by mischance' Mistake, as the term is used in jurisprudence, is an erroneous mental condition, conception or conviction induced by ignorance, misapprehension or misunderstanding of the truth, and resulting in some act or omission done or suffered erroneously by one or both of the parties to a transaction, but without its erroneous character being intended or known at that time." It may be laid down as a general rule that an alleged offender is deemed to have acted under that state of things which he in good faith and on reasonable grounds believed to exist when he did the act alleged to be an offence; *State of Orissa* v. *Bhagaban Barik*, AIR 1987 SC 1265: 1987 (2) SCR 785: 1987 (1) SCALE 712.

**6. Good faith** – 'Good faith' is defined both in section 3(22) of the General Clauses Act (No. X of 1897), and also in section 52 of the Penal Code. According to the General Clauses Act:

**7. Good Faith – Meaning of** – A thing shall be deemed to be done in "good faith" where it is in fact done honestly whether it is done negligently or not; *Mangtu Ram* v. *State of Rajasthan*, 2003 Cr LJ 4733: 2003 (1) Cr LR 707: 2004 (1) Raj LW 226 (Raj).

**68. Power to make rules.**—(1) The State Government may, by notification in the Official Gazette, make rules to carry out the purposes of this Act:

[1][Provided that the Central Government may, frame model rules in respect of all or any of the matters with respect to which the State Government may make rules under this section, and where any such model rules have been framed in respect of any such matter, they shall apply to the State until the rules in respect of that matter is made by the State Government and while making any such rules, so far as is practicable, they conform to such model rules.]

(2) In particular, and without prejudice to the generality of the foregoing powers, such rules may provide for all or any of the following matters, namely:—

(i) the term of office of the members of the Board and the manner in which such member may resign under sub-section (4) of section 4;

(ii) the time of the meetings of the Board and the rules of procedure in regard to the transaction of business at its meeting under sub-section (1) of section 5;

(iii) the management of observation homes including the standards and various types of services to be provided by them and the

1. Ins. by Act 33 of 2006, sec. 26 (w.e.f. 22-8-2006).

circumstances in which and the manner in which, the certification of the observation home may be granted or withdrawn and such other matters as are referred to in section 8;

(iv) the management of special homes including the standards and various types of services to be provided by them and the circumstances in which and the manner in which, the certification of the special home may be granted or withdrawn and such other matters as are referred to in section 9;

(v) persons by whom any juvenile in conflict with law may be produced before the Board and the manner of sending such juvenile, to an observation home under sub-section (2) of section 10;

(vi) matters relating to removal of disqualifications attaching to conviction of a juvenile under section 19;

(vii) the qualifications of the Chairperson and members, and the tenure for which they may be appointed under sub-section (3) of section 29;

(viii) the time of the meetings of the Committee and the rules of procedure in regard to the transaction of business at its meeting under sub-section (1) of section 30;

(ix) the manner of making the report to the police and to the Committee and the manner of sending and entrusting the child to children's home pending the inquiry under sub-section (2) of section 32;

(x) the management of children's homes including the standards and nature of services to be provided by them, and the manner in which certification of a children's home or recognition to a voluntary organisation may be granted or withdrawn under sub-section (2) [1][and the manner of registration of institutions under sub-section (3)] of section 34;

(xi) appointment of inspection committees for children's homes, their tenure and purposes for which inspection committees may be appointed and such other matters as are referred to in section 35;

(xii) facilities to be provided by the shelter homes under sub-section (3) of section 37;

[1][(xiia) rehabilitation mechanism to be resorted to in adoption under sub-section (2), notification of guidelines under sub-section (3) and the manner of recognition of specialised adoption agencies under sub-section (4) of section 41;]

(xiii) for carrying out the scheme of foster care programme of children under sub-section (3) of section 42;

(xiv) for carrying out various schemes of sponsorship of children under sub-section (2) of section 43;

(xv) matters relating to after-care organisation under section 44;

(xvi) for ensuring effective linkages between various agencies for facilitating rehabilitation and social integration of the child under section 45;

---

1. Ins. by Act 33 of 2006, sec. 26 (w.e.f. 22-8-2006).

(xvii) the purposes and the manner in which the Fund shall be administered under sub-section (3) of section 61;

(xviii) any other matter which is required to be, or may be, prescribed.

[1][(3) Every rule made by the Central Government under this Act shall be laid, as soon as may be after it is made, before each House of Parliament, while it is in session, for a total period of thirty days which may be comprised in one session or in two or more successive sessions, and if, before the expiry of the session immediately following the session or the successive sessions aforesaid, both Houses agree in making any modification in the rule or both Houses agree that the rule should not be made, the rule shall thereafter have effect only in such modified form or be of no effect, as the case may be; so, however, that any such modification or annulment shall be without prejudice to the validity of anything previously done under that rule.]

[2][(4)] Every rule made by a State Government under this Act shall be laid, as soon as may be after it is made, before the Legislature of that State.

SYNOPSIS



COMMENTS

**1. Legislation – Intention of –** The proviso to section 68(1) of the Act further makes it clear that the rule making power of the Central Government is essentially to make model rules and even where such model rules have been made, they shall apply to a State until such time as the State Government may make rules on the same subject-matter. Where, therefore, on a subject-matter, comprehended by sections 68(1) and 68(2) of the Act, the State Government has already made Rules, a model rule framed by the Central Government on the same subject-matter, obviously would not have application to the State; since the State has already exercised its rule making authority. It is also relevant in this context to take note of the fact that it is only by Amendment Act 33/06 that a proviso has been inserted to section 68(1) of the Act. At the same time, section 68(1) has remained in tact. Thus, the Legislature did not contemplate a contemporaneous conferment of rule making power on the State Government and the Central Government with regard to the same subject-matter. The proviso to section 68(1) brought about by Act 33/06 makes it clear that the rule making power of the Central Government would essentially be to make model rules lending guidance as it were to the State Government when they exercise their rule making power. Obviously, the power under the proviso to section 68(1) of the Act is not contemplated as available or required to be exercised, as the case may be, in a case where the concerned State has already framed the rule concerning the same subject-matter; *Rohit Sitapatikumar Verma* v. *State of Gujarat*, 2013 (1) GLR 766 Guj (DB).

**2. Modal Rules – Significance of –** The proviso to section 68(1) is a fairly unique provision. While section 68(1) specifically confers power on the State Government to make rules to carry out the purposes of the Act, at first blush the Central Government

1. Ins. by Act 33 of 2006, sec. 26 (w.e.f. 22-8-2006).
2. Sub-section (3) renumbered as sub-section (4) by by Act 33 of 2006, sec. 26 (w.e.f. 22-8-2006).

is also contemporaneously conferred with the power to make rules in respect of all or any of the matters with respect to which the State Government may make rules under the section. But, such model rules shall apply to the State only until the rules in respect of that matter is made by the State Government. A guideline is also mentioned in this regard in the proviso where it is stated that the State Government may, while making such rules under section 68(1) and 68(2) of the Act as far as practical, conform to such model Rules. The Central Rules, therefore, declare that the said Rules would apply in a State until rules are framed by the concerned State Government under section 68 of the Act; *Rohit Sitapatikumar Verma* v. *State of Gujarat,* 2013 (1) GLR 766 Guj (DB).

**3. Model Rules – Purpose of –** The determination of application of the Rules has to be made in the light of provisions contained in section 68 of the Act. This empowers the State Government to frame rules, and the Central Government could also frame model rules in respect of or any of the matters with respect to which the State Government may make Rules under this section, but it has been provided that where any such model Rules have been framed in respect of any such matter, they shall apply to the State until the rules in respect of that matter are made by the State Government. Rule 96 of the Central Rules ingeminates it. The Act came into force on 1st April, 2001 and the State Government framed the rules under section 68 which came into force on 1-5-2004. Central Rules inured on 26-10-2007. The Central rules or model rules are meant to apply to the matters in respect of which the State Government has not framed rules. But the U.P. Government having already framed Rules, the model rules cannot have any application unless the State Rules are inconsistent with the model rules. The model rules may serve as guidance for the States that have not framed Rules. They are in the nature of stop-gap arrangement; *Jai Prakash Tiwari* v. *State of Uttar Pradesh,* 2012 (10) ADJ 478: 2013 (2) ACrR 1383 (All).

**4. Model Rules – Importance of –** The proviso to section 68(1) is a fairly unique provision. While section 68(1) specifically confers power on the State Government to make rules to carry out the purposes of the Act, at first blush the Central Government is also contemporaneously conferred with the power to make rules in respect of all or any of the matters with respect to which the State Government may make Rules under the section. But, such model Rules shall apply to the State only until the rules in respect of that matter is made by the State Government. A guideline is also mentioned in this regard in the proviso where it is stated that the State Government may, while making such Rules [under section 68(1) and 68(2) of the Act] as far as practical, conform to such model Rules; *Vidya* v. *Government of India,* 2010 Cr LJ 1387: 2010 (3) AICLR 308: 2009 (4) Ker LT 937 (Ker).

**5. Provisions of Model Rules Framed by Central Government – Comments on –** A perusal of the proviso shows that the Central Government have been authorized only to frame model Rules in respect of matters for which the State Government may make Rules. Such model Rules framed by the Central Government are to apply to the State only till the Rules in respect of that matter is made by the State Government and while making any such Rules, only so far as is practicable the State Government may conform to such model Rules. Clearly superiority has been conferred upon the Rules made by the State Government. The Rules of the Central Government are only described as model Rules and they are to hold the field if it is vacant and once the State Government has framed the Rules; only such Rules are to be followed by the Courts within the State of Bihar. The superior status of the State Government in the matter of framing of Rules is also clear from the proviso according to which the State Government is required to conform to the model Rules only as far as is practicable. Clearly the State Government is not bound to follow the entire provisions of the Model Rules framed by the Central Government; *Chandrika Sao* v. *State of Bihar,* 2012 (4) East CriC 58: 2014 (1) PLJR 589 (Pat) (DB).

**6. Rules – Comments on –** section 68 of the Juvenile Justice (Care and Protection of Children) Act of 2000 provides that the State Government may by notification in the official gazette, make Rules to carry out the purposes of this Act. Provided that the Central Government may frame model Rules in respect of all or any of the matters with respect to which the State Government may make Rules under this section, and where any such model Rules have been framed in respect of any such matter, they shall apply to the State until the Rules in respect of the matter are made by the State Government and while making any such rules, so far as is practicable, they conform to such model Rules. Under the power granted by section 68 of the Act, the State Government framed Rules which are 'The Uttar Pradesh Juvenile Justice (Care and Protection of Children) Rules, 2004. The Central Government also framed Rules or model Rules which are the Rules of 2007. Under which the provisions of rule 12 have been referred to, and which are applicable to the State only where the States have not framed any Rule under the Act. And where the States have framed their Rules, the model Rules will not apply; *Amit Kumar* v. *State of Uttar Pradesh,* 2013 (5) All LJ 672: 2013 (6) ADJ 21: 2013 (3) ACrR 3146.

**7. Rules Framed by State Government – Primacy of –** section 68(1) makes it clear that the primary Rule making authority under the JJ Act is the State Government. The proviso to section 68(1) of the Act further makes it clear that the rule making power of the Central Government is essentially to make model Rules and even where such model Rules have been made, they shall apply to a State until such time as the State Government may make Rules on the same subject-matter. Where therefore on a subject-matter, comprehended by sections 68(1) and 68(2) of the Act, the State Government has already made Rules, a model rule framed by the Central Government on the same subject-matter, obviously would not have application to the State; since the State has already exercised its rule making authority. It is also relevant in this context to take note of the fact that it is only by Amendment Act 33/06 that a proviso has been inserted to section 68(1) of the Act. At the same time, section 68(1) has remained in tact. Thus, the Legislature did not contemplate a contemporaneous conferment of rule making power on the State Government and the Central Government with regard to the same subject-matter. The proviso to section 68(1) brought about by Act 33/06 makes it clear that the rule making power of the Central Government would essentially be to make model Rules lending guidance as it were to the State Government when they exercise their rule making power. Obviously, the power under the proviso to section 68(1) of the Act is not contemplated as available or required to be exercised, as the case may be, in a case where the concerned State has already framed the rule concerning the same subject-matter; *Vidya* v. *Government of India,* 2010 Cr LJ 1387: 2010 (3) AICLR 308: 2009 (4) Ker LT 937 (Ker).

**8. Rules of State – Comments –** The proviso to section 68(1) specifically provides that the model Rules framed by Central Government shall apply to the State until the Rules in respect of the matter is made by the State Government. The State of Uttar Pradesh has framed the Rules in the year 2004 which have come into force on 1-5-2004; *Vinod* v. *State of Uttar Pradesh,* 2014 (2) ADJ 167: 2014 (1) ACr 647: 2014 (85) ACC 466 (All).

**9. School Certificate with Dubious Date of Birth – Law on –** As regards the consideration of medical opinion over and above the school certificate, the medical opinion is simply estimation and that estimation is based on physical development dependent on so many factors. The certificate giving date of birth is definite and precise information about the date of birth and, therefore, the date of birth given in the School certificate and same sustained through out the school career shall prevail over the mere medical estimation. Conversely School Certificate with dubious date of birth cannot have precedence over medical opinion given by a duly constituted Board of doctors; *Amit Kumar* v. *State of Uttar Pradesh,* 2013 (5) ALJ 672: 2013 (6) ADJ 21: 2013 (3) ACrR 3146: 2013 (81) ACC 899 (All).

**10. State Governments – Obligations of –** Language of the proviso of sub-section (1) of section 68 makes it clear that wherever the State has made no Rules, the model Rules framed by the Central Government would apply and that the State Governments would make endeavor to make Rules in conformity to such model Rules; *Amit Thapar, S/o Baldev Singh Thapar, R/o Guru Road, P.S. Dalanwala* v. *State of Uttarakhand*, 2013 (1) UC 760 (Uttra) (Nainital Bench).

**69. Repeal and savings.**—(1) The Juvenile Justice Act, 1986 (53 of 1986) is hereby repealed.

(2) Notwithstanding such repeal, anything done or any action taken under the said Act shall be deemed to have been done or taken under the corresponding provisions of this Act.

**70. Power to remove difficulties.**—(1) If any difficulty arises in giving effect to the provisions of this Act, the Central Government may, by order, not inconsistent with the provisions of this Act, remove the difficulty:

Provided that no such order shall be made after the expiry of the period of two years from the commencement of this Act.

(2) However, order made under the section shall be laid, as soon as may be after it is made, before each House of Parliament.

# THE JUVENILE JUSTICE (CARE AND PROTECTION OF CHILDREN) RULES, 2007[1]

WHEREAS the Constitution has, in several provisions, including clause (3) of article 15, article 21, article 21A, clauses (1) and (2) of article 22, articles 23 and 24, clauses (e) and (f) of article 39, article 39A, articles 45, 47 and 51A(k), impose on the State a primary responsibility of ensuring that all the needs of children are met and that their basic rights are fully protected;

AND WHEREAS, the Convention on the Rights of the Child adopted by the General Assembly of the United Nations on the 20th November, 1989 and ratified by India on 11th December, 1992, emphasizes conferment of rights on children, and reintegration of juveniles and care and protection of vulnerable children, with a view to furthering their right to survival, development, protection and participation;

AND WHEREAS, the United Nations Standard Minimum Rules for the Administration of Juvenile Justice, 1985 (the Beijing Rules) and the United Nations Rules for the Protection of Juveniles Deprived of their Liberty (1990) set the minimum standard to be adhered to in the administration of juvenile justice in respect of juveniles in conflict with law;

AND WHEREAS, the United Nations Guidelines for the Prevention of Juvenile Delinquency (Riyadh Guidelines) and all other relevant international instruments focus on the prevention of juvenile delinquency and provide guidelines for it;

AND WHEREAS, to give effect to the provisions of the Constitution and relevant international instruments, the Juvenile Justice (Care and Protection of Children) Act, 2000 (56 of 2000) as amended by the Juvenile Justice (Care and Protection of Children) Amendment Act, 2006 (33 of 2006) was enacted to consolidate and amend the law relating to juveniles in conflict with law and children in need of care and protection, by providing for proper care, protection and treatment by catering to their developmental needs, and by adopting a child friendly approach in the adjudication and disposition of matters in the best interest of children and for their ultimate rehabilitation and for matters connected therewith or incidental thereto, through institutional as well as non-institutional measures enumerated under the said Act;

NOW, THEREFORE, with a view to provide for better implementation and administration of the provisions of the said Act in its true spirit and substance, the Central Government in pursuance of the above said provisions and in exercise of the powers conferred by the proviso to sub-section (1) of section 68 of the Juvenile Justice (Care and Protection of Children) Act, 2000 (56 of 2000) hereby makes the following rules and lays down the fundamental principles to be applied in administration of juvenile justice, namely:—

## *CHAPTER I*

## PRELIMINARY

**1. Short title and commencement.**—(1) These rules may be called the Juvenile Justice (Care and Protection of Children) Rules, 2007.

1. *Vide* G.S.R. 679(E), dated 26th October, 2007, published in the Gazette of India, Extra., Pt. II, Sec. 3(i), dated 26th October, 2007.

(2) They shall come into force on the date[1] of their publication in the Official Gazette.

**2. Definition.**—In these rules, unless the context otherwise requires,—

(a) "abandoned" means an unaccompanied and deserted child who is declared abandoned by the Committee after due inquiry;

(b) "Act" means the Juvenile Justice (Care and Protection of Children) Act, 2000 (56 of 2000) as amended by the Juvenile Justice (Care and Protection of Children) Amendment Act, 2006 (33 of 2006);

(c) "best interest of the child" means a decision taken to ensure the physical, emotional, intellectual, social and moral development of juvenile or child;

(d) "child friendly" means any process and interpretation, attitude, environment and treatment, that is humane, considerate and in the best interest of the child;

(e) "community service" implies service rendered to the society by juveniles in conflict with law in lieu of other judicial remedies and penalties, which is not degrading and dehumanizing. Examples of this may include:

(i) cleaning a park;

(ii) getting involved with Habitat for Humanity;

(iii) serving the elderly in nursing homes;

(iv) helping out a local fire or police department;

(v) helping out at a local hospital or nursing home; and

(vi) serving disabled children.

(f) "detention" in case of juveniles in conflict with law means "protective custody" in line with the principles of restorative justice;

(g) "Form" means the Form annexed to these rules;

(h) "individual care plan" is a comprehensive development plan for a juvenile or child based on age specific and gender specific needs and the case history of the juvenile or child, prepared in consultation with the juvenile or child, in order to restore the juvenile's or child's self-esteem, dignity and self-worth and nurture him into a responsible citizen and accordingly the plan shall address the following needs of a juvenile or a child:—

(i) Health needs;

(ii) Emotional and psychological needs;

(iii) Educational and training needs;

(iv) Leisure, creativity and play;

(v) Attachments and relationships;

(vi) Protection from all kinds of abuse, neglect and maltreatment;

(vii) Social mainstreaming; and

(viii) Follow-up post release and restoration.

1. Came into force on 26-10-2007.

(i) "institution" means an observation home, or a special home, or a children's home or a shelter home set-up, certified or recognized and registered under sections 8, 9, 34, sub-section (3) of section 34 and section 37 of the Act respectively;

(j) "Officer-in-charge" or such other nomenclature as issued by the State Government, means a person appointed for the control and management of the institution;

(k) "orphan" means a child who is without parents or willing and capable legal or natural guardian;

(l) "place of safety" means any institution set-up and recognized under sub-section (3) of section 12 and sub-section (1) of section 16 of the Act for juvenile in conflict with law or children;

(m) "recognised" means a person found fit by the competent authority or, an institution found fit by the State Government on the recommendation of the competent authority as per clauses (h) and (i) of section (2) of the Act; or, recognition of an institution or agency or voluntary organisation by the State Government to operate as a children's home, observation home and special home; or a shelter home, specialised adoption agency or after care organization under sub-section (1) of section 37, sub-section (4) of section 41 and clause (a) of section 44 of the Act;

(n) "registered" means all institutions or agencies or voluntary organisations providing residential care to children in need of care and protection registered under sub-section (3) of section 34;

(o) "State Government" in relation to a Union territory means the Administrator of that Union territory appointed by the President under article 239 of the Constitution;

(p) "street and working children" means children without ostensible means of livelihood, care, protection and support in accordance with the provisions laid down under clause (d)(1) of section 2 of the Act;

(q) "surrendered child" means a child, who in the opinion of the Committee, is relinquished on account of physical, emotional and social factors beyond the control of the parent or guardian;

(r) all words and expressions defined in the Act and used, but not defined in these rules, shall have the same meaning as assigned to them in the Act.

## *CHAPTER II*

## FUNDAMENTAL PRINCIPLES OF JUVENILE JUSTICE AND PROTECTION OF CHILDREN

**3. Fundamental principles to be followed in administration of these rules.**—(1) The State Government, the Juvenile Justice Board, the Child Welfare Committee or other competent authorities or agencies, as the case may be, while implementing the provisions of these rules shall abide and be guided by the principles, specified in sub-rule (2).

(2) The following principles shall, *inter alia,* be fundamental to the application, interpretation and implementation of the Act and the rules made hereunder:

**I. Principle of presumption of innocence**

(a) A juvenile or child or juvenile in conflict with law is presumed to be innocent of any *mala fide* or criminal intent up to the age of eighteen years.

(b) The juvenile's or juveniles in conflict with law or child's right to presumption of innocence shall be respected throughout the process of justice and protection, from the initial contact to alternative care, including aftercare.

(c) Any unlawful conduct of a juvenile or a child or a juvenile in conflict with law which is done for survival, or is due to environmental or situational factors or is done under control of adults, or peer groups, is ought to be covered by the principles of innocence.

(d) The basic components of presumption of innocence are:

(i) ***Age of innocence***

Age of innocence is the age below which a juvenile or child or a juvenile in conflict with law cannot be subjected to the criminal justice system. The Beijing rule 4(1) clearly lays down that "the beginning of the age of criminal responsibility shall not be fixed at too low an age level bearing in mind the facts of mental and intellectual maturity". In consonance with this principle, the mental and intellectual maturity of juvenile or child or a juvenile in conflict with law below eighteen years is considered insufficient throughout the world.

(ii) ***Procedural protection of innocence***

All procedural safeguards that are guaranteed by the Constitution and other statutes to the adults and that go in to strengthen the juvenile's or child's right to presumption of innocence *shall be guaranteed to juveniles or the children or juveniles in conflict with law.*

(iii) ***Provisions of Legal aid and Guardian Ad Litem***

Juveniles in conflict with law have a right to be informed about the accusations against them and a right to be legally represented. Provisions must be made for guardian *ad litem,* legal aid and other such assistance through legal services at State expense. This shall also include such juveniles' right to present his case before the competent authority on his own.

**II Principle of dignity and worth**

(a) Treatment that is consistent with the child's sense of dignity and worth is a fundamental principle of juvenile justice. This principle reflects the fundamental human right enshrined in Article 1 of the Universal Declaration of Human Rights that all human beings are born free and equal in dignity and rights. Respect of dignity includes not being humiliated, personal identity, boundaries and space being respected, not being labelled and stigmatized, being offered information and choices and not being blamed for their acts.

(b) The juvenile's or child's right to dignity and worth has to be respected and protected throughout the entire process of dealing with the child from the first contact with law enforcement agencies to the implementation of all measures for dealing with the child.

**III. Principle of Right to be heard**

Every child's right to express his views freely in all matters affecting his interest shall be fully respected through every stage in the process of juvenile justice. Children's right to be heard shall include creation of developmentally appropriate tools and processes of interacting with the child, promoting children's active involvement in decisions regarding their own lives and providing opportunities for discussion and debate.

**IV. Principle of Best Interest**

(a) In all decisions taken within the context of administration of juvenile justice, the principle of best interest of the juvenile or the juvenile in conflict with law or child shall be the primary consideration.

(b) The principle of best interest of the juvenile or juvenile in conflict with law or child shall mean for instance that the traditional objectives of criminal justice, retribution and repression, must give way to rehabilitative and restorative objectives of juvenile justice.

(c) This principle seeks to ensure physical, emotional, intellectual, social and moral development of a juvenile in conflict with law or child so as to ensure the safety, well being and permanence for each child and thus enable each child to survive and reach his or her full potential.

**V. Principle of family responsibility**

(a) The primary responsibility of bringing up children, providing care, support and protection shall be with the biological parents. However, in exceptional situations, this responsibility may be bestowed on willing adoptive or foster parents.

(b) All decision making for the child should involve the family of origin unless it is not in the best interest of the child to do so.

(c) The family - biological, adoptive or foster (in that order), must be held responsible and provide necessary care, support and protection to the juvenile or child under their care and custody under the Act, unless the best interest measures or mandates dictate otherwise.

**VI. Principle of Safety (no harm, no abuse, no neglect, no exploitation and no maltreatment)**

(a) At all stages, from the initial contact till such time he remains in contact with the care and protection system, and thereafter, the juvenile or child or juvenile in conflict with law shall not be subjected to any harm, abuse, neglect, maltreatment, corporal punishment or solitary or otherwise any confinement in jails and extreme care shall be taken to avoid any harm to the sensitivity of the juvenile or the child.

(b) The state has a greater responsibility for ensuring safety of every child in its care and protection, without resorting to restrictive measures and processes in the name of care and protection.

**VII. Positive measures**

(a) Provisions must be made to enable positive measures that involve the full mobilization of all possible resources, including the family, volunteers and other community groups, as well as schools and other mainstream community institutions or processes, for the purpose of promoting the well-being of the juvenile or child through individual care plans carefully worked out.

(b) The positive measures shall aim at reducing vulnerabilities and reducing the need for intervention under the law, as well as effective, fair and humane dealing of the juvenile or child.

(c) The positive measures shall include avenues for health, education, relationships, livelihoods, leisure, creativity and play.

(d) Such positive measures must facilitate the development of identity for the child and provide them with an inclusive and enabling environment.

**VIII. Principle of non-stigmatizing semantics, decisions and actions**

The non-stigmatizing semantics of the Act must be strictly adhered to, and the use of adversarial or accusatory words, such as, arrest, remand, accused, charge sheet, trial, prosecution, warrant, summons, conviction, inmate, delinquent, neglected, custody or jail is prohibited in the processes pertaining to the child or juvenile in conflict with law under the Act.

**IX. Principle of non-waiver of rights**

(a) No waiver of rights of the child or juvenile in conflict with law, whether by himself or the competent authority or anyone acting or claiming to act on behalf of the juvenile or child, is either permissible or valid.

(b) Non-exercise of a fundamental right does not amount to waiver.

**X. Principle of equality and non-discrimination**

(a) There shall be no discrimination against a child or juvenile in conflict with law on the basis of age, sex, place of birth, disability, health, status, race, ethnicity, religion, caste, cultural practices, work, activity or behaviour of the juvenile or child or that of his parents or guardians, or the civil and political status of the juvenile or child.

(b) Equality of access, equality of opportunity, equality in treatment under the Act shall be guaranteed to every child or juvenile in conflict with law.

**XI. Principle of right to privacy and confidentiality**

The juvenile's or child's right to privacy and confidentiality shall be protected by all means and through all the stages of the proceedings and care and protection processes.

**XII. Principle of last resort**

Institutionalization of a child or juvenile in conflict with law shall be a step of the last resort after reasonable inquiry and that too for the minimum possible duration.

**XIII. Principle of repatriation and restoration**

(a) Every juvenile or child or juvenile in conflict with law has the right to be re-united with his family and restored back to the same socio-economic and cultural status that such juvenile or child enjoyed before coming within the purview of the Act or becoming vulnerable to any form of neglect, abuse or exploitation.

(b) Any juvenile or child, who has lost contact with his family, shall be eligible for protection under the Act and shall be repatriated and restored, at the earliest, to his family, unless such repatriation and restoration is likely to be against the best interest of the juvenile or the child.

**XIV. Principle of Fresh Start**

(a) The principle of fresh start promotes new beginning for the child or juvenile in conflict with law by ensuring erasure of his past records.

(b) The State shall seek to promote measures for dealing with children alleged or recognized as having impinged the penal law, without resorting to judicial proceedings.

*CHAPTER III*

## JUVENILE IN CONFLICT WITH LAW

**4. Juvenile Justice Boards.**—There shall be one or more Juvenile Justice Boards in every district, which shall be constituted by the State Government as per section 4 of the Act.

**5. Composition of the Juvenile Justice Board.**—(1) The Board shall consist of a Metropolitan Magistrate or a Judicial Magistrate of the first class, as the case may be, and two social v ›rkers of whom at least one shall be a woman, forming a bench:

Provided that the Principal Magistrate of the Board shall review the pendency of cases before the Board and take such steps, as may be necessary in the expeditious disposal of the cases.

(2) Every such bench shall have the powers conferred by the Code of Criminal Procedure, 1973 (2 of 1974).

(3) (i) A Magistrate with special knowledge or training in child psychology or child welfare shall be designated as the Principal Magistrate of the Board.

(ii) In case the Principal Magistrate with such special knowledge or training is not available, then, the State Government shall provide for such short-term training in child psychology or child welfare as it considers necessary.

(4) The two social workers, of whom at least one shall be a woman, shall be appointed by the State Government on the recommendation of the Selection Committee set-up under rule 91 of these rules.

(5) The State Government shall provide for such training and orientation in child psychology, child welfare, child rights, national and international standards for juvenile justice to all members of the Board as it considers necessary, in accordance with the Integrated Child Protection Scheme of the Central Government.

**6. Tenure of the Board.**—(1) The Board shall have a tenure of three years and the appointment of members shall be co-terminus with the tenure of the Board.

(2) A social worker being a member of the Board shall be eligible for appointment for a maximum of two consecutive terms.

(3) Any extension of the tenure of members of the Board shall be on the basis of their performance appraisal by the District Child Protection Unit of the State Government and on the recommendation of a Selection Committee constituted for the purpose and the performance appraisal of members of the Board shall necessarily assess their participation in the proceedings of the Board and contribution in case disposal.

(4) A member may resign any time, by giving one month's advance notice in writing or may be removed from his office as provided in sub-section (5) of section 4 of the Act.

(5) Any vacancy in the Board may be filled by appointment of another person from the panel of names prepared by the Selection Committee, and shall hold office for the remaining term of the Board.

**7. Qualifications for members of the Board.**—(1) The social worker to be appointed as a member of the Board shall be a person not less than 35 years of age, who has a post-graduate degree in social work, health, education, psychology, child development or any other social science discipline and has been actively involved and engaged in planning, implementing and administering measures relating to child welfare for at least seven years.

(2) No person shall be considered for selection as a Member of the Board, if he,—

(a) has been convicted under any law;

(b) have ever indulged in child abuse or employment of child labour or any other human rights violations or immoral act;

(c) is holding such other occupation that does not allow him to give necessary time and attention to the work of the Board;

(d) does not fulfil the qualification and experience prescribed in the Act and the rules made thereunder and in such a case the Selection Committee shall after due inquiry and on establishment of such fact, reject his application and recommend the name of the next person from the list of names prepared for filling the vacancies.

**8. Sitting and conveyance allowances.**—The social worker members of the Board shall be paid such travel and sitting allowance, as the State Government may determine, but it shall not be less than rupees five hundred per sitting.

**9. Sittings of the Board.**—(1) The Board shall hold its sittings in the premises of an Observation Home or, at a place in proximity to the observation home or, at a suitable premise in any institution run under the Act, and in no circumstances shall the Board operate from within any court premises.

(2) The premises where the Board holds its sittings shall be child-friendly and shall not look like a court room in any manner whatsoever; for example, the Board shall not sit on a raised platform and the sitting arrangement shall be uniform, and there shall be no witness boxes.

(3) The Board shall meet on all working days of a week, unless the case pendency is less in a particular district and concerned authority issues an order in this regard.

(4) A minimum of three-fourth attendance of the Chairperson and Members of the Board is necessary in a year.

(5) Every member of the Board shall attend a minimum of five hours per sitting.

**10. Functions of the Board.**—The Board shall perform the following functions to achieve the objectives of the Act, namely:—

(a) adjudicate and dispose cases of juveniles in conflict with law;

(b) take cognizance of crimes committed under sections 23 to 28 of the Act;

(c) monitoring institutions for juveniles in conflict with law and seeking compliance from them in cases of any noticeable lapses and improvement based on suggestions of the Board;

(d) deal with non-compliance on the part of concerned government functionaries or functionaries of voluntary organizations, as the case may be, in accordance with due process of law;

(e) pass necessary direction to the district authority and police to create or provide necessary infrastructure or facilities so that minimum standards of justice and treatment are maintained in the spirit of the Act;

(f) maintain liaison with the Committee in respect of cases needing care and protection;

(g) liaison with Boards in other districts to facilitate speedy inquiry and disposal of cases through due process of law;

(h) take suitable action for dealing with unforeseen situations that may arise in the implementation of the Act and remove such difficulties in the best interest of the juvenile;

(i) send quarterly information about juveniles in conflict with law produced before them, to the District, State Child Protection Unit, the State Government and also to the Chief Judicial Magistrate or Chief Metropolitan Magistrate for review under sub-section (2) of section 14 of the Act;

(j) any other function assigned by the State Government from time to time relating with juveniles in conflict with law.

**11. Pre and Post-Production action of police and other agencies.**—(1) As soon as a juvenile alleged to be in conflict with law is apprehended by the police, the concerned police officer shall inform:

(a) the designated Juvenile or the Child Welfare Officer in the nearest police station to take charge of the matter;

(b) the parents or guardian of the juvenile alleged to be in conflict with law about the apprehension of the juvenile, about the address of the Board where the juvenile will be produced and the date and time when the parents or guardian need to be present before the Board;

(c) the concerned probation officer, of such apprehension to enable him to obtain information regarding social background of the juvenile and other material circumstances likely to be of assistance to the Board for conducting the inquiry.

(2) Soon after apprehension, the juvenile shall be placed under the charge of the Juvenile or Child Welfare Officer from the nearest police station, who shall produce the juvenile before the Board within twenty-four hours as per sub-section (1) of section 10 of the Act and where such Juvenile or the Child Welfare Officer has not been designated as per provisions laid down under sub-section (2) of section 63 of the Act or is not available for some official reasons, the police officer who had apprehended the juvenile shall produce him before the Board.

(3) The police apprehending a juvenile in conflict with law shall in no case send the juvenile in lock-up or delay his charge being transferred to the Juvenile or the Child Welfare Officer from the nearest police station, if such an officer has been designated.

(4) A list of all designated Juvenile or the Child Welfare Officers in a district and members of Special Juvenile Police Unit with contact details shall be prominently displayed in every police station.

(5) For gathering the best available information it shall be incumbent upon the Police or the Juvenile or the Child Welfare Officer from the nearest police station, to contact the parents or guardians of the juvenile and also apprise them of the juvenile's law breaking behaviour.

(6) The Police or the Juvenile or the Child Welfare Officer from the nearest police station, shall also record the social background of the juvenile and circumstances of apprehension and offence alleged to have been committed in the case diary of each juvenile, which shall be forwarded to the Board forthwith.

(7) The police or the Juvenile or the Child Welfare Officer from the nearest police station, shall exercise the power of apprehending the juvenile only in cases of his alleged involvement in serious offences (entailing a punishment of more than 7 years imprisonment for adults).

(8) In such cases where apprehension apparently seems to be in the interest of the juvenile, the police or the Juvenile or the Child Welfare Officer from the nearest police station, shall rather treat the juvenile as a child in need of care and protection and produce him before the Board, clearly explaining the juvenile's need for care and protection in its report and seek appropriate orders from the Board under rule 13(1)(b) of these rules.

(9) For all other cases involving offences of non-serious nature (entailing a punishment of less than 7 years imprisonment for adults) and cases where apprehension is not necessary in the interest of the juvenile, the police or the Juvenile or the Child Welfare Officer from the nearest police station, shall intimate the parents or guardian of the juvenile about forwarding the information regarding nature of offence alleged to be committed by their child or ward along with his socio-economic background to the Board, which shall have the power to call the juvenile for subsequent hearings.

(10) In case the Board is not sitting, the juvenile in conflict with law shall be produced before the single member of the Board as per the provisions laid down under the sub-section (2) of section 5 of the Act.

(11) In dealing with cases of juveniles in conflict with law the Police or the Juvenile or the Child Welfare Officer from the nearest police station, shall not be required to register an FIR or file a charge-sheet, except where the offence alleged to have been committed by the juvenile is of a serious nature such as rape, murder or when such offence is alleged to have been committed jointly with adults; instead, in matters involving simple offences, the Police or the Juvenile or the Child Welfare Officer from the nearest police station shall record information regarding the offence alleged to have been committed by the juvenile in the general daily diary followed by a report containing social background of the juvenile and circumstances of apprehension and the alleged offence and forward it to the Board before the first hearing.

(12) The State Government shall recognize only such voluntary organizations that are in a position to provide the services of probation, counselling, case work, a safe place and also associate with the Police or the Juvenile or the Child Welfare Officer from the Special Juvenile Police Unit, and have the capacity, facilities and expertise to do so as protection agencies that may assist the Police or the Juvenile or the Child Welfare Officer from the police at the time of apprehension, in preparation of the report containing social background of the juvenile and circumstances of apprehension and the alleged offence, in taking charge of the juvenile until production before the Board, and in actual production of the juvenile before the Board within twenty-four hours.

(13) The Police or the Juvenile or the Child Welfare Officer from the Special Juvenile Police Unit, or the recognized voluntary organization shall be responsible for the safety and provision of food and basic amenities to the juveniles apprehended or kept under their charge during the period such juveniles are with them.

(14) When a juvenile is produced before an individual member of the Board, and an order obtained, such order shall need ratification by the Board in its next meeting.

**12. Procedure to be followed in determination of age.**—(1) In every case concerning a child or a juvenile in conflict with law, the court or the Board or as the case may be the Committee referred to in rule 19 of these rules shall determine the age of such juvenile or child or a juvenile in conflict with law within a period of thirty days from the date of making of the application for that purpose.

(2) The Court or the Board or as the case may be the Committee shall decide the juvenility or otherwise of the juvenile or the child or as the case may be the juvenile in conflict with law, *prima facie* on the basis of physical appearance or documents, if available, and send him to the observation home or in jail.

(3) In every case concerning a child or juvenile in conflict with law, the age determination inquiry shall be conducted by the court or the Board or, as the case may be, the Committee by seeking evidence by obtaining—

(a) (i) the matriculation or equivalent certificates, if available; and in the absence whereof;

(ii) the date of birth certificate from the school (other than a play school) first attended; and in the absence whereof;

(iii) the birth certificate given by a corporation or a municipal authority or a panchayat;

(b) and only in the absence of either (i), (ii) or (iii) of clause (a) above, the medical opinion will be sought from a duly constituted Medical Board, which will declare the age of the juvenile or child. In case exact assessment of the age cannot be done, the Court or the Board or, as the case may be, the Committee, for the reasons to be recorded by them, may, if considered necessary, give benefit to the child or juvenile by considering his/her age on lower side within the margin of one year.

and, while passing orders in such case shall, after taking into consideration such evidence as may be available, or the medical opinion, as the case may be, record a finding in respect of his age and either of the evidence specified in any of the clauses (a)(i), (ii), (iii) or in the absence whereof, clause (b) shall be the conclusive proof of the age as regards such child or Ihe juvenile in conflict with law.

(4) If the age of a juvenile or child or the juvenile in conflict with law is found to be below 18 years on the date of offence, on the basis of any of the conclusive proof specified in sub-rule (3), the Court or the Board or as the case may be the Committee shall in writing pass an order stating the age and declaring the status of juvenility or otherwise, for the purpose of the Act and these rules and a copy of the order shall be given to such juvenile or the person concerned.

(5) Save and except where, further inquiry or otherwise is required, *inter alia,* in terms of section 7A, section 64 of the Act and these rules, no further inquiry shall be conducted by the court or the Board after examining and obtaining the certificate or any other documentary proof referred to in sub-rule (3) of this rule.

(6) The provisions contained in this rule shall also apply to those disposed of cases, where the status of juvenility has not been determined in accordance with the provisions contained in sub-rule (3) and the Act, requiring dispensation of the sentence under the Act for passing appropriate order in the interest of the juvenile in conflict with law.

**13. Post-production processes by the Board.**—(1) On production of the juvenile before the Board, the report containing social background of the juvenile and circumstances of apprehension and offence alleged to have been committed provided by the officers, individuals, agencies producing the juvenile shall be reviewed by the Board, and the Board shall pass the following order in the first summary inquiry on the same day, namely:—

(a) dispose of the case, if the evidence of his conflict with law appears to be unfounded or where the juvenile is involved in trivial law breaking;

(b) transfer to the Committee, matters concerning juveniles clearly stated to be in need of care and protection in the police report submitted to the Board at the time of production of the juvenile;

(c) release the juvenile in the supervision or custody of fit persons or fit institutions or probation officers as the case may be, through an order in Form I, with a direction to appear or present a juvenile for an inquiry on a next date;

(d) detain the juvenile in an Observation Home or fit institution pending inquiry, only in cases of juvenile's involvement in serious offences as per an order in Form II;

(e) in all cases of release pending inquiry, the Board shall notify the next date of hearing, not later than 15 days of the first summary enquiry and also seek social investigation report from the concerned Probation Officer through an order in Form III;

(2) The Board shall take the following steps to ensure fair and speedy inquiry, namely:—

(a) at the time of initiating the inquiry, the Board shall satisfy itself that the juvenile in conflict with law has not been subjected to any ill-treatment by the police or by any other person, including a lawyer or probation officer and take corrective steps in case of such ill-treatment;

(b) in all cases under the Act the proceedings shall be conducted in as simple a manner as possible and care shall be taken to ensure that the juvenile, against whom the proceedings have been instituted, is given child-friendly atmosphere during the proceedings;

(c) every juvenile brought before the Board shall be given the opportunity to be heard and participate in his inquiry;

(d) cases of petty offences, if not disposed of by the Special Juvenile Police Unit or at the police station itself, may be disposed of by the Board through summary proceedings or inquiry, while in cases of heinous offences entailing punishment of 7 years or more, due process of inquiry in detail may follow;

(e) even in cases of inquiry pertaining to serious offences the Board shall follow the procedure of trial in summons cases.

(3) When witnesses are produced for examination in inquiry relating to a juvenile in conflict with law, the Board shall keep in mind that the inquiry is not to be conducted in the spirit of strict adversarial proceedings and it shall use the powers conferred by section 165 of the Indian Evidence Act, 1872 (1 of 1872) so as to question the juvenile and proceed with the presumptions that favour the juvenile's right to be restored.

(4) While examining a juvenile in conflict with law and recording his statement, the Board shall address the juvenile in a child-friendly manner in order to put the juvenile at ease and to encourage him to state the facts and circumstances without any fear, not only in respect of the offence of which the juvenile is accused, but also in respect of the home and social surroundings and the influence to which the juvenile might have been subjected.

(5) The Board may take into account the report of the police containing circumstances of apprehension and offence alleged to have been committed and the social investigation report in Form IV prepared by the Probation Officer or the voluntary organization on the orders of the Board as per Form III, along with the evidence produced by the parties for arriving at a conclusion about the juvenile.

(6) Every inquiry by the Board shall be completed within a period of four months after the first summary inquiry and only in exceptional cases involving trans-national criminality, large number of accused and inordinate delay in production of witnesses, the period of inquiry may be extended by two months on recording of reasons by the Board.

(7) In all other cases except where the nature of alleged offence is serious, delay beyond four to six months shall lead to the termination of the proceedings.

(8) Where the proceedings are delayed beyond six months on account of serious nature of the offence alleged to have been committed by the juvenile, the Board shall send a periodic report of the case to the Chief Judicial Magistrate or Chief Metropolitan Magistrate stating the reason for delay as well as steps being taken to expedite the matter.

**14. Legal Aid.**—(1) The proceedings before the Board shall be conducted in non-adversarial environment, but with due regard to all the due process guarantees such as right to counsel and free legal aid.

(2) The Board shall ensure that the Legal Officer in the District Child Protection Unit and the State Legal Aid Services Authority shall extend free legal services to all the juvenile in conflict with law.

(3) The Legal Officer in the District Child Protection Unit and the State Legal Aid Services Authority shall be under an obligation to provide legal services sought by the Board.

(4) In the event of shortfall in the State Legal Aid Services support, the Board shall be responsible for seeking legal services from recognized voluntary legal services organisations or the university legal services clinics.

(5) The Board may also deploy the services of the student legal services volunteers and non-governmental organisation volunteers in para-legal tasks such as contacting the parents of juveniles in conflict with law and gathering relevant social and rehabilitative information about the juveniles.

**15. Completion of inquiry and dispositional alternatives.**—(1) The Board shall complete every inquiry within the stipulated time of four months and on recording a finding about juvenile's involvement in the alleged offence, pass one of the seven dispositional orders enumerated in section 15 of the Act.

(2) Before passing an order, the Board shall obtain a social investigation report prepared by the probation officer or by a recognized voluntary organization ordered to do so by the Board, and take the findings of the report into account.

(3) All dispositional orders passed by the Board shall necessarily include an individual care plan for the concerned juvenile in conflict with law, prepared by a probation officer or voluntary organization on the basis of interaction with the juvenile and his family where possible.

(4) Where the Board decides to release the juvenile after advice and admonition or after participation in group counselling or orders him to perform community service, necessary direction may also be made by the Board to the District or State Child Protection Unit or the State Government for arranging such individual counselling, group counselling and community service.

(5) Where the Board decides to release the juvenile in conflict with law on probation and place him under the care of the parent or guardian or fit person, the person in whose custody the juvenile is released may be required to submit a written undertaking in Form V for the good behaviour and well-being of the juvenile for a maximum period of three years.

(6) The Board may order release of a juvenile in conflict with law on execution of a personal bond without surety in Form VI.

(7) In the event of placement of a juvenile in conflict with law in care of a fit institution or special home, the Board shall keep in mind that the fit institution or special home is located nearest to the place of residence of the juvenile's parent or guardian.

(8) The Board, where it releases a juvenile in conflict with law on probation and places him under the care of parent or guardian or fit person or where the juvenile is released on probation and placed under the care of fit institution, may order that the juvenile be placed under the supervision of a probation officer. The period of supervision shall be a maximum of three years.

(9) Where the Board decides that a juvenile in conflict with law ought to be treated as a child in need of care and protection, it shall make necessary orders for production of such juvenile before the nearest Committee for suitable care, protection and rehabilitation.

(10) Where it appears to the Board that the juvenile in conflict with law has not complied with probation conditions, it may order the juvenile to be sent for detention in a special home.

(11) Where a juvenile in conflict with law who has attained the age of sixteen years and the offence committed by him is of such a serious nature that in the satisfaction of the Board, it is neither in the interest of the juvenile himself nor in the interest of other juveniles of the special home, the Board may order the juvenile to be kept in a place of safety and in a manner considered most appropriate by it.

(12) The State Government shall make arrangement for complying with the detention of special category of juveniles in conflict with law in place of safety other than the special home.

(13) In no case the period of detention shall exceed beyond the maximum period provided in clause (g) of sub-section (1) of section 15 of the Act.

**16. Institutions for juveniles in conflict with law.**—(1) The State Government or the voluntary organisation recognised by that State Government shall set-up separate observation homes or special homes for boys and girls.

(2) The observation homes or special homes shall set-up separate residential facilities for boys and girls up to 12 years, 13-15 years and 16 years and above.

(3) Every institution shall keep a copy of the Act, the rules made by the Central Government and the State rules if any, for use by both staff, juveniles and children residing therein.

(4) The State Governments in collaboration with civil society shall develop and make available simplified and child friendly versions of the Act and the rules in regional languages.

(5) All facilities and services for juveniles in conflict with law shall be made available and maintained as per the provisions of the Act and the State rules. In case the State Rules have not been notified, the provisions of these rules shall apply.

**17. Release.**—(1) The Officer-in-charge shall maintain a roster of the cases of juveniles in conflict with law to be released on the expiry of the period of stay as ordered by the Board.

(2) Each case shall be placed before the Management Committee set-up under rule 55 of these rules by the concerned probation officer or child welfare officer or case worker for ensuring proper release and social mainstreaming of the juvenile post-release.

(3) The release shall be as per the pre-release and post-release plan prepared under the individual care plan and reviewed from time to time by the management committee set-up under rule 55 of these rules and in all cases of release, necessary action and preparation shall be initiated well before the time of release and shall include preparation for post-release follow-up.

(4) The timely information of the release of a juvenile and of the exact date of release shall be given to the parent or guardian and the parent or guardian shall be invited to come to the institution to take charge of the juvenile on that date.

(5) If necessary, the actual expenses of the parent's or guardian's journey both ways and of the juvenile's journey from the institution shall be paid to the parent or guardian by the Officer-in-charge at the time of the release of the juvenile.

(6) If the parent or guardian, as the case may be, fails to come and take charge of the juvenile on the appointed date, the juvenile shall be taken by the escort of the institution; and in case of a girl, she shall be escorted by a female escort.

(7) At the time of release or discharge, a juvenile shall be provided with a set of summer or winter clothing and essential toiletries, if the Officer-in-charge considers it necessary.

(8) If the juvenile has no parent or guardian, he may be sent to an aftercare organization, or in the event of his employment, to the person who has undertaken to employ the juvenile.

(9) The Officer-in-charge of a girls' institution may, subject to the consent of the girl and the approval of the competent authority, help the girl with her social re-integration by way of sending a girl above the age of eighteen years to an after care programme or, helping her with some vocation or gainful employment or, helping her settle into family life according to the procedure laid down by the competent authority from time to time.

(10) The Officer-in-Charge shall order the discharge in Form VII of any juvenile whose detention period has come to an end and inform the competent authority within seven days of the action taken and if the date of release falls on a Sunday or a public holiday, the juvenile may be discharged on the preceding day with an entry to that effect being made in the register of discharge.

(11) The Officer-in-charge shall in appropriate cases, order the payment of subsistence money, at such rates as may be fixed from time to time, by the State or the District Child Protection Unit or the State Government, and the railway or road, or both, fares, as the case may be.

(12) In deserving cases, the Officer-in-charge may provide the juvenile with such small tools, as may be necessary, to start a work or business subject to such maximum cost as may be fixed by the institution which shall also form part of the post-release plan.

(13) Where a girl has no place to go after release and requests for stay in the institution after the period of her stay is over, the Officer-in-charge may, subject to the approval of the competent authority, allow her stay till the time some other suitable arrangements are made.

**18. Procedure to be followed in respect of sections 21, 22, 23, 24, 25 and 26 of the Act.**—(1) In the event of violation of provisions laid down under section 21 of the Act,—

(a) the Board shall take cognizance of such violation by print or electronic media and shall initiate necessary inquiry and pass appropriate orders as per provisions contained in sub-section (2) of section 21 of the Act; and

(b) where the National or the State Commission for Protection of Child Rights takes *suo motu* cognizance of violation under section 21 of the Act, it shall inform the District or the State Child Protection Unit of the concerned district and the State directing them to initiate necessary action through the Board.

(2) In the event of an escape of a juvenile in conflict with law or a child, the following action shall be taken within twenty-four hours,—

(a) the Officer-in-Charge of any institution shall immediately send a report to the area Police Station or Special Juvenile Police Unit along with the details and description of the juvenile or child, with identification marks and a photograph, with a copy to the Board, District Child Protection Unit and other authorities concerned;

(b) the Officer-in-charge of institutions other than shelter homes or drop-in-centres shall send the guards or concerned staff in search of the juvenile, at places like railway stations, bus stands and other places where the juvenile is likely to go;

(c) the parents or guardians shall be informed immediately about such escape; and

(d) the Officer-in-Charge of an institution other than a shelter home or drop-in-centre shall hold an inquiry about such escape and send his report to the Board or Committee and the authorities concerned and the report shall be placed before the Management Committee set-up under rule 55 of these rules in the next meeting for review.

(3) The offences against a juvenile in conflict with law or a child specified in sections 23, 24, 25 and 26 shall be either bailable or non-bailable besides being cognizable under the provisions of the Code of Criminal Procedure, 1973 (2 of 1974) and the procedures shall apply on the Police, the Board and the concerned authorities and functionaries accordingly.

## *CHAPTER IV*

## CHILD IN NEED OF CARE AND PROTECTION

**19. Child Welfare Committee.**—There shall be a Child Welfare Committee in every district, which shall be constituted by the State Government through a notification in the Official Gazette as per sub-section (1) of section 29 of the Act.

**20. Composition of the Child Welfare Committee.**—(1) The Committee shall consist of a Chairperson and four other members, of whom at least one shall be a woman.

(2) The Chairperson and members of the Committee shall be appointed on the recommendation of a Selection Committee set-up by the State Government, for the purpose under rule 91.

(3) The Selection Committee, while selecting the Chairperson and Members of the Committee, shall as far as possible ensure that none of them are from any adoption agency.

(4) The State Government shall provide for such training and orientation in child psychology, child welfare, child rights, national and international standards for juvenile justice to all members of the Committee as it considers necessary.

**21. Tenure of the Committee.**—(1) The Committee shall have a tenure of three years and the tenure of Chairperson and Members shall be co-terminus with the tenure of the Committee.

(2) The Chairperson and Members of the Committee shall be eligible for appointment for a maximum of two consecutive terms.

(3) Extension of the tenure of members of the Committee shall be on the basis of their performance appraisal by the District Child Protection Unit or the State Government and on the recommendation of the Selection Committee.

(4) With a view to ensuring continuity on completion of the tenure of a Committee, the State Government shall constitute a new Committee before the expiry of the term of the existing Committee; where after the existing Committee shall handover all records and information to the newly formed Committee.

(5) The Chairperson and Members may resign at any time by giving one month's notice in writing or may be removed from office as provided in sub-section (4) of section 29 of the Act.

(6) Any casual vacancy in the Committee may be filled by appointment of another person from the panel of names prepared by the Selection Committee, and shall hold office for the remaining term of the Committee.

**22. Qualifications for Chairperson and Members of the Committee.**—(1) A person to be selected as a Chairperson or Member of the Committee shall have either of the following qualifications, in addition to a minimum of seven years experience in their respective field:

(i) a person with post graduate degree in social work, psychology, child development, education, sociology, law, criminology and, where such a person is not available, a person with at least a graduate degree in any of the social science disciplines;

(ii) a teacher, doctor or a social worker who has been involved in work concerning children.

(2) The Chairperson or Member of the Committee shall be a person not less than 35 years of age.

(3) No person shall be considered for Selection as a Chairperson or Member of the Committee, if he,—

(i) has a previous conviction record;

(ii) has been involved in any immoral act or in an act of child abuse or employment of child labour;

(iii) is holding such full-time occupation that may not allow him to give necessary time and attention to the work of the Committee as per the Act and these rules;

(iv) does not fulfil the qualification and experience prescribed in the Act and the rules made thereunder, and in such a case the Selection Committee shall after due inquiry and on establishment of such fact, reject his application and recommend the name of the next person from the list of names prepared for filling the vacancies.

**23. Sitting and conveyance allowances.**—The Chairperson and Members of the Committee shall be paid such travel and sitting allowance, as the State Government may determine, but it shall not be less than rupees five hundred per sitting per member.

**24. Sitting of the Committee.**—(1) The Committee shall hold its sittings in the premises of the children's home or, at a place in proximity to the children's home or, at a suitable premise in any institution run under the Act.

(2) On receiving information about child or children in need of care and protection, if circumstances are such that the child or children cannot be produced before the Committee, the Committee may move out to reach the child or children and hold its sitting at a place that is convenient for such child or children.

(3) The premises where the Committee holds its sittings shall be child-friendly and shall not look like a court room in any manner whatsoever; for example, the Committee shall not sit on a raised platform and the sitting arrangement shall be uniform and there shall be no witness boxes.

(4) The Committee shall meet a minimum of three days a week, which may be extended by the State Government depending on case and pendency of work.

(5) A minimum of three-fourth attendance of the Chairperson and Members of the Committee is necessary in a year.

(6) The duration of a sitting is dependent on the pendency of work before the Committee.

(7) Every member of the Committee shall attend a minimum of four hours per sitting.

**25. Functions and powers of the Committee.**—The Committee shall perform the following functions to achieve the objectives of the Act, namely:—

(a) take cognizance of and receive children produced before the Committee;

(b) decide on the matters brought before the Committee;

(c) reach out to such children in need of care and protection who are not in a position to be produced before the Committee, being in difficult circumstances, with support from the District Child Protection Unit or State Child Protection Unit or the State Government;

(d) conduct necessary inquiry on all issues relating to and affecting the safety and well being of the child;

(e) direct the Child Welfare Officers or Probation Officers or non-governmental organisations to conduct social inquiry and submit a report to the Committee;

(f) ensure necessary care and protection, including immediate shelter;

(g) ensure appropriate rehabilitation and restoration, including passing necessary directions to parents or guardians or fit persons or fit institutions in this regard, in addition to follow-up and co-ordination with District Child Protection Unit or State Adoption Resource Agency and other agencies;

(h) direct the Officer-in-charge of children's homes to receive children requiring shelter and care;

(i) document and maintain detailed case record along with a case summary of every case dealt by the Committee;

(j) provide a child-friendly environment for children;

(k) recommend 'fit institutions' to the State Government for the care and protection of children;

(l) declare'fit persons';

(m) declare a child legally free for adoption;

(n) keep information about and take necessary follow-up action in respect of missing children in their jurisdiction;

(o) maintain liaison with the Board in respect of cases needing care and protection;

(p) visit each institution where children are sent for care and protection or adoption at least once in three months to review the condition of children in institutions, with support of the State Government and suggest necessary action;

(q) monitor associations and agencies within their jurisdiction that deal with children in order to check on the exploitation and abuse of children;

(r) co-ordinate with the Police, Labour Department and other agencies involved in the care and protection of children with the support of District Child Protection Unit or State Child Protection Unit or State Government;

(s) liaison and network with the corporate sector and non-governmental organisations for any of the above, including for social inquiry, restoration and rehabilitation, as and when required; and

(t) maintain a suggestion box to encourage inputs from children and adults alike and take necessary action.

**26. Procedure in relation to Committee.**—(1) The quorum for the meeting shall be three members attending, which may include the Chairperson.

(2) Any decision taken by an individual member, when the Committee is not sitting, shall require ratification by the Committee in its next sitting.

(3) The Committee shall take into consideration the age, developmental stage, physical and mental health, opinion of the child and the recommendation of the child welfare officer or caseworker, prior to disposal of cases.

(4) For final disposal of a case, the order of the Committee shall be signed by at least two members, including the Chairperson.

**27. Production of a child before the Committee.**—(1) A child in need of care and protection shall be produced before the Committee within twenty-four hours, excluding journey time, by one of the following persons—

(a) any police officer or Special Juvenile Police Unit or a designated police officer;

(b) any public servant;

(c) childline, a registered voluntary organization or by such other voluntary organization or an agency as may be recognized by the State Government;

(d) social worker;

(e) any public spirited citizen; or

(f) by the child himself.

(2) In case of a child under two years of age, who is medically unfit, the person or the organization shall send a written report along with the photograph of the child to the Committee within twenty-four hours and produce the child before the Committee as soon as the child is medically fit along with a medical certificate to that effect.

(3) The Committee can *suo motu* take cognizance of cases brought to their notice and reach out to a child in need of care and protection where necessary and the District or the State Child Protection Unit or the State Government shall provide necessary support and assistance to the Committee for carrying out such functions.

(4) In case the Committee is not sitting, the child may be produced before the single member of the Committee as per the provisions laid down under the sub-section (2) of section 30 of the Act for being placed in safe custody of parent or guardian or fit person or fit institutions, as the case may be, till such time that the child can be produced before the Committee.

(5) In case the single member is also not accessible, or that the hours are odd, the child shall be taken by an non-governmental organisation or Childline or Police to an appropriate institution for children registered under the Act with all the necessary documents, and placed in such institution till the time of production before the Committee.

(6) The concerned institution shall inform the Chairperson or a member of the Committee about such child and produce the child before the Committee within twenty-four hours and in such cases, it may not be necessary for the

person who brings a child in need of care and protection to an institution to be present at the time of production of the child before the Committee.

(7) Whoever produces a child before the Committee shall submit a report on the circumstances under which the child came to their notice and efforts made by them on informing the police and the missing persons squad and in cases where a recognized voluntary organization or any police personnel produce a child before the Committee, they shall also submit a report on the efforts made by them for tracing the family of the child.

(8) Any general medical or gynaecological examination of children shall not be a pre-requisite for production of the child before the Committee or admission in an institution.

(9) The Committee shall facilitate the filing of a police complaint and First Information Report in cases of missing children as well as matters of violence, exploitation and abuse of children and arrange for required legal aid through the Legal Officer in the District Child Protection Unit or District or State Legal Aid Services Authority or voluntary organisations.

(10) Each Committee shall send quarterly information about children in need of care and protection received by them to the District or State Child Protection Unit or State Government.

(11) Children shall be provided a child-friendly environment during the proceedings of the Committee.

(12) The Committee shall have an empanelled list of lawyers, social workers and mental health expert who may assist the Committee in dealing with cases of abused children and who may also interface with the Public Prosecutor or Assistant Public Prosecutor to facilitate legal services to the abused children, when the cases relating to such children are taken up in regular criminal courts.

(13) Every possible effort shall be made to trace the family with support from the District Child Protection Unit, and assistance of recognized voluntary organizations, childline or police may also be taken.

(14) The Committee shall send the child to the designated place of safety, with age and gender appropriate facilities, pending inquiry and in such eventuality, the District Child Protection Unit or State Child Protection Unit or State Government shall provide transport or make necessary budgetary allocations for such expenses based on the actual fare.

(15) The child may be escorted by the police officer or representative of the voluntary organization or by any other arrangement as considered appropriate by the Committee with support from the District Child Protection Unit and in case of a girl child, a female escort shall accompany the child.

(16) A list of all recognized child care institutions along with their capacity and appropriate facilities as prescribed under section 34 of the Act, a list of all childs related resource services and a list of contact details of all Child Welfare Committees across the country shall be provided to the Committee by the District Child Protection Unit or State Government.

(17) The Committee may, while making an order in Form VIII placing a child under the care of a parent, guardian or fit person pending inquiry or at the time

of restoration, as the case may be, direct such parent, guardian or fit person to enter into an undertaking in Form IX.

(18) Whenever the Committee orders a child to be kept in an institution, it shall forward to the Officer-in-Charge of such institution a copy of the order of short-term placement pending inquiry, in Form X with particulars of the home and parents or guardian and previous record.

(19) Whenever the Committee orders a child to be kept in a fit institution as part of restoration under clause (f) of sub-section (3) of section 39 of the Act, it shall forward a copy of its order of restoration in Form XI to the Officer-in-Charge of such institution.

(20) The child shall be placed in an institution closest to where his parents or guardians belong as far as possible, unless the child has been subjected to abuse or exploitation by parents or guardians.

**28. Procedure for inquiry.**—(1) When a child is brought before the Committee, the Committee shall assign the case to a social worker or caseworker or child welfare officer or Officer-in-Charge as the case may be, of the institution or any recognized agency for conducting the inquiry through an order in Form XII.

(2) The Committee shall direct the concerned person or organization about the details or particulars to be enquired into for developing an individual care plan and suitable rehabilitation.

(3) All inquiries conducted by a social worker or caseworker or child welfare officer or Officer-in-Charge of the institution or any recognized agency shall be as per Form XIII and must provide an assessment of the family situation of the child in detail, and explain in writing whether it will be in the best interest of the child to restore him to his family.

(4) The inquiry must be completed within four months or within such shorter period as may be fixed by the Committee:

Provided that the Committee may, in the best interest of the child and for the reasons to be recorded in writing, extend the said period under special circumstances.

(5) After completion of the inquiry, if, the child is under orders to continue in the children's home, the Committee shall direct the Officer-in-Charge of the home to submit quarterly progress report of such child and produce the child before the Committee for an annual review of the progress.

**29. Children's homes.**—(1) The State Government itself or in association with voluntary organizations, shall set-up separate homes for children in need of care and protection, in the manner specified below:—

(a) all children's homes shall be registered as child care institutions under sub-section (3) of section 34 of the Act and rule 71 of these rules;

(b) all children's homes shall be certified as per the procedure laid down in rule 70;

(c) all children's homes shall report to the concerned Committee about every child in need of care and protection received by them;

(d) children of both sexes below ten years may be kept in the same home but separate facilities shall be maintained for boys and girls in the age group 5 to 10 years;

(e) every children's home shall include separate facilities for children in the age group of 0-5 years with appropriate facilities for the infants;

(f) separate children's homes shall be set-up for boys and girls in the age group 10 to 18 years;

(g) children in the age group of 10 to 18 shall be further segregated into two groups of 10 to 15 years and 15 to 18 years.

(2) Each children home shall be a comprehensive child care centre with the primary objective to promote an integrated approach to child care by involving the community and local Non-Governmental Organisations through the Management Committee set-up under rule 55 of these rules and the District Child Protection Unit or State Child Protection Unit or the State Government shall make an annual performance review of functioning of the children's homes.

(3) The activities of such centre shall focus on:

(a) preparing and following individual care plans for every child, with rights based approach, specifically addressing the child's physical and mental health, emotional needs, education, skill development, protection and special needs if any;

(b) family based non-institutional services, such as, foster family care, adoption and sponsorship;

(c) specialized services in situations of conflict or disaster and for juvenile or children affected by terminal or incurable disease to prevent neglect by providing family counselling, nutrition, health interventions, psycho-social interventions and sponsorship;

(d) emergency outreach service through childline (Toll free Help Line No. 1098);

(e) linkages with Integrated Child Development Services to cater to the needs of children below six years;

(f) linkages with organizations and individuals who can provide support services to children; and

(g) opportunities to volunteers willing to provide various services for children.

**30. Shelter homes.**—(1) For children in urgent need of care and protection, such as street children and run-away children, the State Government shall support creation of requisite number of shelter homes or drop-in-centres through the voluntary organizations.

(2) Shelter homes shall include:

*(g) short-stay homes for children needing temporary shelter, care and protection for a maximum period of one year,

*(h) transitional homes providing immediate care and protection to a child for a maximum period of four months,

*(i) 24 hour drop-in-centres for children needing day care or night shelter facility.

---

* **Ed.**—It appears clauses (g), (h) and (i) have been wrongly so lettered, they ought to have been lettered as (a), (b) and (c) respectively.

(3) The shelter homes or drop-in-centres shall have the minimum facilities of boarding and lodging, besides the provision for fulfilment of basic needs in terms of clothing, food, health care and nutrition, safe drinking water and sanitation.

(4) There shall be separate shelter homes for girls and boys as per rule 40(2)(d) of these rules.

(5) All shelter homes shall provide requisite facilities for education, vocational training, counselling and recreation or make arrangements for it in collaboration with voluntary organizations or corporate sector.

(6) The Committee, Special Juvenile Police Units, public servants, childlines, voluntary organizations, social workers and the children themselves may refer a child to such shelter homes.

(7) All shelter homes shall submit a report of children using the shelter home facility along with a photograph of the child to the Committee, the missing persons bureau or special juvenile police unit and the District Child Protection Unit or the State Child Protection Unit.

(8) The requirements of producing a child received by a shelter home before the Committee, inquiry and disposal under sections 32, 33, 38 and 39 of the Act shall apply only to shelter homes other than drop-in-centres as specified in rule 30(2)(c) of these rules.

(9) The services of Officer-in-charge, child welfare officer, social worker shall be provided for the proper care, protection, development, rehabilitation and reintegration needs of children in shelter homes.

(10) No child shall ordinarily stay in a short stay home for more than a year except in special circumstances with the approval of the Committee.

**31. Guidelines for prevention of sexual abuse of children.**—The Central Government, State Government, the Juvenile Justice Board, the Child Welfare Committee, other competent authorities and agencies shall, in the best interest of children, ensure that every person, school or such other educational institutions abide by the guidelines issued from time to time by Central Government and State Government.

## *CHAPTER V*

## REHABILITATION AND SOCIAL REINTEGRATION

**32. Rehabilitation and Social Reintegration.**—The primary aim of rehabilitation and social reintegration is to help children in restoring their dignity and self-worth and mainstream them through rehabilitation within the family where possible, or otherwise through alternate care programmes and long-term institutional care shall be of last resort.

**33. Adoption.**—(1) The primary aim of adoption is to provide a child who cannot be cared for by his biological parents with a permanent substitute family.

(2) For all matters relating to adoption, the guidelines issued by the Central Adoption Resource Agency and notified by the Central Government under sub-section (3) of section 41 of the Act, shall apply.

(3) In case of orphaned and abandoned children the following procedure shall apply, namely:—

(a) Specialized Adoption Agencies shall produce all orphaned and abandoned children who are to be declared legally free for adoption before the Committee within twenty-four hours of receiving such children, excluding the time taken for journey;

(b) a child becomes eligible for adoption when the Committee has completed its inquiry and declares the child legally free for adoption;

(c) such declaration shall be made in Form XIV;

(d) a child must be produced before the Committee at the time of declaring such child legally free for adoption;

(e) whenever intimation is received by the police about an abandoned infant, the police shall take charge of the infant and arrange to provide immediate medical assistance and care;

(f) subsequently, the child shall be placed in a specialized adoption agency or recognized and certified children's home or in a paediatric unit of a Government hospital followed by production of the child before the Committee within twenty-four hours;

(g) procedure for declaring a child abandoned and certifying him legally free for adoption:

(i) in case of an abandoned child, the recognized agency shall within twenty-four hours, report and produce the child before the Committee with the copy of the report filed with the police station in whose jurisdiction the child was found abandoned;

(ii) the Committee will institute a process of inquiry, which shall include a thorough inquiry conducted by the Probation Officer or Child Welfare Officer, as the case may be and who shall give report in Form XIII to the Committee containing the findings within one month;

(iii) there shall be a declaration by the specialized adoption agency, stating that there has been no claimant for the child even after making notification in at least one leading national newspaper and one regional language newspaper for children below two years of age and for children above two years, an additional television or radio announcement and notification to the missing persons squad or bureau shall be made;

(iv) the steps stated in (iii) shall be taken within a period of sixty days from the time when the child is found in case of a child below two years of age and in case of children above two years of age, this period shall be four months;

(v) the period of notification shall run concurrently with the inquiry to be conducted and report submitted under clause (ii) of this sub-rule;

(vi) the Committee shall declare the child legally free for adoption on completion of the process of inquiry, including declaration of the specialized adoption agency made under clauses (ii) and (iii) of this sub-rule;

(vii) no child above seven years who can understand and express his opinion shall be declared free for adoption without his consent.

(4) In case of surrendered children the following procedure shall apply, namely:—

(a) a surrendered child is one who had been declared as such after due process of inquiry by the Committee and in order to be declared legally free for adoption, a 'surrendered' child shall be any of the following:—

(i) born as a consequence of non-consensual relationship;

(ii) born of an unwed mother or out of wedlock;

(iii) a child in whose case one of the biological parents is dead and the living parent is incapacitated to take care;

(iv) a child where the parents or guardians are compelled to relinquish him due to physical, emotional and social factors beyond their control;

(b) serious efforts shall be made by the Committee for counselling the parents, explaining the consequences of adoption and exploring the possibilities of parents retaining the child and if, the parents are unwilling to retain, then, such children shall be kept initially in foster care or arranged for their sponsorship;

(c) if the surrender is inevitable, a deed of surrender in Form XV shall be executed on a non-judicial stamp paper in the presence of the Committee;

(d) the adoption agencies shall wait for completion of two months reconsideration time given to the biological parent or parents after surrender;

(e) in case of a child surrendered by his biological parent or parents, the document of surrender shall be executed by the parent or parents before the Committee;

(f) after due inquiry, the Committee shall declare the surrendered child legally free for adoption in Form XIII as the case may be after a sixty days' reconsideration period as per Central Adoption Resource Agency guidelines.

(5) For the purposes of section 41 of the Act, 'court' implies a civil court, which has jurisdiction in matters of adoption and guardianship and may include the court of the district judge, family courts and city civil court.

**34. Foster care.**—(1) For children who cannot be placed in adoption, order shall be issued by the competent authority in Form XVII for carrying out foster care, as given in sub-section (2) of section 42 of the Act and rule 35(1) of these rules, under the supervision of a probation officer or case worker or social worker, as the case may be, and the period of foster care shall depend on the need of the child.

(2) Every State Government shall design its own foster care programme so as to reduce institutionalization of children and enable a nurturing family environment for every child.

(3) The State Government shall consult the Boards or Committees, non-governmental organisations, academicians and organisations working on alternative care for children in developing the foster care programme.

**35. Criteria for selection of families for foster care.**—(1) In case of the children covered under rule 34 of these rules, the following criteria shall apply for selection of families for foster care, namely:—

(i) foster parents should have stable emotional adjustment within the family;

(ii) foster parents should have an income in which they are able to meet the needs of the child and are not dependent on the foster care maintenance payment;

(iii) the monthly family income shall be adequate to take care of foster children and approved by the Committee;

(iv) medical reports of all the members of the family residing in the premises should be obtained including checks on Human Immuno Deficiency Virus (HIV), Tuberculosis (TB) and Hepatitis B to determine that they are medically fit;

(v) the foster parents should have experience in child caring and the capacity to provide good child care;

(vi) the foster parents should be physically, mentally and emotionally stable;

(vii) the home should have adequate space and basic facilities;

(viii) the foster care family should be willing to follow rules laid down including regular visits to pediatrician, maintenance of child health and their records;

(ix) the family should be willing to sign an agreement and to return the child to the specialized adoption agency whenever called to do so;

(x) the foster parents should be willing to attend training or orientation programmes; and

(xi) the foster parents should be willing to take the child for regular (at least once a month in the case of infants) checkups to a pediatrician approved by the agency.

(2) There shall be no discrimination in selection of foster-parents on the basis of caste, religion, ethnic status, disability, or health status and the best interest of the child shall be paramount in deciding foster care placement.

(3) The foster-parents shall be declared 'fit persons' by the Committee before placing the child as per the provisions laid down in clause (i) of section 2 of the Act after thorough assessment done by the Child Welfare Officer or Social Worker as per Form XVI.

**36. Pre-adoption foster care.**—In case of pre-adoption foster care, the provisions contained in sub-section (1) of section 42 and the corresponding guidelines notified under sub-section (3) of section 41 of the Act, shall apply.

**37. Sponsorship.**—(1) The State Government shall prepare sponsorship programme in consultation with the Non-Governmental Organisations, Child

Welfare Committees, other relevant government agencies and the corporate sector.

(2) The State Government, with the help of District or State Child Protection Units shall identify families and children at risk and provide necessary support services in the form of sponsorship for child's education, health, nutrition and other developmental needs.

(3) The children's homes and special homes shall promote sponsorship programmes as laid down in section 43 of the Act.

(4) The institutions receiving sponsorship, shall maintain proper and separate accounts of all the receipts and payments for the programme.

(5) The Board or the Committee shall make an order in Form XVIII for support to a juvenile or child through sponsorship and send a copy to the District or State Child Protection Unit or the State Government for appropriate action.

**38. After Care Organisation.**—(1) The State Government shall set-up an after care programme for care of juveniles or children after they leave special homes and children's homes with the objective to facilitate their transition from an institution-based life to mainstream society for social reintegration.

(2) After care programmes shall be made available for 18-21 years old persons, who have no place to go to or are unable to support themselves, by the District or State Child Protection Units in collaboration with voluntary organizations for the purpose of section 44 of the Act and this rule.

(3) Once the Board or the Committee passes an order in Form XIX for placing a juvenile or a child completing 18 years of age under the after care programme, a copy of such order shall be sent to the District and the State Child Protection Unit and the State Government, who shall be responsible for arranging after care.

(4) The Board or the Committee shall have jurisdiction over persons placed in after care programme.

(5) The objective of these organisations shall be to enable such children to adapt to the society and during their stay in these transitional homes these children will be encouraged to move away from an institution-based life to a normal one.

(6) The key components of the programme shall include:—

(a) community group housing on a temporary basis for groups of young persons aged 18-21 years;

(b) encouragement to learn a vocation or gain employment and contribute towards the rent as well as the running of the home;

(c) encouragement to gradually sustain themselves without state support and move out of the group home to stay in a place of their own after saving sufficient amount through their earnings;

(d) provision for a peer counsellor to stay in regular contact with these groups to discuss their rehabilitation plans and provide creative outlets for their energy and to tide over crisis periods in their life.

(7) During the course of vocational training a stipend may be provided till such time that the youth gets employment.

(8) Loans may be arranged for the youth in an after care programme aspiring to set-up entrepreneurial activities on the basis of an application made by them and due verification of the need for such a loan, and necessary professional advice and training shall be made available to the youth in the after care programme in this regard.

(9) The structure shall include 6 to 8 youths in each group home who may opt to stay together on their own and one peer counsellor for a cluster of five group homes.

**39. Linkages and co-ordination.**—(1) The State Government shall circulate a copy of the Act and the rules framed thereunder to establish effective linkages between various government, non-government, corporate and other community agencies for facilitating the rehabilitation and social reintegration of juveniles or children through the Board or the Committee as the case may be.

(2) The State Government with the help of State or District Child Protection Unit shall identify the roles and responsibilities of each department at State or district levels for effective implementation of the Act and the rules and inform them through a notification.

(3) The State Government with the help of State or District Child Protection Unit shall arrange for appropriate training and sensitization of functionaries of these departments from time to time in co-ordination with National Institute of Public Co-operation and Child Development and its Regional Centres.

(4) The State Government with the help of State or District Child Protection Unit shall develop effective networking and linkages with local non-governmental organisations for specialized services and technical assistance like vocational training, education, health care, nutrition, mental health intervention, drug de-addition and legal aid services.

## *CHAPTER VI*

## STANDARDS OF CARE FOR INSTITUTIONS

**40. Physical infrastructure.**—(1) The homes for juveniles in conflict with law and children in need of care and protection shall function from separate premises.

(2) The accommodation in each institution shall be as per the following criteria, namely:—

**(a) Observation Home:**

(i) Separate observation homes for girls and boys;

(ii) Classification and segregation of juveniles according to their age group preferably 7-11 years, 12-16 years and 16-18 years, giving due consideration to physical and mental status and the nature of the offence committed.

**(b) Special Home:**

(i) Separate special homes for girls above the age of 10 years and boys in the age groups of 11 to 15 and 16 to 18 years;

(ii) Classification and segregation of juveniles on the basis of age and nature of offences and their mental and physical status.

**(c) Children's Home:**

(i) While children of both sexes below 10 years can be kept in the same home, separate bathing and sleeping facilities shall be maintained for boys and girls in the age group of 5-0 years;

(ii) Separate children's homes for boys and girls in the age group of 7-11 and 12-18 years;

(iii) Separate facilities for children in the age group of 0-5 years with appropriate facilities for infants.

**(d) Shelter Home:**

(i) Separate shelter homes for girls and boys;

(ii) Separate shelter homes for girls above the age of 10 years and boys in the age groups of 11 to 15 and 16 to 18 years.

(3) The norms for building or accommodation for an institution with 50 juveniles or children shall be as under:

| | | |
|---|---|---|
| (i) | 2 Dormitories | Each 1000 Sq. ft. for 25 juveniles/children *i.e.* 2000 Sq. ft. |
| (ii) | 2 Classrooms | 300 Sq. ft. for 25 juveniles/children *i.e.* 600 Sq. ft. |
| (iii) | Sickroom/First aid room | 75 Sq. ft. per juvenile/children for 10 *i.e.* 750 Sq. ft. |
| (iv) | Kitchen | 250 Sq. ft. |
| (v) | Dining Hall | 800 Sq. ft. |
| (vi) | Store | 250 Sq. ft. |
| (vii) | Recreation room | 300 Sq. ft. |
| (viii) | Library | 500 Sq. ft. |
| (ix) | 5 bath rooms | 25 Sq. ft. each *i.e.* 125 Sq. ft. |
| (x) | 8 toilets/latrines | 25 Sq. ft. each *i.e.* 200 Sq. ft. |
| (xi) | Office rooms | (a) 300 Sq. ft. (b) Superintendent's room 200 sq. fit |
| (xii) | Counselling and guidance room | 120 Sq. ft. |
| (xiii) | Workshop | 1125 Sq. ft. for 15 juvenile @ 75 Sq. ft. per trainee |
| (xiv) | Residence for Superintendent | (a) 2 rooms of 250 Sq. ft. each (b) kitchen 75 Sq. ft. (c) bathroom-cum-Toilet/latrine 50 Sq. ft |
| (xv) | 2 Rooms for Juvenile Justice Board/Child Welfare Committee | 300 Sq. ft. each *i.e.* 600 Sq. ft. |
| (xvi) | Play ground | Sufficient area according to the total number of juveniles or children |
| | **Total** | **8495 Sq.ft.** |

(4) The Superintendent shall stay within the institution and be provided with quarters and in case he is not able to stay in the home for legitimate reasons (to be permitted by Director, Child Protection), any other senior staff member of the hstitution shall stay in the institution and be in a position to supervise the overall care of the children or juveniles and, take decisions in the case of any crisis and emergency.

(5) (i) the standards of accommodation as per the norms laid down in rule 40(2) shall be observed to the extent possible and shall include a minimum of following facilities:—

| | |
|---|---|
| (a) Dormitory: | 40 Sq. ft. per juvenile or child |
| (b) Classroom: | 300 Sq. ft for 25 juvenile or child |
| (c) Workshop: | 75 Sq. ft. per juvenile or child |
| (d) Play ground: | Sufficient play ground area shall be provided in every institution according to the total number of juveniles in institution |

(ii) there shall be proper and smooth flooring for preventing accidents.

(iii) there shall be adequate lighting, ventilation, heating and cooling arrangements, safe drinking water and clean toilets, in terms of gender, age appropriateness and accessibility.

(iv) all institutions under the Act shall make provision of first aid kit, fire extinguishers in kitchen, dormitories, store rooms, counselling room, periodic review of electrical installations, proper storage and inspection of articles of food stuffs, stand-by arrangements for water storage and emergency lighting.

(6) The Observation homes and special homes shall be child-friendly and in no way shall they look like a jail or lock-up.

**41. Clothing and bedding.**—The clothing and bedding shall be as per the scale and climatic conditions. The requirements of each juvenile or child and the minimum standards for clothing and bedding are laid down in Schedule I of these rules.

**42. Sanitation and hygiene.**—Every institution shall have the following facilities, namely:—

(a) sufficient treated drinking water; water filters shall be installed;

(b) sufficient water for bathing and washing clothes, maintenance and cleanliness of the premises;

(c) proper drainage system;

(d) arrangements for disposal of garbage;

(e) protection from mosquitoes by providing mosquito nets;

(f) annual pest control;

(g) sufficient number of well lit and airy toilets in the proportion of at least one toilet for seven children;

(h) sufficient number of well lit and airy bathrooms in the proportion of at least one bath room for ten children;

(i) sufficient space for washing;

(j) clean and fly-proof kitchen and separate area for washing utensils;

(k) sunning of bedding and clothing;

(l) maintenance of cleanliness in the Medical Centre.

**43. Daily routine.**—(1) Every institution shall have a daily routine for the juveniles or children developed in consultation with the Children's Committees, which shall be prominently displayed at various places within the institution.

(2) The daily routine shall provide, *inter alia,* for a regulated and disciplined life, personal hygiene and cleanliness, physical exercise, yoga, educational classes, vocational training, organized recreation and games, moral education,

group activities, prayer and community singing and special programmes for Sundays and holidays.

**44. Nutrition and Diet Scale.**—The following nutrition and diet scale shall be followed by the institutions, namely:—

(a) the children shall be provided four meals in a day including breakfast;

(b) the menu shall be prepared with the help of a nutritional expert or doctor to ensure balanced diet and variety in taste as per the minimum nutritional standard and diet scale set out in Schedule II of these rules;

(c) every institution under this Act shall strictly adhere to the minimum nutritional standard and diet scale specified in Schedule II;

(d) juveniles or children may be provided special meals on holidays and festivals;

(e) infants and sick juveniles or children shall be provided special diet according to the advise of the doctor on their dietary requirement.

**45. Medical care.**—Every institution shall:

(a) maintain a medical record of each juvenile or child on the basis of monthly medical check-up and provide necessary medical facilities;

(b) ensure that the medical record includes weight and height record, any sickness and treatment, and other physical or mental problem;

(c) have arrangement for the medical facilities, including a doctor on call available on all working days for regular medical check-ups and treatment of juveniles or children;

(d) have sufficient medical equipments to handle minor health problems including first aid kit with stock of emergency medicines and consumables;

(e) train all staff in handling first aid;

(f) tie-up with local Primary Health Centre, government hospital, medical colleges, other hospitals, clinical psychologists and psychiatrists and mental health institutes for regular visits by their doctors and students and for holding periodic health camps within the institutions;

(g) make necessary arrangements made for the immunization coverage;

(h) take preventive measures in the event of out break of contagious or infectious diseases;

(i) set-up a system for referral of cases with deteriorating health or serious cases to the nearest civil hospital or recognised treatment centres;

(j) keep sick children under constant medical supervision;

(k) admit a juvenile or child without insisting on a medical certificate at the time of admission;

(l) arrange for a medical examination of each juvenile or child admitted in an institution by the Medical Officer within twenty-four hours and in special cases or medical emergencies immediately;

(m) arrange for a medical examination of the juvenile or child by the Medical Officer at the time of transfer within twenty-four hours before transfer;

(n) not carry out any surgical treatment on any juvenile or child without the previous consent of his parent or guardian, unless either the parent or guardian cannot be found and the condition of the juvenile or child is such that any delay shall, in the opinion of the medical officer, involve unnecessary suffering or injury to the health of the juvenile or child, or otherwise without obtaining a written consent to this effect from the Officer-in-Charge of the institution;

(o) provide or arrange for regular counselling of every juvenile or child and ensure specific mental health interventions for those in need of such services, including separate rooms for counselling sessions within the premises of the institution;

[1][(p) refer such children who are addicted to alcohol or other drugs which lead to behavioural change in a person, to an Integrated Rehabilitation Centre for Addicts or similar centres maintained by the State Government for mentally ill persons (including the persons addicted to any narcotic drug or psychotropic substance) for the period required for in-patient treatment of such juvenile or child.]

**46. Mental health.**—(1) A mental health record of every juvenile or child shall be maintained by the concerned institutions.

(2) Both milieu-based interventions that is creating an enabling environment for children and individual therapy are must for every child and shall be provided in all institutions.

*Explanation.*—For the purpose of this sub-rule, milieu-based intervention is a process of recovery, which starts through providing an enabling culture and environment in an institution so as to ensure that each child's abilities are discovered and they have choices and right to take to decisions regarding their life and thus, they develop and identify beyond their negative experiences and such intervention has a critical emotional impact on the child.

(3) The environment in an institution shall be free from abuse, allowing juveniles or children to cope with their situation and regain confidence.

(4) All persons involved in taking care of the juveniles or children in an institution shall participate in facilitating an enabling environment and work in collaboration with the therapists.

(5) Individual therapy is a specialized process and each institution shall make provisions for it as a critical mental health intervention.

(6) Every institution shall have the services of trained counsellors or collaboration with external agencies such as child guidance centres, psychology and psychiatric departments or similar government and non-governmental agencies, for specialized and regular individual therapy for every juvenile or child in the institution.

(7) A mental health care plan shall be developed for every juvenile or child by the child welfare officers in consultation with mental health experts

---

1. Subs. by G.S.R. 903(E), dated 26th December, 2011 (w.e.f. 27-12-2011). Clause (p), before substitution, stood as under:

"(p) refer such children who require specialized drug abuse prevention and rehabilitation programme, to an appropriate centre administered by qualified personnel where these programmes shall be adopted to the age, gender and other specifications of the concerned child.".

associated with the institution and integrated into the individual care plan of the concerned juvenile or child.

(8) The recommendations of mental health experts shall be maintained in every case file and integrated into the care plan for every child.

(9) All care plans shall be produced before the Management Committee set-up under rule 55 of these rules every month and before the Child Welfare Committee every quarter.

[1][(10) No juvenile or child shall be administered medication for psychiatric problems without a psychological evaluation and diagnosis by a trained medical health professional.]

**47. Education.**—(1) Every institution shall provide education to all juveniles or children according to the age and ability, both inside the institution or outside, as per the requirement.

(2) There shall be a range of educational opportunities including, mainstream inclusive schools, bridge school, open schooling, non-formal education and learning and input from special educators where needed.

(3) Wherever necessary, extra coaching shall be made available to school going children in the institutions by encouraging volunteer services or tying up with coaching centers.

**48. Vocational Training.**—(a) Every institution shall provide gainful vocational training to juveniles or children.

(b) The institutions shall develop networking with Institute of Technical Instruction, Jan Shikshan Sansthan, Government and Private Organization or Enterprises, Agencies or non-governmental organisations with expertise or placement agencies.

**49. Recreation facilities.**—(1) A provision of guided recreation shall be made available to all juveniles or children in the institutions.

(2) It shall include indoor and outdoor games, music, television, picnics and outings, cultural programmes and library.

**50. Institutional management of juveniles or children.**—(1) The following procedure shall be followed in respect of the newly admitted juveniles:

(a) receiving and search;

(b) disinfection and storing of juvenile's personal belongings and other valuables;

(c) bath and haircut (unless prohibited by religion);

(d) issue of toiletry items; new set of clothes, bedding and other outfit and equipment (as per scales);

(e) medical examination and treatment where necessary and in case of every juvenile suspected to be suffering from contagious or infectious diseases, mental ailments or addiction;

(f) segregation in specially earmarked dormitories or wards or hospitals in case of a child suffering from contagious disease requiring special care and caution;

---

1. Subs. by G.S.R. 903(E), dated 26th December, 2011, for sub-rule (10) (w.e.f. 27-12-2011). Sub-rule (10), before substitution, stood as under:

"(10) No juvenile or child shall be administered medication for mental health problems without a psychological evaluation and diagnosis by appropriately trained mental health professionals.".

(g) attending to immediate and urgent needs of the juveniles like appearing in examinations, interview letter to parents, personal problems and verification by the Officer-in-Charge of age of juvenile as per order of the Board.

(2) Every newly admitted juvenile or child shall be allotted a case worker from amongst the probation officers or child welfare officers or social workers or counsellors attached to the institutions or voluntary social workers or counsellors.

(3) Every newly admitted juvenile shall be familiarized with the institution and its functioning and shall receive orientation in the following areas:—

(a) personal health, hygiene and sanitation;

(b) institutional discipline and standards of behaviour, respect for elders and teachers;

(c) daily routine, peer interaction, optimum use of developmental opportunities; and

(d) rights, responsibilities and obligations within the institution.

(4) The designated officer shall enter the name of the juvenile or child in the Admission Register and allocate appropriate accommodation facility.

(5) The photograph shall also be taken immediately for records and the case worker or probation officer or welfare officer shall begin the investigation and correspondence with the person, the juvenile or child might have named.

(6) The Officer-in-Charge shall see that the personal belongings of the juvenile or child received by the institution is kept in safe custody and recorded in the Personal Belonging Register and the item must be returned to the juvenile or child when he leaves the institution.

(7) The girl juvenile or child shall be searched by a female member of the staff, and with due regard to decency and dignity of the juvenile or child.

(8) The educational level and vocational aptitude of the juvenile admitted, may be assessed on the basis of test and interview conducted by the teacher, the workshop supervisor and other technical staff and necessary linkages may also be established with outside specialists and community-based welfare agencies, psychologist, psychiatrist, child guidance clinic, hospital and local doctors, open school or Jan Sikshan Sansthan.

(9) A case history of the juvenile or the child admitted to an institution shall be maintained as per Form XX, which shall contain information regarding his socio-cultural and economic background and these informations may invariably be collected through all possible and available sources, including home, parents or guardians, employer, school, friends and community.

(10) A well-conceived programme of pre-release planning and follow up of cases discharged from special homes shall be organized in all institutions in close collaboration with existing governmental and voluntary welfare organizations.

(11) In the event of a juvenile or child leaving the institution without permission or committing an offence within the institution, the information shall be sent by the Officer-in-Charge of the concerned institution to the police and the family, if known; and the detailed report of circumstances alongwith the efforts to trace the juvenile or child where the juvenile or child is missing, shall be sent to the Board or Committee, as the case may be.

(12) An individual care plan for every juvenile or child in institutional care shall be developed with the ultimate aim of the child being rehabilitated and re-

integrated based on their case history, circumstances and individual needs and the individual care plan shall be based on following guidelines:—

(a) the Officer-in-Charge, counsellor along with the child welfare officer or case worker, or social worker shall prepare an individual care plan for every child in an institution within one month of his admittance as per Form XXI;

(b) all care plans shall include a plan for the juvenile's or child's restoration, rehabilitation, reintegration and follow-up;

(c) the care plan shall be reviewed quarterly by the Management Committee set-up under rule 55 of these rules for appropriate development and rehabilitation including options for release or restoration to family or foster care or adoption;

(d) juveniles or children shall be consulted while determining their care plan;

(e) continuity of care plan shall be ensured in cases of transfer or repatriation or restoration.

**51. Prohibited articles.**—No person shall bring into the institution the following prohibited articles, namely:—

(a) fire-arms or other weapons, whether requiring license or not (like knife, blades, lathi, spears and swords);

(b) alcohol and spirit of any description;

(c) bhang, ganja, opium or other narcotic or psychotropic substances;

(d) tobacco; or

(e) any other article specified in this behalf by the State Government by a general or special order.

**52. Articles found on search and inspection.**—(1) The Officer-in-Charge shall see that every juvenile received in the institution is searched, his personal belongings inspected and money or any valuables found with the juvenile is kept in the safe custody of the Officer-in-Charge.

(2) The girls shall be searched by a female member of the staff and both the girls and boys shall be searched with due regard to decency and dignity.

(3) In every institution, a record of money, valuables and other articles found with a juvenile shall be maintained in the "Personal Belongings Register".

(4) The entries made in the Personal Belongings Register, relating to each juvenile, shall be read over to juvenile in the presence of a witness, whose signature shall be obtained in token of the correctness of such entries and it shall be countersigned by the Officer-in-Charge.

**53. Disposal of articles.**—The money or valuables belonging to a juvenile received or retained in an institution shall be disposed of in the following manner, namely:—

(a) on an order made by the competent authority in respect of any juvenile, directing the juvenile to be sent to an institution, the Officer-in-Charge shall deposit such juvenile's money together with the sale proceeds in the manner laid down from time to ime in the name of the juvenile;

(b) the juvenile's money shall be kept with the Officer-in-Charge and valuables, clothing, bedding and other articles, if any, shall be kept in safe custody;

(c) when such juvenile is transferred from one institution to another, all his money, valuables and other articles, shall be sent along with the juvenile to the Officer-in-Charge of the institution to which he has been transferred together with a full and correct statement of the description and estimated value thereof;

(d) at the time of release of such juvenile, the valuables and other articles kept in safe custody and the money deposited in name of the juvenile shall be handed over to the parent or guardian, as the case may be, with an entry made in this behalf in the register and signed by the Officer-in-Charge;

(e) when a juvenile in an institution dies, the valuable and other articles left by the deceased and the money deposited in the name of the juvenile shall be handed over by the Officer-in-Charge to any person who establishes his claim thereto and executes an indemnity bond;

(f) a receipt shall be obtained from such person for having received such valuables and other articles and the amount;

(g) if no claimant appears within a period of six months from the date of death or escape of such juvenile, the valuables and other articles and amount shall be disposed of as per the decision taken by Management Committee set-up under rule 55 of these rules.

**54. Maintenance of case file.**—(1) The case file of each juvenile and child shall be maintained in the institution containing the following information:—

(a) report of the person or agency who produced the juvenile before the Board;

(b) Officer-in-Charge's, probation officer's or child welfare officer's, counsellor's and case-workers reports;

(c) information from previous institution;

(d) report of the initial interaction with the juvenile, information from family members, relatives, community, friends and miscellaneous information;

(e) source of further information;

(f) observation reports from staff members;

(g) regular health status reports from Medical Officer, drug de-addiction progress reports, progress reports *vis-a-vis* psychological counselling or any other mental health intervention, where applicable;

(h) Intelligence Quotient (I.Q.) testing, aptitude testing, educational or vocational tests;

(i) social history;

(j) summary and analysis by case-worker and Officer-in-Charge;

(k) instruction regarding training and treatment programme and about special precautions to be taken;

(l) leave and other privileges granted;

(m) special achievements and violation of rules, if any;

(n) quarterly progress report;

(o) individual care plan, including pre-release programme, post-release plan and follow-up plan as prescribed in Form XXI;

(p) leave of absence or release under supervision;

(q) final discharge;

(r) follow-up reports;

(s) annual photograph;

(t) case history duly filled in prescribed Form XX;

(u) follow-up report of post-release cases as per direction of the competent authority if any; and

(v) remarks.

(2) All the case files maintained by the institutions and the Board or Committee shall, as far as possible, be computerised and networked so that the data is centrally available to the State and the District Child Protection Unit and the State Government.

**55. Management Committee.**—(1) Every institution shall have a Management Committee for the management of the institution and monitoring the progress of every juvenile and child.

(2) In order to ensure proper care and treatment as per the individual care plans, a juvenile or child shall be grouped on the basis of age, nature of offence or kind of care required, physical and mental health and length of stay order.

(3) The Management Committee shall consist of the following personnel:—

| | | |
|---|---|---|
| District Child Protection Officer (District Child Protection Unit) | – | Chairperson |
| Officer-in-Charge | – | Member-Secretary |
| Probation Officer or Child Welfare Officer or Case-Worker | – | Member |
| Medical Officer | – | Member |
| Psychologist or Counsellor | – | Member |
| Workshop Supervisor or Instructor in Vocation | – | Member |
| Teacher | – | Member |
| Social Worker Member of Juvenile Justice Board or Child Welfare Committee | – | Member |
| A juvenile or child representative from each of the Children's Committees (on a monthly rotation basis to ensure representation of juveniles or children from all age groups) | – | Member |

(4) In the districts where District Child Protection Unit is not constituted the District Magistrate or Collector or his nominee shall be the Chairperson of this Committee.

(5) Where voluntary organizations are involved in providing professional and technical services like education, vocational training, psychosocial care, mental health intervention and legal aid, the Management Committee may invite a representative of such voluntary organizations as a special invitee to the Management Committee meetings.

(6) (a) The Management Committee shall meet every month to consider and review—

(i) custodial care or care in the institution, housing, area of activity and type of supervision or interventions required;

(ii) medical facilities and treatment;

(iii) food, water, sanitation and hygiene conditions;

(iv) mental health interventions with the juveniles and children;

(v) individual problems of juveniles and children, provision of legal aid services and institutional adjustment, leading to the quarterly review of individual care plans;

(vi) vocational training and opportunities for employment;

(vii) education and life skills development programmes;

(viii) social adjustment, recreation, group work activities, guidance and counselling;

(ix) review of progress, adjustment and modification of residential programmes to the needs of the juveniles and children;

(x) planning post-release or post-restoration rehabilitation programme and follow up for a period of two years in collaboration with aftercare services;

(xi) pre-release or pre-restoration preparation;

(xii) release or restoration;

(xiii) post-release or post-restoration follow-up;

(xiv) minimum standards of care, including infrastructure and services available;

(xv) daily routine;

(xvi) community participation and voluntarism in the residential life of children such as education, vocational activities, recreation and hobby;

(xvii) oversee that all registers as required under the Act and rules are maintained by the institution, check and verify these registers, duly stamped and signed in the monthly review meetings;

(xviii) matters concerning the Children's Committees;

(xix) any other matter which the Officer-in-Charge may like to bring up.

(b) The Officer-in-Charge or child welfare officer shall file a quarterly progress report of every juvenile or child in the case file and send a copy to the District Child Protection Unit and Board or Committee, as the case may be.

(7) The Management Committee shall set-up a complaint and redress mechanism in every institution and a Children's Suggestion Box shall be installed in every institution at a place easily accessible to juveniles and children away from the office set-up and closer to the residence or rooms or dormitories of the children.

(8) (a) The Children's Suggestion Box, whose key shall remain in the custody of the Chairperson of the Management Committee, shall be checked every week

by the Chairperson of the Management Committee or his representative from District Child Protection Unit, in the presence of the members of the Children's Committees.

(b) If there is a problem or suggestion that requires immediate attention, the Chairperson of the Management Committee shall call for an emergency meeting of the Management Committee to discuss and take necessary action.

(c) The quorum for conducting the emergency meetings shall be five members, including two members of Children's Committees, Chairperson of the Management Committee, Member of Committee or the Board as the case may be and the Officer-in-Charge of the institution.

(d) In the event of a serious allegation or complaint against the Officer-in-Charge of the institution, he shall not be part of the emergency meeting and another available member of the Management Committee shall be included in his place.

(e) All suggestions received through the suggestion box and action taken as a result of the decisions made in the emergency meeting or action required to be taken shall be placed for discussion and review in the monthly meeting of the Management Committee.

(9) A Children's Suggestion Book shall be maintained in every institution where the complaints and action taken by the Management Committee are duly recorded and such action and follow up shall be communicated to the Children's Committees after every monthly meeting of the Management Committee.

(10) The Board or Committee shall review the Children's Suggestion Book at least once in three months.

**56. Children's Committees.**—(1) Officer-in-Charge of every institution for juveniles or children shall facilitate the setting up of Children's Committees for three different age groups of children, *viz.*, 6-10 years, 11-15 years and 16-18 years and these Children's Committees shall be constituted solely by children.

(2) Such Children's Committee shall be encouraged to participate in following activities:—

(a) improvement of the condition of the institution;

(b) reviewing the standards of care being followed;

(c) preparing daily routine and diet scale;

(d) developing educational, vocational and recreation plans;

(e) supporting each other in managing crisis;

(f) reporting abuse and exploitation by peers and caregivers;

(g) creative expression of their views through wall papers or newsletters or paintings or music or theater;

(h) management of institution through the Management Committee.

(3) The Officer-in-Charge shall ensure that the Children's Committees meet every month and maintain a register for recording its activities and proceedings, and place it before the Management Committee in their monthly meetings.

(4) The Officer-in-Charge shall ensure that the Children's Committees are provided with essential support and materials including stationary, space and guidance for effective functioning.

(5) The Officer-in-Charge shall, as far as possible, seek assistance from local voluntary organization or child participation experts for the setting up and functioning of the Children's Committees.

(6) The local voluntary organization or child participation expert shall support the Children's Committees in the following:—

*(j) selecting their leaders;

*(k) conducting the monthly meetings;

*(l) developing rules for the functioning of Children's Committees and following it;

*(m) maintaining records and Children's Suggestion Book and other relevant documents;

*(n) any other innovative activity.

(7) The Management Committee shall seek a report from the Officer-in-Charge on the setting up and functioning of the Children's Committees, review these reports in their monthly meetings and take necessary action where required.

**57. Rewards and earnings.**—The rewards to a juvenile or child, at such rates as may be fixed by the management of the institution from time to time, may be granted by the Officer-in-Charge as an encouragement to steady work and good behaviour; and at the time of release, the reward shall be handed over after obtaining a receipt from the parent or the guardian who comes to take charge of the juvenile or child or juvenile or child himself.

**58. Visits to and communication with juveniles or children.**—(1) The parents and relatives of the juveniles or children shall be allowed to visit once in a month or in special cases, more frequently at the discretion of the Officer-in-Charge as per the visiting hours laid down by him, except where parents or relatives or guardian have been found to be responsible for subjecting the juvenile or child to violence, abuse and exploitation.

(2) The receipt of letters by the juveniles or children of the institution shall not be restricted and they shall have freedom to write as many letters as they like at all reasonable times; and the institution shall ensure that where parents, guardians or relatives are known, at least one letter is written by the juvenile or children every month for which the postage shall be provided by the institution.

(3) The Officer-in-Charge may peruse any letter written by or to the juvenile or children, and may for the reasons that he considers sufficient refuse to deliver or issue the letter and forward it to the Committee after recording his reasons in a book maintained for the purpose.

(4) The Officer-in-Charge shall, in special circumstances or as per orders of the Board or Committee, allow a juvenile or child to make telephonic communication with his parents or guardians or relatives.

**59. Death of a juvenile or child.**—On the occurrence of any case of death or suicide in an institution the procedure to be adopted shall be as under:

(1) In the event of an unnatural death or suicide of a juvenile or child in an institution it is imperative for the institution to ensure that an inquest and post-mortem examination is held at the earliest.

---

* **Ed.**—It appears clauses (j), (k), (l), (m) and (n) have been wrongly so lettered, they ought to have been lettered as (a), (b), (c), (d) and (e) respectively.

(2) In case of natural death or due to illness of a juvenile or child, the Officer-in-Charge shall obtain a report of the Medical Officer stating the cause of death and a written intimation about the death shall be given immediately to the nearest Police Station, the Board or Committee, the National or State Commission for Protection of Child Rights, District Child Protection Unit or State Child Protection Unit or any other concerned authority and the parents or guardians or relatives of the juvenile or child.

(3) Whenever a sudden or violent death or death from suicide or accident takes place, immediate information shall be given by the case-worker or probation officer or welfare officer to the Officer-in-Charge and the Medical Officer and the Officer-in-Charge shall immediately inform the nearest police station, Board or Committee and parents or guardians or relatives of the deceased juvenile or child.

(4) If a juvenile or child dies within twenty-four hours of his admission to the institution, the Officer-in-Charge of the institution shall report the matter to the Officer-in-Charge of the Police Station having jurisdiction and the District Medical Officer or the nearest Government Hospital and the parents or guardians or relatives of such juvenile or child without delay.

(5) The Officer-in-Charge shall also immediately give intimation to nearest Magistrate empowered to hold inquests and to the Board or as the case may be the Committee.

(6) The Officer-in-Charge and the Medical Officer at the institution shall record the circumstances of the death of the child and send a report to the concerned Magistrate, the Officer-in-Charge of the police station having jurisdiction, the Committee and the District Medical Officer or the nearest government hospital where the dead body of the juvenile or child is sent for examination, inspection and determination of the cause of death and the Officer-in-Charge and the Medical Officer shall also record in writing their views on the cause of the death if any, and submit it to the concerned Magistrate and the Officer-in-Charge of the police station having jurisdiction.

(7) The Officer-in-Charge and the Medical Officer shall make themselves available for any inquiries initiated by the police or the Magistrate concerning the cause of death and other details regarding such juvenile or child.

(8) As soon as the inquest is held, the body shall be handed over to the parents or guardian or relatives or, in the absence of any claimant, the last rituals shall be performed under the supervision of the Officer-in-Charge in accordance with the known religion of the juvenile or child.

**60. Abuse and exploitation of the juvenile or child.**—(1) Every institution shall have systems of ensuring that there is no abuse, neglect and maltreatment and this shall include the staff being aware of what constitutes abuse, neglect and maltreatment as well as early indicators of abuse, neglect and maltreatment and how to respond to these.

(2) In the event of any physical, sexual or emotional abuse, including neglect of juveniles and children in an institution by those responsible for care and protection, the following action shall be taken:—

(i) the incidence of abuse and exploitation must be reported by any staff member of the institution immediately to the Officer-in-Charge on receiving such information;

(ii) when an allegation of physical, sexual or emotional abuse comes to the knowledge of the Officer-in-Charge, a report shall be placed before the Board or Committee, who in turn, shall order for special investigation;

(iii) the Board or Committee shall direct the local police station or Special Juvenile Police Unit to register a case, take due cognizance of such occurrences and conduct necessary investigations;

(iv) the Board or Committee shall take necessary steps to ensure completion of all inquiry and provide legal aid as well as counselling to the juvenile or child victim;

(v) the Board or Committee shall transfer such a juvenile or child to another institution or place of safety or fit person;

(vi) the Officer-in-Charge of the institution shall also inform the Chairperson of the management committee and place a copy of the report of the incident and subsequent action taken before the management committee in its next meeting;

(vii) in the event of any other crime committed in respect of juveniles or children in institutions, the Board or Committee shall take cognizance and arrange for necessary investigation to be carried out by the local police station or Special Juvenile Police Unit;

(viii) the Board or Committee may consult Children's Committee set-up in each institution to enquire into the fact of abuse and exploitation as well as seek assistance from relevant voluntary organizations, child rights experts, mental health experts or crisis intervention centres in dealing with matters of abuse and exploitation of juveniles or children in an institution.

**61. Juvenile or child suffering from dangerous diseases or mental health problems.**—(1) When a juvenile or a child placed under the care of a fit person or a fit institution under the provisions of the Act, is found to be suffering from a disease or physical or [1][psychiatric problems requiring prolonged medical treatment or found addicted to alcohol or other drugs which lead to behavioural changes in a person], the juvenile or the child may be sent by an order of the competent authority to an appropriate place for such period as may be certified by medical officer to be necessary for proper treatment of the juvenile or the child or for the remainder of the term for which he has to stay.

(2) When the juvenile or the child is cured of the disease or physical or [2][psychiatric] problems, the competent authority may, if the juvenile or child is still liable to stay, order the juvenile or the child to be placed back in the care of

1. Subs. by G.S.R. 903(E), dated 26th December, 2011, for "mental health problems requiring prolonged medical treatment, or is found addicted to a narcotic drug or psychotropic substance" (w.e.f. 27-12-2011).
2. Subs. by G.S.R. 903(E), dated 26th December, 2011, for "mental health" (w.e.f. 27-12-2011).

fit person or institution from where the juvenile or child was removed for treatment and if the juvenile or the child is no longer liable to be kept under the care of fit person or institution, the competent authority may order him to be discharged.

[1][***]

(4) Where there is no organization either within the jurisdiction of the competent authority, or nearby District or State for care and protection of juveniles or children suffering from serious psychiatric or physical disorder [2][***], as required under section 58 of the Act, necessary organization shall be set-up by the State Government at such places, as it may deem fit to cater to the special needs of such juveniles or children.

**62. Leave of absence of a juvenile or child.**—(1) A juvenile or child in an institution may be allowed to go on leave of absence or released under supervision for examination or admission, special occasions like marriage or emergencies like death or accident or serious illness in the family.

(2) While the leave of absence for short period generally not exceeding seven days excluding the journey time may be recommended by the Officer-in-Charge, but granting of such leave shall be by the Board or Committee.

(3) The parents or guardian of the juvenile or the Officer-in-Charge on behalf of the juvenile or child may submit an application to the Board or Committee requesting for relieving the juvenile or child on leave, stating clearly the purpose for the leave and the period of leave.

(4) While considering the application of leave of absence, the Board or Committee shall hear the juvenile or child or the parents or guardians of the juvenile or child and if the Board or Committee considers that granting of such leave is in the interest of the juvenile or child, appropriate order shall be made and the Board or Committee may call for a report from the probation officer or child welfare officer in case the preliminary information gathered from the juvenile or child or concerned parent or guardian is not sufficient for the purpose.

(5) While issuing orders sanctioning the leave of absence or relieving under supervision, as the case may be, the competent authority shall mention the period of leave and the conditions attached to the leave order, and if any of these conditions are not complied with during the leave period, the juvenile or child may be called back to the institution.

(6) The parent or guardian shall arrange to escort the juvenile or child from and to the institution and where this is not possible, the Officer-in-Charge may arrange to escort the juvenile or child to the place of the family and back. In case the parents or guardian is willing to arrange escort but does not have requisite financial means, the Officer-in-Charge shall arrange for the travelling expenses as admissible under the rules.

---

1. Sub-rule (3) omitted by G.S.R. 903(E), dated 26th December, 2011 (w.e.f. 27-12-2011). Sub-rule (3), before omission, stood as under:

   "(3) The order of restoration of a juvenile or a child suffering from an infectious or contagious disease to his parents or guardian shall be based on the principle of best interest of the juvenile or child, keeping in mind the risk of stigmatization and discrimination and discontinuation of treatment.".

2. The words "and infection" omitted by G.S.R. 903(E), dated 26th December, 2011 (w.e.f. 27-12-2011).

(7) If the juvenile or child runs away from the family during the leave period, the parent or guardian is required to inform the Officer-in-Charge of the institution immediately, and try to trace the juvenile or child and if found, the juvenile or child shall be brought back to the institution immediately.

(8) If the juvenile or child is not found within twenty-four hours, the Officer-in-Charge shall report the matter to the nearest police station and missing person's bureau, but no adverse disciplinary action shall be taken against the juvenile or child and procedure laid down under the Act shall be followed.

(9) If the parent or guardian does not take proper care of the juvenile or child during the leave period or does not bring the juvenile or child back to the institution within the stipulated period, such leave may be refused on later occasions.

(10) If the juvenile or child does not return to the institution on expiry of the sanctioned leave, the Board or Committee shall refer the case to police for taking charge of the juvenile and bring him back to the institution.

(11) The period of such leave shall be counted as a part of the period of stay in the institution and the time which elapses after the failure of a juvenile to return to the institution within the stipulated period, shall be excluded while computing the period of his stay in the institution.

**63. Inspection.**—(1) The State Government shall constitute State, District or city level inspection committee on the recommendation of the Selection Committee constituted under rule 91 of these rules.

(2) The inspection committees shall visit and oversee the conditions in the institutions and appropriateness of the processes for safety, well being and permanence, review the standards of care and protection being followed by the institutions, look out for any incidence of violation of child rights, look into the functioning of the Management Committee and Children's Committee set-up under rules 55 and 56 of these rules and give appropriate directions.

(3) The team shall also make suggestions for improvement and development of the institution.

(4) The team shall consist of a minimum of five members with representation from the State Government, the Board or Committee, the State Commission for the Protection of Child Rights or the State Human Rights Commission, medical and other experts, voluntary organizations and reputed social workers.

(5) The inspection shall be carried out at least once in every three months.

(6) The inspection visit shall be carried out by not less than three members.

(7) The team may visit the institutions either by prior intimation or make a surprise visit.

(8) The team shall interact with the children during the visits to the institution, to determine their well-being and uninhibited feed back

(9) The follow-up action on the findings and suggestion of the children shall be taken by all concerned authorities.

(10) The action taken report, findings and suggestions from the Inspection Committee shall be sent to the District Child Protection Unit and the State Government.

**64. Social Audit.**—(1) The Central Government or the State Government shall monitor and evaluate the implementation of the Act annually by reviewing matters concerning establishment of Board or Committee or Special Juvenile Police Unit where required, functioning of Board or Committee or Special

Juvenile Police Unit, functioning of institutions and staff, functioning of adoption agencies, child friendly administration of juvenile justice and any other matter concerning effective implementation of the Act in the State.

(2) The social audit shall be carried out with support and involvement of organizations working in the field of mental health, child care and protection and autonomous bodies like the National Institute of Public Co-operation and Child Development, Indian Council for Child Welfare, Childline India Foundation, Central and State level Social Welfare Boards, School of Social Work and School of Law.

**65. Restoration and Follow-up.**—(1) The order for restoration of the juvenile or child shall be made by the Board or Committee on the basis of a fair hearing of the juvenile or child and his parents or guardian, as well as on the reports of the Probation Officers or Child Welfare Officers or non-governmental organisations directed by the Board or Committee to conduct the home study and any other relevant document or report brought before the Board or Committee for deciding the matter.

(2) The Board or Committee shall send a copy of the restoration order along with a copy of the order for escort as per Form XXII to the District Child Protection Unit or State Government who shall provide funds for restoration of the juvenile or child.

(3) Every restoration shall be planned for as part of the individual care plans prepared by the case-workers or counsellors or child welfare officers or probation officer, as the case may be, and shall be based on the review and recommendations of the Management Committee set-up under rule 55 of these rules.

(4) Besides police, the Board or Committee shall seek collaboration with non-governmental organisations to accompany juveniles or children back to their family for restoration.

(5) In case of girls, the juvenile or child shall necessarily be accompanied by female escorts.

(6) The expenses incurred on restoration of a juvenile or child, including travel and other incidental expenses, shall be borne by the District Child Protection Unit or State Government.

(7) When a juvenile or child expresses his unwillingness to be restored back to the family, the Board or Committee shall make a note of it in its records in writing and such juvenile or child shall not be coerced or persuaded to go back to the family, particularly if the social investigation report of the child welfare officer or probation officer establishes that restoration to family may not be in the best interest of the juvenile or child or, if the parents or guardians refuse to accept the juvenile or child back.

(8) A follow-up plan shall be prepared as part of the individual care plans by the Child Welfare Officers or Probation Officers or non-governmental organisations assigned by the Board or Committee to assist in restoration of the child.

(9) A quarterly follow-up report shall be submitted to the Board or Committee by the concerned Child Welfare Officer or Probation Officer or non-

governmental organisation for a period of two years with a copy to the Officer-in-Charge of the institution from where the juvenile or child is restored.

(10) The follow-up report shall clearly state the situation of the juvenile or child post restoration and the juvenile's or child's needs to be met by the State Gbvernment in order to reduce further vulnerability of the juvenile or child.

(11) The Officer-in-Charge shall file the follow-up report in the case-file of the juvenile or child and place the report before the management committee set-up under rule 55 of these rules in its next meeting.

(12) The Officer-in-Charge shall also send a copy of the follow-up reports to the District Child Protection Unit.

(13) Where a follow-up is not possible due to unavailability of government functionaries or non-governmental organisations, the concerned District Child Protection Unit shall provide necessary assistance and support to the concerned Board or Committee.

**66. Visitor's Book.**—(1) A Visitor's Book shall be maintained, in every institution, in which the person visiting the home shall record the date of his visit with remarks or suggestions, which he may think proper.

(2) The Officer-in-Charge shall forward a copy of every such entry to the District Child Protection Unit or State Government, with such remarks as he may desire to offer in explanation or otherwise; and thereon, the designated authority shall issue such orders as he may consider necessary.

**67. Maintenance of Registers.**—The Officer-in-Charge shall maintain in his office, such registers and forms, as required by the Act and as specified by these rules made thereunder and the list of registers or files or books to be maintained shall minimally comprise of:

(a) Admission and discharge register;
(b) Supervision register;
(c) Medical file or medical report;
(d) Nutrition diet file;
(e) Stock register;
(f) Log book;
(g) Order book;
(h) Meeting book;
(i) Cash book;
(j) Budget statement file;
(k) Inquiry report file;
(l) Individual case file with individual care plan;
(m) Children's Suggestion book;
(n) Visitor's book;
(o) Staff movement register;
(p) Personal belongings register;
(q) Minutes register of Management Committee;

(r) Minutes register of Children's Committees; and

(s) Attendance register for staff and juveniles or children.

**68. Personnel or Staff of a Home.**—(1) The personnel strength of a home shall be determined according to the duty, posts, hours of duty per day and category of children that the staff is meant to cater to.

(2) The institutional organizational set-up shall be fixed in accordance with the size of the home, the capacity, workload, distribution of functions and requirements of programmes.

(3) The whole-time staff in a home may consist of Officer-in-Charge, Probation Officer (in case of Observation home or Special home), Case-Workers (in case of Children's home or shelter home or after care organization), Child Welfare Officers, Counsellor, Educator, Vocational Training Instructor, Medical Staff, Administrative staff, Care Takers, house father and house mother, child mentors, volunteers, store keeper, cook, helper, washerman, safai karamchari, gardener as required.

(4) The part-time staff, shall include Psychiatrist, Psychologist, Occupational therapist, and other professionals as may be required by time to time.

(5) The staff of the home shall be subject to control and overall supervision of the Officer-in-Charge who by order, shall determine their specific responsibilities and shall keep the concerned authority informed of such orders made by him from time to time.

(6) The duties and responsibilities of the staff under the Officer-in-Charge shall be fixed in keeping with the statutory requirements of the Act.

(7) The Officer-in-Charge and such other staff who may be required, shall live in the quarters provided for them within the premises of the home.

(8) The number of posts in each category of staff shall be fixed on the basis of capacity of the institution; and the staff shall be appointed in accordance with the educational qualifications, training and experience required for each category.

(9) The suggested staffing pattern for an institution with a capacity of 100 juveniles or children could be as mentioned below:

| Sl. No. | Staff/Personnel | No. of Posts |
|---|---|---|
| (1) | (2) | (3) |
| 1. | Officer-in-Charge (Superintendent) | 1 |
| 2. | Counsellor | 2 |
| 3. | Probation Officer or Child Welfare Officer or Case-Worker | 3 |
| 4. | House Mother or House Father | 4 |
| 5. | Educator | 2 (voluntary or part time) |
| 6. | Doctor | 1 |
| 7. | Paramedical staff | 1 |
| 8. | Store-keeper-cum-Accountant | 1 |
| 9. | Art & Craft-cum-Music Teacher | 1 (part time) |

| (1) | (2) | (3) |
|---|---|---|
| 10. | PT Instructor cum Yoga Trainer | 1 (part time) |
| 11. | Driver | 1 |
| 12. | Cook | 2 |
| 13. | Helper | 2 |
| 14. | Housekeeping | 2 |
| 15. | Gardener | 1 (part time) |
| | Total | 25 |

(10) The number of posts in the category of counsellor, case-worker or probation officer, house father or house mother, educator and vocational instructor shall proportionally increase with the increase in the capacity of the institution.

(11) In case of institutions housing infants, provision for *ayahs* and paramedical staff shall be made as per the need.

## *CHAPTER VII*

## MISCELLANEOUS

**69. Recognition of fit persons or fit institution.**—(1) Any individual who is willing temporarily to receive a juvenile or child in need of care, protection or treatment for a period as may be necessary, may be recognized by the competent authority as a fit person after due verification of their credentials and reputation.

(2) Any suitable place or institution, the manager of which is willing temporarily to receive a juvenile or child in need of care and protection for a period as may be necessary, may be recognized by the State Government as a fit institution on the recommendation of the competent authority.

(3) An institution recognized as a fit institution shall,—

(a) meet the standards of care laid down in the Act and the rules made thereunder;

(b) have the capacity and willingness to meet the standards of care laid down in the Act and the rules;

(c) receive and provide basic services for care and protection of the juveniles and children;

(d) prevent subjection of juvenile or child to any form of cruelty or exploitation or neglect; and

(e) abide by the orders of the competent authority.

(4) A list of fit institutions approved by the State Government shall be kept in the office of the Board and the Committee.

(5) A fit institution with collateral branches may send the juvenile or child placed therein by an order of the competent authority to any of its branches after seeking permission from the competent authority.

(6) Before declaring any person as a fit person or recommending an institution as a fit institution, the competent authority shall hold due enquiry and only on being satisfied, recognition shall be given.

**70. Certification or recognition and transfer of Management of Institutions and after care organizations.**—(1) Any organization desiring certification under the Act shall make an application together with a copy each of the rules, bye-laws articles of association, list of members of the society or the association running the organization, office bearers and a statement showing the status and past record of specialized childcare services provided by the organization, to the State Government, who shall after verifying the provisions made in the organization for the boarding and lodging, general health, educational facilities, vocational training and treatment services may grant certification or recognition under sections 8, 9, 34, 37, 41 or 44 of the Act, as the case may be, on the condition that the organization shall comply with the standards or services as laid down under the Act and the rules framed their under, from time to time and to ensure an all round growth and development of juvenile or child placed under its charge.

(2) Any organization desiring recognition under the Act shall make an application to the Competent Authority, who shall after due inquiry, recommend the State Government for such recognition.

(3) The State Government may, transfer the management of any State run institution under the Act to a voluntary organization of repute, who has the capacity to run such an institution; and certify or recognize the said voluntary organization as a fit institution to own the requisite responsibilities under a Memorandum of Understanding for a specified period of time.

(4) The State Government may, if dissatisfied with the conditions, rules, management of the organization certified or recognized under the Act, at any time, by notice served on the manager of the organization, declare that the certificate or recognition of the organization, as the case may be, shall stand withdrawn as from a date specified in the notice and from the said date, the organization shall cease to be an organization certified or recognised under sections 8, 9, 34, 37, 41 or 44 of the Act, as the case may be:

Provided that the concerned organization shall be given an opportunity of making a representation in writing, within a period of thirty days, against the grounds of withdrawal of certificate or recognition of that organization.

(5) The decision to withdraw or to restore the certificate or recognition of the organization may be taken, on the basis of a thorough investigation by a specially constituted advisory board under section 62 of the Act.

(6) On the report of the advisory board, the Officer-in-Charge of the institution shall be asked to show cause so as to give an explanation within thirty days.

(7) When an organization ceases to be an organization, certified or recognised under sections 8, 9, 34, 37, 41 or 44 of the Act, the juvenile or the child kept therein shall, be transferred to some other institution of repute, certified or recognized under sections 8, 9, 34, 37, 41 or 44 of the Act or discharged, in accordance with the provisions of the Act and the rules relating to their discharge and transfer by giving intimation of such discharge or transfer to the Board or the Committee, as the case may be.

**71. Registration under the Act.**—(1) All institutions and organisations running institutional or non-institutional care services for children in need of care and protection, whether run by the government or voluntary organization, shall get themselves registered under sub-section (3) of section 34 of the Act.

(2) All such institutions shall make an application together with a copy each of rules, bye-laws, memorandum of association, list of governing body, office bearers, balance sheet of past three years, statement of past record of social or public service provided by the institution or organization to the State Government, who shall after verifying that provisions made in the institution or organization for the care and protection of children, health, education, boarding and lodging facilities, if any, vocational facilities and scope of rehabilitation, may issue a registration certificate to such organization under sub-section (3) of section 34 of the Act and as per this rule.

**72. Grant-in-aid to certified or recognized organization.**—(1) An organization certified or recognized or registered under sections 8, 9, 34, sub-section (3) of section 34, 37 or 44 of the Act, may during the period when certification or recognition or registration is in force, may apply for grants-in-aid by the State Government, for the maintenance of juvenile or child received by them under the provisions of the Act; and for expenses incurred on their education, treatment, vocational training, development and rehabilitation.

(2) The grants-in-aid may be admissible, at such rates, which shall be sufficient to meet the prescribed norms, in such manner and subject to such conditions as may be mutually agreed to by both the parties.

(3) In case of transfer of management of government-run homes under sections 8, 9, 34, sub-section (3) of sections 34, 37 or 44 of the Act to a voluntary organization, the same budget which the Government was spending on that home, shall be given to the voluntary organization as grant-in-aid under the Memorandum of Understanding signed between both the parties describing their role and obligations.

**73. Admission of outsiders.**—(1) No stranger shall be admitted to the premises of the institution, except with the permission of the Officer-in-Charge or on an order from the Board or Committee.

(2) In special cases, where parents or guardians have travelled a long distance from another state or district, the Officer-in-Charge shall allow parents or guardians entry into the premises and a meeting with their children, provided they possess proper identification and are not reported to have subjected the juvenile or child to abuse and exploitation.

**74. Identity photos.**—(1) On admission to a home established under the Act, every juvenile or child shall be photographed.

(2) One photograph shall be kept in the case file of the juvenile or the child, one shall be fixed with the index card, a copy shall be kept in an album serially numbered with the negative in another album, and a copy of the photograph shall be sent to the Board or Committee as case may be, as well as to the district or State Child Protection Unit.

(3) In case of a child missing from an institution or in case of lost children received by an institution, a photograph of the child with relevant details shall be sent to the missing person's bureau and the local police station.

**75. Police Officers to be in plain clothes.**—While dealing with a juvenile or a child under the provisions of the Act and the rules made thereunder, except at the time of arrest, the Police Officer shall wear plain clothes and not the police uniform.

**76. Prohibition on the use of handcuffs and fetters.**—No child or the juvenile in conflict with law dealt with under the provisions of the Act and the rules made there under shall be handcuffed or fettered.

**77. Procedure to be followed by a Magistrate not empowered under the Act.**—(1) When any juvenile or child is produced before a Magistrate other than Board or Committee, and the Magistrate is of the opinion that such person is a juvenile or child, he shall record his reasons and send the juvenile or child to the appropriate competent authority.

(2) In case of a juvenile produced before a Magistrate not empowered under this Act, such Magistrate shall direct the case to be transferred to the Board for inquiry and disposal.

(3) In case of a child in need of care and protection produced as a victim of a crime before a Magistrate not empowered under the Act, such Magistrate shall transfer the matter concerning care and protection, rehabilitation and restoration of the child to the appropriate Committee.

**78. Transfer.**—(1) During the inquiry, if it is found that the juvenile or child hails from a place outside the jurisdiction of the Board or Committee, the Board or Committee shall order the transfer of the juvenile or child and send a copy of the order to the State Government or State or District Child Protection Unit:

Provided that:

(i) such transfer is in the best interest of the juvenile or child;

(ii) no child shall be transferred or proposed to be transferred only on the ground that the child has created problems or, has become difficult to be managed in the existing institution or, is suffering from a chronic or terminal illness or, on account of disability;

(iii) such transfer shall only take place after the completion of evidence and cross-examination that may be required in a legal proceeding involving a juvenile or child; and

(iv) the reasons for and circumstances of such transfer are recorded in writing.

(2) The State Government or State or District Child Protection Unit shall accordingly:

(i) send the information of transfer to the appropriate competent authority having jurisdiction over the area where the child is ordered to be transferred by the Board or Committee; and

(ii) send a copy of the information to the Officer-in-Charge of the institution where the child is placed for care and protection at the time of the transfer order.

(3) On receipt of copy of the information from the State Government or State or District Child Protection Unit, the Officer-in-Charge shall arrange to escort the child at government expenses to the place or person as specified in the order.

(4) On such transfer, case file and records of the juvenile or child shall be sent along with the juvenile or child.

**79. Procedure for sending a juvenile or child outside the jurisdiction of the competent authority.**—(1) In the case of a juvenile or a child whose ordinary place of residence lies outside the jurisdiction of the competent authority, and if the competent authority considers it necessary to take action under section 50 of the Act, it shall direct a probation officer or case worker or child welfare officer, as the case may be, to make enquiries as to the fitness and willingness of the relative or other person to receive the juvenile or the child at the ordinary place of residence, and whether such relative or other fit person can exercise proper care and control over the juvenile or the child.

(2) Where a juvenile or child is ordered to be sent to the ordinary place of residence or to a relative or fit person, execution of a bond by the juvenile or child without any surety, in Form VI, is necessary along with an undertaking by the said relative or fit person in Form V or IX as the case may be.

(3) Any breach of a bond or undertaking or of both given under sub-rule (2) of this rule, shall render the juvenile liable to be brought before the competent authority, who may make an order directing the juvenile to be sent to an institution home.

(4) Any juvenile or a child, who is a foreign national and who has lost contact with his family shall also be entitled for protection.

(5) The juvenile or the child, who is a foreign national, shall be repatriated, at the earliest, to the country of his origin in co-ordination with the respective Embassy or High Commission.

(6) The Board or Committee shall keep the Ministry of External Affairs informed about repatriation of every juvenile or child of foreign nationality carried out on the orders of the Board or Committee.

(7) A copy of the order passed by the competent authority under section 50 of the Act shall be sent to—

- (a) the probation officer or child welfare officer who was directed to submit a report under sub-rule (1) of this rule;
- (b) the probation officer or child welfare officer, if any, having jurisdiction over the place where the juvenile or the child is to be sent;
- (c) the competent authority having jurisdiction over the place where the juvenile or the child is to be sent; and
- (d) the relative or the person who is to receive the juvenile or the child.

(8) During the pendency of the order under sub-rule (6) of this rule, the juvenile or the child shall be sent by the competent authority to an observation home or children's home as the case may be.

(9) Where the competent authority considers it expedient to send the juvenile or the child back to his ordinary place of residence under section 50, the competent authority shall inform the relative or the fit person, who is to receive the juvenile or the child accordingly; and shall invite the said relative or fit person to come to the home, to take charge of the juvenile or the child on such date, as may be specified by the competent authority.

(10) The competent authority inviting the said relative or fit person under sub-rule (8) of this rule may also direct, if necessary, the payment to be made by the Officer-in-Charge of the home, of the actual expenses of the relative or fit person's journey both ways, by the appropriate class and the juvenile's or child's journey from the home to his ordinary place of residence, at the time of sending the juvenile or the child.

(11) If the relative or the fit person fails to come to take charge of the juvenile or the child on the specified date, the juvenile or the child shall be taken to his ordinary place of residence by the escort of the observation home and in the case of a girl, at least one escort shall be a female.

**80. State Child Protection Unit.**—The specific functions of the State Child Protection Unit shall include:

(a) implementation of the Act and supervision and monitoring of agencies and institutions under the Act;

(b) set-up, support and monitor the District Child Protection Units;

(c) represent State Child Protection Unit as a member in the Selection Committee for appointment of members of Boards or Committees;

(d) make necessary funds available to the District Child Protection Units for providing or setting up required facilities to implementation the Act;

(e) network and co-ordinate with all government departments to build inter-sectoral linkages on child protection issues, including Departments of Health, Education, Social Welfare, Urban Basic Services, Backward Classes & Minorities, Youth Services, Police, Judiciary, Labour, State AIDS Control Society, among others;

(f) network and co-ordinate with civil society organizations working for the effective implementation of the Act;

(g) training and capacity building of all personnel (Government and Non-government) working under the Act;

(h) establish Minimum Standards of Care and ensure its implementation in all institutions set-up under the Act;

(i) review of the functioning of Committees; and

(j) all other functions necessary for effective implementation of the Act.

**81. District Child Protection Unit.**—(1) The District Child Protection Unit shall co-ordinate and implement all child rights and protection activities at district level.

(2) The specific functions of the District Child Protection Unit shall include:

(a) ensure effective implementation of the Act at district or city levels by supporting creation of adequate infrastructure, such as, setting up Boards, Committees, Special Juvenile Police Units and homes in each district;

(b) identify families at risk and children in need of care and protection;

(c) assess the number of children in difficult circumstances and creating district-specific databases to monitor trends and patterns of children in difficult circumstances;

(d) periodic and regular mapping of all child related services at district for creating a resource directory and making the information available to the Committees and Boards from time to time;

(e) implement family based non-institutional services including sponsorship, foster care, adoption and after care;

(f) ensure setting up of District, Block and Village Level Child Protection Committees for effective implementation of programmes as well as discharge of its functions;

(g) facilitate transfer of children at all levels for either their restoration to their families or placing the child in long or short-term rehabilitation through institutionalization, adoption, foster care and sponsorship;

(h) supporting State Adoption Resource Agency in implementation of family based non-institutional services at district level;

(i) network and co-ordinate with all government departments to build inter-sectoral linkages on child protection issues, including Departments of Health, Education, Social Welfare, Urban Basic Services, Backward Classes & Minorities, Youth Services, Police, Judiciary, Labour, State AIDS Control Society, among others;

(j) network and co-ordinate with civil society organizations working under the Act;

(k) develop parameters and tools for effective monitoring and supervision of agencies and institutions in the district in consultation with experts in child welfare;

(l) supervise and monitor all institutions or agencies providing residential facilities to children in district;

(m) train and build capacity of all personnel (Government and Non-government) implementing the Act to provide effective services to children;

(n) organize quarterly meeting with all stakeholders at district level including CHILDLINE, Specialised Adoption Agencies, Officer-in-Charges of homes, non-governmental organisations and members of public to review the progress and implementation of the Act; and

(o) liaison with the State Child Protection Unit, State Adoption Resource Agency at State level and District Child Protection Units of other districts.

**82. Setting of the Child Welfare Committee.**—(1) The State Government shall set-up by notification in Official Gazette Child Welfare Committees under section 29 of the Act in every district with requisite infrastructure, personnel, and finances for smooth running, as listed below:

(a) the infrastructure shall consist of a sitting hall, a separate room for the Committee, room for office staff, waiting room for children, waiting room for parents or guardian, room for personal interaction between the child or parents and the Committee, a record room, safe drinking water facility and toilets;

(b) the State Government shall provide necessary human resource support for every Committee, including welfare officer, steno-typist or computer operator, peon, safai karamchari.

(2) The allowances of the Chairperson and Members shall be disbursed by the District Child Protection Unit or State Government as per rule 23 of these rules.

**83. Setting up of Juvenile Justice Board.**—The State Government shall set-up by notification in Official Gazette, Juvenile Justice Board in every district, with requisite infrastructure, personnel, besides the Principal Magistrate and Members and Finances as listed below:

(1) Infrastructure shall consist of a Board Room, waiting room for children, a room for Principal Magistrate and Members, a record room, room for Probation Officers, waiting room for parents and visitors, safe drinking water facility and toilets.

(2) The State Government shall provide necessary human resource support for every Board, including probation officer, steno-typist or computer operator, peon, safai karamchari.

**84. Special Juvenile Police Unit.**—(1) The State Government shall appoint a Special Juvenile Police Unit at the District level within four months of the notification of these rules and the unit shall consist of a juvenile or child welfare officer of the rank of police inspector and two paid social workers having experience of working in the field of child welfare, of whom one shall be a woman.

(2) The District Child Protection Unit or the State Government shall provide services of its two social workers to the Special Juvenile Police Unit for discharging their duties.

(3) The juvenile or child welfare officer at the police station shall be a person with aptitude and appropriate training and orientation to handle the cases of juveniles or children in terms of the provisions of the Act.

(4) The transfer and posting of the designated Juvenile or Child Welfare Officer shall be within the Special Juvenile Police Units of other police stations or district unit, unless there is an exceptional case of promotion and in such cases, other police officer must be designated and deputed in the unit so that there is no shortfall.

(5) Special Juvenile Police Unit at district level shall co-ordinate and function as a watch-dog for providing legal protection against all kinds of cruelty, abuse and exploitation of child or juvenile.

(6) The unit shall take serious cognizance of adult perpetrators of crimes against children and see to it that they are without delay apprehended and booked under the appropriate provisions of the law and for this purpose the district level units shall maintain liaison with other units of police station.

(7) The Special Juvenile Police Units shall seek assistance from the voluntary organizations, panchayats and Gram Sabhas or Resident Welfare Associations in identifying juveniles in conflict with law as well as reporting cases of violence against children, child neglect and child abuse.

(8) The Special Juvenile Police Units shall particularly seek assistance from voluntary organizations recognized as protection agencies by the State Government for the purpose of assisting Special Juvenile Police Units and local police stations at the time of apprehension, in preparation of necessary reports, for taking charge of juveniles until production and at the time of production before the Board as per rule 11(12) of these rules.

(9) The Superintendent of Police in a district shall head the Special Juvenile Police Unit and oversee its functioning from time to time.

(10) A Nodal Officer from Police not less than the rank of Inspector-General of Police shall be designated in each State to co-ordinate and upgrade role of police on all issues pertaining to care and protection of children or juveniles under Act.

(11) Any police officer found guilty, after due inquiry, of torturing a child, mentally or physically, shall be liable to be removed from service, besides being prosecuted for the offence.

**85. Honorary or Voluntary Welfare Officers and Probation Officers.**—To augment the existing probation service, honorary or voluntary welfare officers and probation officers may be appointed from the voluntary organization and social workers found fit for the purpose by the competent authority and their services may also be co-opted into the implementation machinery by the orders of the competent authority.

**86. Duties of the Officer-in-Charge of an institution.**—(1) The Officer-in-Charge shall have the primary responsibility of maintaining the institution and shall stay within the institutional premises to be readily available as and when required by the juveniles or children and the staff and in case where an accommodation is not available within the institutional premises, the Officer-in-Charge shall stay at a place in close proximity to the institution till such time that such an accommodation is made available within the institution.

(2) The general duties and functions of the Officer-in-Charge shall include:

(a) compliance with provisions of the Act and the rules and orders made thereunder;

(b) compliance with the orders of the Board or Committee;

(c) providing homely atmosphere of love, affection, care, development and welfare for juveniles or children;

(d) maintaining minimum standards of care in the institution;

(e) proper maintenance of buildings and premises;

(f) security measures and periodical inspection, including daily inspection and rounds of the institution, proper storage and inspection of food stuffs as well as food being served;

(g) supervision and monitoring of juveniles' or children's discipline and well being;

(h) planning implementation and co-ordination of all institutional activities, programmes and operations, including training and treatment programmes or correctional activities as the case may be;

(i) prompt action to meet emergencies;

(j) ensuring accident and fire preventive measures within the institutional premises;

(k) stand-by arrangements for water storage, power plant, emergency lighting;

(l) careful handling of plants and equipments;

(m) segregation of a juvenile or child suffering from contagious or infectious diseases;

(n) observance and follow-up of daily routine;

(o) filing of monthly report of juvenile or child in the case file;

(p) organize local and national festivals in the institution;

(q) organize trips or excursions or picnics for juveniles or children;

(r) preparation of budget and control over financial matters;

(s) allocation of duties to personnel;

(t) supervision over office administration, including attending to personnel welfare and staff discipline;

(u) prompt, firm and considerate handling of all disciplinary matters;

(v) organize the meetings of the Management Cbmmittee set-up under rule 55 of these rules and provide necessary support;

(w) maintenance of all records and registers required under the Act and the rules and monthly verification of the same by the Management Committee set-up under rule 55 of these rules;

(x) liaison, co-ordination and co-operation with the District Child Protection Unit or State Government as and when required; and

(y) co-ordination with the legal officer in the District Child Protection Unit to ensure that every juvenile is legally represented and provided free legal aid and other necessary support or, where the District Child Protection Unit has not been set-up, services of the District or State Legal Services Authority shall be made available.

**87. Duties of a Probation Officer or Child Welfare Officer or Case-Worker.**—(1) Every probation officer or child welfare officer or case-worker shall carry out all directions given by the Board or Committee or concerned authority and shall perform the following duties, functions and responsibilities:—

(a) making social investigation of the juvenile (Form IV) or the child (Form XIII) through personal interview and from the family, social agencies and other sources;

(b) attending the proceedings of the Board or Committee and submitting reports as and when required;

(c) clarifying problems of the juvenile or the child and dealing with their difficulties in institutional life;

(d) participating in the orientation, monitoring, education, vocational and rehabilitation programmes;

(e) establishing co-operation and understanding between the juvenile or the child and the Officer-in-Charge;

(f) assisting the juvenile or the child to develop contacts with family and also providing assistance to family members;

(g) developing a care plan for every child in consultation with the juvenile or child and following up its implementation;

(h) participating in the pre-release programme and helping the juvenile or the child to establish contacts which can provide emotional and social support to juvenile or child after their release;

(i) establishing linkages with voluntary workers and organizations to facilitate rehabilitation and social reintegration of juveniles and to ensure the necessary follow-up;

(j) follow-up of juveniles after their release and extending help and guidance to them;

(k) visiting regularly the residence of the juvenile or child under their supervision and also places of employment or school attended by such juvenile or child and submitting fortnightly reports as prescribed in Form XXI;

(l) accompanying juveniles or children wherever possible, from the office of the Board to observation home, special home, children's home or fit person, as the case may be; and

(m) maintaining case file and such registers as may be specified from time to time.

(2) On receipt of information from the Police or Juvenile or Child Welfare Officer of the Police under clause (b) of section 13 of the Act, the probation officer shall inquire into the antecedents and family history of the juvenile or the child and such other material circumstances, as may be necessary and submit a social investigation report as early as possible, in Form IV or XIII, to the Board.

**88. Duties of House Father or House Mother.**—(1) The general duties, functions and responsibilities of a house father, house mother and other care takers shall be as follows:—

(a) handling juvenile or child with love and affection;

(b) taking proper care and welfare of juvenile or child;

(c) maintaining discipline among the juveniles or children;

(d) maintenance, sanitation and hygiene;

(e) implementing daily routine in an effective manner and ensuring children's involvement;

(f) looking after the security and safety arrangements of the home; and

(g) escorting juveniles or children, whenever they go out of the home.

**89. Disqualification for Officer-in-Charge, probation officer or child welfare officer or case-worker, house father or house mother and other care givers and staff.**—(1) The Officer-in-Charge, probation officer or child welfare officer or case-worker, house father or house mother and other care givers and staff shall not employ a juvenile or child under their supervision or care and protection for their own purposes or take any private service from them.

(2) Any report of physical, sexual or emotional abuse of a juvenile or a child in an institution or outside, by a caregiver, shall hold them liable for disqualification after due inquiry.

**90. Training of personnel.**—(1) The State Government or the Officer-in-Charge shall provide for training of personnel of each category of staff, in keeping with their statutory responsibilities and specific jobs requirements.

(2) The training programme shall include—

(a) orientation and induction training of the newly-recruited staff,

(b) refresher training courses and skill enhancement programmes for all care givers once a year, and

(c) staff conferences, seminars, workshops.

(3) The State Government with the help of the State Child Protection Unit, National Institute of Public Co-operation and Child Development and its Regional Centres shall organize regular training and capacity building of personnel involved in the implementation of the Act and the rules made thereunder.

**91. Selection Committee and its composition.**—The State Government shall constitute a Selection Committee by notification in the Official Gazette, for a period of five years, consisting of the following seven members, namely:—

(a) a retired judge of High Court as the Chairperson;

(b) one representative from the concerned Department of State Government not below the rank of Director as the Member-Secretary;

(c) two representatives from a reputed non-governmental organization, working in the area of child welfare;

(d) two representatives from academic bodies concerned with social work, psychology, sociology, child development, education, law, criminology and with experience of working on children's issues; and

(e) a representative of the National or State Human Rights Commission or, National or State Commission for Protection of Child Rights or, National or State Commission for Women.

**92. Functions of the Selection Committee.**—(1) (a) In making appointment of members of the Board or Committee, the Selection Committee shall take into consideration the applications received in this regard in response to a public advertisement to this effect by the District or State Child Protection Unit or the State Government; and

(b) The Selection Committee shall select and recommend a panel of names to the State Child Protection Unit or State Government for appointment as members of the Board or Committee from amongst the applications received.

(2) In the event of any complaint against a member of the Board or Committee, the Selection Committee shall hold necessary inquiry and recommend termination of appointment of such member to the State Child Protection Unit or State Government, if required.

(3) (a) The Selection Committee, at the time of recommending names for appointment as member of Board or Committee shall also prepare a panel of names for each Board or Committee to fill in vacancies, which may arise during the tenure of the Board or Committee.

(b) In the event of a vacancy in the Board or Committee, the District Child Protection Unit shall inform the State Child Protection Unit or State Government for filling up such vacancy.

(c) The State Child Protection Unit or State Government shall fill the vacancies on the basis of the panel of names recommended by the Selection Committee.

(4) The Selection Committee shall recommend names for constitution of the State or District or City Level Inspection Committees as required under section 35 of the Act.

**93. Advisory Boards.**—(1) The Central Government and the State Government shall constitute Advisory Board at Central, State, District, City levels for a period of three years.

(2) The Central Advisory Board shall be constituted through the Union Ministry of Women and Child Development.

(3) The State Government shall constitute the State Advisory Board, District Advisory Board and the City Advisory Board.

(4) All the Advisory Boards shall hold at least two meetings in a year.

(5) These Advisory Boards shall inspect the various institutional or non-institutional services in their respective jurisdictions; and the recommendations made by them, shall be acted upon by the Central Government and the State Government.

(6) The Central Government through the Central Ministry of Women and Child Development shall set-up the Central Advisory Board to be headed by the Minister concerned and shall consist of the Secretary of the Ministry aforesaid, representatives from State Governments, representative members from the competent authority, leading non-governmental organisations, experts in child or juvenile care, children's institution and academic institutions as members.

(7) A designated official of the Central Ministry of Women and Child Development shall function as the Member-Secretary of the Central Advisory Board.

(8) The State Government, through the Selection Committee constituted under rule 91 of these rules, shall set-up State, District and City level Advisory Boards, which shall consist of representatives of the State Government, members of the competent authority, academic institutions, locally respectable and spirited citizens, representatives of non-governmental organizations.

(9) The District or City level Advisory Board constituted in terms of sub-section (3) of section 62 of the Act shall also function as the inspection committee under section 35 of the Act.

(10) The termination, resignation, or other vacancy caused in an advisory board and appointment of new members therein shall be done in the same manner as is done in case of the competent authority.

**94. Openness and Transparency.**—(1) All Children's homes shall be open to visitors with the permission of the Officer-in-Charge and the Committee or Officer-in-Charge as the case may be, may consider appropriate to allow representatives of local self-government, voluntary organizations, social workers, researchers, medicos, academicians, prominent personalities, media and any other persons as visitors, as the Officer-in-Charge considers appropriate keeping in view the security, welfare and the interest of the children.

(2) The Officer-in-Charge of the home shall encourage active involvement of local community in improving the conditions in the homes, if, the members of the community want to serve the institution or want to contribute through their expertise.

(3) The Officer-in-Charge shall maintain a visitors book and the remarks of the visitors given therein shall be considered by the advisory inspecting authority.

(4) While visiting an institution, the visitors will not say or do anything that undermines the authority of the Officer-in-Charge or is in contravention of the Act or rules or impinges on the dignity of the children.

(5) The visitors may be allowed to visit observation homes and special homes with the permission of the competent authority.

**95. Juvenile Justice Fund.**—(1) The State Government shall create a Fund at the State level under section 61 of the Act to be called the 'Juvenile Justice Fund' (hereinunder referred to as the Fund) for the welfare and rehabilitation of the juvenile or the child dealt with under the provisions of the Act.

(2) In addition to donations, contributions or subscriptions coming under sub-section (2) of section 61, the Central Government shall also make contribution to the Fund.

(3) The Fund shall be applied:

(a) to implement programmes for the welfare, rehabilitation and restoration of juveniles or children;

(b) to pay grant-in-aid to non-governmental organizations;

(c) to meet the expenses of State Advisory Board and its purpose;

(d) to do all other things that are incidental and necessary for the above purposes.

(4) The management and administration of the Fund shall be under the control of the State Advisory Board under sub-section (3) of section 61 of the Act.

(5) The assets of the Fund shall include all such grants and contributions, recurring or non-recurring, from the Central Government and State Government or any other statutory or non-statutory bodies set-up by the Central or State Government as well as the voluntary donations from any individual or organization.

(6) All withdrawals shall be made by cheques or requisitions, as the case may be, signed by the secretary-cum-treasurer and in the case of amounts exceeding rupees one thousand, they shall be signed duly by the secretary-cum-treasurer and a member of the board of management to be nominated by the State Advisory Board.

(7) The regular accounts shall be kept of all money and properties, and all incomes and expenditure of the Fund and shall be audited by a notified firm of Chartered Accountants, or any other recognized authorities as may be appointed by the Board.

(8) The auditors shall also certify the expenditure from the Fund made by the secretary-cum-treasurer.

(9) All contracts and other assurances shall be in the name of the board of management and signed on their behalf by the secretary-cum-treasurer and one member of the board of the management authorised by it for the purpose.

(10) The board of management shall invest for the time being the proceeds of sale or other disposal of the property, as well as any money or property not immediately required to be used to serve the objective of the Fund, in any one or more of the modes of investment authorised by law for the investment of trust moneys as the board of management may think proper.

(11) The board of management may delegate to one or more of the members such of its powers, which in its opinion are merely a procedural arrangement.

**96. Application of these rules.**—It is hereby declared that until the new rules conforming to these rules are framed by the State Government concerned under section 68 of the Act, these rules shall *mutatis mutandis* apply in that State.

**97. Pending cases.**—(1) No juvenile in conflict with law or a child shall be denied the benefits of the Act and the rules made thereunder.

(2) All pending cases which have not received a finality shall be dealt with and disposed of in terms of the provisions of the Act and the rules made thereunder.

(3) Any juvenile in conflict with law, or a child shall be given the benefits under sub-rule (1) of this rule, and it is hereby clarified that such benefits shall be made available to all those accused who were juvenile or a child at the time of commission of an offence, even if they cease to be a juvenile or a child during the pendency of any inquiry or trial.

(4) While computing the period of detention or stay or sentence of a juvenile in conflict with law or of a child, all such period which the juvenile or the child has already spent in custody, detention, stay or sentence of imprisonment shall be counted as a part of the period of stay or detention or sentence of imprisonment contained in the final order of the court or the Board.

**98. Disposed off cases of juveniles in conflict with law.**—The State Government or as the case may be the Board may, either *suo motu* or on an application made for the purpose, review the case of a person or a juvenile in conflict with law, determine his juvenility in terms of the provisions contained in the Act and rule 12 of these rules and pass an appropriate order in the interest of the juvenile in conflict with law under section 64 of the Act, for the immediate release of the juvenile in conflict with law whose period of detention or imprisonment has exceeded the maximum period provided in section 15 of the said Act.

**99. Disposal of records or documents.**—The records or documents in respect of a juvenile or a child or a juvenile in conflict with law shall be kept in a safe place for a period of seven years and no longer, and thereafter be destroyed by the Officer-in-Charge or Board or Committee, as the case may be.

**100. Repeal.**—The Juvenile Justice (Care and Protection of Children) Rules, 2001, notified *vide* F.No.1-3/2001-SD, dated the 22nd June, 2001 in the Gazette of India, Extraordinary, Part I, Section 1 of the same date is hereby repealed.

*SCHEDULE I*

(*See* rule 41)

## CLOTHING, BEDDING, TOILETRIES AND OTHER ARTICLES

(1) Juveniles or children shall be provided with the following articles:—

**Bedding**

| S.No. | Article | Quantity to be provided per child |
|---|---|---|
| 1. | Towels | 4 per Years |
| 2. | Cotton Bed Sheets | 2 per 2 Years |
| 3. | Pillow (Cotton stuffed) | 1 per 2 Years |
| 4. | Pillow Covers | 2 per 2 Years |
| 5. | Woollen blankets | 2 per 2 years |
| 6. | Cotton Durry | 2 per 2 years |
| 7. | Cotton filled quilt | 1 per 2 years (in cold regions) |
| 8. | Mattress | 1 per 2 years |
| 9. | Mosquito Net | 1 per 2 years |

**Clothing for girls**

| | | |
|---|---|---|
| 1. | Skirts & Blouse or Salwar Kameez or Half Sari with blouses and petticoats | 5 sets per year for girls depending on age and regional preferences |
| 2. | Banyans (1 Metre each) | 6 per year for younger girls |
| 3. | Brassieres | 6 per year for older girls |
| 4. | Panties (1 Metre Cloth each) | 6 per year |
| 5. | Sanitary Towels | 12 packs per year for older girls |
| 6. | Woollen Sweaters | 2 in 2 years (in cold regions) |
| 7. | Woollen Shawls | 1 in 2 years (in cold regions) |

**Clothing for boys**

| | | |
|---|---|---|
| 1. | Shirts | 5 sets per year |
| 2. | Shorts | 5 sets per year for younger boys |
| 3. | Pants | 5 sets per year for older boys |
| 4. | Vest | 4 sets per year |
| 5. | Underwear | 4 sets per year |
| 6. | Woolen Jerseys | 2 in 2 years (for cold regions) |
| 7. | Scarfs | 2 in 2 years (for cold regions) |

**Miscellaneous Articles**

| | | |
|---|---|---|
| 1. | Slippers | 1 pair per year |
| 2. | Shoes | 1 pair per year |
| 3. | School Uniform | 2 sets per year for children attending outside schools |
| 4. | School Shoes | 1 pair per year for children attending outside schools |
| 5. | School Bag and Stationery | 1 set per year for children attending outside schools |
| 6. | Handkerchiefs | 6 per year |

**Note.**—(a) In addition to the clothing specified above, each child shall be provided, once in three years, with a suit consisting of one white shirt, one pair of Khaki shorts or pants, one pair of white canvas shoes and one blazer (for cold regions) for use during ceremonial occasions. In the case of girls it shall be one white half sari or one salwar kameez or one white skirt and one white blouse, a pair of white canvas shoes and a blazer (for cold regions).

(2) In every hospital attached to the institution where there is provision for in-patient cots, the following scale has to be followed:—

| *Night clothing & bedding* | *Scale for supply* |
|---|---|
| 1. Mattress | One per bed per 3 years |
| 2. Cotton Bed Sheets | Four per bed per year |
| 3. Pillows | One per bed per two year |
| 4. Pillow Covers | Four per bed per year |
| 5. Woollen blankets | One per bed per 2 years |
| 6. Pyjamas and loose shirts (Hospital type for boys) | 3 pairs per child per year |
| 7. Skirts and blouses or salwar kameez for girls | 3 pairs per child per year |
| 8. Cotton durry | One per bed per three years |

**Note.**—(i) When a child is admitted as an in-patient in the institution Hospital, the Institution Doctor shall issue the in-patient with the hospital clothing, the clothes on body being preserved, duly washed and handed back, at the time of the child's discharge from the hospital.

(ii) Each child shall be provided with Kit Box or a Locker, as per convenience and necessity.

(iii) The Superintendent shall make arrangements for two-tier bed system in place of conventional cots, as per convenience and necessity.

(3) *Toiletry:* Every resident of the Home shall be issued with oil, soap and other material for in accordance with the following scales:—

| | |
|---|---|
| Hair oil for grooming the hair | 100 mgs per month |
| Toilet soap or carbolic soap | 1 large bar per month |
| Tooth paste and brush | 1 Brush per 3 months 50 gms paste per month |
| Comb | 1 per year |

**Note.**—(a) For washing of cloth and towels, bed-sheet etc., the following scale may be followed:—

| | |
|---|---|
| (i) Washing Soap | 1 soap for one month (125 gms) |
| (ii) Whitening/bleaching agent | to the extent required only for white clothing |

Provided, however, the hospital clothing is not mixed with other clothing at the time of washing and if necessary, the Superintendent can issue the above items separately for washing of hospital clothing.

(b) The children attending school outside the institution may be issued with one additional bar of washing soap (100 gms) per head per month for washing their school uniform.

(4) The following items shall be provided for maintaining the Homes in a healthy and sanitary condition:

| **Item** | **Scale of supply** |
|---|---|
| (1) Broom Stick | 25 to 40 Nos. per month depending on the area of the institution |
| (2) DDT spray | As per the institution Doctor's advice |
| (3) Effective bugs killing agent | As required |
| (4) Phenyl and cleaning acid (daily) | Depending on the area of lavatories to be cleaned as per institution Doctor's advice |

SCHEDULE II

(*See* rule 44)

**NUTRITION AND DIET SCALE**

| *Name of the articles of diet* | *Scale per head per day* |
|---|---|
| (1) Rice/Wheat/Ragi/Jowar | 600 Gms, (700 Gms for 16-18 yrs age) of which atleast 100 gms to be either Wheat or Ragi or Jowar |
| (2) Dal/Rajma/Chana | 120 Gms |
| (3) Edible Oil | 25 Gms |
| (4) Onion | 25 Gms |
| (5) Salt | 25 Gms |
| (6) Turmeric | 05 Gms |
| (7) Coriander Seed Powder | 05 Gms |
| (8) Ginger | 05 Gms |
| (9) Garlic | 05 Gms |
| (10) Tamarind/Mango powder | 05 Gms |
| (11) Milk (at breakfast) | 150 ml |
| (12) Dry Chillies | 05 Gms |
| (13) Vegetables Leafy | 100 Gms |
| Non-leafy | 130 Gms |
| (14) Curd or Butter Milk | 100 Gms/Ml |
| (15) Chicken once a week or Eggs 4 days | 115 Gms |
| (16) Jaggery & Ground Nut Seeds or Paneer (vegetarian only) | 60 Gms each (100 Gms for paneer) Once in a week |
| (17) Sugar | 40 Gms |
| ***Following items for 50 Children per day*** | |
| (18) Pepper | 25 Gms |
| (19) Jeera Seeds | 25 Gms |
| (20) Black Gramdal | 50 Gms |
| (21) Mustard Seeds | 50 Gms |
| (22) Ajwain Seeds | 50 Gms |
| ***On Chicken Day for 10 Kg. of Chicken*** | |
| (23) Garam Masala | 10 Gms |
| (24) Kopra | 150 Gms |
| (25) Khas Khas | 150 Gms |
| (26) Groundnut Oil | 500 Gms |
| ***For Sick Children*** | |
| (27) Bread | 500 Gms |
| (28) Milk | 500 Ml |
| ***Other Items*** | |
| (29) LP Gas for Cooking only | |

**Instructions:**

**(2) Variation in Diet**

(a) Three varieties of Dal *i.e.,* Toor (Tuvari), Moong (Green Gram) and Chana (Bengal Gram) may be issued alternatively.

(b) The Superintendent may also arrange to substitute chicken with fish at his discretion, provided that there is no extra expenditure to Government.

(c) On non-vegetarian days, vegetarian children shall be issued with either 60 Gms of Jaggery and 60 Gms of Groundnut seeds per head in the shape of laddus or any other sweet dish or 100 gms paneer.

(d) Potatoes shall be issued in lieu of vegetables once in a week.

(e) Leafy vegetables such as Fenugreek (Methi), Spinach (Palak), Sarson (Mustard leaves) Gongura Thotakura or any other saag etc., may also be issued once in a week. If a kitchen garden is attached to any institution leafy vegetables, in addition to drumstick trees, curry leaves trees and coriander leaves, should be grown and issued and the Superintendent should try to issue variety of vegetables and see that the same vegetable is not repeated for at least a period of one week.

(f) The Superintendent may make temporary alternations in the scale of diet in individual cases when considered necessary by him, or on the institution Doctor's advice subject to the condition that the scale laid down is not exceeded.

**(3) Meal Timing and Menu:**

(a) Breakfast after 8:00 a.m.

(i) Upma or chapattis made of Wheat or Ragi or any other dish.

(ii) Chutneys from Gongura or fresh curry leave or fresh coriander or Coconut and Putnadal etc., Dal/vegetable may be issued as a dish.

(iii) Milk

(iv) Any seasonal fruit in sufficient quantity

(b) Lunch at 1:00 P.M. and Dinner After 7:00 P.M.

(i) Rice/Chapattis or combination of both

(ii) Vegetable Curry

(iii) Sambar or Dal

(iv) Butter Milk or curd

**(4) Others:**

(a) Depending on the season, the Superintendent shall have the discretion to alter the time for distribution of food.

(b) On the advise of the Institution Doctor, every sick child who is prevented from taking regular food, on account of his ill-health, may be issued with medical diet, as indicated in diet scale.

(c) Extra diet for nourishment like milk, eggs, sugar and fruits shall be issued to the children on the advice of the Institution Doctor in addition to the regular diet, to pick up weight or for other health reasons and for the purpose of calculation of the daily ration, the sick children shall be excluded from the day's strength.

(d) On the following national and festival occasions, sweet dishes may be distributed to all the children at the Home at the rate fixed by the Commissioner, from time to time.

1. Republic Day (26th January)
2. Ambedkar's Birthday (14th April)

3. Independence Day (15th August)
4. Mahatma Gandhi's Birth Day (2nd October)
5. Children's Day (14th November)
6. Child Rights Day (20th November)
7. Dussehra (Vijayadasami)
8. Deepavali
9. Ramzan (Id-Ul-Fitr)
10. Bakrid (Id-Ul-Zuha)
11. Christmas (25th December)

The States may specify additional festivals depending upon local preferences.

## FORM I

[Rule 13(1)(c)]

## SUPERVISION ORDER

When the Juvenile is placed under the care of a parent, guardian or other fit person/ fit institution Profile No. of............................................20........................................ .

Whereas (name of the juvenile/) has this day found to have committed an offence and has been placed under the care of (name)..................................................(address) ............................................... on executing a bond by he said ............................................ and the Board is satisfied that it is expedient to deal with the said juvenile by making an order placing him/her under supervision.

It is hereby ordered that the said juvenile be placed under the supervision of...................................................probation officer/case worker, for a period of ..............................................................subject to the following conditions:—

1. that the juvenile along with the copies of the order and the bond executed by the said.........................................................................shall be produced before the probation officer/caseworker named therein............................................. .
2. that the juvenile shall be submitted to the supervision of the aforesaid probation officer/case worker.
3. that the juvenile shall reside at...........................for a period of................. .
4. that the juvenile shall not be allowed to quit the district jurisdiction of.........................without the permission of the probation officer/case-worker.
5. that the juvenile shall not be allowed to associate with bad characters.
6. that the juvenile shall live honestly and peacefully; and will go to school regularly/endeavour to earn an honest livelihood.
7. that the juvenile shall attend the attendance centre regularly.
8. that the person under whose care the juvenile is placed shall arrange for the proper care, education and welfare of the juvenile.
9. that the preventive measures will be taken by the person under whose care the juvenile is placed to see that the juvenile does not commit any offence punishable by any law in India.
10. that the juvenile shall be prevented from taking narcotic drugs or psychotropic substances or any other intoxicants.
11. That the directions given by the probation officer/case-worker from time to time, for the due observance of the conditions mentioned above, shall be carried out.

Dated this............................................day of...........................................20......... .

..................

(signature)

Principal Magistrate, Juvenile Justice Board

Additional, conditions, if any may be inserted by the Juvenile Justice Board

## FORM II

[Rule 13(l)(d)]

Order of detention under sub-section..................of section.............., sub-section ...........................of section..........................and sub-section.........of section......... .

To

The Officer in charge

...................................

...................................

Whereas on the...........................day of.................................20........., ..................... .................(name of the juvenile), son/daughter of..............................aged................, residing at..........................................being found in Profile No. ..............................to be juvenile in conflict with law/section..............................is ordered by me..................... Principal Magistrate, Juvenile Justice Board under section..................................of Juvenile Justice Act, 2000 to be kept in the Observation Home/Special Home/ .................................................................................for a period of..................

This is to authorize and require you to receive the said juvenile; into your charge, and to keep him/her in the Observation Home/Special Home/..........................for the aforesaid order to be carried into execution according to law.

Given under my hand and the seal of Juvenile Justice Board

This......................................day of......................................20.........

..................

(signature)

Principal Magistrate, Juvenile Justice Board

Encl:

Copy of the judgment, if any, or orders, particulars of home and case-history and individual care plan, if any:

Strike which is not required.

## FORM III

[Rules 13(1)(e) and (5)]

### ORDER OF SOCIAL INVESTIGATION/INQUIRY

To

Probation Officer/Case-Worker/Person in-charge of Voluntary Organization/Case-Worker

---

Whereas a report/complaint under section..............................of the Juvenile Justice (Care and Protection of Children) Act, 2000 has been received from.................in respect of..............................(name of the juvenile), son/daughter of....................................... approximate age.................residing at......................................................, who has been produced before the Board.

You are hereby directed to enquire into the social antecedents, family background and circumstances of the alleged offence by the said juvenile and submit your social investigation report on or before.................or within such time allowed to you by the Board.

You are also hereby directed to consult an expert in child psychology, psychiatric treatment or counselling for their expert opinion if necessary and submit such report along with your Social Investigation Report.

Dated this.........................day of...............................20............. .

..................

(signature)

Principal Magistrate, Juvenile Justice Board

# FORM IV

[Rules 13(5) and 87(1)(a) and (2)]

## SOCIAL INVESTIGATION REPORT

Sl. No. ...........................

Submitted to the Juvenile Justice Board.....................................................(address).

Probation Department/Concerned State Government Authority/Voluntary Organisation..................................................................(Signature and Stamp)

Profile No.

Under section:

Title of Profile:

Police Station:

Nature of offence charged:

---

| | |
|---|---|
| Name | Religion |
| Father's Name | Caste |
| Permanent Address | Year of birth |
| Last address before apprehension | Age |
| | Sex |

---

Previous institutional/case history and individual care plan, if any

FAMILY

| Members of family | Name | Age | Health | Education | Occupation | Monthly earnings | Disabilities | Any other *e.g.* social habits |
|---|---|---|---|---|---|---|---|---|
| Father | | | | | | | | |
| Step-Father | | | | | | | | |
| Mother | | | | | | | | |
| Step-mother | | | | | | | | |
| Siblings | | | | | | | | |
| Any other legal guardian/relative | | | | | | | | |

If married, relevant particulars

..........................................................................................................................

Other near relatives or agencies

Interested.................................................................................................................

Attitude towards religion normal

And ethical code of the home etc.........................................................................

Social and economic status..................................................................................

Delinquency record of members of family............................................................

Present living conditions...................................................................................................
Relationship between parents/
Parents and children especially
With the juvenile under investigation.............................................................................
Other factors of importance if any..................................................................................

**JUVENILES HISTORY**

Mental condition
(Present and past)................................................................................................
Physical condition
(Present and past)................................................................................................
Habits, interests
(moral, recreational etc.)....................................................................................
Outstanding characteristics and personality traits...........................................................
Companions and their influence.........................................................................................
Truancy from home, if any................................................................................................
School (attitude towards school, teachers, class mates and *vice-versa*)............................
..........................................................................................................................................
Work record (jobs held, reasons for leaving, vocational interests, attitude towards job or employers)................................................................................................................
Neighbourhood and neighbours report..................................................................................
Parent's attitude towards discipline in the home and child's reaction..........................
..........................................................................................................................................
Any other remarks

---

**RESULT OF INQUIRY**

Emotional factors
Physical condition
Intelligence
Social and economic factors
Religious factors
Suggested causes of the problems
Analysis of the case including reasons for delinquency
Opinion of experts consulted
Recommendation regarding treatment and its Plan by Probation Officer

..........................................................................
Signature of the Probation Officer/Case-Worker

## FORM V

[Rules 15(5) and 79(2)]

### UNDERTAKING/BOND TO BE EXECUTED BY A PARENT/GUARDIAN/ RELATIVE/FIT PERSON IN WHOSE CARE A JUVENILE IS PLACED

Whereas I..................................being the parent, guardian, relative or fit person under whose care...................................(name of the juvenile) has been ordered to be placed by the Juvenile Justice Board..............................., have been directed by the said Board to execute an undertaking/bond with surety in the sum of Rs. .............. (Rupees..............................................................) or without surety. I hereby bind myself on the said...........................................................being placed under my care. I shall have the said....................................................properly taken care of and I do further bind myself to be responsible for the good behaviour of the said...............................................

and to observe the following conditions for a period of...............................years w.e.f................. .

1. that I shall not change my place of residence without giving previous intimation in writing to the Juvenile Justice Board through the Probation Officer/Case-Worker;
2. that I shall not remove the said juvenile from the limits of the jurisdiction of the Juvenile Justice Board without previously obtaining the written permission of the Board;
3. that I shall send the said juvenile daily to school/to such vocation as is approved by the Board unless prevented from so doing by circumstances beyond control;
4. that I shall send the said juvenile to an Attendance Centre regularly unless prevented from doing so by circumstances beyond my control;
5. that I shall report immediately to the Board whenever so required by it;
6. that I shall produce the said juvenile in my care before the Board, if he/she does not follow the orders of Board or his/her behaviour is beyond control;
7. that I shall render all necessary assistance to the Probation Officer/Case-Worker to enable him to carry out the duties of supervision;
8. in the event of my making default herein, I undertake to produce myself before the Board for appropriate action or bind myself, as the case may be, to forfeit to Government the sum of Rs. ................(Rupees................................................).

Dated this..................................day of..........................20...........

.......................................................................................

Signature of person executing the Undertaking/Bond.

(Signed before me)

Principal Magistrate, Juvenile Justice Board

Additional conditions, if any, by the Juvenile Justice Board may be entered numbering them properly;

(Where a bond with sureties is to executed add)

I/We.............................................of........................................................(place of residence with full particulars) hereby declare myself/ourselves as surety/sureties for the aforesaid..........................................(name of the person executing the undertaking/bond) to adhere to the terms and conditions of this undertaking/bond. In case of ..........................................(name of the person executing the bond) making fault therein, I/We hereby bind myself/ourselves jointly or severally to forfeit to government the sum of Rs.................(Rupees..........................................................................) dated this the ................day of................20................in the presence of.............................................. .

........................................

Signature of Surety(ties)

(Signed before me)

....................................

Principal Magistrate, Juvenile Justice Board

## FORM VI

[Rules 15(6) and 79(2)]

## PERSONAL BOND BY JUVENILE/CHILD

Personal Bond to be signed by juvenile/child who has been ordered under Clause................of sub-section..........................................of section......................of the Act.

Whereas, I..........................................................inhabitant of...............................(give full particulars such as house number, road, village/town, tehsil, district, state) ...............................have been ordered to be sent back/restored to my native place by the Juvenile Justice Board/Child Welfare Committee.........................................................under section............................of the Juvenile Justice (Care and Protection of Children) Act, 2000 on my entering into a personal bond under sub-rule...............of rule...............and sub-rule...............of rule...............of these Rules to observe the conditions mentioned herein below. Now, therefore, I do solemnly promise to abide by these conditions during the period....................................... .

I hereby bind myself as follows:—

1. That during the period...............I shall not ordinarily leave the village/town/ district to which I am sent and shall not ordinarily return to..........................or go anywhere else beyond the said district without the prior permission of the Board/ Committee;
2. That during the said period I shall attend school/vocational training in the village/town or in the said district to which I am sent;
3. That in case of my attending school/vocational training at any other place in the said district I shall keep the Board/Committee informed of my ordinary place of residence.

I hereby acknowledge that I am aware of the above conditions which have been read over/explained to me and that I accept the same.

(Signature or thumb impression of the juvenile/child)

Certified that the conditions specified in the above order have been read over/ explained to (Name of juvenile/child)....................................................and that he/she has accepted them as the conditions upon which his/her period of detention/placement in safe custody may be revoked.

Certified accordingly that the said juvenile/child has been released/relived on the......................................... .

...............................................................................

Signature and Designation of the certifying authority
*i.e.* Officer-in-Charge of the institution

## FORM VII

[Rule 17(10)]

## DISCHARGE ORDER

I.........................................name and designation of the discharging authority...............................State Government/Union Territory Administration, do by this order permit..............................son/daughter of..................................................................... residence..............................................Profile Number..............................who was ordered to be detained/placed in a observation home/special home/after care home by the Juvenile Justice Board..............................under section...............of the Juvenile Justice (Care and Protection of Children) Act, 2000, for a term of...............on the...............day of...............20...............and who is now in the...............home, at..............................to be discharged from the said...............home and supervision and the authority of....................................................during the remaining period of stay.

This order is granted subject to the conditions hereon, upon the breach of any of which it shall be liable to be revoked.

Dated........................ ..........................................................................

Place......................... Signature and Designation of Releasing Authority

**Conditions:**

1. The discharged person shall proceed to...............and live under the supervision and authority of...............until the expiry of the period of his/her detention unless the remission is sooner cancelled.
2. He/She shall not, without the consent of the...............remove himself/herself from that place or any other place, which may be named by the said.......................... .

3. He/she shall obey such instruction as he/she may receive from the said..............................with regard to punctual and regular attendance at school/ vocation or otherwise.
4. He/She shall attend the Attendance Centre located at..............................regularly.
5. He/She shall abstain from committing any offense and shall lead a sober and industrious life to the satisfaction of............... .
6. In the event of his/her committing a breach of any of the above conditions the remission of the period of detention hereby granted shall be liable to be cancelled and on such cancellation he/she shall be dealt with under sub-section (3) of section 59 of the Juvenile Justice (Care & Protection of Children) Act, 2000.

I hereby acknowledge that I am aware of the above conditions which have been read over/explained to me and that I accept the same.

..........................................................................

(Signature or mark of the released juvenile)

Certified that the conditions specified in the above order have been read over/ explained to (Name of juvenile/child)..............................and that he/she has accepted them as the conditions upon which his/her period of detention may be revoked.

Certified accordingly that the said juvenile/child has been discharged on the..................... .

..........................................................................

Signature and Designation of the certifying authority
*i.e.* Officer-in-Charge of the institution

## FORM VIII
[Rule 27(17)]
## SUPERVISION ORDER

When the Child is placed under the case of a parent/guardian or other fit person

Case No..........................................................of...................................20..............

Whereas (name of the child)........................................has this day been found to be in need of care and protection, and has been placed under the care and supervision of (name)..............................(address)..............................on executing a bond by the said...................................and the Committee is satisfied that it is expedient to deal with the said child by making an order placing him/her under supervision.

It is hereby ordered that the said child be placed under the supervision of (name)...............................................(address).......................................................for a period of.........................subject to the following conditions that:—

1. the child along with the copies of the order and the bond, if any, executed by the said..............................shall be produced before the Committee as and when required by the person executing the bond.
2. the child shall be placed under the supervision of the aforesaid parent/guardian/ fit person.
3. the child shall reside at..............................for a period of...............
4. the child shall not be allowed to quit the district jurisdiction of...................with the permission of the Committee.
5. the child shall go to school regularly/endeavour to earn an honest livelihood.
6. the person under whose care the child is placed shall arrange for the proper care, education and welfare of the child.
7. the child shall not be allowed to associate with undesirable characters and shall be prevented from coming in conflict with law.
8. the child shall be prevented from taking narcotic drugs or psychotropic substances or any other intoxicants.

9. the directions given by the Committee from time to time, for the due observance of the conditions mentioned above, shall be carried out.

Dated this........................day of............................20...............

.................

(Signature)

Chairperson, Child Welfare Committee

- Additional conditions, if any may be interested by the Child Welfare Committee

## FORM IX

[Rules 27(17) and 79(2)]

### UNDERTAKING BY THE PARENT OR 'FIT PERSON' TO WHOM CHILD IS RESTORED

I...............................................resident of House No. ........................................Street ........................Village/Town...............District..........................State..........................do hereby declare that I am willing to take charge of (name of the child)........................................Aged..............under the orders of the Child Welfare Committee..........................subject to the following terms and conditions:—

(i) If his/her conduct is unsatisfactory I shall at once inform the Committee.

(ii) I shall do my best for the welfare and education of the said child as long as he/she remains in my charge and shall make proper provision for his/her maintenance.

(iii) In the event of his/her illness, he/she shall have proper medical attention in the nearest hospital

(iv) I undertake to produce him/her before the competent authority as and when required.

Dated this..............day of....................20............

................

Signature

Signature and address of witness(es)

(Signed before me)

Chairperson, Child Welfare Committee

## FORM X

[Rule 27(18)]

### ORDER OF SHORT-TERM PLACEMENT PENDING INQUIRY

Name of the child :

Sex :

Age :

Father's Name :

Mother's Name :

Address :

Date of receiving by Organization/Institution :

Produced by :

This is to authorize and direct you to receive the said child in your charge, and keep her/him in the Shelter Home/Children's Home for care and protection under section 33(1) of the Juvenile Justice Act, 2000.

Next Date:

..................

(Signature)

Chairperson/Member

Child Welfare Committee

## FORM XI

[Rule 27(19)]

## ORDER OF RESTORATION OF A CHILD TO AN INSTITUTION

To

The Officer-in-Charge

Whereas on the..........................day of..........................20...............(name of the child) ..............................................., son/daughter of..................................aged................residing at................................being in care and protection under section 33(4) of the Juvenile Justice (Care and Protection) Act, 2000 is ordered by the Child Welfare Committee....................................................., to be kept in the Children's Home/Shelter Home..............................................................for a period of.......................... .

This is to authorize and require you to receive the said child in your charge, and to kept him/her in the Children's Home/Shelter Home.....................................for the aforesaid order to be carried into execution according to law.

Given under my hand and the seal of Child Welfare Committee.

This..............................day of................................20.......... ..................

(Signature)
Chairperson/Member
Child Welfare Committee

Encl:

Copy of the orders, particulars of home and previous record, case-history and individual care plan, whichever is applicable:

## FORM XII

[Rule 28(1)]

## ORDER FOR ENQUIRY

To

Child Welfare Officer/Person in-charge of Voluntary Organization/Social Worker/ Case-Worker

---

Whereas a report under section..........................of the Juvenile Justice (Care and Protection of Children) Act, 2000 has been received from.........................................in respect of (name of the child)..............................., aged (approximate).........., son/daughter of.............................................residing at..............................., who has been produced before the Committee under section...............of the Juvenile Justice (Care and Protection of Children) Act, 2000.

You are hereby directed to enquire into the social and family background of the said child and submit your inquiry report on or before..........................or within such time allowed to you by the Committee.

You are also hereby directed to consult an expert in child psychology, psychiatric treatment or counselling for their expert opinion if necessary and submit such report along with your Inquiry Report.

You are hereby directed to enquire into the character and social antecedents of the said juvenile and submit your social investigation report on or before.................................. or within such time allowed to you by the Board/Committee.

Dated this...........................day of.........................20.......... . ..................

(Signature)
Chairperson/Member
Child Welfare Committee

SEAL

## FORM XIII

[Rules 28(3); 33(3)(g)(ii) and (4)(f); 87(1)(a) and (2)]

## FORMAT FOR INQUIRY REPORT

Sl. No. ........................

Produced before the Child Welfare Committee..........................................(address).

Case No.

Concerned Government Department/Voluntary Organisation

Category of child in need of care and protection:

| | |
|---|---|
| Name | Religion |
| Father's Name | Caste |
| Permanent Address | Year of birth |
| Address of last residence | Age |
| | Sex |

Previous institutional/case history and individual care plan, if any

FAMILY

| Members of family | Name | Age | Health | Education | Occupation | Monthly earnings | Disabilities | Any other *e.g.* social habits |
|---|---|---|---|---|---|---|---|---|
| Father | | | | | | | | |
| Step-Father | | | | | | | | |
| Mother | | | | | | | | |
| Step-mother | | | | | | | | |
| Siblings | | | | | | | | |
| Any other legal guardian/ relative | | | | | | | | |

If married, relevant particulars

..........................................................................................

Other near relatives or agencies interested..........................................................................

Attitude towards religion normal and ethical code of the home etc. ..............................

Social and economic status..................................................................

Delinquency record of members of family......................................................

Present living conditions.....................................................................

Relationship between parent/ parents and children especially with the said child...........................................................

Other factors of importance if any..........................................................

### CHILD'S HISTORY

Mental condition
(Present and past)..........................................................................................................
Physical condition
(Present and past)..........................................................................................................
Habits, interests
(moral, recreational etc.).................................................................................................
Outstanding characteristics and personality traits.........................................................
Companions and their influence......................................................................................
Truancy from home, if any................................................................................................
School (attitude towards school, teachers, class mates and *vice-versa*)............................
.............................................................................................................................................

Work record (jobs held, reasons for leaving, vocational interests, attitude towards job or employers)....................................................................................................................
Neighbourhood and neighbours report.............................................................................
Parent's attitude towards discipline in the home and child's reaction..........................
.............................................................................................................................................

Any other remarks

---

### RESULT OF INQUIRY

Emotional factors
Physical condition
Intelligence
Social and economic factors
Religious factors
Reasons for child's need for care and protection
Opinion of experts consulted
Recommendation of Child Welfare Officer/Case-Worker/Social Worker regarding psychological support, rehabilitation and reintegration of the child and suggested plan.

..............................................................................................
Signature of the Child Welfare Officer/Case-Worker/Social Worker

## FORM XIV

[Rule 33(3)(c)]

### ORDER FOR DECLARING CHILD LEGALLY FREE FOR ADOPTION

1. In exercise of the powers vested in the Child Welfare Committee........................... constituted under sub-section...........................of section...........................of the Juvenile Justice (Care and Protection of Children) Act, 2000 and sub-rule............of rule...........of these rules, minor...........................born on (date)...........................placed in custody of Specialised Adoption Agency (name & address)..........................,...........................*vide* order................dated....................of the Chairperson, Child Welfare Committee.................. ..............................................................., has been declared legally free for adoption on the basis of details furnished through:

(a) Inquiry/home study conducted by Child Welfare Officer/Social Worker/Case-Worker.

(b) Document of surrender executed by the parent(s) and surrender deed signed in the presence of the Committee under sub-rules...........of rule..........of these rules.

(c) Declaration submitted by the Specialised Adoption Agency under sub-rules............of rule.........of these rules.

2. ....................................................(name of the Specialised Adoption Agency) shall fulfil all conditions specified in Juvenile Justice (Care and Protection of Children) Act, 2000 and the rules relating thereto and furnish a copy of adoption decree/guardianship order in respect of the minor as may be required by Committee and the concerned Department of the State Government of......... .

..........................................

Date..........................                                        Chairperson/Member

Place.........................                                        Child Welfare Committee

For completion by the Specialised Adoption Agency.

i. I have read and understood Chapters III and IV of Juvenile Justice (Care and Protection of Children) Act, 2000 and the rules thereunder and agree to abide/be bound by the same while placing said minor in adoption.

ii. I further declare that the particulars stated in the declaration submitted by me on...........................true and correct. In case they are found to be false or incorrect, the Committee has right to suspend this Release Order for (name of the minor)....................................................and ask for production of said minor before the Committee.

Date........................

Place.......................                                        ..............................................................

Child Welfare Officer/Social Worker

**FORM XV**

[Rule 33(4)(c)]

**DEED OF SURRENDER**

I....................................................d/o or s/o.......................................................residing at........................................................................................am not in a position due to social reasons/due to being single/ill/disabled to take care of my child (name, if any)....................................................approximate age......years. I am explained the consequences of surrendering my child by the Child Welfare Officer/Social Worker (name)...........................and the Child Welfare Committee.................... . In full knowledge of all these facts, I am surrendering my child before the Committee today, dated........................... . Within two months from this stated date if I do not revise my decision to take back my child and do not approach the said Committee for the same, the Committee shall declare my child legally free for adoption and I shall have no further claim on my child.

..................................................

Signature of parent/guardian

Date..............................

That I....................................................Child Welfare Officer/Social Worker have explained the procedure and the consequences of surrendering the child to the concerned parent/guardian on (date)........................... .

...........................................................................

Signature of Child Welfare Officer/Social Worker

Date.............................

(Signed before me)

....................................

Chairperson/Member

Child Welfare Committee

## FORM XVI

[Rule 35(3)]

### A. FOSTER CARER'S ASSESSMENT

**1. Agency Details**

Name of the Agency

Address

Telephone

Fax

E-mail

Name of the Social Worker

Tel

Date............................(Form Completed)

**2. Details of the Applicant**

Surname

Full Name

Date of Birth

Religion

Language(s) spoken at Home

Occupation

(a) Nature of Work

(b) Hours of Work

Address

Telephone

**3. Description of a preferred child**

The type of child, the foster-carer would consider

(To be filled after a full discussion with the Foster-carer)

Age Range Under 2 years 3-6 years 7-12 years 13-15 years 16-18 years

| Sl. No. | Type of Placement | Duration |
|---|---|---|
| (i) | Pre-adoption | |
| (ii) | Emergency | |
| (iii) | Short-term | |
| (iv) | Assessment | |
| (v) | Long-term | |

The Child an applicant can care for (Please Tick)

**A child who is:**

(i) Neglected

(ii) Orphaned

(iii) With Physical impairment

(iv) Mental impairment

(v) Hearing impairment

(vi) Speech impairment

(vii) Special Education needs

(viii) Learning difficulties

(ix) Physical abuse

(x) Sexual abuse
(xi) Who does not relate easily
(xii) Who needs control/may defy authority
(xiii) Born of rape/incest
(xiv) Who's parent(s) is suffering from disease
(xv) Whose parent(s) is HIV positive
(xvi) Whose parent(s) is AIDS patient
(xvii) Whose parent(s) are alcoholic
(xviii) Drug addicts
(xix) Are in jail
(xx) Relinquished
(xxi) Belong to another caste
(xxii) Are of different religion

**4. Profile of the family**

| Brief Family Profile | | | | | |
|---|---|---|---|---|---|
| Name | Gender | Approx. Age | Occupation | Education | Relationship with the applicant |
| | | | | | |
| | | | | | |

(Give details of personalities, family life, experiences etc. Also highlight specific qualities of the family that can match with a child's needs. The details should facilitate initial identification of a potential match with a specific child.)

Accommodation (House)

(Details of type, size, own/rented space, amenities etc.)

Neighbourhood

(Details of composition, amenities and facilities, public transport etc.)

**5. Verification of applicant's identity**

Place of residence

Period of stay

Nationality

Marital status (date/length of marriage)

Has either of the applicant had a previous marriage? Details

If children from previous marriage? Details

Specify documents seen with date

**6. Career History**

(Details of education, employment, voluntary work, part-time work, leisure activities)

**7. Agency Inquiries**

Medical check

Police check

Employer

8. Personal references (from 2 persons)

This section to be completed after interviews with two references; information gathered through these interviews should include:

- Length of time known
- Relationship to the applicant

- Provide evidence on the applicants ability to perform the tasks involved in.............
- Caring for children
- Providing a safe and caring environment
- Applicant as a neighbour
- Interests, talents, personality

Assessment of the social worker for these references

**B. HOME STUDY REPORT**

A Home Study Report of the foster carer(s) being a crucial document being prepared by the social worker of the Specialised Adoption Agency based on the information collected by the format given above should broadly include the following information:—

- Social status and family background
- Description of the home
- Standard of living as it appears in the home
- Current relations amongst the members in the home
- Status of development of the children already in the home
- Employment and economic status
- Health details
- Details of facilities of education, medical, vocational trainings available in the neighbourhood
- Reasons for wanting a child in foster care
- Attitudes of the grandparents and other relatives
- Anticipated plans for the foster child
- Legal status of the foster carer(s)
- Willingness to undergo training.

**C. DETAILS OF APPLICANT(S)**

**1. Background**

Family structure with details of parents and siblings, significant details of other family members, childhood experiences, etc.

**2. Relationships:**

If couple - Length of married life, what qualities does each applicant bring to the partnership, what makes the relationship positive for each other? Within the relationship how do applicants cope with problems/stress/anger? How do applicants support each other? What is each applicant's assessment of how the foster placement will affect his or her relationship?

**3. Decision-making:**

How is decision – making exercised in this relationship and how does each of the applicants view this? Is there wider extended family involvement in the couple's decision-making process? If so, how will this affect the child to be placed?

What are the strengths and vulnerabilities of this partnership?

- Children
- Children and their parent's relationships
- Children's attitude and readiness for a foster placement sibling. Describe each child and their temperament, any special talent and need, how children have been involved in preparation.

**4. Applicants support networks:**

Give a general picture of support systems currently used by the applicants including extended family, friends, neighbours, religious activities, community groups etc., include details of the location etc.

**5. Other significant members of the family:**

Living in the house or not. Their relationship to the applicants, how much time they spent within the home, their attitude to the proposed placement? How important is their acceptance of placement to the applicant.

**6. Description of the family life style:**

Outline what family considers important *e.g.*, how important are religious and cultural practices. How is affection shown in the family? How do the members spend their time? What expectations family members have with regard to personal space? What value is placed on education/Hobbies and leisure activities that the whole family undertakes?

**7. Parenting capacities:**

Experience of the applicants of caring and working with children. Describe their adjustment to parenthood. What is their understanding of how children develop?

Using their own childhood experiences what patterns of parenting would they repeat and what would they change? What is their understanding of their own parenting strengths/potentials and about their parenting skills to meet the needs of individual child. To what extent they would expect other family members to be involved in parenting of their children/placed children.

How will they ensure that a child will be safe from physical sexual abuse in their family and within wider support networks?

**8. Managing Unacceptable Behaviour:**

What are rules in the household? How do the applicants show approval/ disapproval? What are discipline measures they use? Their attitude towards punishment?

What do they anticipate would be the issues and difficulties and themselves for their own children and for their support network? What do they anticipate would be the issues and difficulties for the child? Which changes do they anticipate would need in their lifestyle?

**Social workers assessment:**

It should provide an analysis of all the information collected through the format and its significance with regard to the capacity of the applicant to carryout fostering task: (What skills do the applicants have in relating to and working with children? How well will the applicant work with the agency, with biological parents? What are the strengths and resources of the applicants and which are the areas where they may experience difficulty? Also the point of disagreement between the social worker and the applicants should be recorded here)

Recommendations of the Child Welfare Officer/Social Worker

....................

(Signature)

**FORM XVII**

[Rule 34(1)]

**ORDER OF FOSTER CARE PLACEMENT**

The child (name and address)................................approximate age..........d/o or s/o Mr. ......................................and Mrs. .....................................or Ms. .................................... is in need of care and protection of a family. Mr. ...................and Mrs. ...................or Ms. ...................resident of (complete address and contact numbers) .................................... ..................................................is/are declared fit person/persons for foster-care placement of the child based on the home study report of the Child Welfare Officer/ Social Worker Ms./Mr. ...................of the organization (address).......................................

The child (name).......................................is placed in foster care for a period of...................(days/months), under the supervision of the aforesaid Child Welfare Officer/Social Worker (name and contact)....................................... .

.....................................

Chairperson/Member
Child Welfare Committee

**FORM XVIII**

[Rule 37(5)]

**ORDER OF SPONSORSHIP PLACEMENT**

The juvenile/child (name and address).........................................approximate age............d/o or s/o Mr. ......................................and Mrs. .......................................or Ms. .......................................has been identified by the State/District Child Protection Unit as a juvenile/child at risk needing urgent care and protection. On the basis of the Inquiry Report submitted by the State/District Child Protection Unit/Child Welfare Officer/Social Worker it is established that the said juvenile/child needs sponsorship support for education/health/nutrition/other developmental needs.......................................*(please specify)*. The State/District Child Protection Unit is hereby directed to release Rs...............per month/Rs. ..........as one time sponsorship support to the said juvenile/child for a period of.................(days/month) and carryout necessary follow up.

The State/District Child Protection Unit is also directed to clearly lay down the terms and conditions for sponsorship support and follow-up.

..........................................................................................

Principal Magistrate, Juvenile Justice Board/
Chairperson/Member, Child Welfare Committee

Copy to: State/District Child Protection Unit or concerned Department of the State Government

**FORM XIX**

[Rule 38(3)]

**ORDER OF AFTER CARE PLACEMENT**

The juvenile/child (name)....................d/o or s/o.......................................has/will be completing 18 years of age on (date)............ . She/he is still in need of care and protection for the purpose of rehabilitation and reintegration. She/he is placed in (name of organization)....................for providing aftercare. The in-charge of the Organization is directed to admit the child and provide all possible opportunities for her/his rehabilitation and reintegration in its truest sense. The person shall be provided all these opportunities maximum till the age of 21 years only or till reintegration in the society, whichever is earlier. The in-charge will send half yearly report on the status of the child/youth to the Child Welfare Committee.

The State/District Child Protection Unit is hereby directed to arrange for aftercare for the said juvenile/child for a period of...................(days/month) and carryout necessary follow-up. The State/District Child Protection Unit is also directed to clearly lay down the terms and conditions for aftercare programme and carryout necessary follow-up.

..........................................................................................

Principal Magistrate, Juvenile Justice Board/
Chairperson/Member, Child Welfare Committee

Copy to: State/District Child Protection Unit or concerned Department of the State Government

## FORM XX

[Rules 50(9) and 54(1)(t)]

## CASE HISTORY FORM FOR CHILDREN IN NEED OF CARE AND PROTECTION

Case/Profile No. ..................

Date & Time..........................

Affix a latest photograph here

### A. PERSONAL DATA

1. Name
2. Male/Female (tick the appropriate category)
3. (a) age at the time of admission
   (b) present age:
4. Category:
   - Separated from family
   - Abandoned/deserted
   - Victim of exploitation and violence (give detail)
   - Run-away
   - Any other
5. Religion Hindu (OC/BC/SC/ST)
   Muslim/Christian/Other (pl. specify)
6. Location of Residence Urban/Sub-urban/Rural/Slum/
   Industrial/Other (pl. specify)
7. Native District & State:
8. Description of the Housing:
   (i) Concrete building Tiled House/Hut/On the street/Others (please specify)
   (ii) Three-bed room/two-bed room/one-bed room/no separate bed room
   (iii) Owned/rental
9. By whom the juvenile was brought before the Child Welfare Committee:
   (i) Police-Local Police/Special Juvenile Police Unit/Railway Police/Women Police
   (ii) Probation Officers
   (iii) Social Welfare Organization
   (iv) Social Worker
   (v) Parent(s)/Guardian(s) (please specify the relationship)
   (vi) Child himself/herself
10. Reasons for leaving the family
    (i) Abuse by parent(s)/guardian(s)/step-parents(s)
    (ii) In search of employment
    (iii) Peer group influence
    (iv) Incapacitation of parents
    (v) Criminal behaviour of parents
    (vi) Separation of Parents
    (vii) Demise of parents
    (viii) Poverty
    (ix) Others (please specify)
11. Types of abuse met by the child
    (i) Verbal abuse – Parents/siblings/employers/others (pl. specify)
    (ii) Physical abuse

(iii) Sexual abuse parents/siblings/Employers/others pl. specify)
(iv) Others – parents/siblings/employers/others (pl. Specify)

12. Types of ill-treatment met by the child.
   (i) Denial of food – parents/siblings employers/other (pl. specify)
   (ii) Beaten mercilessly – parents/siblings/employers/other (pl. specify)
   (iii) Causing injury – parents/siblings/employers/other (pl. specify)
   (iv) Other (pl. specify) – parents/siblings/employers/others (pl. specify)
13. Exploitation faced by the child
   (i) Extracted work without payment
   (ii) Little (low) wages with longer duration of work
   (iii) Others (pl. specify)
14. Health status of the child before admission.
   (i) Respiratory disorders - present/not known/absent
   (ii) Hearing impairment - present/not known/absent
   (iii) Eye diseases - present/not known/absent
   (iv) Dental disease - present/not known/absent
   (v) Cardiac diseases - present/not known/absent
   (vi) Skin disease - present/not known/absent
   (vii) Sexually transmitted diseases - present/not known/absent
   (viii) Neurological disorders - present/not known/absent
   (ix) Mental handicap - present/not known/absent
   (x) Physical handicap - present/not known/absent
   (xi) Others (pl. specify) - present/not known/absent
15. With whom the child was staying prior to admission
   (i) Parent(s) – Mother/Father/Both
   (ii) Guardian(s) – Relationship
   (iii) Friends
   (iv) On the street
   (v) Night shelter
   (vi) Orphanages/Hostels/Similar Homes
   (vii) Other (pl. specify)
16. Visit of the parents to meet the child
   (i) Prior to institutionalization – Frequently/Occasionally/Rarely/Never
   (ii) After institutionalization - Frequently/Occasionally/Rarely/Never
17. Visit of the child to his family
   (i) Prior to institutionalization -
   Frequently/Occasionally/Rarely/During festival times/During summer holidays/Whenever fallen sick/Never
   (ii) After institutionalization –
   Frequently/Occasionally/Rarely/During festival times/During summer holidays/Whenever fallen sick/Never
18. Correspondence with parents—
   (i) Prior to institutionalization -
   Frequently/Occasionally/Rarely/During festival times/During summer holidays/Whenever fallen sick/Never

(ii) After institutionalization –

Frequently/Occasionally/Rarely/During festival times/During summer holidays/Whenever fallen sick/Never

**B. CHILDHOOD HISTORY (up to the age of 12 years)**

19. Diet of mother during pregnancy:
    (i) Taken nutritious diet
    (ii) Ordinary diet
    (iii) Inadequate food intake
20. Health during pregnancy
    (i) Mother infected with contagious diseases
    (ii) Mother consumed/used contraceptives
    (iii) Intake of antibiotics
    (iv) No such details available
21. Birth details
    (i) Normal delivery/prolonged delivery/caesarian
    (ii) Under weight/normal weight/over weight
22. Details of immunization provided
23. Details of handicap
    (i) Hearing impairment — By birth/After accident/diseases
    (ii) Speech impairment — By birth/After accident/diseases
    (iii) Physical handicap — By birth/After accident/diseases
    (iv) Mental handicap — By birth/After accident/diseases
    (v) Others (please specify)

**C. FAMILY DETAILS:**

24. Household Composition:

| S. No. | Name & Relationship | Age | Sex | Education | Occupation | Income |
|---|---|---|---|---|---|---|
| 1 | 2 | 3 | 4 | 5 | 6 | 7 |

| Health | History of Mental illness | Handicap | Habit | Socialization |
|---|---|---|---|---|
| 8 | 9 | 10 | 11 | 12 |

25. Type of family:
    Nuclear family/joint family/broken family
26. Relationship among the family members:
    (i) Father & mother — Cordial/Non Cordial/Not known
    (ii) Father & child — Cordial/Non Cordial/Not known
    (iii) Mother & child — Cordial/Non Cordial/Not known
    (iv) Father & siblings — Cordial/Non Cordial/Not known
    (v) Mother & siblings — Cordial/Non Cordial/Not known
    (vi) Juvenile & siblings — Cordial/Non Cordial/Not known
27. History of crime committed by family members:

| S. No. | Relationship | Nature of crime | Arrest if any made | Period of confinement | Punishment awarded |
|---|---|---|---|---|---|
| 1. | Father | | | | |
| 2. | Step-father | | | | |
| 3. | Mother | | | | |
| 4. | Step-mother | | | | |
| 5. | Brother<br>(a)<br>(b)<br>(c)<br>(d) | | | | |
| 6. | Sister<br>(a)<br>(b)<br>(c)<br>(d) | | | | |
| 7. | Child | | | | |
| 8. | Others (uncle/ aunty/ grandparents) | | | | |

28. Properties owned by the family:
    (i) Landed properties (pl. specify the area)
    (ii) Household articles-Cows/Cattle/Bull
    (iii) Vehicles-two wheeler/three wheeler/four wheeler (lorry/bus/car/tractor/ jeep)
    (iv) Others (please specify)
29. Marriage details of family members:
    (i) Parents Arranged/Special Marriage/Local Union
    (ii) Brothers Arranged/Special Marriage/Local Union
    (iii) Sisters Arranged/Special Marriage/Local Union
30. Social activities of family members:
    (i) Participate in social and religious functions
    (ii) Participate in cultural activities
    (iii) Does not participate in social and religious functions
    (iv) Not known
31. Parental care towards juvenile before admission:
    (i) Over protection
    (ii) Affectionate
    (iii) Attentive
    (iv) Not affectionate
    (v) Not attentive
    (vi) Rejection

**D. ADOLESCENCE HISTORY (Between 12 and 18 years)**

32. Puberty
    Early
    Middle age
    Late

33. Details of delinquent behaviour if any
    (i) Stealing
    (ii) Pick pocketing
    (iii) Arrack selling
    (iv) Drug pedalling
    (v) Petty offences
    (vi) Violent crime
    (vii) Rape
    (viii) None of the above
    (ix) Others (please specify)
34. Reason for delinquent behaviour
    (i) Parental neglect
    (ii) Parental overprotection
    (iii) Parents criminal behaviour
    (iv) Parents influence (negative)
    (v) Peer group influence
    (vi) To buy drugs/alcohol
    (vii) Others (pi. specify)
35. Habits

A
(i) Smoking
(ii) Alcohol consumption
(iii) Drug use (specify)
(iv) Gambling
(v) Begging
(vi) Any other

B
(i) Watching TV/movies
(ii) Playing indoor/outdoor games
(iii) Reading books
(iv) Religious activities
(v) Drawing/painting/acting/singing
(vi) Any other

**E. EMPLOYMENT DETAILS**

Employment details of the juveniles prior to entry into the Home:

| S.No. | Details of employment | Duration | Wages earned |
|---|---|---|---|
| (i) | Cooly | | |
| (ii) | Rag picking | | |
| (iii) | Mechanic | | |
| (iv) | Hotel work | | |
| (v) | Tea shop work | | |
| (vi) | Shoe polish | | |
| (vii) | Household works | | |
| (viii) | Others (pl. specify) | | |

36. Details of income utilization:
    (i) Sent to family to meet family need
    (ii) For dress materials
    (iii) For gambling
    (iv) For prostitution
    (v) For alcohol
    (vi) For drug

(vii) For smoking
(viii) Savings

37. Details of savings
(i) With employers
(ii) With friends
(iii) Bank/Post Office
(iv) Others (pls. specify)

38. Duration of working hours
(i) Less than six hours
(ii) Between six and eight hours
(iii) More than eight hours

**F. EDUCATIONAL DETAILS**

39. The details of education of the juvenile prior to the admission to Children's Home
(i) Illiterate
(ii) Studied up to V Standard
(iii) Studied above V Std but below VIII Standard
(iv) Studied above VIII Std but below X Standard
(v) Studied above X Standard

40. The reason for leaving the School
(i) Failure in the class last studied
(ii) Lack of interest in the school activities
(iii) Indifferent attitude of the teachers
(iv) Peer group influence
(v) To earn and support the family
(vi) Sudden demise of parents
(vii) Rigid school atmosphere
(viii) Absenteeism followed by running away from school
(ix) Others (pls. specify)

41. The details of the school in which studied last:
(i) Corporation/Municipal/Panchayat Union
(ii) Government/SC Welfare School/BC Welfare School
(iii) Private management
(iv) Convents

42. Medium of instruction:
Hindi/English/Urdu/Tamil/Malayalam/Kannada/Telugu
Other language (please specify)

43. After admission to Children's Home, the educational attainment from the date of admission till date;

| No. of years | Class studied | Promoted/detained |
|---|---|---|

44. Vocational training undergone form the date of admission into Children's Home till date.

| No. of years | Name of Vocational Trade | Proficiency Attained |
|---|---|---|

45. Extra curricular activities developed from the date of admission into the Children's Home till date
(i) Scout
(ii) Sports (please specify)

(iii) Athletics (please specify)
(iv) Drawing
(v) Painting
(vi) Others (pl. specify)

## G. MEDICAL HISTORY

46. Height and weight at the time of admission:
47. Physical condition:
48. Medical history of child (gist):
49. Medical history of parent/guardian (gist):
50. Present health status of the child:

| Sl. No. | Annual Observation | 1st Quarter | 2nd Quarter | 3rd Quarter | 4th Quarter |
|---|---|---|---|---|---|
| 1. | Date of review | | | | |
| 2. | Height | | | | |
| 3. | Weight | | | | |
| 4. | Nutritious diet given | | | | |
| 5. | Stress disease | | | | |
| 6. | Dental | | | | |
| 7. | ENT- Tonsils | | | | |
| 8. | External eye problem: vision | | | | |
| | Left | | | | |
| | Right | | | | |

51. Height and Weight Chart:

| Date, Month & Year | Height | Admissible weight | Actual weight |
|---|---|---|---|
| | | | |
| | | | |
| | | | |
| | | | |
| | | | |
| | | | |
| | | | |
| | | | |
| | | | |

## H. SOCIAL HISTORY

52. Details of friendship prior to admission into Children's Home:
    i. Co-workers
    ii. School/Classmate
    iii. Neighbours
    iv. Others (pl. specify)
53. Majority of the friends are
    i. Educated
    ii. Illiterate

iii. The same age group
iv. Older in age
v. Younger in age
vi. Same sex
vii. Opposite sex

54. Details of membership in group (please specify details)
    i. Associated with cine fans association
    ii. Associated with religious group
    iii. Associated with arts and sports club
    iv. Associated with gangs
    v. Associated with voluntary social service league
    vi. Others (please specify)
55. The position of the child in the groups/league
    i. Leader
    ii. Second level leader
    iii. Middle level functionary
    iv. Ordinary member
56. Purpose of taking membership in the group:
    i. For social service activities
    ii. For leisure time spending
    iii. For pleasure seeking activities
    iv. For deviant activities
    v. Others (please specify)
57. Attitude of the group/league
    i. Respect the social norms and follow the rules
    ii. Interested in violating the norms
    iii. Impulsive in violating the rules
58. The location/meeting point of the groups
    i. Usually at fixed place
    ii. Places are changed frequently
    iii. No specific places
    iv. Meeting point is fixed conveniently
59. The reaction of the society when the child first came out of the family
    i. Supportive
    ii. Rejection
    iii. Abuse
    iv. Ill-treatment
    v. Exploitation
60. The reaction of the police towards children
    i. Passionate
    ii. Cruel
    iii. Abuse
    iv. Exploitation
    v. Ill-treatment
61. The response of the general public towards the child

**HISTORY OF THE CHILD (GIST)**

i. Education

ii. Health

iii. Vocational training

iv. Extra curricular activities

v. Others

Suggestion of Child Welfare Officer/Probation Officer after orientation to juvenile/child and the response towards orientation.

Follow-up by Child Welfare Officer/Probation Officer/Case-Worker/Social Worker

Quarterly Review of Case History by Management Committee

..........................................................................................

Superintendent/Welfare Officer/Probation Officer

## FORM XXI

[Rules 50(12)(a), 54(1)(o) and 87(1)(k)]

## INDIVIDUAL CARE PLAN

Individual care plan for each child shall be prepared following the principle of the best interest of the child. In preparing individual care plan the care options in the following order of preferences shall be considered:—

(i) Preserving the biological family

(ii) Kinship Care

(iii) In-country adoption

(iv) Foster Care

(v) Inter-country Adoption

(vi) Institutional Care

Case/Profile No. of 20..........(year) of the Board/Committee

Admission No.

Date of Admission:

**A. PERSONAL DETAILS**

1. Name of the Child:
2. Age:
3. Sex: Male/Female
4. Father's/Mother's name:
5. Nationality:
6. Religion/caste:
7. Educational Attainment:
8. Summary of Case History:
    - Health needs
    - Emotional and psychological support needed
    - Educational and Training needs
    - Leisure, creativity and play
    - Attachments and Relationships
    - Religious beliefs
    - Protection from all kinds of abuse, neglect and maltreatment
    - Social mainstreaming
    - Follow-up post release/restoration

### B. FORTNIGHTLY PROGRESS REPORT OF PROBATIONER

Part One

1. Name of the Probation Officer/Case-Worker
2. For the month of
3. Registration No.
4. Competent Authority
5. Profile No.
6. Name of the Child
7. Date of Supervision Order
8. Address of the Child
9. Period of Supervision

Part Two

| Places of interview | Dates |
|---|---|
| .......................... | .......................... |
| .......................... | .......................... |
| .......................... | .......................... |

1. Where the child is residing?
2. Progress made in any educational/training course.
3. What work he/she is doing and his/her monthly average earning, if employed.
4. Savings kept in the Post Office.
5. Savings Bank Account in his/her name.
6. Remarks on his/her general conduct and progress.
7. Whether property cared for?

Part Three

1. Any proceedings before the competent authority of or
   (a) Variation of conditions of bond
   (b) Change of residence
   (c) Other matters
2. Period of supervision completed on..........................
3. Result of supervision with remarks (if any)
4. Name and Addresses of the parent or guardian or fit person under whose care the juvenile is to live after the supervision is over.

Date of report................Signature of the Probation Officer/Case-Worker..................

### C. PRE-RELEASE REPORT

**Tick whichever is applicable**

Final Release ☐ Transfer ☐

1. Details of place of transfer and concerned authority responsible in the place of transfer/release
2. Details placement of the juvenile/child in different institutions
3. Training undergone and skills acquired
4. Final progress report of the Officer-in-Charge/probation officer/child welfare officer/case-worker/social worker (to be attached)
5. Date of release/transfer
6. Date of repatriation

7. Requisition for escort if required
8. Identification of escort
9. Recommended rehabilitation plan including possible placements
10. Sponsorship requirement and report, if applicable
11. Identification of Probation Officer/Case-worker/social worker/non-governmental organisation for post-release follow-up
12. Memorandum of Understanding with non-governmental organisation identified for post-release follow-up
13. Identification of sponsorship agency/individual sponsor for the child post-release, if any
14. Memorandum of Understanding between the sponsoring agency and individual sponsor
15. Details of Savings Account of the child, if any
16. Details of child's earnings and belongings if any
17. Details of awards/rewards due to the child if any
18. Opinion of the child
19. Any other information

**Note.**—Pre-release report shall be prepared 6 months prior to the date of release/ transfer of juvenile/child and shall take into account the recommendations of the last review report and all other relevant information.

**D. POST-RELEASE REPORT**

1. Status of Bank Account: Closed/Transferred
2. Earnings and belongings of the child: handed over to the child or his/her parents/guardians - Yes/No
3. First interaction report of the probation officer/child welfare officer/case-worker/ social worker/non-governmental organisation identified for follow-up with the child post-release
4. Placement of the juvenile/child if any
5. Family's behaviour towards the child
6. Social milieu of the child, particularly attitude of neighbours/community
7. How is the child using the skills acquired?
8. Whether the child has been admitted to a school or vocation? Give date and name of the school/institute/any other agency
9. Report of second and third follow-up interaction with the child after two months and six months respectively

## FORM XXII

[Rule 65(2)]

**ESCORT ORDER**

Case No. ........................

In the matter of Boy/Girl Child

..................................................

Aged about.........year taken charge for sole custody under section 33(3) of the Juvenile Justice Act, 2000

The Parents of the boy/girl child are reported to be residing at:

He/She therefore be sent under supervision of a proper police/non-governmental organisation escort to the................................................................................ .

For tracing and for handing over to the parents or close relatives of the said Boy Child/Girl Child residing at the aforesaid address or at other Place which may be shown by the Child, if no such parents or relative are traced or if traced but they are unwilling to take charge of the boy/girl be kept in the custody of the Superintendent ..................................Children's Home and the said Boy/Girl child be produced before the concerned Child Welfare Committee for further orders.

**Orders**

Pending Escort, the said Boy/Girl Child shall remain in Children's Home, residing at present at....................................... The State/District Child Protection Unit, or Police Department or non-governmental organisation/Childline shall positively make immediate arrangement not less than 15 days from the date of receipt of this order by him and send the said Boy Child/Girl Child at his/her aforesaid place of residence.

Dated this..............................day of...............................20........... .

.......................................

Chairperson/Member
Child Welfare Committee

CC to:

1. The Superintendent, Children Home.
2 The State/District Child Protection Unit or non-governmental organisation or Childline

Ref.: 1. Order of admission of minor.............born on.........Profile No. .................. .

# NATIONAL CHARTER FOR CHILDREN, 2003[1]

*The Government of India have had for consideration the question of adopting a National Charter for Children to reiterate its commitment to the cause of the children in order to see that no child remains hungry, illiterate or sick. After the consideration, it has been decided to adopt the National Charter for Children enunciated below:—*

**National Charter for Children, 2003.**—Whereas the Constitution of India enshrines both in Parts III and IV the cause and the best interest of children, insofar that:

The State can make special provisions for children, (Art. 15(3))

The State shall provide free and compulsory education to all children of the age of six to fourteen years, (Art. 21A)

No child below the age of 14 years shall be employed to work in a factory, mine or any other hazardous employment, (Art. 24)

The tender age of children is not abused and that citizens are not forced by economic necessity to enter avocations unsuited to their age or strength (Art. 39e), and that

Children are given opportunities and facilities to develop in a healthy manner and in conditions of freedom and dignity and that youth are protected against exploitation and against moral and material abandonment (Art. 39f),

The State shall endeavour to provide early childhood care and education for all children until they complete the age of six years, (Art. 45)

Whereas it is a Fundamental Duty of a parent or guardian to provide opportunities for education to his child or ward between the age of six and fourteen years, (Art. 51A)

Whereas through the National Policy for Children, 1974, we are committed to providing for adequate services to children, both before and after birth and throughout the period of growth, to ensure their full physical, mental and social development,

Whereas we affirm that the best interest of children must be protected through combined action of the State, civil society, communities and families in their obligations in fulfilling children's basic needs,—

Whereas we also affirm that while State, Society, Community and Family have obligations towards children, these must be viewed in the context of intrinsic and attendant duties of children and inculcating in children a sound sense of values directed towards preserving and strengthening the Family, Society and the Nation.

And whereas we believe that by respecting the child, society is respecting itself,

Now, therefore, in accordance with our pledge in the National Agenda of Governance, the following National Charter for Children, 2003 is announced.

Underlying this Charter is our intent to secure for every child its inherent right to be a child and enjoy a healthy and happy childhood, to address the root

1. Resolution No. 6-15/98-C.W., dated 9th February, 2004, Issued by Ministry of Human Resource Development.

causes that negate the healthy growth and development of children, and to awaken the conscience of the community in the wider societal context to protect children from all firms of abuse, while strengthening the family, society and the Nation.

**1. Survival, Life and Liberty.**—(a) The State and community shall undertake all possible measures to ensure and protect the survival, life and liberty of all children.

(b) In particular, the State and community will undertake all appropriate measures to address the problems of infanticide and foeticide, especially of female child and all other emerging manifestations that deprive the girl child of her right to survive with dignity.

**2. Promoting High Standards of Health and Nutrition.**—(a) The State shall take measures to ensure that all children enjoy the highest attainable standards of health, and provide for preventive and curative facilities at all levels especially immunisation and prevention of micronutrient deficiencies for all children.

(b) The State shall take measures to cover, under primary health facilities and specialised care and treatment, all children of families below the poverty line.

(c) The State shall take measures to provide adequate pre-natal and post-natal care for mothers along with immunization against preventable diseases.

(d) The State shall undertake measures to provide for a national plan that will ensure that the mental health of all children is protected.

(e) The State shall take steps to ensure protection of children from all practices that are likely to harm the child's physical and mental health.

**3.** The State shall take steps to provide all children from families below the poverty line with adequate supplementary nutrition and undertake adequate measures for ensuring access to safe drinking water and environmental sanitation and hygiene.

**4. Assuring Basic Minimum Needs and Security.**—(a) The State recognizes that the basic minimum needs of every child must be met, that foster full development of the child's faculties.

(b) In order to ensure this, the State shall in partnership with the community provide social security for children, especially for abandoned children and street children.

(c) State and community shall try and remove the fundamental causes which result in abandoned children and children living on streets, and provide infrastructure and material support by way of shelter, education, nutrition and recreation.

**5. Play and Leisure.**—The State and community shall recognize that all children require adequate play and leisure for their healthy development and must ensure means to provide for recreational facilities and services for children of all ages and social groups.

**6. Early Childhood Care for Survival, Growth and Development.**—(a) The State shall in partnership with the community provide early childhood care for all children and encourage programmes which will stimulate and develop their physical and cognitive capacities.

(b) The State shall in partnership with the community aim at providing a child care centre in every village where infants and children of working mothers can be adequately cared for.

(c) The State will make special efforts to provide these facilities to children from SCs/STs and marginalised sections of society.

**7. Free and Compulsory Primary Education.**—(a) The State recognises that all children shall have access to free and compulsory education. Education at the elementary level shall be provided free of cost and special incentives should be provided to ensure that children from disadvantaged social groups are enrolled, retained and participate in schooling.

(b) At the secondary level, the State shall provide access to education for all and provide supportive facilities from the disadvantaged groups.

(c) The State shall in partnership with the community ensure that all the educational institutions function efficiently and are able to reach universal enrolment, universal retention, universal participation and universal achievement.

(d) The State and community recognise that a child be educated in its mother tongue.

(e) The State shall ensure that education is child-oriented and meaningful. It shall also take appropriate measures to ensure that education is sensitive to the healthy development of the girl child and to children of varied cultural backgrounds.

(f) The State shall ensure that school discipline and matters related thereto do not result in physical, mental, psychological harm or trauma to the child.

(g) The Stale shall formulate special programmes to spot, identify, encourage and assist the gifted children for their development in the field of their excellence.

**8. Protection from Economic Exploitation and All Forms of Abuse.**—(a) The State shall provide protection to children from economic exploitation and from performing tasks that are hazardous to their well-being.

(b) The State shall ensure that there is appropriate regulation of conditions of work in occupations and processes where children perform work of a non-hazardous nature and that their rights are protected.

(c) The State shall move towards a total ban of all forms of child labour.

**9.** (a) All children have a right to be protected against neglect, maltreatment, injury, trafficking, sexual and physical abuse of all kinds, corporal punishment, torture, exploitation, violence and degrading treatment.

(b) The State shall take legal action against those committing such violations against children even if they be legal guardians of such children.

(c) The State shall in partnership with the community set up mechanisms for identification, reporting, referral, investigation and follow-up of such acts, while respecting the dignity and privacy of the child.

(d) The State shall in partnership with the community take up steps to draw up plans for the identification, care, protection, counselling and rehabilitation of child victims and ensure that they are able to recover, physically, socially and psychologically, and re-integrate into society.

**10.** (a) The State shall take strict measures to ensure that children are not used in the conduct of any illegal activity, namely, trafficking of narcotic drugs and psychotropic substances, begging, prostitution, pornography or violence. The State in partnership with the community shall ensure that such children are rescued and immediately placed under appropriate care and protection.

(b) The State and community shall ensure protection of children in distress for their welfare and all round development.

(c) The State and community shall ensure protection of children during the occurrence of natural calamities in their best interest.

**11. Protection of the Girl Child.**—(a) The State and community shall ensure that crimes and atrocities committed against the girl child, including child marriage, discriminatory practices, forçing girls into prostitution and trafficking are speedily eradicated.

(b) The State shall in partnership with the community undertake measures, including social, educational and legal, to ensure that there is greater respect for the girl child in the family and society.

(c) The State shall take serious measures to ensure that the practice of child marriage is speedily abolished.

**12. Empowering Adolescents.**—The State and community shall take all steps to provide the necessary education and skills to adolescent children so as to equip them to become economically productive citizens. Special programmes will be undertaken to improve the health and nutritional status of the adolescent girl.

**13. Equality, Freedom of Expression, Freedom to Seek and Receive Information, Freedom of Association and Peaceful Assembly.**—The State and community shall ensure that all children are treated equally without discrimination on grounds of the child's or the child's parents or legal guardian's race, colour, caste, sex, language, religion, political or other opinion, national, ethnic or social origin, disability, birth, political status, or any other consideration.

**14.** All children shall be given every opportunity for all round development of their personality, including expression of creativity.

**15.** (a) Every child shall have the freedom to seek and receive information and ideas. The State and community shall provide opportunities for the child to access information that will contribute to the child's development.

(b) The State and community shall undertake special measures to ensure that the linguistic needs of children are taken care of and encourage the production and dissemination of child-friendly information and material in various forms.

(c) The State and community shall be responsible for formulating guidelines for the mass media in order to ensure that children are protected from material injuries to their well-being.

**16.** All children shall enjoy freedom of association and peaceful assembly, subject to reasonable restrictions and in conformity with social and family values.

**17. Strengthening Family.**—(a) Every child has a right to a family. In case of separation of children from their families, the State shall ensure that priority is given to re-unifying the child with its parents. In cases where the State perceives adverse impact of such a re-unification, the State shall make alternate arrangements immediately, keeping in mind the best interests and the views of the child.

(b) All children have a right to maintain contact with their families, even when they are within the custody of the State for various reasons.

(c) The State shall undertake measures to ensure that children without families are either placed for adoption, preferably intra-country adoption, or foster care or any other family substitute services.

(d) The State shall ensure that appropriate rules with respect to the implementation of such services are drafted in a manner that are in the best interest of the child and that regulatory bodies are set up to ensure the strict enforcement of these rules.

(e) All children shall have the right to meet their parents and other family members who may be in custody.

**18. Responsibilities of Both Parents.**—The State recognizes the common responsibilities of both parents in rearing their children.

**19. Protection of Children with Disabilities.**—(a) The State and community recognise that all children with disabilities must be helped to lead a full life with dignity and respect. All measures would be undertaken to ensure that children with disabilities are encouraged to be integrated into the mainstream society and actively participate in all walks of life.

(b) State and community shall also provide for their education, training, health care, rehabilitation, recreation in a manner that will contribute to their overall growth and development.

(c) State and community shall launch preventive programmes against disabilities and early detection of disabilities so as to ensure that the families with disabled children receive adequate support and assistance in bringing up their children.

(d) The State shall encourage research and development in the field of prevention, treatment and rehabilitation of various forms of disabilities.

**20. Care, Protection, Welfare of Children of Marginalized and Disadvantaged Communities.**—The State and community shall provide care, protect and ensure the welfare of children from marginalized and disadvantaged communities, support them in preserving their identity, and encourage them to adopt practices that promote their best interest.

**21.** The State recognises that children from disadvantaged communities and weaker/vulnerable sections of the society are in need of special interventions and support in all matters pertaining to education, health, recreation and supportive services. It shah make adequate provisions for providing such groups with special attention in all its policies and programmes.

**22. Ensuring Child Friendly Procedures.**—All matters and procedures relating to children, *viz.*, judicial, administrative, educational or social, should be child friendly. All procedures laid down under the juvenile justice system for children in conflict with law and for children in need of special care and protection shall also be child-friendly.

•••